International Political Communication

International Political Communication

W. PHILLIPS DAVISON

Published for the
COUNCIL ON FOREIGN RELATIONS

FREDERICK A. PRAEGER, *Publishers*
New York • Washington • London

For Holley and Stowe

FREDERICK A. PRAEGER, PUBLISHERS
111 Fourth Avenue, New York 3, N.Y., U.S.A.
77–79 Charlotte Street, London W. 1, England
Published in the United States of America in 1965
by Frederick A. Praeger, Inc., Publishers

Library of Congress Catalog Card Number: 65-24723

The Council on Foreign Relations is a nonprofit organization devoted to the study of political, economic, and strategic problems as related to American foreign policy. It takes no stand, expressed or implied, on American policy.

The authors of books published under the auspices of the Council are responsible for their statements of fact and expressions of opinion. The Council is responsible only for determining that they should be presented to the public.

For a list of Council publications see page 401.

Printed in the United States of America

Preface and Acknowledgments

If one does not begin an exploration such as this with a sense of modesty, it will be thrust upon him as he gradually realizes the extent of the task. The amount of literature and experience relating to political aspects of international communication is so great that any one student can tap only a portion of it. Two extensive bibliographies on the subject have appeared, but these were selective to begin with and an enormous quantity of excellent material has appeared since the second one was published.* Much relevant experience has never been committed to writing, or is inaccessible because it is contained in confidential documents. Research that is basic to an understanding of the communication process is scattered throughout the literature of psychology, sociology, political science, and several other disciplines. The attempt that is made in this book to summarize current thinking on international communication must therefore remain incomplete.

Several relevant areas of knowledge either have been excluded from this treatment or have been touched on only briefly. Among these are the processes involved in using verbal or other symbols to encode messages that can then be transferred to another eye or ear and decoded, the field of comparative semantics, and the wide range of technical questions involved in communicating with people of other countries: for example, the properties of short-wave broadcasting, the economics of book translation, and the administration of foreign students. Psychological warfare, or the use of communications in conjunction with military operations, has also been excluded, although a few examples from the

* Bruce Lannes Smith, Harold D. Lasswell, and Ralph D. Casey, *Propaganda, Communication, and Public Opinion* (Princeton, N.J.: Princeton University Press, 1946); and Bruce Lannes Smith and Chitra M. Smith, *International Communication and Political Opinion* (Princeton, N.J.: Princeton University Press, 1956).

literature of psychological warfare have been used. Even if these and some other specialized areas are bypassed, international political communication remains an extraordinarily difficult subject to encompass.

The imperfections in this book do not, however, result from lack of generous assistance from a wide variety of sources. Indeed, it is difficult to acknowledge them all. The author's greatest debt is to those whose prior investigation and thought made this book possible, and this indebtedness is only partially acknowledged in the footnotes. Particular thanks are also due to members of a study group of the Council on Foreign Relations, which met in 1962-63 to discuss international communication under the chairmanship of John S. Dickey, and included Charles E. Allen, Frank Altschul, Edward W. Barrett, James P. Baxter III, Robert Blum, Robert O. Carlson, Louis G. Cowan, Martin F. Herz, Harold Kaplan, S. Holt McAloney, Porter McKeever, Lester Markel, Philip E. Mosely, Waldemar A. Nielsen, Ithiel DeSola Pool, George E. Probst, Leo Rosten, Col. Marshall E. Sanders, Howland H. Sargeant, Abe Sirkin, Hans Speier, Shepard Stone, and Ralph K. White. While the writer has not in every case followed the advice offered by members of this group, individually and collectively they have provided a major source of ideas and stimulation. In addition, invaluable suggestions have been received from those who indulgently consented to read portions of the manuscript at various stages, including Robert Blum, Lloyd A. Free, George S. Franklin, Jr., Alexander George, David W. MacEachron, Abe Sirkin, Hans Speier, Charles A. H. Thomson, and Ralph K. White. A draft of the entire manuscript was read by Henry M. Wriston and Shepard Stone, greatly to the profit of the writer. The author is also indebted to John C. Campbell and William Diebold, his colleagues on the Studies Staff of the Council on Foreign Relations, and to several former colleagues at The RAND Corporation, including Herbert S. Dinerstein, Joseph M. Goldsen, Leon Gouré, Herbert Goldhamer, and Paul Kecskemeti, some of whose ideas have been incorporated without explicit citations. Special thanks are due to Philip E. Mosely, who was director of the studies program of the Council on Foreign Relations at the time this book was started, and without whose encouragement it would not have been completed.

Numerous officials of the U. S. Information Agency, the Department of State, the Agency for International Development, and other governmental offices have been extremely helpful and patient in providing information and checking figures: especially Lowell Bennett, Leo P.

Crespi, Morton Glatzer, John P. McKnight, and Edward Savage of the U. S. Information Agency; Donald B. Cook of the Department of State; and Gale C. Griswold and Gerald F. Winfield of the Agency for International Development. None of these, needless to say, bears any responsibility for the opinions expressed herein, or for any errors that may have crept in despite their assistance.

Among the many who have assisted in preparing the manuscript for publication, the writer would like to thank Barbara A. Hanes, Mary L. Ryan, and Mrs. Mary E. Woodring in particular. The book has benefited greatly from the editing of Robert W. Valkenier.

More than the credit customarily assigned an author's spouse should go to Betty Davison, whose criticisms have combined wifely insights with experience from the world of commercial publishing, thereby sparing the reader much that he otherwise would have had to undergo.

W. P. D.

June, 1965

Contents

International Political Communication

I

Introduction: Communication as a Tool of Foreign Policy

This book searches for ways in which the United States can use public communication more effectively to advance its foreign policies. If the approach followed here were to be summarized in a single sentence, it might read something like this: Let us forget our preconceptions about "propaganda" and try to make a realistic evaluation of the political effects that newspapers, radio, films, the exchange of persons, and other means of international communication can achieve; let us then examine the ways in which these capabilities can be used by our democracy in the present-day world.

How does one make a realistic estimate of what international communication can be expected to accomplish? There is no accepted formula. Instead, a bevy of further questions immediately present themselves. First of all, one must gain a picture of the network of channels through which ideas flow throughout the world. How extensive is it, and how accurately does it transmit ideas from one country to another? Is a democratic government that tries to engage in propaganda whistling in a storm, emitting feeble pipes that are destined to be swallowed up by the torrent of words and images from other sources, or can one take advantage of existing currents to ride the winds?

Then there is the question of what happens when people are exposed to ideas that reach them through the mass media, or even by word of mouth. When are these ideas likely to have an effect, and when not? What kinds of effects can they achieve? Why is it that the most loudly repeated idea sometimes has little or no impact, while another one that is whispered softly produces a volcanic reaction? Under what conditions can mass media spark the formation of political parties?

Some reasons for the varied effects that can be achieved by communications are clearly rooted in the differences among nations. Any attempt to explain what can be accomplished through information and cultural programs must therefore take into account the ways that communications are used in different areas, and what happens to ideas when they are transmitted to another political environment. In Communist countries, for example, ideas from abroad have to penetrate a screen of ideological indoctrination, as well as border controls. Ideas that are directed to emerging countries are frequently misunderstood because the background information needed to interpret them is lacking. Those that arrive in industrialized democracies have to compete for the attention of the harassed citizenry with a flood of other ideas on all possible subjects.

If one can establish approximately what the potentialities of communications to any given area are, the next step is to ask how these can best be employed in the service of foreign policy. Just how can the desired effects be achieved? Here one may draw on the experience of the United States and other democracies, and also examine techniques used by totalitarian states. Most accounts dealing with the use of communications to advance national policies are, however, disappointing. They merely describe what has been done, and do not tell us very much about the resulting effects. The available records on American activities, although voluminous, still leave many questions unanswered. It would be convenient if we could take a simple pragmatic approach and find out what has been done right, so that we could do more of it, and what has been done badly, so that our mistakes could be avoided. But this is impossible, except in rare cases. The United States has been conducting information and cultural programs on a large scale for some twenty-five years, but we have only a vague notion of what has been accomplished—a fact that is as frustrating to those who set out to prove that this country has been losing the "battle of ideas" by default as to those who defend the effectiveness of our efforts. In the abstract, we know that communications can be extremely powerful, but when it comes to a particular case we find it difficult to prove their effectiveness.

The present analysis is intended to lead both to greater awareness of the role that international communication can play in many widely varying situations and to a number of general recommendations regarding the use of communications in support of foreign policy. The former aim is possibly the more important. It is the hope of the author that those who are professionally concerned with one or more aspects of the flow of ideas among nations will find it useful to look at their interests in a broader context, even though their own experience in a given field may go beyond anything that can be presented here. Those who are only occasionally concerned with foreign audiences may find a treatment such as this even more useful. Relatively few Americans devote themselves full time to international information or cultural activities, but ever-increasing numbers of us are involved in the international communication network in one way or another, whether as travelers, hosts to foreign visitors, participants in business enterprises, or actors in events that become known abroad. This analysis will have served its purpose if it succeeds in assisting members of any of these groups to find better ways of using communications to help achieve the kind of world we want to live in.

As for general recommendations, a few that are presented in more detail in the concluding chapter may be summarized here by way of example. First, the United States should build more purposefully on its traditions of free public discussion and should regard freedom of information as the cornerstone of its international communication policy. Every effort should be made to see that government programs adhere to the standards of objectivity and truthfulness that are observed by the best of the private media, recognizing that most ideas which flow abroad from this country pass through nonofficial channels and that it is self-defeating to apply one set of standards to government activities and another to the private sector. We should remove those barriers to the free flow of ideas that we have erected ourselves, and should use all available instrumentalities to break down other barriers and to increase freedom of communication throughout the world. We should place more emphasis on a two-way exchange between the United States and other nations, and encourage other peoples to speak to us. Where communication is inadequate, the government should step in to provide information and interpretation, and should pave the way for private initiative to fill the gap as soon as possible. In short, we should work toward creating a situation in which public discussion on an international level can facilitate cooperation, compromise, and the formation of public opinion, much as it does at home.

The principle of free communication does not exclude special pleading or the dissemination of ideas to help attain predetermined ends in the international arena any more than in the domestic arena. It is a proper function of official information and cultural programs, both of the United States and of other countries, to advance the foreign policies of their respective governments, and to do so as efficiently as possible within the bounds of truthfulness and good taste. A second general recommendation is, therefore, that emphasis should be placed on increasing the effectiveness with which communications are used in American official programs.

More efficient use of the communication facilities at the disposal of the U. S. Government will require four kinds of improvements: a clearer realization of the kinds of political effects that can be achieved through the dissemination of ideas; a better understanding of the audiences to which we are speaking; more careful planning of all government programs on an integrated basis; and more attention to improving the quality and usefulness of our communications.

To achieve a more realistic understanding of the capabilities of communication means abandoning some commonly held preconceptions. We usually think of information or propaganda programs primarily as instruments of persuasion, although this is only one of their functions, and not necessarily the major one. They are often more important as the means to tell people how to do things they want to do already, or to provide them with ammunition to support existing opinions. We also tend to think of communications primarily as affecting individuals, although in fact their effects on organizations may be more significant. They frequently make it possible for organizations to form by rallying people to a flag or a cause, or by enabling widely separated individuals to join in a common effort; or they provide existing organizations with information that enables them to function more efficiently. We see communication as an instrument for winning over those who oppose us, although experience shows that our words are more likely to be heeded by those who are already sympathetic or are uncommitted. People have an almost unlimited capacity to ignore information they find unwelcome or irrelevant.

We must also learn to know our audiences better. If we are to originate communications that will receive attention and be acted upon, we should be able to anticipate how people will make use of the ideas we are transmitting to them. Will the circumstances under which they live allow them to respond even if they want to? Will our communications assist existing organizations or help new ones to form? In our personal relationships we almost instinctively appreciate the necessity of knowing as much as possible about people we are talking to, but this requirement is given much less emphasis in our international communication programs. Indeed, the detailed study of foreign audiences is one of the most neglected aspects of current information and cultural activities, public and private.

More careful audience analysis will make improved planning possible. One of the principal steps in the planning of communication programs is to predict which ideas will receive attention, and what kinds of actions or reactions they will evoke. This goal will never be completely attained, but if it is not accepted as the basis for planning there is little possibility that operations can be improved. Furthermore, planning for each geographical area should be conducted on a government-wide basis, rather than being segmented along agency lines; in spite of a network of coordinating committees, the activities of different government agencies are still poorly integrated.

But perhaps the most important improvements could be made in the content of American programs directed abroad. Our emphasis has traditionally been on quantity: How many hours a week are we broadcasting, how many students have been exchanged, and how many publications distributed? The growth in the facilities we have built for speaking to other nations has not been matched by an increase in the importance and usefulness of what we have to say to them. Many of the materials we send abroad to explain the United States and its policies and to assist developing nations in building modern societies were created for American audiences and do not take the requirements of foreign audiences into account. More attention—and money—should be devoted to the preparation of high-quality materials and the design of programs that are specially adapted to the needs and interests of those to whom they are directed.

A third general recommendation is that increased efforts should be made to bring government and private American communications to other peoples into a more harmonious relationship. Those who expect the United States Information Agency and the State Department to bear the entire burden of conducting our end of the international political dialogue are barking up only one tree in a very large forest. In many areas, the words and actions of private individuals and groups have a greater political impact than do those of the government. Some of these groups, especially those that are in basic sympathy with our foreign policies, could use greater assistance from official agencies; for instance, they need more information about their audiences in other countries, about our own foreign policies, and about what is already being done to advance these. Conversely, private citizens who are actively engaged in international communication could be of greater help in guiding government activities in this field.

Under a democratic system, most communications from the United States will never be harnessed to political goals, and there will always be some that produce a dissonant ring. Even so, greater harmony can be achieved by stimulating an awareness on the part of those who are in touch with foreign audiences of the political side-effects of what they say and do. If we know what these side-effects are, it will be possible in many cases to emphasize the desirable ones and to reduce those that are less desirable. Already, through voluntary action and the pressure of domestic public opinion, many Americans in business and other spheres of activity are showing greater sensitivity to the feelings of other peoples than was once the case. Much more can be done to encourage this trend.

In addition, further emphasis can be given to putting dissonant ideas into perspective, so that they will not loom larger than they are. One of the major functions of public and private information and cultural programs that have a political purpose is to interpret the total flow of international communications, so that films, news reports, and other materials can be judged in context. Already, efforts of the U. S. Information Agency to give an accurate picture of race relations in the United States appear to have made reports of individual racial incidents less disturbing to our friends abroad. Greater efforts by both public and private bodies to ensure that people in other countries can understand the meaning of ideas from the United States would be rewarding.

A final note concerns vocabulary. "Communication" is a cumbersome word. It would be a pleasure to avoid it. Furthermore, it has been employed in such a variety of contexts that it has a large number of connotations. A generation ago it was firmly established as part of the professional language of engineers, who applied it to the telephone, telegraph, and radio; and of physicians, who spoke of communicable diseases. Social scientists then began to find the term useful in describing human interaction; some defined communication as including all those processes by which people influence those around them, and others treated whole societies as communication systems. No wonder that librarians, faced with the necessity of classifying a book with "communication" in its title are tempted to hide it instead. In the following pages an effort will be made to hew close to one of the dictionary definitions of the term: the transfer of ideas by words or other symbols. "Communication," in the singular and as an adjective, will be used to refer to the whole *process* by which meaning is transferred; the plural, "communications," will refer to the messages themselves.

In spite of its noneuphonious ring, communication is an almost indispensable word if one wishes to discuss international exchanges of ideas, since other available terms refer to only parts or aspects of the process, and some are emotionally weighted. "News," "information," "education," "entertainment," "culture," and "propaganda" are all involved in international communication, yet none of these expressions is broad enough to include all the others.

Much of what we will be discussing in the following pages could properly be defined as "propaganda"—that is, as an attempt to influence the attitudes or behavior of others through the systematic use of words or other symbols. There is nothing inherently disreputable about propaganda. It can be used in the service of good causes as well as bad ones. A propagandist can be completely open and honorable, as, for instance, is the case with spokesmen for health associations who try to persuade the public to cooperate in disease prevention. Nevertheless, however much the purist insists that "propaganda" is not a pejorative term, in popular use it is one. In practice, propaganda is subjectively defined as "a persuasive statement that I don't like," and the first line of defense against any unwelcome political communication is to label it propaganda. Educators, artists, and newsmen, some of whom are engaged in activities that would have to be labeled as propaganda under a strict definition of the term, usually object strenuously to being included in the same category as political hucksters. For all these reasons the term is best used sparingly.

Even if one avoids the word "propaganda," however, it is still useful to distinguish between communications that are primarily intended to have a political effect and those that are not, and a further distinction should be made between government and nongovernment sources. Thus, ideas in international traffic fall into four broad categories:

1. Official communications that are intended to influence foreign audiences—for example, those of the U. S. Information Agency.

2. Official communications that are not intended to exert a political influence abroad—such as those of the U. S. Armed Forces Radio and Television Network overseas.

3. Private communications that are intended to have a political influence on foreign audiences—such as those of groups working to promote international understanding.

4. Private communications that do not have a political purpose—such as those of international news services or business enterprises with interests abroad.

These categories are not always clear and distinct. A single communication from either a private or official source may have both a political and a nonpolitical purpose, or its purpose may be unclear. And in some cases it is difficult to determine whether a source is governmental or nongovernmental.

A further problem is that there is no easy way to label those communications that do in fact have a political effect, whether they are designed to do so or not. Indeed, some messages with no political purpose may influence power relationships appreciably. This is especially likely to be true in the case of important news stories or information about scientific developments. Conversely, some messages that are designed to exert a political influence fall on deaf ears and achieve no effects at all.

In the following discussion, we shall be concerned with all communications that have a political impact, whether or not this is intended. The first half of the book is devoted to exploring certain characteristics of the world communication network as it exists today, the kinds of effects that communications can have, and the different roles they play in democracies, Communist states, and emerging countries. The second half deals more directly with the use of ideas to advance foreign policy: the structural requirements of an information or cultural program that is intended to exert political influence, the communication activities of the Communist countries and the United States, and the ways in which Americans, both in and out of government, might employ communications more effectively to support national goals. While the two halves of the book thus take different approaches to the subject matter, they are heavily interdependent, since the properties of communication affect its capabilities, and the policies that are adopted toward it help to shape the international network.

PART ONE

The Flow and Effects of Communications

II

The International Network

The principal channels through which ideas are exchanged among nations include international news services and the press, radio, and television; films and film-strips; books and other publications; cultural events and exhibitions; and personal contacts across national boundaries. These mechanisms, as well as subsidiary ones such as international mail services, telecommunications, and recordings, are patched together to form a tangled network.*

Several characteristics of this network affect the role that international communication plays in political life. One is its unevenness of coverage. In industrialized countries the network is dense, and brings an indigestible volume of ideas into almost every home, while in areas where modernization has just started the bounds of the known universe may extend only slightly beyond the edge of the village. Indeed, UNESCO has estimated that two-thirds of the world's population still lack the barest means of being informed of domestic news, let alone foreign news.

Also noteworthy is the extent to which the total volume of communications among nations has mushroomed in recent years, while technological developments have contributed to greater speed and wider dispersal. Although still thinly covered, the emerging countries of Africa, Asia, and Latin America have experienced a surprisingly rapid growth of the mass media, and more of their populations are now exposed to the stream of world events than ever before. The number of newspapers printed in these areas has increased by about one-third during the past decade, and the number of radio receivers has more than doubled.

At the same time, the United States has received a constantly increas-

* A brief description of the principal international communication channels is found in the Appendix.

ing share of attention in international communications. Except in Communist states, the press is likely to devote substantially more space to the United States than to any other foreign country, and American news tends to dominate the wires of the international news services.[1] In general, other peoples know far more about us than we about them.

Another important characteristic of systems for exchanging ideas among nations is that they all depend on facilities beyond the control of the person or organization originating a given message. Short-wave radio requires that suitable receivers be accessible to the audience. Most other radio and television transmissions must be rebroadcast if they are to reach people in distant areas. Information sent through news service facilities is subject to extensive processing before it is available in newscasts or newspapers. Films, recordings, books and other publications, as well as letters, are dependent on the international mails, or other forwarding services. International personal contacts involve travel facilities, passports, and visas. For a message to reach an audience in another country, the cooperation of a large number of third parties, including foreign government agencies, is usually required.

The international network is thus likely to be effective in transmitting ideas to large numbers of people only insofar as it is tied in with national and local networks. For a speech of a government official to reach a substantial audience abroad, it is usually necessary that the text, or a story about it, be carried by local newspapers, radio, or other media. A foreign book or magazine is more widely read if it is available in the native language at local bookstores or newsstands. To reach the widest possible audience, any idea must be talked about, and many areas that have poorly developed modern media partially make up for this by more extensive use of person-to-person channels.

Barriers to the Exchange of Ideas

Of greater interest than the extent of the international network is its quality: the degree to which it is able to transmit ideas from one nation to another accurately and comprehensibly. The quality of communication naturally varies as between any two countries, but in few cases is it outstandingly good. Even if semantic difficulties can be overcome, messages may be distorted or inhibited in a large number of ways. Among the principal barriers to the free flow of ideas are incompetence, bias, efforts to give the consumer what he wants, censorship of many kinds, various regulatory activities, and technical and economic factors.

Incompetence in international reporting has most frequently been criticized by newsmen who are interested in raising journalistic standards. As an example of the difficulties that can be caused by poor reporting, an International Press Institute study described the effects of news stories from London that failed to give an accurate rendition of Prime Minister Attlee's remarks during a British foreign-policy debate in 1953. These stories immediately led to angry reactions in the United States. A U. S. Senator said of the British: "Let them . . . be damned." Newspapers across the country began to take pro- or anti-British positions without really knowing what had been said in London. The flurry ended when the British Information Service released the text of Attlee's speech, most of which was printed by *The New York Times*.[2] The *Nieman Reports,* published by the Nieman Foundation at Harvard, contain numerous similar examples. The less developed countries, in particular, suffer from a lack of professionally trained journalists, with the result that instances of misleading news stories are relatively frequent. A former Latin American newspaperman has complained that "What we read in our papers is not only questionable as to truth but lacking in imagination." [3]

An even more serious form of distortion results when those who control communication channels allow a systematic bias to be introduced. The extent to which this has been true in the United States has received apoplectic attention from a number of American writers. Distortion of this type is often traced to the pressure of advertisers and powerful interest groups, and to the prejudices and political preferences of publishers and editors. Upton Sinclair saw journalism as one of the devices whereby industrial autocracy maintained control over political democracy. Writers in liberal journals of opinion frequently complain about bias in the American mass media, charging, for example, that some editors and publishers are more interested in fighting the Cold War than in bringing their readers full and accurate reports.[4]

European students of the press have given extensive attention to specific areas where coverage has been restricted or biased by pressure groups. A survey conducted by a Swiss scholar found that the most widespread form of pressure was the threat to withdraw advertising. A single unfavorable review of a film could cause motion-picture exhibitors or theater owners to cancel their advertisements, and a railroad official was even on record as suggesting that no funds should be spent for advertising in papers that gave extensive attention to accidents at grade crossings. A German journalism trade periodical complained that if a paper published anything derogatory to "a cattle-dealer, a professor, or, for that matter, a bicycle rider," then all cattle-dealers, professors, and bicycle riders felt insulted and threatened to cancel their subscriptions.[5]

Communication content may also be affected by nationalistic or other emotions, or by conventions governing the media in a given area. It has been alleged that coverage of American affairs in the postwar British press has been colored by frustration over Great Britain's reduced power status and resentment of the role in international affairs played by the United States; and a distinguished Latin American journalist has been quoted as saying that in his country one never attacks the armed forces, the Catholic Church, old and distinguished families, or large corporations and banks.[6]

In many cases, bias is introduced unintentionally. Neither a reporter nor a scholar can completely free himself from his background and predilections. Even on television, where an event is seen by the viewer as it happens, complete objectivity seems to be impossible. When researchers systematically monitored television coverage of the 1952 Democratic Party national convention in Chicago, they found that each of three networks covering the proceedings gave a very different impression as to what was going on. One network left the viewer with a feeling that sinister forces in the background were manipulating events on the convention floor, a second network gave a picture of confusion, while the third added enough interpretive comment to give an air of rationality to developments as they unfolded.[7] Other studies of television coverage have yielded similar observations.

As in the case of journalistic incompetence, it is not difficult to find examples of distortion introduced by bias. Nevertheless, as far as the free world is concerned, it is doubtful whether this is among the most important barriers to the flow of accurate information among nations. The large, independent news agencies have pointed out again and again that they serve clients of all shades of opinion, and are subject to vigorous competition among themselves and from other media. Deliberate bias is a luxury they cannot afford. While distortions, sometimes frequent, on the part of individual publications or electronic media can be cited, the relative ease with which these lapses are detected suggests that less distorted presentations are not too difficult to find elsewhere. Free-world governments, likewise, are subject to a multiplicity of checks on most of the information that passes through official or government-controlled channels, and they cannot afford to acquire reputations for consistent mendacity. Agencies and channels controlled by authoritarian governments have worse records; here a heavy political coloration can be expected.

Another source of distortion in international communication is the effort to sell news and entertainment. The box-office and audience ratings are, of course, of great importance in commercial films, radio, and television. Wire agencies transmit what they believe is likely to be used in the media they serve. One student of the press visited a bilingual newspaper in Strasbourg that received both the German and the French services of one American agency. The disparity of the two news files almost made him wonder if the two could stem from the same source.[8] Apparently, the agency in question had selected items to fit what it regarded as the varying interests of French and German audiences.

Estimation of reader or listener interests and prejudices is especially important in molding the contents of media that reach the consumer directly. No matter how faithfully wire agencies may seek to report international news, this material usually will not be used unless the local editor thinks it will be given attention by his public. Furthermore, since most media receive much more information than they can handle in the limited space or time available to them, editors must in any case make a rigorous selection. A newspaperman who compared American press coverage of the Castro revolt in Cuba with the original AP and UPI reports about the revolt that were sent to subscribing newspapers found that the papers received enough wire copy to tell the long, involved story, but they made little use of this material until the last six days before Batista's regime fell.[9] Those who control the content of other channels—the film exhibitor, the bookstore proprietor, or even the librarian—also make selections based in part on audience interest.

Box-office pressure has apparently been partially successful in preventing Hollywood from making films that might be offensive to Communist elements. A newspaper survey of major film producers in 1961 found that only two of them could remember having produced movies during the preceding decade that were critical of any aspect of Soviet life. One explanation for this anomaly, at a time when most studios denied employment to any actor or writer considered pro-Communist, is that Hollywood executives feared lowered attendance in countries such as France and Italy, where Communist parties were strong. Some industry spokesmen recalled that there had been difficulty in finding theaters in Italy to show *Ninotchka* because of the opposition of the large Italian Communist Party to this famous Garbo film's mild spoofing of the Soviets.[10]

Censorship constitutes an even more serious barrier to international communication than bias or the effort to sell, especially if both direct and indirect forms of censorship are included. One authority, in the course of a survey of press freedom throughout the world, identified the following major means of government control of information in addition to direct censorship: punitive action against information personnel, licensing or selection of information personnel, licensing of publication, restriction of vital supplies such as newsprint, seizure of publications, limitations on access to news, control of distribution, and regulation of policy and format.[11] Such restrictive practices, in one form or another, are found both in authoritarian countries and in a great many nations that have a fairly democratic form of government. As of 1961, the International Press Institute concluded that only thirty-five of the United Nations' member states could claim to have a free press, and that in at least as many the press was fully controlled. The IPI's observation at the end of 1962 was that this had been a grim year for believers in press freedom, and it was joined in this dour judgment by the Associated Press. The AP survey at the end of 1963 was no more cheerful.[12]

In addition to exercising domestic controls, most countries try to regulate some categories of incoming information. Democracies ordinarily seek to exclude certain materials—pornography, for instance—although political criteria are also used on occasion. During World War II, the U. S. Post Office Department started holding up Nazi propaganda materials at ports of entry, and similar measures have been applied to Communist propaganda. Other democracies have arrangements for controlling incoming ideas that are sometimes more strict than those of the United States and sometimes more lax. Dictatorships tend toward much more stringent measures, including jamming of radio broadcasts and threats against those who read or listen to foreign communications, as well as strict border controls applying both to the movement of people and to information and cultural materials.[13]

Measures to keep domestic information from flowing out are also frequent. In many areas, especially in Communist states, foreigners are limited in their freedom of movement and in the sources they can consult. Newsmen who succeed in gathering information may be prevented from transmitting it by threats of retaliation against themselves or their employers. A foreign correspondent who refuses to see the error of his ways may be expelled from the country.

Some states apply direct censorship to outgoing information. In 1961, Brazil announced that films made within the country would have to pass the censor before being sent abroad. A law to this effect had been on the books since 1946, but had not been enforced. Its revival was brought about by a film made by *Life* magazine showing conditions among Brazilian families in the northeast drought area. American film-makers in Southeast Asia have found that the nations of this region usually make permission to shoot sequences on their territory contingent on submission of the complete script for approval.

In addition to censorship and other intentional restrictions, governments frequently impose regulations that are not designed to limit the flow of information but may actually do so. For instance, national trade and tariff policies often hamper communication. A UNESCO study that catalogued these regulations as of the mid-1950's noted that the general trend toward economic controls had engulfed materials of education, science, and culture along with other commodities.[14] At the time of this survey, the United States, for instance, had a 10 per cent tariff on certain categories of books, a duty of 1 cent per foot on most entertainment and news films, and a 15 per cent tariff on phonograph recordings. Many other states had higher imposts. Official regulations in some countries limit the proportion of certain materials that can be brought in from abroad or provide that information may be distributed only through certain channels. Great Britain permits a television network to give only 12 per cent of its time to imported programs; Canada prescribes that 55 per cent of TV programs be produced locally, and Japan allows importers to pay no more than $450 for an imported half-hour television show.[15] Several countries have ruled that foreign news services must distribute their product through national agencies, and not directly to the mass media.

Cost factors also play a large part in determining what information reaches the consumer through the international network, and not infrequently cause omissions and distortions. A 1956 UNESCO study of the international telecommunication rate structure found that charges for transmitting a given message between equidistant points might vary by over 300 per cent. Sometimes it costs twice as much to send a message in one direction rather than the other between the same two points. The rate was 25 cents per word to send a press telegram from Sweden to Paraguay, and 15 cents per word to send the same message from Paraguay to Sweden. From Spain to New York, the charge was 13 cents per word; from New York to Switzerland, 6.5 cents. Although technological advances since World War II have made it physically possible for domestic media almost anywhere in the world to receive extensive international coverage, these advances cannot be fully exploited because of political and economic restrictions.[16]

Barriers to the movement of people from one country to another are at least as great as those inhibiting the flow of information and cultural materials. To begin with, only certain categories of people can travel: those who can afford it, those in certain occupations, those who are not tied down by domestic responsibilities or ill-health, and so on. In addition, governments have made foreign travel more difficult and expensive by cumbersome regulations and by imposing a variety of charges, such as passport fees and debarkation taxes. Most Communist countries are highly restrictive when it comes to allowing people either to enter or leave. Their citizens must often show a "need to travel" in order to go abroad, and visas for incoming foreign visitors are granted on a selective basis. In January, 1958, Poland adopted a schedule of costs for a passport that almost cut off the flow of Poles visiting the West, except on official business. A passport for travel to America was to cost $292—a charge equal to three or four months' pay for the average worker—while the charge for a passport good for a visit to Western Europe was fixed at $210. Those going to Communist countries, on the other hand, could obtain passports for $17. There was, however, a strong adverse public reaction to this price schedule, and passports to all Western countries were reduced to about $42. Even this lower fee still limited sharply the number of those who could afford to travel to the West.[17]

Some of the effects of the various biases and selective mechanisms that influence the international flow of ideas are highlighted when one compares the way different media treat the same events, or events occurring during the same time period. For example, a comparison of the issues published by fourteen newspapers in different countries on November 2, 1956, the day the Anglo-French invasion of Suez and Soviet intervention in Hungary became known, showed strikingly different ways of handling the news. All free-world papers covered both stories on their front pages, but Sweden's *Dagens Nyheter* was the only one giving top billing to Soviet intervention. *Pravda* devoted nearly its entire front page to a denunciation of the Anglo-French invasion, but ignored events in Hungary almost entirely: a 250-word item on page fourteen entitled "The Situation in Hungary" said nothing at all about the involvement of Soviet forces.[18]

An earlier UNESCO study of comparative coverage in seventeen newspapers also found wide variations in the treatment given major events. *O Estado* of São Paulo covered all but one of the nineteen principal stories of the week, the best record of the papers examined. New York's *Daily News* missed five, and Moscow's *Pravda* (which provided the best coverage of any Communist paper in the sample) missed nine. The study concluded that news was seldom presented in a way that made understanding of world events easy; the reader had to make a considerable effort if he wanted to be informed.[19]

Another way of evaluating the role of distortion in international communication is to ask how accurate and adequate a picture of any given country is provided by the media in a second country. This approach was used by the International Press Institute in its study of how nations are presented to each other in the press. Each researcher, after assembling a picture of Country B as given by the press of Country A, then passed his report to a newsman from Country B and asked, in effect, whether the latter could recognize the portrait of his own nation. This was done for ten free-world countries. Only rarely were the factual elements of the picture criticized, and relatively little willful bias was found, but in most cases the pictures tended to be incomplete and unbalanced; adequate interpretation was lacking. All the judges were dissatisfied with the reporting about their own countries.[20]

Completeness and absolute accuracy are ideals that individual media can never achieve. Nevertheless, when the channels for the international flow of ideas are so constituted that they supplement each other, it is more likely that people can be adequately informed if they wish to be. No one medium can be expected to do the whole job by itself, but many of the biases that are built into the communication network can be offset when a multiplicity of channels are allowed to function independently. Books and foreign travel can be particularly valuable in providing a background against which ideas received from other sources can be interpreted. Personal letters, short-wave broadcasts, magazines, films, international exhibitions, the remarks of visitors from abroad, and information from other specialized sources, sometimes spread by word of mouth, often can be used to supplement or verify reports carried by the local press, TV, and radio. Furthermore, just as there are powerful forces that tend to inhibit or distort ideas flowing through international communication channels, there are also forces working in the opposite direction.

Forces Promoting Freedom of Information

Several factors tending to facilitate the flow of accurate information through the international network have already been touched upon. Most commercial media and some government sources try to give as accurate and complete a picture as they can. Commercial undertakings know that they will suffer loss of credibility if their reports are consistently too wide of reality. Government offices require fairly accurate information, at least for internal use, and some of this reaches a broader public. Censorship and inhibition of information has in it an implication of fear and weakness which, even if it does not ensure freedom, nevertheless sometimes brings about a relaxation of restrictions.

Furthermore, countries that have attempted to maintain controls over communication have experienced great difficulty in making these controls watertight. Just as it is technically difficult to assure a completely free flow of ideas among nations, it is also difficult to inhibit this flow entirely. A senior foreign correspondent has reported that, although censorship had been attempted in many countries which he had covered, he could not recall a single instance when he was effectively blocked from sending out important news in one way or another. At the most, the censor caused delay and inconvenience. Sometimes this correspondent filed stories after leaving the country in question; on other occasions he found that one channel was censored while a second was not. Another reporter, noting that the press in South Viet-Nam, Laos, and Cambodia was heavily influenced by government controls, observed that people could supplement press reports with information received from foreign radios, rumors, foreign embassy information centers, and foreign correspondents.[21] The U. S. Central Intelligence Agency, in an experiment to see how much secret information could be obtained from open sources, contracted with a group of university scholars to produce a picture of the U.S. order of battle from unclassified publications, speeches, and press releases. The picture proved to be surprisingly complete, and included some important defense secrets.[22] Even during the time of the most stringent Stalinist controls in the

Soviet Union, foreigners who were stationed there reported that a large amount of fairly accurate information about the outside world was available through person-to-person channels, even though it was not mentioned in the official Soviet media.

In addition to these limitations on the suppression of information, a number of efforts have been made by international organizations, governments, and private associations to break down barriers to international communication. The principal international organizations concerned are the United Nations and some of its specialized agencies. Although the U.N. has not taken as strong a stand on freedom of information as its more liberal members might wish, it has nevertheless consistently upheld the principle, and has stimulated an immense number of debates, conferences, and reports on the subject.[23] The U.N. Declaration of Universal Human Rights recognizes freedom to receive and impart information as one of man's basic rights, and the Commission on Human Rights decided in 1960 to review developments affecting freedom of information as a regular item on its agenda. Pursuant to this resolution, the Economic and Social Council requested the Secretary General to make an annual report on developments affecting communication media, and the first such report was submitted to the Economic and Social Council in December 1961.[24] The United Nations conducted a seminar on freedom of information in 1962, and in 1963 it convened a conference on international travel and tourism that unanimously affirmed the right of freedom of movement and called for lower travel costs and the easing of travel curbs. Several routine U.N. operations also promote the flow of ideas among nations. For example, its debates are heard by representatives of nearly all nations, and are carried further not only by commercial and governmental networks but by broadcasting and publishing programs under the direct control of the world body.

All the U.N. specialized agencies encourage the international exchange of ideas in the areas for which they are responsible, but UNESCO has been especially active in promoting freedom of information in many fields and in numerous ways. Its charter contains the statement that the member states "are agreed and determined to develop and to increase the means of communication between their peoples." UNESCO has worked for international agreements to promote the free flow of ideas "by word and image" and to remove existing barriers; it has assisted in the international exchange of students; it has sponsored conferences to improve competence, standards, coverage, and cooperation among media in various countries; it has encouraged the development of adequate information services in emerging areas; and it has been foremost in collecting information about the channels through which ideas pass.

An example of a private organization that is doing a remarkable amount to promote journalistic freedom and competence is the International Press Institute, founded in 1952.[25] The Institute's membership of 1,500 represents more than 600 newspapers in some 48 "free press" countries. Its headquarters are in Zurich, where a small secretariat is maintained on a tiny budget, and annual conferences of members have been held in major cities throughout the free world. The Institute has eschewed the support of any government, and has been financed largely by contributions from publishers and by the Ford, Rockefeller, and Asia foundations. It has given its attention primarily to countries where freedom of the press exists at least in principle—on the premise that it can accomplish more in such countries than in nations that are overtly authoritarian.[26]

The IPI has developed some ingenious methods of improving the objectivity and completeness of reporting. For example, during the days when the debate on the European Defense Community was causing acrimonious comment in both France and Germany, the Institute assembled a group of French and German newspapermen and showed them how each country was being treated in the press of the other. Both groups were shocked at the distorted picture of opinion in their own country that they found in the press of their neighbor, and resolved to try to combat distortion in their own coverage. A substantial improvement in balance on both sides could be observed after the confrontation. Similar efforts have been made by the IPI in the case of the Greek and Turkish press, although with less striking results.

Other activities of the IPI have included conducting seminars and training courses for newsmen in emerging countries, sponsoring "traveling consultants" to assist publishers with the technical and business side of running a newspaper, organizing discussions of specialized subjects such as science reporting and European economic integration, and encouraging the growth of national press institutes to promote a free and competent press on an individual-country basis. As of 1964, national institutes had been founded in India, Korea, and the Philippines. IPI's work has also involved cataloguing violations of press freedom and attempting to mobilize free-world opinion to have these restrictions removed. Success has been achieved in several cases—for instance, in Ceylon, where the Institute played an important role in persuading the government to lift a rigid censorship that was imposed in 1959, and in India, where three Portuguese newsmen were released from internment as a result of IPI intervention following the invasion of Goa.

Private international news services and professional associations have also played an important part in promoting the free flow of information. Of these, the Associated Press has been particularly active in opposing governmental information restrictions, as well as monopolistic practices on the part of publishers.[27] Many of the professional and trade associations to which communication personnel and agencies belong, such as the Inter-American Press Association, seek to improve facilities and standards and to break down barriers as part of their activities. UNESCO has listed 64 international professional associations in the mass media, as well as 1,049 national organizations of this type in 93 states.[28]

Various governments have contributed to greater freedom of international communication, either individually or through intergovernmental associations. Most democracies have supported resolutions in the United Nations aimed at increasing freedom of both domestic and international information media. In order to find a majority, however, such resolutions have usually been watered down to the point of ambiguity. As one critic has pointed out, these texts are based on the lowest level of freedom allowed by the supporting states.[29] More important are specific agreements between or among nations that facilitate travel, telecommunications, the exchange of cultural materials, or various forms of information activities. In addition, several intergovernmental associations are engaged substantially in promoting cultural relations—for example, the Council of Europe, the Organization of American States, and the Arab League.[30] Many other intergovernmental bodies are involved in cultural and information exchanges to a lesser degree.

The most important forces working against barriers to international communication are human ingenuity and man's desire to know. In authoritarian countries, people who are curious about the outside world have developed to a high degree the art of "reading between the lines," and they often draw surprisingly accurate conclusions from very sparse information. Conversely, where there is little interest about foreign areas, even the most highly developed system of communication is unlikely to bring ideas from abroad to a wide audience. Apathy is an even greater barrier to international communication than are political or economic restrictions. This, and some of the other psychological factors that affect the exchange of ideas, will be discussed in the following chapter.

III

Impact of Communications on the Individual

Even though the global network of international communication channels is growing rapidly, it does not follow that the ideas flowing through this network automatically have an effect. Indeed, the extent to which people can remain ignorant in the face of easily available information, whether from foreign or domestic sources, is impressive. In 1947-48, an analysis of replies to public-opinion polls showed that about 30 per cent of the American electorate were unaware of almost any given event in American foreign affairs. Some 45 per cent could be considered aware of major issues, but were not informed about their nature. Only about 25 per cent consistently showed some knowledge of foreign-policy problems. Another study, conducted at about the same time, disclosed a similar picture: a "hard core of chronic know-nothings" amounted to about a third of the adult population, another third had a smattering of information about foreign-policy issues, and the rest could be considered relatively well-informed.[1]

Repeated public-opinion soundings taken during the past fifteen years suggest that the level of information about foreign policy in the United States is gradually increasing, but that the rate of increase is slow.[2] Increasing interest is borne out by other indexes. When Cordell Hull was Secretary of State in the 1930's, about a dozen newspapermen could be expected to turn up for his press conferences, while those of John Foster Dulles in the 1950's might draw as many as 175. Mail coming to the State Department for reply has greatly increased in quantity: in 1958, the number of letters approximated 40,000; in 1961, about 180,000 such letters were received; and in 1963, the total was expected to exceed 300,000. The sheer quantity of foreign news in the American press has also risen, presumably reflecting greater reader interest.[3] Nevertheless, as of 1961, only 22 per cent of a national cross-section said that they had heard or read anything about the European Common Market, and in 1964 one out of four American adults did not know that mainland China had a Communist government.[4]

In other countries where the communication network is dense and where at least rudimentary knowledge about principal foreign policy issues is easily available, the public at large does not appear to be any better informed about foreign affairs than is the American public. In 1955, six years after the founding of NATO, slightly more than 50 per cent of a cross-section of West German voters said they knew what it was, but when questioned more closely about half of the "yesses" could not give a statement of NATO's purpose.[5] The English and French publics have likewise shown high proportions either unaware of or uninformed about most questions affecting the foreign relations of their countries, apart from occasional matters of burning interest. In countries where the mass media are thinly spread, and illiteracy is relatively high, awareness of foreign affairs is even lower.

Nor is it a simple matter to raise the level of information, as indicated by an experiment conducted in 1947-48 by the American Association for the United Nations in cooperation with the Stephen H. Wilder Foundation and the United Nations Association of Cincinnati. This experiment involved organizing a campaign to make every adult in the Greater Cincinnati area conscious of and informed about the United Nations. The campaign lasted six months, and during this period Cincinnati's citizens were deluged with information about the world organization. Mass media, advertisers, schools, religious groups, and civic groups combined to din into the ears and minds of southern Ohio residents facts about the United Nations, including the slogan of the campaign: "Peace begins with the United Nations—the United Nations begins with you." Display cards carried the message in buses; newspapers stepped up U.N. coverage and features; thousands of matchbooks and blotters with the campaign slogan on them were distributed; and radio stations plugged the theme, one of them scheduling as many as 150 spot announcements each week.[6]

In spite of this vigorous and ably conducted effort, the campaign had an almost imperceptible effect on the level of information about the U.N. in Cincinnati. A survey conducted by the National Opinion Research Center of the University of Chicago *before* the publicity started found 30 per cent of the area's population almost totally ignorant about the purposes of the United Nations. After the campaign, a second survey found the percentage essentially unchanged. Further techniques were used to evaluate the impact of the campaign, in addition to the two waves of surveys, but they all reinforced the same conclusion: the level of information about the United Nations in Cincinnati had not been affected appreciably. Those who had been ignorant before remained ignorant.

A similiar experiment was conducted in West Germany, where officials of the South German Radio decided to see if they could raise the level of information among their listeners about the upper house of the Federal Legislature in Bonn, the Bundesrat. Polls showed that at that time only 10 per cent of the station's listeners could give a satisfactory definition of what the Bundesrat was. For two years, Radio Stuttgart seized every opportunity to insert mentions of the German upper house in its news and public-affairs broadcasts, together with a one-sentence description of what the Bundesrat was and what it did. Listeners were tested about their knowledge of this constitutional body at the end of the first year and again at the end of the second. On neither occasion could a statistically significant change in the level of information be detected.[7]

In contrast to such instances as these, where large doses of information seem to have had little impact, cases can be cited in which publicity has had very important effects. Skilled public-relations men have succeeded in making budding film or TV personalities familiar to a large proportion of the population, advertisers have had remarkable successes in selling, and history is replete with stories of stirring messages that swayed millions.

To understand why some messages have an impact and others do not, it is necessary to consider some of the psychological processes that affect attention and comprehension. These processes condition our reactions to all kinds of communications—whether domestic or international—and have been examined in connection with advertising, education, and behavior in small groups, as well as in the context of political affairs. Observations that have been made in a wide variety of social and psychological studies are thus helpful in explaining the impact of international communications on the individual.

Selectivity of Attention

One of the major reasons for the wide range in the effects of communications is that people are highly selective in the choice of objects for their attention. This selectivity is essential if a human being is to behave in a rational manner. A person who tried to attend to *all* the communications available to him would run the danger of becoming completely disoriented.

Fortunately, from a very early age, each individual learns ways of sorting out the communications to which he is exposed, so that he gives his attention primarily to those that are likely to have significance for him. William James refers to this "narrowness of consciousness" as one of the most extraordinary facts of our life: "although we are besieged at every moment by impressions from our whole sensory surface, we notice so very small a part of them." [8]

Such a felicitous constriction of perception is achieved in part by the fact that a person's mental picture of the world helps him to select for attention those incoming communications that are likely to be useful to him. This mental picture is a complicated structure, consisting of factual knowledge, attitudes, and images. It is based largely on experience; its various components have proved useful guides to action in the past, and they ordinarily remain unchanged until further experience shows that they are not helping a person achieve the things he wants, or until he develops new goals and desires.[9]

Most people have constructed a fairly accurate mental picture of those aspects of their environment that they have found significant. It is interesting to dwell on inaccurate and grotesque ideas that sometimes are widespread, but to do so distorts the true situation. A person would find it difficult to survive if his knowledge, attitudes, and beliefs did not give him a reasonably good guide to reality. Even when it comes to specialized areas, such as economics, researchers have found that most people have a fairly sound, if unsophisticated, picture of their situation. They therefore are not swayed easily by rumors and unfounded statements; nor are they puppets in the hands of those who would manipulate their behavior.[10] Their existing picture of the world provides a yardstick against which they can measure the importance and accuracy of the communications to which they are exposed.

Another characteristic of our internalized road map is that it must maintain a fair degree of consistency, although this consistency does not have to be perfect, especially with regard to questions on which we are not called to act frequently or directly. For instance, a study of attitudes toward Russia held by men who had no immediate involvement in foreign affairs found that most of them thought that relations between the United States and the Soviet Union would improve during the next few years, but they also believed that in the long run war with Russia was inevitable. Their short-term and long-term perspectives were not well integrated. This seeming remoteness of international affairs from the daily life of most people makes it possible for them to entertain inconsistent views.[11] Nevertheless, attitudes, stereotypes, and beliefs relating to matters of immediate concern ordinarily form a harmonious structure. Psychologists can often infer unstated attitudes by reasoning that these are likely to be consistent with known attitudes, and students of opinion can sometimes relate answers to various questions so as to derive insights into a respondent's total personality.[12] The pressure to maintain consistency leads people to attend to messages that are harmonious with their internalized picture of the environment; conversely, they tend to avoid ideas that conflict with this picture.

When a person entertains sets of attitudes or beliefs that impel him in two different directions at once, he experiences a feeling of discomfort, especially if he is forced to take some action. We sometimes speak of being "torn" between two inclinations. A series of ingenious experiments has shown that when people act in a way that is inconsistent with what they already know or believe, they actively seek to reduce the resulting internal disharmony by finding a formula that will reconcile the conflicting elements.[13] Sometimes the strain can be reduced by acquiring new attitudes or information; sometimes by giving up some of the ideas one already has.

No two individuals have exactly the same picture of the world, but those who live in close association often develop similar bodies of attitudes and information. There tends to be a harmony of belief within social groups as well as within individuals.[14] The desirability—sometimes amounting to a necessity—of preserving this harmony has a strong influence on the kinds of ideas to which any group member gives his attention. He is likely to seek out communications that are useful in his social relations and to avoid those that would be socially disruptive.

Citizens of each nation tend to develop certain patterns of belief that are similar in many respects to those of their fellow nationals. Important individual and social differences remain, but one can still speak of national characteristics and ways of thinking. This is especially true in regard to mental pictures of other countries, and a great deal of effort has been devoted to identifying and describing the images that citizens of different nations have of each other.[15] These images affect our attention to information about other nations: we are more likely to notice facts that fit in with our stereotypes than those that conflict with them.

The mental content that helps us guide our actions as individuals, as members of social groups, and as citizens of a given country thus also sensitizes us to the importance of certain communications and predisposes us to disregard others. When an information film on NATO was shown in Germany, for instance, it was found that those who already were familiar with NATO learned more from the film than those who were not.[16] It is difficult to interest people in things that are completely new to them, unless it can be shown that these are somehow relevant to their existing wants and needs. (As the author of the above study points out, if the NATO film had been shown to young soldiers in the new German army the results might have been different.) Ordinarily, we rely on the existence of prior attitudes or knowledge of certain subjects to alert us to the potential usefulness of further information about these same subjects.

Communication Habits

Our existing view of the world gives us a great many clues as to *what kinds* of information we require; a closely related mechanism helps us determine *how to get* information. This mechanism consists of a body of "communication habits"—that is, the knowledge, attitudes, and practices that govern our use of communication channels.

In the course of his lifetime, each person learns to pay attention to certain sources of information that help him satisfy his wants and needs. Some people become accustomed to relying on radio or TV for current news; others, on the press. In the United States, the higher the educational level of a person, the more attention he is likely to pay to the daily newspaper.[17] Studies of consumer behavior have indicated that some population categories obtain much of their information about goods and services from the mass media, while others tend to consult knowledgeable individuals. For instance, women with large families are likely to read advertising about consumer goods, while other people often seek the advice of these women before doing their shopping. Businessmen rely to a surprising extent on word of mouth to keep in touch with what is going on in the economic sphere.[18] All these communication habits, sometimes formed on the basis of experience and sometimes learned because they reflect a prevailing practice, play a large part in helping people choose the sources of information to which they will expose themselves.

Communication habits also help to determine how much importance or credence will be attached to information that is received from certain sources. Some people and media are regarded as reliable; others as less so. For example, in one experiment an opinion was more often accepted when it was attributed to an American scientist than when it was attributed to *Pravda*. In another experiment, a cartoon chart of "The Four Goals of Labor" was taken from a labor newspaper and equipped with a legend explaining that it came from a publication of the National Association of Manufacturers. It was then shown to twenty union members, most of whom criticized it as "patronizing," "loaded," or "paternalistic." Polls have indicated that some groups among the American public place more trust in news heard over TV, while others are more likely to believe information from the press.[19] A face-to-face communication often has a greater impact than substantially the same message in another form. The weight attached to the words of different speakers varies, however, and people usually learn a number of cues that enable them to evaluate the statements of persons they do not know. Some people tend to deduce the status of a speaker from his voice and to believe "high-status speakers" more readily than "low-status speakers."[20]

Cultural differences in the use of communication media are marked, even when substantially the same channels are available to members of the societies being compared. In a Norwegian election survey, 19 per cent of the respondents reported that they did not follow the campaign in any of the mass media, while a similar survey in the United States found that only 8 per cent of Americans gave such a response. On the other hand, 23 per cent of the Norwegians were members of political parties, and presumably received campaign information through their party organizations, while in the United States only 0.4 per cent reported a party affiliation. Nearly half of another cross-section of Americans said they regularly followed electoral news in the press, while only one in five French respondents did.[21] Americans usually regard a press report as more authoritative than a rumor, while in countries with a controlled press the reverse is often the case. In societies having a strong oral tradition, meetings and assemblies may have more appeal than the mass media. A study of communication in Samoa found that, even though press and radio were fairly widely available, the traditional pattern of holding ceremonial gatherings in the districts and villages continued to be the most effective method for reaching the population.[22]

The simplest way to appreciate the working of communication habits and the other psychological mechanisms that guide our attention is through introspection. Why did you notice certain things in the newspaper and ignore others? Which were the stories that "jumped out at you"? What can you remember from the radio and TV fare to which you were recently exposed? Does your attention tend to wander when some people are talking and become focused when others speak? The reasons for your behavior will not always be immediately clear, but by and large you will find either that you gave your attention to messages that were relevant to your existing interests—that you could "use" in some way—or that you were following habits that had led you to useful information in the past.

Processing Incoming Information

The mechanisms by which we sort out incoming communications operate fairly efficiently, but they still allow some boring, meaningless, or disturbing ideas to come to our attention. The selective process is never perfect. Most people therefore develop a variety of psychological devices that help to make incoming ideas more interesting and less disturbing.

Rational methods for dealing with communications that conflict with established attitudes and knowledge are familiar. We decide that the conflicting information is overbalanced by other factors, has little importance, comes from an unreliable source, or is simply untrue. Sometimes we actively look for proof that an incoming communication is false. A striking illustration of this "checking" process was provided by a study of reactions to Orson Welles's famous radio dramatization in 1938 of an invasion of the United States by creatures from Mars. The play was presented in such a way that it could be mistaken for a news broadcast by those who tuned in after the beginning. The finding of the study that is of most relevance here is not that some people were deceived, but that the overwhelming majority of listeners found the story simply too fantastic to believe, or else looked for other sources of information to verify it. Those listeners who were deceived by the broadcast were, for the most part, people to whom the disturbing information was in some way welcome—for example, those whose view of the world included the possibility of strange and cataclysmic events.[23]

In addition to dismissing information that we can easily label as untrue or unimportant, we are likely to forget even relevant facts if they conflict with our internalized picture. This seems to involve a process of subconscious rejection. For example, in one experiment subjects more readily forgot ratings of themselves that did not fit in with their own self-images than ratings that did. In another study, students who were given information to correct wrong answers that they had previously given on a test were found to remember the corrective information less well than completely new information.[24] A researcher who interviewed Soviet soldiers who had entered Poland in 1939 and again in 1945 found that many of them had been surprised both times at the high standard of living. His explanation for the fact that they tended to forget their first experience in Poland was that this recollection conflicted with the picture of a capitalist society that was necessary for their satisfactory adjustment in the Soviet Union.

The suspiciousness with which efforts to change existing ideas or attitudes are usually greeted often leads to effects that are quite different from those intended by the would-be persuader. A college professor who participated in a three-year experimental program on the improvement of teaching in international relations reported that the course failed to teach many of the participants to think more critically or even to acquire more knowledge about foreign affairs. Instead, it often seemed to generate distrust of the instructors and the sources used. The students tended to absorb only the information that fitted their own image of international relations and to reject other information. Similarly, a film designed to warn viewers about the dangers of racism in the United States left some people who saw it more complacent than those who had not seen the film.[25] Psychological-warfare personnel in World War II found that surrender appeals to enemy troops could have the effect of making them fight harder if these appeals were seen by the soldiers as damaging to their honor.

Suspicion can sometimes be partially dispelled by emphasis on candor and factualness, or by allowing people to choose whether or not to expose themselves to ideas with which they differ. In one experiment, students who were given a choice of whether or not to listen to propaganda opposed to their own views (in this case, on early marriage) changed their opinions in response to the message more than those who were exposed to it without being given a choice.[26] And during the early years of the Cold War, analysts of international propaganda concluded that candor and factualness were more likely to be effective in radio broadcasts than slanted newscasts and emotional appeals. There were found to be substantial differences among audiences, however, some being less hospitable to candor than others.[27]

Instead of consciously or subconsciously rejecting an incoming communication, a person may be able to make it accord more closely with his existing attitudes and knowledge by changing or misunderstanding it a little. All of us do this occasionally. The writer has experimented with distortion by showing subjects a selection of newspaper headlines and then asking them later to write down the headlines they remember. Usually the recalled headlines are changed according to well-defined patterns. Almost half of a group of military officers changed the headline "Senator Hits Military Pay Scale" into some variant of "Senator Opposes Military Pay Rise." The headline as remembered in this form was more in harmony with the stereotype of legislators entertained by most government employees. On two occasions, the experiment was conducted shortly after the press had contained prominent stories about aviation disasters, and both times the headline "Worst Rail Crash Kills 60" was changed by a large proportion of the subjects to "Worst *Air* Crash Kills 60." When air crashes had *not* been in the headlines, this change was infrequent. Similarly, studies of rumor dissemination have shown that as a rumor is passed from mouth to mouth, the story tends to be changed so as to conform better to the preconceptions of those persons making up the chain.[28]

Another subconscious way of dealing with information that is not harmonious with existing knowledge and attitudes is to interpret it so that it supports, or at least conflicts less, with ideas that are already established. A well-known experiment involved showing a series of cartoons ridiculing ethnic prejudice to both prejudiced and unprejudiced subjects. Most of the unprejudiced subjects understood the cartoons with no difficulty. Many of the prejudiced ones, on the other hand, read meanings into the cartoons that had nothing to do with the primary message. Instead of seeing ethnic prejudice as the target, some subjects saw the cartoons as being directed against people with old-fashioned ideas. Others could see no meaning in the cartoons at all.[29] A study conducted among Hungarian refugees who had been involved in the anti-Communist risings of 1956 showed that half the respondents thought that American broadcasts had promised help to the rebellion. No such assurances had been given. Nevertheless, the hope of the Hungarians that they would hear promises of support apparently led many of them to read into the broadcasts meanings that were not there.[30]

While the tendency to ignore, forget, distort, or interpret communications that conflict with an established picture of the world provides a powerful brake on the ability of such messages to influence action or attitudes, this does not mean that they are always without effect. Even a very unsettling idea, if it is useful to a person in achieving something he wants, is likely to receive attention and be acted upon. Threatening communications, for example, are often ignored or forgotten, but if they also suggest an acceptable method of avoiding the impending danger they are more likely to have an effect.[31] Those involved in politics, or any form of controversy, have to familiarize themselves with the arguments of the opposition, even though these may be very distasteful. That disturbing communications sometimes have to be given attention, even at considerable emotional cost, is illustrated by the experience of a French broadcaster who spoke to Nazi-occupied France over British Broadcasting Corporation facilities during World War II. He knew that he should be aware of what was being broadcast over stations in France, but hearing French voices praising the enemy was more than he could stand. So he stopped trying to listen to the Paris radio and read transcripts of the broadcasts instead.[32]

The Uses of Ideas

In the foregoing pages, we have referred occasionally to "utility," in the sense that a communication is useful to a person if it helps him directly or indirectly to achieve something he wants, or helps him satisfy a conscious or subconscious need. In many cases, information may be useful in the short run but damaging in a longer perspective. A sign pointing to a bar would be considered "useful" to an alcoholic, even though the end result of this information might be contrary to his best interests. Flattery is useful to most of us. By "useful information" we thus refer to ideas that can be used, even though in some cases they may be untrue or misleading.

Since the kinds of information that a person can use are determined by his wants and needs, and by the situation in which he finds himself, no two people have exactly the same requirements. For example, legislators who have economic or personal ties with another country are likely to pay more attention to information from that country than other legislators. Their international links open them to messages they would otherwise never hear.[33] Nevertheless, several categories of information useful to most people can be distinguished.

The first category might be called instrumental information. We are likely to pay attention to communications that tell us how to do something we want to do: how to make a living, be the life of the party, build a sailboat, achieve inner harmony, and so on. Early newspaper publishers, in their efforts to attract readers, emphasized the economic utility of the information provided by their publications. Théophraste Renaudot, who in 1631 founded the first newspaper in France, pointed out that his journal would enable a merchant to avoid trying to do business with a city that was under siege or had been destroyed, and keep a professional soldier from looking for employment in lands that were at peace. He added that the paper would also help to simplify correspondence, since it would no longer be necessary for letter-writers to give their friends exhaustive accounts of events.[34] Updated versions of Renaudot's appeal for subscribers are still part of the promotional material of modern publishers.

A second obvious category consists of entertainment material. All of us turn to communications for purposes of relaxation, or to escape from the mundane world in which we find ourselves. Furthermore, since entertainment is not incompatible with other uses to which communications can be put, the story or program that is both entertaining and instructive is highly sought after.

It is also quite apparent that people make use of ideas they obtain from communications to assist them in their social relations. If our friends are interested in baseball, we are more likely to read the sports page so that we can talk with them about yesterday's game. Some opinion leaders use information from news magazines to prepare themselves to answer questions and converse in the manner that others have come to expect of them.[35] In social relations, information can be a form of barter—that is, it can be used in conversation and traded for expressions of interest or other indications of social approval.

Researchers have been most impressed, however, with the degree to which we use ideas from incoming communications to achieve internal consistency, harmony, and self-confidence. People seem to require constant reassurance that the beliefs, attitudes and images that make up their internal guidance systems are indeed good and correct ones. Numerous observations have confirmed that a person is likely to expose himself to political communications he expects to agree with, and to sources he approves of. People more readily learn materials that support their attitudes than facts that are inconsistent with these attitudes. Republicans pay more attention to Republican campaign propaganda than to opposing propaganda, and Democrats behave similarly with regard to political materials. Those who are in favor of civil defense are more likely to read pamphlets on the subject than those who are not. Prejudiced people will learn arguments that prove the correctness of their prejudice more easily than those that tend to show its falsity.[36] If a person's opinions or beliefs are shaken, although not changed, by arguments or events, he is likely to look for ideas that will tend to confirm in his own mind that he is indeed right.[37]

The same communications may be used by different people for different purposes. Studies of the effects of television on children, for example, have shown that what a child sees and the way he interprets it depend on the problems he is faced with in his family, school, or play group. "It is they who use television, rather than television that uses them." [38] Similar observations have been made about the ways children react to material in comic books: "The same media materials appeared to be interpreted and used differently by children in different social positions." [39] When the All India Radio organized a series of experimental farm-radio forums, it was found that the broadcasts appealed to a diversity of interests among the farmers. All the farmers listened to the same programs, but no two sets of reactions were identical. One village reported increased contributions toward a new school building; another organized a four-day camp for youth leaders; in a third, farmers started inoculating poultry. A city reporter who visited one of the forums was so impressed by the discussions following the radio program that he remarked: "We city people must now give up the idea that the farmers are ignorant." [40]

A message that is requested or sought out by a person because he has an immediate use for it is likely to have an effect. Or, even though the message is not sought out, it may fill a need. An effect is then still probable. But when a message is both unsought for and unusable after it arrives, an effect is unlikely. An example of a communication in the first category is the advice given by an information clerk in a railroad station; his record of success in influencing behavior is difficult to beat. Most advertisements could be placed in the second category; those who want the product being advertised are likely to respond. The third category includes propaganda for a new doctrine that is spread among people who are quite satisfied with their existing religion. Its success is likely to be minimal.

Effects of Public Communications

Because people make use of ideas for a number of different purposes, public communications are able to achieve several kinds of effects. They can increase factual knowledge, reinforce or change attitudes, focus attention, confer prestige, produce bewilderment, and influence behavior in a number of other ways. In any given case, the effect that a communication has depends on the use that is made of it.

The fact that communications can influence behavior by increasing factual knowledge is often ignored, possibly because it is so obvious. Magazines that recommend recipes or provide home-improvement hints, for example, often secure compliance by millions.[41] While the actions brought about by such communications are usually nonpolitical, the political implications of following advice regarding crop productivity or personal hygiene in underdeveloped countries, or even in industrialized societies, are clear. The same is true of information on how to organize a parent-teachers association or how to oppose Communist infiltration of trade unions. During World War II, Allied radio operators devoted substantial efforts to giving information to underground movements in occupied territories on techniques of opposing the Nazis. They did this primarily not by overt instruction but by "cross-reporting" the activities of one resistance group to another. Combat psychological-warfare personnel, rather than exhorting well-motivated soldiers to lay down their arms, found that it was more valuable to tell those who already wanted to surrender how they could do so. In short, factual knowledge in the minds of those who want to use it can be a powerful force in inducing and shaping action.

A much more dramatic effect of communications is that of changing attitudes. Most national information and cultural programs are based in large part on the assumption that they can alter the attitudes of people in other countries and thereby influence their actions. Yet, paradoxically, despite the popular image of the propagandist as a molder of opinion, communications by themselves are rather poor instruments for changing attitudes, especially in view of the powerful forces at work within each individual that protect the picture of the world he has already established.

Nevertheless, under some conditions, communications *can* shape attitudes, although these conditions are more often absent than present. When the attention of an audience can be secured, communications may help to form attitudes toward new subjects. They can also influence attitudes that are weakly held, or, when several attitudes are fairly evenly balanced, they may be able to strengthen one of them at the expense of the others. They can even change attitudes that are strongly held when they are able to report new facts about the environment, or when they can suggest courses of action that a person believes will satisfy his wants and needs better than his present behavior.

One of the first experimental studies testing the ability of communications to form new attitudes was carried out at the University of Iowa. Students were divided into two groups, one of which was given material to read that praised Prime Minister Hughes of Australia. The other group was exposed to anti-Hughes material. Attitudes in both groups were strongly influenced in the direction suggested by the material.[42] The rather striking effects observed in this case seem to have been due to the fact that very few of the students had ever heard of Mr. Hughes before. Forced to adopt an opinion, most of them had nothing on which to base it except the material to which they had recently been exposed.

Similar observations have been made in local elections where the candidates were virtually unknown. In such cases, newspaper support for one candidate is likely to be important. Students observing a local election in Cambridge, Mass., noted that when people knew very little about any of the candidates, even a small amount of information was enough to enable a voter to form an attitude and vote accordingly. This information often came through person-to-person channels.[43]

Attitudes that are not strongly held can sometimes be modified by persuasive communications. For example, when the public is fairly apathetic on an issue, the editorial stand of a newspaper can often tip the scales in one or the other direction.[44] Studies of troop orientation materials in World War II found that documentary films were able to change attitudes of military personnel on such questions as how long the war would last or how important the contribution of the Royal Air Force was, but that basic attitudes remained unaffected. Similarly, an educational TV program entitled "The Roots of Prejudice" brought about some changes in the behavior of nonethnocentric viewers, but did not alter the attitudes of those who were strongly prejudiced.* When attitudes are firmly held, as often is the case in race relations, a persuasive campaign may not only fail to influence these attitudes but may bring reprisals against the source advocating the changes.[45]

In addition to being able to promote new attitudes and to shape lightly held preconceptions, communications can often influence even strongly held attitudes if they are able to report a significant alteration in the environment, or a previously unknown fact about the environment. This is because people tend to change their internal guidance mechanisms to adjust to new situations. The dynamic effect of political developments on attitudes is suggested by a study of the 1940 Presidential election in Erie County, Ohio. On the basis of a series of polls taken at short intervals during the campaign, a researcher saw the voting preference of many German-Americans swing from the Democratic column into the Republican column.[46] This was presumably a result of Roosevelt's steps to support the Western Allies in the European war. In another instance, opinion researchers found that news reports about remarks of Jacob Malik in 1951, indicating that the Soviets favored an end to the Korean War, brought about a substantial shift in opinions about the future of Soviet-American relations among people in the United States. Indian attitudes toward both the Western and the Communist powers were appreciably affected by the Chinese attack on India's northern border in 1962. And public sentiment in those parts of the United States where racial integration in the schools has been started has tended to become more favorable toward integration *following* action by school officials, thus accommodating to the new situation.[47]

Because of the impact that events can have on attitudes, propagandists usually seek out and report developments that they think will favor their cause. "You have been cut off," was one of the messages frequently carried by psychological-warfare leaflets in World War II. Or

* Whether an attitude is strongly or weakly held seems to depend largely on the reasons why a person holds that attitude. If it serves as an important behavioral guide or assists a person in adjusting to those around him, it is much less likely to be changed by communications than if it merely reflects his prior experience with an object or event. (See M. Brewster Smith, "Opinions, Personality and Political Behavior," *American Political Science Review,* March 1958, pp. 10-12; also M. Brewster Smith, Jerome S. Bruner, and Robert W. White, *Opinions and Personality* [New York: John Wiley & Sons, 1956].)

"The unit on your flank has already surrendered." Politicians often try to influence opinion by revealing that a respected personality or organization has come out in favor of this or that cause. Advertisers do much the same thing when they use testimonials for products. In such cases, it is the change in the social environment, or the new information about it, that is expected to produce the desired results. Whether these tactics achieve their intended effect depends on the degree to which the audience actually regards the judgment of the public figures or organizations concerned as a significant factor.

Usually, however, information about important political developments reaches people through normal news channels. The shifts in attitudes that are brought about by word of these developments can be attributed to communications insofar as the information network is responsible for bringing events to people's attention, but it is clearly the event itself that is the basic causative factor. The primacy of events in changing attitudes has often led official propagandists to seek a greater measure of influence over what the government of their country says and does. This, in turn, has brought on bureaucratic struggles of substantial proportions.

A third way in which communications can modify attitudes is by presenting a method of interpreting the environment that helps a person satisfy his needs better than he can with his existing attitude structure. Political and religious conversions usually take place as a result of a change in the social environment (e.g., a marriage, a new job, or a move to a different community), but sometimes the environment remains the same and a person comes gradually or suddenly to the conclusion that a new doctrine will help him achieve his goals better than the one he has been following. Studies of conversion to and defection from Communism have presented examples of persons who experienced changes of this type. In many of these cases, the persuasive communications were primarily of a person-to-person nature, but books and other literature sometimes played an important part.[48]

As with a shift in attitude caused primarily by a change in the environment, it is usually difficult to decide how much one should consider a conversion of this type as being caused by communications and how much by the idea or doctrine that is communicated. Who is more influential: the creative thinker or the publicist who makes the thinker's ideas known? Both are necessary to bring about the attitude changes that result from a new doctrine.

Under certain conditions, communications can thus play a part in changing attitudes, but ordinarily their persuasive power is modest. The study of the 1940 Presidential election in Erie County, Ohio, showed that about 5 per cent of the electorate changed their political attitudes as a result of the campaign.[49] A similar investigation in Elmira, N.Y., in 1948, showed a change of 8 per cent.[50] Of 560 residents of Springfield, Mo., who were interviewed before and after a week-long campaign designed to create a more favorable attitude toward the oil industry, 78 per cent retained their original "pro" or "anti" classification.[51] Students of the press have made much the same point by reminding us that overwhelming editorial support is not enough to elect political candidates. In 1932, 1936, and 1940, a large proportion of the American press backed the Republican Presidential candidate, but each time Franklin D. Roosevelt was easily elected. In 1960, John F. Kennedy won with the support of only 15 per cent of the American dailies.[52] Events in Western Europe have generally borne out the American experience in this regard.

Similar observations have been made about person-to-person communication, even though this is generally regarded as having a greater impact than messages received through the mass media. A study of lobbying in the Vermont legislature, for instance, found that lobbyists were likely to be effective only when attitudes were still fluid, or when there was already a tendency in the legislature to favor a measure. One of the senior lawmakers queried could not think of a single instance where a switch in voting was brought about by lobbying. Washington lobbyists, also, have been found to have only a marginal impact on major issues commanding public attention.[53]

The most frequent effect of political communications on attitudes is not to change them, but to strengthen them. Often this strengthening process brings people to a point where they are willing to act. Election campaigns are significant not so much because they convert a few people but because they are able to persuade those who already lean in a given direction to go to the polls. Typically, campaigns are built on tendencies already present. Thus, in the 1952 Senatorial election in Maryland, Senator Butler's manager found that there was some doubt among the electorate as to whether the conservative Democratic incumbent, Millard Tydings, was sufficiently anti-Communist. Senator Butler's campaign literature therefore nourished this doubt. It never directly accused Senator Tydings of pro-Communist sympathies, but managed to strengthen the latent suspicion on the part of the voters to a point where it apparently had a substantial effect on the election outcome.[54] One tactic was to publicize rhetorical questions to Senator Tydings: *Why* didn't you ask Secretary of State Dean Acheson to testify about loyalty? *Why* is there all the talk about your keeping parts of the hearing out of the official record?

Another campaign that fanned latent emotions was conducted unintentionally by a number of large German newspapers and magazines in 1956. Partly as a circulation-building device, they began to publicize crimes committed by American military personnel stationed in Germany. This whipped up emotions to such a pitch that at least one town council officially requested the withdrawal of American forces from the area.[55] It later turned out that the "crime wave" represented no more than the usual number of violations to which German and American authorities were accustomed, and that the publicity had not been intended to spur political action. Nevertheless, the news stories achieved a powerful effect because they fanned the suspicion of foreigners, and especially foreign military personnel, that exists in almost all populations.

As these examples suggest, the ability of communications to trigger actions toward which predispositions already exist is considerable. Popular radio and television figures have been able to cause members of their audiences who agree with them to deluge Congressmen with letters for or against legislation. The success of advertising in selling goods and services is built much more on its ability to reinforce the desires of a person who already wants something than on its ability to persuade him that he should have it.*

Communications can also serve to focus attention. As a student of the press has pointed out, newspapers may not be very successful in telling people what to think, but they are extraordinarily successful in telling them what to think about. Since people tend to stick to certain sources of information, the subjects that are prominently discussed in these sources often come to occupy the center of attention. When newspapers give prominence to a particular foreign-policy issue, it tends to climb higher on the list of matters claiming the attention of State De-

* Edward L. Bernays has noted that no advertisement, no matter how shrewdly conceived, is likely to convert a person who is passive and disinterested into a potential customer. (Peter Bart, "Advertising: Bernays Discounts Persuasion," *The New York Times,* September 25, 1962.)

partment officials. Indeed, one of the most influential documents circulated in the State Department is a daily summary of the main foreign-policy stories in principal American newspapers, furnishing those who read it with a list of questions that are in the public eye. One or more of the items on this list is likely to be raised each day in the Department's Executive Staff meeting.[56]

The importance of capturing headlines, of getting everybody talking about a given subject, and of flooding the channels of communication with news about a particular event has long been recognized by political publicists. During World War II, for instance, when news from different parts of the world sometimes favored the Allies and at other times the Axis, a favorite device of each side was to use communication media to focus public attention on areas where its own forces were advancing, while placing less emphasis on other areas.

Numerous other effects of communications on individuals have been noted, some of these being compounds or variants of the effects discussed above. For example, communications can confer prestige—or take it away. Favorable references to ideas, persons, or organizations give them a certain status or significance among those who pay attention to these references. As two leading authorities put it, if you are important you will be a subject of mass attention, and if you are a subject of mass attention you will be important. A wartime study of a war-bond sales campaign conducted by a popular radio personality found that her success was due to a substantial degree to the way in which the mass media had previously built her up as a person of sincerity and competence. The ability of the public-relations profession to make public figures out of nonentities through the use of the mass media is such that even those who have helped create the illusion are frequently deceived.[57]

The ability of communications to cause bewilderment has been given relatively little attention by scholars, but has often been noted in political contexts. The Nazis released contradictory reports during their rapid military advances during World War II, presumably to lower confidence in all news about the fighting and to increase despair when the truth was finally known. The Soviets have been accused of trying to stimulate bewilderment by their techniques of alternately blowing hot and cold. Critics of American information policy have alleged that a similar, if unintended, result is achieved when prominent government officials almost simultaneously make conflicting pronouncements regarding the position of the United States. There are, however, limitations on the ability of communications to produce bewilderment, since sources that are so unreliable as to be of little use ordinarily come to be disregarded.

That the mass media can provide entertainment that may either enrich or debase popular tastes has long been acknowledged, and considerable attention has been paid to the effects that this entertainment content has on individuals and society. Discussions of mass culture more and more tend to become discussions of mass communications.[58]

The entertainment and cultural impact of communications is of interest to those concerned primarily with political ideas for several reasons. One is that entertainment and art can assemble large audiences, which then can be exposed to political materials. Most propaganda programs make extensive use of this principle. In addition, communications that entertain or enrich frequently include politically significant ideas, and are particularly important in international communication, where they play a significant part in shaping the image that peoples have of other nations. This has led to concern about American motion-picture and television exports, and to efforts to bring a better-balanced picture of American culture to foreign audiences.*

"Escapism" in entertainment offers relief from the unpleasant and monotonous realities of life. Virtually any material may be escapist for some part of its audience; what primarily worries critics is material that is not in accord with reality and thus may make people less able to cope with their environment. The available research on escapist entertainment suggests that it does indeed make some people more disoriented; for others, it can promote relaxation and even provide information that is useful in certain contexts.[59] Escapism, as do other effects of communications, depends on the use that people make of the ideas to which they are exposed.

* Students of literature and art have approached the relationship between politics and culture from a different point of view, noting that many seemingly apolitical creations have been influenced by well-defined political attitudes. Even the pleasure dome of Coleridge's "Kubla Khan," we find, was not devoid of political symbolism, having been partially inspired by the poet's anger at Catherine the Great of Russia, who forced one of her courtiers to marry a particularly ill-favored lady and then expose himself on a cake of ice with his ugly bride. (Carl R. Woodring, *Politics in the Poetry of Coleridge* [Madison, Wisc.: University of Wisconsin Press, 1961], pp. 49-52.)

Subliminal Stimulation and Pavlovianism

The popular imagination has, from time to time, been aroused by the idea that there are techniques that can be used to magnify the effects of communications and make it possible for the skilled (and usually Machiavellian) communicator to mold the attitudes and actions of his audience at will. One of the techniques mentioned in recent years is that of subliminal stimulation. This involves confrontation of an audience with stimuli that are below the threshold of conscious perception but nevertheless register on the sensory organs. The most common method of studying subliminal perception is to flash words or symbols on a motion-picture or television screen so briefly that a person does not realize he has seen them, although in fact his eye does perceive them. It has been hypothesized that this technique might make it possible for an idea to penetrate the mind without being inhibited or modified by the psychological defenses that a person sets up to protect his established attitudes. Subliminal stimulation thus might be used to sell a product or convey a political idea.

Another technique sometimes mentioned in the same context is that of the conditioned response. Following the experimental work of Pavlov, who was able to train dogs to salivate at the sound of a bell, it is argued that human beings can be similarly conditioned so that they will react in predictable ways to verbal or visual stimuli. One of the best-known exponents of what might be called "political Pavlovianism" was Serge Chakotin, who guided the propaganda of the German Social Democratic Party during much of the Weimar Republic.[60] Hitler, said Chakotin, was no more than a trainer who set out to create living robots. He believed that Mussolini and the Communists followed the same tactic, and that advertising also relied heavily on conditioning.

Subliminal stimulation and the conditioned response are based on careful psychological observation, and both can lead to observable effects. Nevertheless, when they are transferred from the laboratory to the realm of everyday experience, or even to more realistic laboratory situations, both lose much of the power that has been attributed to them. Indeed, in most situations, more conventional means of influencing behavior appear to be not only equally effective, but even more so.

Experiments with subliminal stimulation suggest strongly that communications that are received without registering in the consciousness encounter subconscious barriers very similar in nature to those with which other communications have to contend. Most studies to date have suggested that subliminal stimulation is a relatively inefficient means of communication, although it sometimes can influence attitudes or action if the subject matter is noncontroversial. When two groups of subjects were given the subliminal instructions "Write more," or "Don't write," these exhortations seemed to influence the number of words put down in response to ambiguous Thematic Apperception Test pictures more than vocal instructions did. A review of research on subliminal communication by the London Institute of Practitioners in Advertising concluded that most reports of results achieved by this form of stimulation had been greatly overdrawn and that subliminal communications appeared to be subject to limitations similar to those affecting other communications.[61] Subliminal messages may, however, have some practical applications: as advocates of subliminal television commercials have pointed out, they could be presented without interrupting entertainment programs.

Pavlovian psychology appears to have equal limitations in most situations encountered in everyday experience. In laboratory experiments, in prisons, and whenever the communicator exercises substantial and continuous control over the environment, subjects can sometimes be conditioned successfully, although this does not mean that Pavlovian theories are necessarily being used. The Chinese Communists, for instance, seem to have evolved their brainwashing techniques in a pragmatic, trial-and-error fashion.[62] Ordinarily, however, the extent of possible conditioning is limited by people's ability to disregard or distort communications that have little meaning or relevance for them, and to select sources of information that are more congenial to their existing attitudes.[63]

Conditioning does, of course, play a role in human response to communications. Particularly over a long period of time, associations are learned between politicians and programs, between products and slogans, and between appearances and values. This learning, however, seems to be subject to the checks and balances that have been discussed above. Even in totalitarian states, propagandists have experienced great difficulties in affecting the basic conceptions of their captive audiences by conditioning.

International Travel as a Channel for Communications

A person who travels abroad is bombarded by a series of highly diverse communications. He sees new things, meets different people, and is often exposed to the mass media and educational systems of the country he is visiting. In addition, he is partially cut off from his old sources of information, he forms new social relationships, and some of his social relationships at home tend to atrophy with the passage of time.

Because so many factors are involved, it is difficult to say which ones are responsible for the observable effects of travel and residence abroad. One communication cannot easily be disentangled from another, and all that the visitor sees and hears is mediated by his new social and geographical environment, and by the new desires and needs to which this environment gives rise.

Nevertheless, the extent to which the effects of international travel seem to conform to the observations that can be made about the impact of communications in general is remarkable. Travelers are guided in their perception by the mental picture of the world that they have built up in the past, and change this picture only reluctantly when it proves to be a poor guide to action. What they learn from their foreign experience is heavily influenced by the psychological organization they bring with them.[64] Travel agents have reported that foreign visitors to the United States ask to see those aspects of America about which they have heard at home, and what foreign students learn from a sojourn at American colleges depends in part on their past experience and on how they expect to be able to use the new information when they return to their own countries. As a rule, the most impressive result of foreign experience is an increase in factual knowledge. Indeed, foreign students and leaders who have visited the United States under State Department auspices usually mention the acquisition of professionally useful information as the most valuable aspect of their trip.[65]

As with other forms of exposure to communications, travel has the effect of reinforcing attitudes, creating attitudes on new subjects, and changing some attitudes that are weakly held, but it is less likely to bring about fundamental changes in basic preconceptions.[66] State Department escort-interpreters who have accompanied foreign leaders on their travels through the United States have concluded that exposure to new information in itself is unlikely to affect a closed or hostile mind. For example, members of a Soviet delegation who arrived with the conviction that workers' children in the United States could not afford a higher education were simply unable to hear evidence to the contrary.[67]

Nevertheless, this does not mean that basic attitudes are completely unaffected. Stereotypes that travelers bring with them about the country they are visiting are usually modified and sharpened by the elimination of some shadings and the adoption of new ones.[68] These images are thus changed so that they conform more closely to reality and provide a more useful guide to action. Foreign travel may also lead people to evaluate their own situations differently, and this may result in attitudinal shifts. For instance, American businessmen who have changed their views on foreign economic policy following repeated trips abroad seem to have done so mainly because they have come to see themselves as representatives of the United States as a whole, rather than of a particular industry or geographical section.[69] And just as other communications can affect attitudes by reporting a significant alteration in the environment, travel can lead to changes in outlook when a person finds himself forced to cope with a new environment.

The Audience for International Communications

Since most people feel that they don't need a great deal of information from abroad to satisfy their immediate requirements, they are unlikely to give very much attention to international communications. Cross-section surveys in many parts of the world have shown that popular interest in foreign affairs nearly always takes a back seat to interest in domestic politics, which, in turn, are of far less concern than personal problems.

Although Americans pay more attention to international matters than citizens of many countries, a survey of available studies in 1959 concluded that no more than 15 per cent of adult Americans displayed a significant interest in world affairs, and that the proportion of those who were almost completely apathetic approached 50 per cent. About 10 per cent typically mention international questions as among those most important for determining their voting behavior.[70] Congruent results were reached by a 1954 study, in which respondents were asked what kinds of things they worried about most. Only 8 per cent mentioned the international situation or world affairs, while 80 per cent replied in terms of personal or family problems.[71] It is probable that the intensive publicity campaign in Cincinnati was unable to raise the level of information about the United Nations appreciably because only a limited number of people felt a need for more information. Those who wanted to know about the U.N. were apparently able to learn as much as they wished from the sources regularly available to them; those who had no interest in such information simply disregarded it. The publicity campaign flowed over Cincinnati like water over a saturated sponge; little more information was absorbed.

Survey results from other countries show similar tendencies, and are reinforced by reports from political observers. A story from travelers who drove to Budapest not long after the Hungarian uprising may be indicative. On the way through Hungary, they left their obviously foreign car parked in the square of a very dusty town, and returned to find that one or more persons had written something in the dust on the side of the automobile. Feeling sure that these must be either Communist or anti-Communist slogans, but not knowing Hungarian, the travelers laboriously copied the words and then dusted off the car. When the inscriptions were deciphered by friends in Budapest, they turned out to reflect the opinions of adherents of two rival football teams. Studies in India have shown that relatively few people are familiar with facts about the Cold War. Even those who have access to newspapers are likely to be uninformed, since they tend to forget information that has no meaning for them.[72] A recent West German investigation of the motives that play a part in the political decisions of the average voter found that foreign policy matters entered into these decisions in fewer than one-fifth of the cases. About two-thirds of the respondents felt themselves involved "not very much" or "not at all" in political events, and could remember very little political information. In another survey, only 16 per cent of a West Germany cross-section said they discussed politics fairly regularly; 37 per cent claimed they never did.[73]

Even in times of crisis, political matters, and especially international ones, are likely to receive less attention than the affairs of everyday life. A news dispatch from Paris during the height of the Algerian turmoil in 1962 pointed out that, although he may have been conscious that history was being made, the average Parisian devoted more attention to the details of daily living than to political affairs. In the newspapers, weather reports and crossword puzzles were scrutinized at least as carefully as the doings of the Secret Army Organization.[74] Very similar behavior could be noted in Berlin during the Soviet blockade of 1948-49. While aware of political matters, Berliners were still primarily concerned with personal problems.[75]

The audience for international communications is thus a relatively small one, but it includes a disproportionate number of influential people, since these are the ones who are likely to be able to use information from abroad. In a university city of northen Spain, for instance, it was found that a majority of journalists, civil servants, professional people, and students said that they read the foreign press occasionally. Nearly nine out of ten of these read the French press, one out of five mentioned the English press, and one out of seven the American.[76]

Furthermore, a small proportion of a population may amount to a rather large absolute number. In a sample of 204 well-to-do households in one Midwest community of the United States, for instance, five households were found to include one or more listeners to international broadcasts.[77] If projected to cover all middle- and upper-class households in the United States, this survey would indicate an audience for international broadcasts of several hundred thousand. (The sample is unrepresentative, but at least suggests an order of magnitude.)

There are, of course, exceptions to the general rule that only a fraction of a population will be interested in communications from abroad. If these are relevant to widely felt needs they will have a large audience, regardless of their point of origin. Thus, Western jazz and Western fashions seem to have gained wide acceptance among young people in Eastern Europe, and foreign ideas about agriculture and hygiene are given attention in emerging areas by millions who have little concern with political affairs. A communication that is useful to large segments of any population is likely to find a substantial audience, regardless of its point of origin.

A related implication of the selective manner in which people approach communications is that most audiences are well disposed toward the sources of ideas to which they expose themselves. Thus, the Voice of America is listened to mainly by people who already have pro-American attitudes. The same is ordinarily true of people who read American publications or visit the United States. Furthermore, those who are favorable toward a source are likely to learn more from it. When the U. S. Information Service in Greece inserted a series of advertisements about the United Nations Declaration of Universal Human Rights in Salonika newspapers, in order to test this means of spreading ideas, it was found not only that those who noted the advertisements tended to be more favorable to the United States than those who did not, but that they learned a number of facts to support their pro-American beliefs. The campaign thus helped them strengthen preexisting attitudes.[78]

Although most audiences for international communications are basically friendly, there are some, usually much smaller, that are unfriendly or neutral. Individuals who require information from abroad for professional purposes will seek out such information even if they do not approve of the source. This is often the case with government officials. During World War II, for instance, it was known that Germany maintained a monitoring system for foreign broadcasts, and Allied broadcasters were fairly sure that even if they couldn't reach a large audience in Germany, they would have the attention of the influential group of German government officials who read the monitoring reports. After the war, it was found that this assumption was correct. Indeed, the Nazi Propaganda Minister was so concerned about the effect of the monitoring reports on top government echelons that he constantly tried to restrict their circulation.[79] Allied psychological warfare attempted to make use of the German monitoring service in various ways—for instance, by incorporating hints in London broadcasts that German Air Force personnel were deserting in their planes. It was assumed that these hints would reach Luftwaffe authorities through German government channels, and that increased security restrictions and suspicion would lead to lowered flying efficiency.[80]

Students and newsmen are also likely to be found among unfriendly or neutral audiences for international communications. Translations of American works are widely used in Soviet technical and scientific education, and some of the bitterest opponents of colonialism in emerging nations have sought an education in the schools of the country they regarded as their principal enemy. Probably the most important neutral audience for international communications is the news industry. Indeed, foreign affairs correspondents in Washington are among the principal users of the daily reports on broadcasts from other countries issued by the U. S. Government.

Finally, it is apparent that all generalizations about the way people use communications and the various effects communications can have must be modified in view of detailed knowledge about each audience. All individuals differ, each group of people differs from every other group, and societies and nationalities show characteristic differences. Generalizations can provide only rules of thumb and an indication of the kinds of specific facts that are required to explain the impact of any given communication. Above all, the available body of knowledge reminds us to ask whether an audience can use the ideas that are made available, and just how they will be used. Will they help people to satisfy a need or attain a goal? If not, they are likely to be disregarded or forgotten.

IV

Communication and Organization

Most of us tend to think of the effects of communications mainly in terms of their impact on individuals. Yet the part they play in the creation and functioning of organizations is frequently of greater political significance, since so much of the world's work requires mobilization and coordination of individual efforts. Anyone interested in the political role of international communication should therefore concern himself with the way organizations, as well as individuals, make use of ideas from abroad.

In general, the more complicated an organization, whether political, economic, or social, the more communication facilities it requires. In traditional societies, where most of a person's activities are predetermined by the situation into which he is born, communication systems can be simple. But societies that embrace many highly differentiated activities require complicated communication systems to link their various parts. These systems usually extend to persons and organizations outside the society as well.

Dependence of Organizations on Communications

Formal organizations (such as factories or government agencies) that are constituted according to a set pattern, with certain members assigned to certain jobs, make use of communications both to keep the internal machinery running and in their external relations. Within the organization it is necessary that instructions flow from those in charge to those below, that the managers and key people be sufficiently acquainted with what is going on in the organization as a whole, that necessary technical information be available to all concerned, and that everyone be motivated to do his job properly. Communications to and from outside groups and individuals are used in arriving at policy decisions, recruiting new members, soliciting supporters or buyers, and maintaining good relations with other relevant publics. Sometimes technical information necessary for the performance of the work can be obtained only from outside sources.

The requirements of each organization for both internal and external communications are determined by its structure and functions, as well as by the characteristics of the individuals in it. A college faculty may require formal meetings only rarely, and may receive few messages from the college administration; many political and industrial organizations, on the other hand, require almost constant communication among key officials. An analysis of information exchanged within four Israeli immigrant communities noted that they all seemed to require communications that served substantially the same purposes, but that the communication systems used differed according to the internal division of labor in each group. Studies of whole societies have found that the kinds of communication systems used are closely related to such factors as degree of urbanization, form of government, and literacy rate.[1]

Within formal organizations, the most important communication channel is likely to be the chain of command. Supplementary means for exchanging ideas often include house organs, large and small meetings, suggestion boxes, and individual conferences. The internal communication network is usually dominated by certain centers where information from various sources converges; personnel in such centers tend to be more satisfied in their work than others—to be conscious of a greater "voice" in the organization.[2] In addition, informal channels of communication usually spring up; both executives and other employees obtain much of the information they need in social gatherings or through other personal contacts. If any component of the necessary intra-organizational communication system is lacking, then the enterprise functions less efficiently. It is interesting to note that industrial enterprises in Communist countries seem to have essentially the same intra-organization communication problems as those in the free world.[3]

Public media frequently play an important part in keeping the various parts of a large organization in touch with each other. Administrators of welfare and other civic agencies have often observed that one of the best ways to interest their boards of directors in what they are doing is through publicizing their activities in local newspapers.[4] Similarly, researchers in large enterprises have found that they sometimes can communicate their findings to management more efficiently through publication than through administrative channels. U.S. officials abroad have occasionally resorted to "leaks" to the press to bring certain ideas to the attention of their superiors in Washington.

The mass media play an even more important part in providing organization members with information they need in their work. Some newspapers, such as the *Wall Street Journal* and the *Journal of Commerce,* are especially designed to be of assistance to executives in decision-making positions. Even more specialized are the periodic newsletters and "dope sheets," many of them originating in Washington, that find most of their subscribers among high executives. Such newsletters for executives, which have proliferated in other industrialized countries also, recall the *Fugger Newsletters,* the reports used by the famed Renaissance banking house at Augsburg to keep itself informed of political and other developments that were likely to affect its business.[5] Specialized publications also serve scientists, engineers, and others who help to keep the industrial machinery running. The relatively large circulation figures of these journals and newspapers are frequently surprising to those outside the field concerned.

The role of mass media in selling goods and services, and in recruiting employees and supporters has been widely recognized only in relatively recent times. The efforts of early newspaper publishers to sell advertising indicate that the use of this vehicle to bring information about a product or service to a prospective buyer was not widely accepted before the eighteenth century. Instead, the buyer was expected to go down to the market place and find what he wanted. If he wished to hire someone or to find a business associate, he had to ask around. The princely publisher of the *Nassauisch Saarbrückische Wochen-Blatt* pointed out in about 1750 that anyone with something to sell could save himself a great deal of effort by inserting a notice in the newspaper, and that persons looking for traveling companions to help defray the cost of an expensive journey could do the same. The use of communications in public relations was apparently accepted somewhat earlier. At the time of the crusades, we find accusations that Bishop William of Ely had hired troubadours to come from France to recite poems and sing songs about him that were flattering but untrue. "People spoke of him," says the chronicler, "as if his equal did not exist on earth."[6] Today, use of the public media is accepted as one of the principal ways through which all kinds of organizations recruit employees and supporters. Paid advertisements by religious groups in American publications have drawn as many as 350,000 inquiries in a single year.

Internal communications within government bureaucracies, the largest and ordinarily most important political organizations, are very similar in character to those in large businesses or industries. The same requirements for a flow of information up, down, and laterally within the structure are present, as are the problems of motivating employees. In addition, government personnel often require an even broader range of technical information than do employees in most private organizations, and much of this information originates outside the official structure. Collectively, government policy-makers need to be informed of practically all major developments, both inside their countries and in the world at large. Diplomatic and intelligence reporting services supply some of the necessary information for both technicians and decision-makers, and additional data are received through public channels. Most foreign-policy officials of the U. S. Government rely heavily on *The New York Times* and a few other newspapers.[7] Former West German Chancellor Adenauer repeatedly cited the *Neue Zürcher Zeitung* as a basic source of data.[8] Public officials, like private individuals, establish habits that determine in large measure where they obtain their information.

Communications directed outward by a governmental bureaucracy serve some of the same purposes as those of other organizations—e.g., recruitment, persuasion, and public relations—but many of the messages that are aimed at domestic audiences are also concerned with morale and control.[9] National cohesion cannot be achieved without numerous communication links between government and people, and no state can survive without some form of a domestic information program.[10] Such programs include not only material intended to inform and persuade but also to instruct and command. In this respect, government information, while directed outward from the bureaucratic structure, resembles downward internal messages within industrial organizations.

Dependence of government on communications, both internal and external, is underlined by experience in both ancient and modern times. The relative stability of the Egyptian, Persian, and Roman empires was ensured in part by the ability of their rulers to keep records, send orders swiftly, and coordinate the actions of myriads of officials in widely dispersed communities. In the eleventh century in China, where the principle of printing by movable type was already known, newspapers were being issued by the government for the use of higher officials, and three centuries later a public press was brought into being to bring news about the court to the public. The government of ancient Japan seems to have developed efficient two-way communication between the government and people by 700-800 A.D. Provincial administrators were required to report to the central government not only information that was necessary for administrative purposes, but also news of "unusual interest" to the public; and it was possible for the Emperor to transmit messages rapidly to almost the entire population, through the use of town criers and notice boards. One way the Emperor appealed for continued obedience was by publicly announcing and praising particularly meritorious deeds.[11]

Napoleon was a leading innovator in the use of information for governmental purposes in modern times. Not only did he make significant contributions to military communications and establish an admirable intragovernmental system for the upward and downward flow of instructions and reports, but he also put great emphasis on talking to his subjects directly and frequently, and introduced a system of control over domestic publications, education, and the arts that did not differ in essentials from the system used in some authoritarian states today. In postwar Germany, one of the first measures taken by Allied military authorities was to set up a newspaper and radio network to disseminate instructions and to prevent rumors and unrest. Similarly, whenever Yugoslav partisans gained control of an area during their fight against Hitler, one of their first moves was to procure paper and ink and publish simple newspapers—sometimes in hectographed editions.[12] The Imam of Yemen probably overstated the importance of communications, however, when he commented wryly: "It seems all you need to make a government these days is a radio station and a declaration that you have made a government."[13]

Communication as an Organizing Force

Communications can facilitate organized action by those who are not joined in a formal structure in at least four ways: by mobilizing large groups around widely shared ideas, by promoting and maintaining a sense of identity among people who are separated by space or by political barriers, by providing a mechanism through which those who are unorganized can coordinate their efforts, and by helping to train people for future jobs or roles within formal organizations. Some individual communications are able to perform all these functions at once; others, only one or two.

The ability of communications to mobilize people, to rally them to a flag or a cause, has been vividly illustrated by Gorham B. Munson in his account of twelve great propaganda speeches and documents.[14] Most of these were effective because they put into concise and dramatic form ideas toward which many people were groping, or which they already entertained. Some of these ideas were disreputable, as in the case of the "Protocols of the Elders of Zion" or Mussolini's "We or They" declaration. Others represented higher ideals, as in the case of Thomas Paine's *Common Sense,* Woodrow Wilson's Fourteen Points, or the French Revolution's "Declaration of the Rights of Man." But in each instance the communications served to rally large numbers of people who could then identify themselves more clearly with a cause. Organizations recruited members and supporters from those so identified.

Sometimes it is news about an event that serves to rally and to mobilize. The shots of the American revolutionaries at Lexington and Concord were, according to song and story, heard round the world. The American Declaration of Independence provided a strong impetus for the democratic movement in Europe. News of the action, spread by the press, led to vigorous argument, enthusiastic agreement, and violent criticism in politically conscious circles of the Old World. This impact contrasted with the relative lack of stir made by the Netherlands declaration of 1581, which became known to relatively few people because of the rudimentary development of communication media in the sixteenth century.[15]

The mobilizing effect of communications can be observed almost everywhere in the modern world. The Cairo radio has allegedly been able to touch off riots, inspire sabotage, and spur on Algerian fighters against the French.[16] The Iranian Government has blamed Radio Moscow for rallying crowds against the Teheran Government. Publications have sometimes succeeded in striking a chord of response among readers and leading them to organize either temporarily or permanently. When the *Saturday Review* proposed that a Society for Individual Responsibility be organized to stimulate civic action in public affairs, many readers who approved of the editorial wrote to the magazine asking to be put in touch with likeminded people in their own communities. Within six months, more than 1,000 persons were organized in local groups.[17] A social scientist has made the perceptive observation that audiences of communications assume many of the properties of social groups, and that these audiences sometimes begin to behave in a structured manner, very much like organizations. Because they belong to the same audience, previously unrelated individuals, each responding to the same media content, can interact and sometimes even arrive at a division of labor. Teen-age groups built around a disc jockey or a particular style of music provide cases in point.[18]

A related, but somewhat different, way that communications can pave the way for organization, or can help to preserve a diffuse organization, is to promote a sense of mutual identification among people or groups already having something in common. Some of the very earliest newspapers in Europe seem to have circulated primarily among Calvinists, since they were widely scattered, having frequently been forced by established churches to emigrate. The press was able to keep them informed of matters of common interest, to let each Calvinist settlement know what others were doing, and to preserve a sense of identity among them.[19] A similar function was served by the underground press in occupied Europe during World War II. It reminded its readers that they were Danes or Dutch, Poles or French, and encouraged solidarity in resisting the occupiers. The remarkable extent and persistence of the European underground press, in spite of the fact that all those involved in it ran the danger of death, testifies to the vital importance that members of the submerged nationalities attached to keeping in touch with each other and with current events. As many as 62 different papers with a combined circulation of 57,000 copies appeared during the first year the Netherlands were occupied. In Poland, the underground secretly monitored Allied and neutral broadcasts and printed the news obtained this way first in mimeographed form and later on hidden printing presses.[20] Newspapers and radio stations serving various nationality groups in the United States have sometimes been able to preserve a sense of common identity among members of these minorities, and thus have made it possible for minority-group organizations to recruit members and continue their activities for several generations.

Promoting a sense of identity with a larger group is particularly important in the case of people who feel weak or isolated. During World War II, the resistance press performed this function for the peoples of occupied Europe, along with leaflets and radio messages from England that exhorted them to hold out and promised help. The commandant of the Auschwitz extermination camp reported that many inmates were kept alive by the hope they received from foreign broadcasts heard over radio receivers secretly constructed within the camp.[21] When encouraging messages from the outside did not arrive, resistance leaders sometimes forged them. This was done in Poland, where the underground launched bundles of leaflets into the air attached to balloons that were constructed so as to burst after rising some distance. In the morning it looked as though the messages had been dropped by friendly planes.[22]

A third way that communications can facilitate concerted action is by providing a mechanism for the exchange of ideas and coordination of effort among those who are not formally organized. In some cases, this web of communications serves as a substitute for formal organization or makes it unnecessary; in others, the exchange of ideas brings groups close enough together to make formal organization possible.

Again, the resistance press in occupied Europe can serve as an example. Although governments in exile lost control over most of the administrative apparatus in their homelands, they were able to achieve wide compliance with instructions given through underground channels. When Norwegian young people were ordered by the Nazis to register for labor service, instructions to avoid registration were circulated through the clandestine news media. As a result, some 50,000 young people went into hiding. Similarly, Norwegian teachers and clergymen were advised through the same channels not to join Nazi-controlled professional organizations, and almost all of them complied. Coordinated action made successful resistance possible.[23]

Situations where information media serve as a substitute for formal structures can frequently be observed in American politics. The dues-paying membership in American political parties tends to be small, and at election time party leaders rely to a large extent on publicity to mobilize their supporters. Meetings, newsletters, and grass-roots discussions, as well as political information in the mass media, help to form the electorate into blocs, which partially dissolve again after the election is over. Publicity has played a particularly important part in California politics, since political organization there has remained even more rudimentary than in most other states.[24]

The mass media sometimes provide a mechanism for conducting a dialogue among those who are concerned with a particular area of activity, and make it possible for them to function as a loosely organized group. In Washington, for instance, nearly everyone concerned with foreign policy, both inside and outside the government, reads *The New York Times* and *The Washington Post.* As one observer puts it, these newspapers provide, in effect, "an internal system of foreign policy communication in a widely decentralized policy-making structure."[25] That the coordination function of *The New York Times* goes beyond the capital is indicated by surveys which found that *The Times* was subscribed to by 60 per cent of American news editors, 46 per cent of utility executives, 30 per cent of college presidents, and 28 per cent of bank officers. Nearly half the persons listed in *Who's Who in America* gave it as their favorite paper.[26] Most countries have similar "prestige papers" that perform an analogous function by providing influential citizens with information they need to form opinions on public issues and acquainting them with the thoughts of others in this same group. More specialized publications furnish a forum for those who are concerned with other fields, such as science, medicine, business, or education.

Good internal communication among a whole people seems to be one of the requirements of nationhood. If the inhabitants of a given political unit exchange ideas more with other people in the same unit than with those outside it, prospects for national viability are better than if political lines cut across principal lines of communication. The latter situation is likely to prevail when the living space of an ethnic group has been divided up among two or more states, as has been the case with the Kurds, Armenians, and numerous African tribes. It has been suggested that a lot could be learned about the prospects for developing true nationhood in some of the new African states by mapping basic traffic and communication patterns, market areas, languages, and cultures.[27]

The role of communications in creating nations can be seen most clearly in the modernizing areas of the world, where newspapers and other media have been important in drawing nationalists together and giving them common conceptions. Indeed, many nationalist groupings have been formed around newspapers. During the period of British hegemony in Egypt, for instance, it was common for nationalist papers to stimulate the formation of political parties, rather than for an existing party to create its own organ.[28] In Turkey, one of the important steps toward the creation of a modern nation was the emergence of newspapers and other literature using "prose addressed to the people."

Prior to this development in the second half of the nineteenth century, the exchange of ideas between the small cultural elite in the Ottoman Empire and the mass of the people had been stifled by the fact that the mass media had used a language comprehensible only to the elite.[29] The role of the press in building our own nation has also been commented on. Noting that "since primitive times news has been the spark that welded bonds of mutual interest among men," a veteran executive of the Associated Press observes that American newspapers "helped to integrate democratic forces so that a great nation could be created." [30]

Finally, communications can assist in the formation of organizations by preparing individuals for later activity in them as leaders or members. Although this is one of the principal functions of education, information media outside the formal educational framework also play a vital role. Technical journals, for example, not only provide an important part of the information needed by those already employed in modern industrial organizations; they also help to train a new generation.[31] Popular scientific publications and TV programs have done a great deal to stimulate young people to equip themselves for specialized jobs. The literature of space exploration, including science fiction, has been a factor in motivating some of those who later provided the skills and brain power necessary for the enormous effort involved in space programs. Personnel who create and staff political organizations, also, are motivated and trained, at least in part, by the communication media. Leaders for the burgeoning democratic movements of the eighteenth and nineteenth centuries could not have emerged without the vigorous journalism and discussion of the time, and nationalist movements of the nineteenth and twentieth centuries have been led by men who received much of their stimulation from the nationalist content of European and American information media and educational programs.

Public Opinion: A Form of Organization

In addition to making it possible for both highly structured and diffuse organizations to take shape and function, communications play a part in a more intangible, but no less important form of organization —namely, public opinion. The rise of public opinion as an important political force has usually been associated with the development of the mass media, but it is possible for it to appear even when communication is largely restricted to person-to-person channels, although then it develops much more slowly and is usually confined to a limited area.

Historians have identified phenomena much like public opinion, although they were not yet called by this name, in ancient Egypt, classical Greece and Rome, and medieval Europe.[32]

The expression "public opinion" was popularized shortly before the French Revolution by the French Finance Minister, Necker, who used it to describe the reaction of investors to the securities offered for sale by the crown, and it was during the revolutionary period that both intellectuals and statesmen began to concern themselves with this newly recognized force.[33] The German poet Wieland, a close observer of the revolution, described public opinion as follows:[34]

> I, for my part, understand by it an opinion that gradually takes root among a whole people; especially among those who have the most influence when they work together as a group. In this way it wins the upper hand to such an extent that one meets it everywhere. It is an opinion that without being noticed takes possession of most heads, and even in situations where it does not dare to express itself out loud it can be recognized by a louder and louder muffled murmur. It then only requires some small opening that will allow it air, and it will break out with force. Then it can change whole nations in a brief time and give whole parts of the world a new configuration.

Although public opinion has frequently been referred to since Wieland's day, there is still little agreement on what it is. Some authorities use the expression to denote the distribution of opinion on a public issue that is found by opinion polls or by other means. Others see it as an opinion, shared by a major segment of a population, that comes to the attention of higher authorities.[35] In this discussion public opinion will be treated as a consensus that influences the behavior of individuals who contribute to the consensus. It can be considered a form of organization because it is able to coordinate the thought and action of a large number of people, and because it also leads to a differentiation of roles. This is substantially the view adopted by Charles Horton Cooley: "Public opinion is no mere aggregate of separate individual judgments, but an organization, a cooperative product of communication and reciprocal influence."[36] Within the group of those sharing a public opinion on any given issue one can usually distinguish among leaders, disseminators, spokesmen, and followers; sometimes even more specialized roles appear.

Because public opinion enables large numbers of people to act together, it often represents a powerful force. "Whatever may come to be considered a public opinion," said Ferdinand Tönnies, "it confronts the individual with an opinion which is in part an extraneous power." Alfred Sauvy refers to it as an anonymous power (*"cette puissance anonyme"*), and in popular usage it is often associated with influence or compulsion.[37]

Public opinion forms when people become aware that they share attitudes held by others on a given issue, and begin to take this agreement into account in shaping their actions and developing their own opinions further.[38] Communications play an important role in this process. In his classic description of the development of public opinion, James Bryce pictures a businessman reading a news dispatch at breakfast, talking with acquaintances on a commuter train, reading more news stories and editorials, and discussing the matter with his partner before his individual mind is made up.[39] If people are unaware of the attitudes of others, public opinion cannot grow. A French parliamentarian recalled that on July 10, 1940, when the end of the Third Republic was voted in Vichy, many of those who voted against the measure were amazed to find so many others sharing their position. They had thought of themselves as alone, or as members of small groups. Numerous colleagues who had voted together on this occasion told him later: "If I had only known."[40] Obviously, knowledge of the opinions of others would have affected their behavior, but communication among the members of different parliamentary groups had been inadequate.

Lack of communication also inhibited the formation of public opinion among workers in Hungarian factories during the period prior to the anti-Communist uprising of 1956. Although most workers were opposed to the regime, they could not be sure of the attitudes of others because fear of informers made it difficult for them to talk about political matters outside their immediate circle of close friends.[41] It was only when the rebellion broke out and free discussion was suddenly possible that they discovered how the overwhelming majority of their coworkers felt and were able to coordinate their efforts.*

* An illusion of public opinion may sometimes be created when people are incorrectly informed about the attitudes of those around them. This was the case in a small Massachusetts town studied by a social psychologist in the early 1930's. He noted that public opinion there was strongly opposed to card playing, but that when queried privately people did not share this attitude. Apparently, the illusion that most people were opposed to card playing had led to a situation where public opinion to this effect was assumed to exist. To test this hypothesis, he arranged a

Within their immediate environments, people sometimes become aware of public opinion through a process that might be called "personal sampling." They find out what a few individuals think about an issue through observation or conversation and then project these opinions on the whole community, or on various groups within it. Thus, certain opinions may be ascribed to farmers, businessmen, young people, and so on. On other occasions it is possible to form a picture of public opinion on the basis of local elections, crowd behavior, or other phenomena in the community.

When larger areas are concerned, we are likely to be more dependent on the mass media both for knowledge about issues and for information about the attitudes of others. Reports describing the views of opinion leaders, reactions of organized groups, or mass meetings and demonstrations make it possible to form expectations about the way other people will react with respect to a given issue. These expectations then influence our own behavior. We believe that, as far as this issue is concerned, we are likely to meet with approval or disapproval, support or opposition, if we do or say certain things.

Sometimes public opinion can be manufactured quite successfully by astute use of mass media. For a few weeks during 1960, Israel was divided into two camps over the issue of radios in buses. Controversy raged in newspaper correspondence columns and editorials, and at last the authorities were forced to take notice. It was ordered that bus radios must be turned off if any single passenger raised an objection. This was referred to by at least one editor as a "triumph for public opinion." When a reporter subsequently investigated, he found that the issue had been raised by a young poet and two of his friends, who had written nearly all the letters to the press, using a variety of fictitious names and addresses.[42]

Public opinion on most issues involves only a minority of the population—usually the minority that also is most attentive to the mass media. Thus, during the late eighteenth and early nineteenth centuries, when public opinion achieved some of its greatest victories over the established order, relatively few individuals made up the relevant publics.

---

bridge party and invited a liberal minister to participate. This started vigorous discussions that enabled people to become acquainted with the true attitudes of their neighbors, and led to a change in public opinion in the town as a whole. (Richard L. Schanck, "A Study of Change in Institutional Attitudes in a Rural Community," *Journal of Social Psychology,* February, 1934, p. 126.)

Most of these people, who read political publications, wrote numerous letters, and gathered in the coffee houses and salons to discuss the events of the day, belonged to the newly prosperous but still small middle class.[43] Even the most influential media had what by present standards would be considered tiny circulations. In 1793, for instance, *The Times* of London stated that its regular sale was "now nearly 4,000 daily, a number which was never before attained by any morning paper under any circumstances." This figure, however, gave no indication of total readership, since each copy was seen by numerous persons in the coffee houses, where patrons waited their turn for reading. After they had finished, the copy was then passed from hand to hand outside. Regular subscription by individuals did not become common for some time.[44]

The segment of a population that acts on any given issue today is also likely to be small, even though participants may be drawn from more classes and social groups. The Hungarian revolt of 1956 was based on an extremely broad public opinion, yet as far as can be determined the majority of the adult population was not directly involved. One survey, which sought to reconstruct a picture of how the entire population had behaved, is summarized in Table 1.[45]

TABLE 1

ADULT BEHAVIOR IN HUNGARIAN REVOLUTION

	Percentage of population
Actively fought with gun in hand	11
Actively participated without fighting	16
Supported, without fighting or participating	8
Inactive, although not against revolution	63
Against the revolution	2
	100

This survey indicates that about two-thirds of the adult population remained inactive, although not opposed to the revolution. Further analysis shows that the inactive elements were largely composed of women; more than half the men participated in some way or another. Most of the actual fighting was done by age groups under thirty.

Ordinarily, those who actively take part in public opinion on an issue represent a much smaller minority of the population than was the case in Hungary. If only 5 or 10 per cent of the people are interested in a question, they usually will form public opinion regarding it. On most U.S. foreign-policy issues, strong feelings on the part of a small but interested group determine what public opinion will be. Naturally, the identity of those involved varies from issue to issue.[46]

The political significance of public opinion lies partly in the enormous flexibility of this kind of organization. Public opinion can be mobilized on a wide variety of issues, and among population groups where other forms of organization are rudimentary. It is not necessary that the people involved know each other personally. The only prerequisites are an issue, the means of communication, and a sufficient number of attentive individuals. It may have been this spontaneous character of public opinion that accounted for the mystification, and sometimes terror, with which supporters of the *ancien régime* faced it at the time of the French Revolution. Entrenched in the institutions of church, state, and the feudal system, they suddenly found themselves confronted with a vigorous middle class that behaved as though it were an organized body, even though little organizational structure was visible. Leaders of the middle class could act with the confidence of widespread support, and in the knowledge of the opinions of other leaders. In the end they succeeded in capturing the state apparatus.

Although public opinion plays its most noticeable role in the political sphere, it can lead to significant changes in economic and social areas as well. It frequently brings about adjustments in the goods and services offered the public, and plays a role both in the imposition of racial and religious discrimination and in the struggle against it. Public opinion can lead to the formation of new industries and new communities, to saving or to spending. For instance, wartime surveys of bond-buying habits found that most people knew that their friends, neighbors, or co-workers were buying bonds. This knowledge influenced their own behavior, and saving became an accepted pattern.[47] The part played by public opinion in causing inflation, deflation, and depressions has also been noted. An analysis of financial crises in France and England between 1924 and 1936 indicates that public opinion not only influenced those who had to make decisions about monetary policy during this period but that it helped to shape the economic behavior of investors, speculators, and others who were involved in creating the economic conditions that had to be dealt with.[48]

Movements that start out primarily as efforts to build public opinion frequently result in the creation of formal organizations. Indeed, the process of mobilizing public opinion involves many of the same steps as organization-building: giving expression to widely shared ideas, promoting communication among interested individuals, creating a sense of identity, and training people to play certain roles. If formal organizations result from public opinion, these then may seek to build a larger public opinion, which, in turn, may lead to the creation of even larger associations, the passage of laws, or alterations in the machinery of government. This circular process can be discerned in such developments in American history as the temperance movement, the abolitionist movement, and the trend toward greater social security.

Organizations as Users of International Communications

A major reason for the constant growth in the volume of international communications is the increase in the number and size of organizations that make use of them. Those categories of communications that have shown particularly sharp increases in recent years include technical data required by industrial and professional groups, information needed by political and economic decision-makers, and material for the use of international organizations.

Technical data from abroad are required increasingly by industrial organizations, agricultural producers, military establishments, and all institutions concerned with science. Much of the information sought by underdeveloped countries is of a technical nature, although a far larger volume is consumed by industrialized nations. The official translation programs of major countries stress scientific and economic materials, and professional journals include more and more information from abroad. Soviet exchange programs with the United States place heavy emphasis on the collection of technical data.

The dependence of advanced technology on foreign information is dramatically illustrated when, for one reason or another, the flow of this information is inhibited. A study of military thought in West Germany in the early 1950's found, for instance, that the expertness of German military specialists had been reduced substantially because they had been cut off from foreign military technology during the postwar years.[49] Similar observations could probably have been made in other technical fields in either Germany or Japan.

Another class of organizational users of international communications includes governments and economic organizations with foreign interests, both of which require large quantities of information about what is happening abroad for use in their day-to-day business and for planning purposes. The vital nature of this information is suggested by the lengths that merchants and princes went to gather it before the days of regular international news services. Merchants trading between Italy and Egypt seem to have been among the first to establish something approximating a commercial news service to provide information about crops and market conditions in various parts of the Mediterranean world.[50] The Venetian diplomatic service, which became a model followed by other Western European states from early in the second millennium, provided the government of Venice with voluminous reports of current affairs abroad. Prompt information about events that might affect market prices was so important that enormous prices were paid for it. As late as 1500, the cost of a letter carried from Rome to Venice by the fastest possible means was about 40 ducats—more than a month's salary for a professor of great renown, and half the annual salary of a military instructor or an interpreter who could handle Turkish.[51] Today, the huge consumption of international news and other information materials by governments and business interests testifies to their continually increasing demand for knowledge about what is happening abroad.

International communications are especially important to organizations with members or branches in several countries. Some business organizations have resorted to extensive publishing programs to help link together their scattered employees. The Royal Dutch Shell Group publishes two monthly magazines in English and Dutch with a combined circulation of approximately 80,000 copies for its personnel throughout the world. These magazines have the task of informing employees in all nations "why, for whom, and with whom they are doing their job." Local companies belonging to the group publish an additional 32 magazines with a combined circulation of over 280,000.[52] The International Chamber of Commerce provides a unique forum for the exchange of economic information in its biennial conferences, where business leaders from some 50 nations meet to work through an agenda prepared by a score of international committees and by an international secretariat and staff in Paris.[53] International religious organizations, labor organizations, scientific associations, and many other kinds of groups also use publications, conferences, and other channels to provide their members with some of the information necessary for the conduct of organizational affairs. The *Annuaire des Organisations Internationales* for 1962-63 lists more than 1,300 nongovernmental groups, the overwhelming majority of which sponsor publications or international conferences. It also lists about 150 international organizations in which governments are members. These are concerned primarily with technical matters such as health, mail service, broadcasting, or scientific interchange, and also are prolific publishers. Nongovernmental international organizations in the commercial and industrial sphere have quadrupled during the past decade; those concerned with health and medicine have more than doubled, and intergovernmental organizations have increased by 50 per cent.[54]

All international political organizations rely heavily on communication to maintain cohesion and satisfy organizational needs for information. The multilateral alliances in which the United States is involved have placed great emphasis on developing communication links of all types. NATO has programmed over 26,000 miles of submarine cables, land lines, and radio links in and among its member nations, and both SEATO and CENTO have made similar efforts to assure good military communications; in addition, they have made use of periodic conferences and have sponsored international training and exchange programs. In the case of NATO, a number of periodical publications have also sprung up. The British Commonwealth, an international political organization of a looser type, is largely a nexus of informational exchange. The historical, economic, and emotional ties that form the basis for this grouping are nourished by Commonwealth conferences, the international service of the British Broadcasting Corporation, such specialized journals as *The Round Table: A Quarterly Review of British Commonwealth Affairs,* and the great private media of public information that radiate from London to all parts of the Commonwealth. All countries with important colonial interests established radio service to their overseas dependencies between the world wars. Holland started broadcasts to Dutch settlers in the East Indies in 1927, France began its regular Empire Service over Paris-Colonial in 1931, and Great Britain followed in 1932.[55]

International communications also play a role in training the personnel who staff both governmental and private organizations concerned with international affairs, and in creating human channels through which information can flow among nations. Exchange programs and international educational institutions have already produced a corps of persons throughout the world who are able to talk with each other more easily because they have shared the common experience of learning to live with those of a different national background. A U.S. ambassador, when asked his opinion about the utility of student exchange programs, noted that he was able to call up the premier of the country in which he was stationed and start the conversation with a few reminiscences of shared college experiences.[56]

When the functioning of an alliance is concerned, such a seemingly minor matter as this ability of the personnel involved to talk informally may make the difference between success and failure.* Those interested in closer European integration have emphasized the importance of creating a European bureaucracy, and several proposals have been advanced for educational institutions that would equip students for service in international organizations.[57]

Since communication among two or more nations is necessary for the operation of international organizations, one way of inhibiting the activity of such organizations is to choke off their foreign contacts. Communist countries have used this technique to discourage the operation of bodies with international ties, and some non-Communist nations have used it against the Communist network. In a statement to the House Foreign Affairs Committee on the need for legislation denying passports to Communist supporters, a State Department official observed that "communication and personal contact are essential to the effective operation of any such complex organization." Therefore, he said, the Department sought to deny easy communication to the Communists by the application of passport, visa, and immigration regulations.[58]

International public opinion, as a form of organization, is achieved when substantial numbers of people in various countries coordinate their actions with the actions of other members of the international public as a result of awareness of a consensus on an issue. While communication among free nations makes the development of international public opinion possible, it is difficult to cite cases in which this opinion has exerted appreciable force. Many observers were disappointed when an effective international protest failed to develop following Soviet resumption of atomic testing in 1961, and students of international rela-

* Both British and American information and cultural programs in Germany following World War II helped to build a group of persons who could serve as interpreters between the nations involved. (Raymond Ebsworth, *Restoring Democracy in Germany: The British Contribution* [New York: Frederick A. Praeger, 1961], pp. 173-75; John Gimbel, *A German Community Under American Occupation* [Stanford, Calif.: Stanford University Press, 1961], p. 211.)

tions have pointed out that public opinion within nations is still a far more significant political factor than international public opinion. Indeed, whether states pay attention to world opinion appears to be largely a matter of political convenience.[59] The Communist apparatus has attempted to simulate international public opinion on a number of issues, but usually the artificial nature of the alleged consensus has been apparent. Something approaching a true international public opinion does, however, seem to have developed in Western Europe on the question of intra-European wars. Among political elites and other politically conscious strata of the West European population, such wars are now considered "senseless, fratricidal, and self-destructive." [60] As long as this climate of opinion prevails, war among the countries involved appears to be ruled out. Further cases probably could be cited if more systematic attention had been given to studying the phenomenon.

At the present time it is likely that international public opinion is more influential in such areas as science, literature, and fashion than in the political sphere. One can certainly speak of a consensus on many issues among influential groups of scientists—especially in so far as what problems are worth studying; and in the realms of style, music, or literature, international public opinion has an important effect on individual behavior. The rapid increase in international communication, and the resulting possibility of dialogues and consensuses in more and more areas, suggest that international public opinion will play a larger role in the future.

Communications from abroad are likely to achieve an effect when they serve an existing organizational need or assist in the creation of new organizations or an international public opinion. As is the case with individuals, if information cannot be used it will have little impact. For example, if there is no framework in which an exchange student who has learned new techniques abroad can apply his skills, they will be partially or entirely wasted. Similarly, propaganda in favor of international cooperation is likely to have little political significance without the concurrent growth of institutions and organizations that can give effect to the ideas expressed.[61]

The kinds of organizations that use international communications, and the types of information from abroad that affect their behavior, differ according to the political, social, and economic contexts in which they are located. No two countries display exactly the same organizational patterns, and the differences within a single country may be extreme. Nevertheless, there is no part of the world where organizations are not important users of ideas from abroad, and the implications of international communication for the formation and operation of organized groups are at least as important as their effects on individuals—possibly more important.

V

The Political Role of Communication in Democracies

Domestic practices affecting communications in any state help to determine both the nature of the messages from and about that state that go abroad and the impact that ideas from other countries have on its internal politics. The role of communication in democracies is a particularly complicated one, and imposes a number of limitations on the ways that democratic spokesmen can seek to influence foreign nations. It also causes difficulties for people in other countries when they try to evaluate the significance of news from democracies; and it produces a curious blend of susceptibility and invulnerability to messages from abroad on the part of citizens of democratic states.

Many of the characteristics that we associate with democracy depend on free access of all groups in a population to the channels of communication, both as senders and as receivers. These characteristics include nonviolent competition for political power among various groups within the nation (and the existence of machinery for the orderly transfer of power from one group to another), the ability of those outside the government to influence its actions, and the reliance of the government more on suasion and less on force to accomplish its domestic policies. Because of their political significance, the communication media in democracies are under constant pressure, on the one side from groups seeking preferential access, and on the other from those who feel themselves disadvantaged or who want to maintain freedom of access for all.

Democracies are also characterized by a respect for the individual, who is allowed wide latitude to seek full personal development according to his own inclinations, to pursue his own happiness, and to participate actively in a variety of groups. Satisfaction of personal desires likewise depends in large measure on access to information of many types and on freedom to communicate. Nevertheless, complete freedom for any individual can never be assured, since it may restrict the freedom of others or may conflict with strongly held group values. How much latitude each individual can be allowed is a problem with which democratic theorists have struggled since classical times; they agree only that individual freedom should be as great as possible. This problem is also reflected in the debate over the role of the communication media in democracies: To what extent should they try to give each person what he wants, and to what extent have they a social responsibility? [1]

Communications and the Functioning of Competing Groups

The importance of competing, nongovernmental groups in the functioning of a democracy needs little stress. Indeed, the network of voluntary associations in the United States has been characterized by political observers as a beneficent species of invisible government, and it has been pointed out that those concerned with American democracy should be aware of the necessity of keeping these organizations healthy and alert.[2] Voluntary organizations cannot remain strong, however, if they lack adequate information about the subjects with which they are concerned, or if communication facilities are not available to make possible a full exchange of ideas within and among them.

Since competing groups in a democracy have such diverse political interests, a far greater variety of media is necessary to satisfy their internal and external requirements than is the case in states where only one political point of view is permitted. Officials familiar with communications in India, for instance, have noted that, in proportion to population, much more varied information sources are required than is the case in a totalitarian country such as Communist China. Democratic states that have succumbed to totalitarianism, as Italy did in 1922 and Germany in 1933, witnessed a marked decline in the number of newspapers, magazines, and other information media that previously spoke for nongovernmental points of view. A German commentary on the Italian press after 1922 noted not only that the number of papers had declined, but that the remaining ones had become very dull.[3] When the German press was "coordinated" after 1933, the same serial publication, by then under Nazi influence, recorded a similar decrease in the number of German newspapers, but this time explained that it was undesirable to have so many political points of view expressed, because this interfered with the formation of a single national will. Between 1932 and 1937, the number of newspapers appearing in Germany sank from 4,703 to 2,527.[4]

Recent trends toward the consolidation of the mass media in industrialized democracies have led to fears that in these countries, too, the media will no longer be able to give adequate expression to all principal points of view. In the United States, for instance, only sixty-five cities still had competing daily newspapers in 1960,[5] and today there are even fewer. Cities with only one daily paper increased from 1,107 in 1945 to 1,222 in 1960, although during this period total daily newspaper circulation rose by more than 12 million, and as of 1960, about 750 American radio and TV stations were affiliated with newspapers, thus further increasing centralized control of the mass media.

Nevertheless, it can be argued that this centralization is more apparent than real. Since 1945 the proportion of radio and TV stations affiliated with newspapers has been declining, and as of 1960 there were only 355 "single voice" cities in the United States, as opposed to 3,324 "competing voices" in 1,106 cities.[6] Furthermore, the daily press, radio, and TV do not constitute the only channels of information open to competing groups in a democratic society. News magazines, periodicals, books, newsletters, public meetings, and other channels play an important role. It is quite possible that in the United States and Western Europe more varied points of view are now available to the public than was the case twenty years ago.

Perhaps equally important is the fact that many large media are hospitable to a broad range of opinions in their news coverage, even if they have become hesitant in expressing their own opinion. This has increasingly been the case with radio, TV, and large newspapers in the United States, and the same trend has been observed in other major democracies. A leading editor has observed that in an earlier era of American history a large number of papers assured that there was "a journalistic advocate for every noticeable point of view, every substantial interest . . . in the body politic." Now, the large, independently edited newspapers are assuming more and more of this function.[7]

The willingness of the "great press" to serve as a common carrier of information and opinion is in part a concession to the widely held concept, as expressed by the Commission on the Freedom of the Press in

1947, that the individual citizen deserves access to principal conflicting ideas about major issues, and that those who have something to say about these issues should be able to reach the public.[8] At the same time, it is good business for the mass press to serve as many groups as possible. A large newspaper requires a large constituency and this is likely to be made up of people with varying interests.[9] With regard to radio and television, there is steady governmental pressure—sometimes gentle and sometimes stronger—to ensure that the airwaves are open to the expression of differing points of view.[10]

Opportunities for competing groups to make use of communication channels are never perfect; some groups are better served than others. Nevertheless, most democracies have facilities for the dissemination of a wide range of information and attitudes, usually excluding material that is repugnant to moral values held by the overwhelming majority.[11] This variety of expression enables individuals to nourish their own points of view by finding support for them in the stream of communications; it makes it possible for those with similar attitudes to learn about each other and to get in touch with each other; and it thus facilitates the growth of public opinion, the formation of new political groupings, and the modification of the programs of existing groups.

A democracy is, however, more than a network of contending groups. It is itself a larger group, and as such requires a communication network that will help ensure internal cohesion, reinforce democratic values, and assist in the formation of a national public opinion on vital issues. Plato's observation that democracy was possible only in small states may have been related to the fact that in his day effective communication via the mass media was not possible, and that a sufficient exchange of ideas through person-to-person channels could not be achieved throughout a large realm.[12] The Commission on the Freedom of the Press and other commentators have stressed that, in the interest of democracy, the major media should clarify the values, goals, and common understandings of the society in which they operate, and should help to bridge the gaps that separate geographical, religious, and social groups by explaining these groups to each other.[13] Content studies of American mass media have indicated that these do in fact tend to reiterate certain values that are held by the majority. This has been deplored as leading to undue uniformity, but it is also a force for unity. A German student of the 1920's, seeking an explanation for the fact that the United States had achieved such unity of outlook despite its diverse population, found the answer primarily in the work of the information media. German media had fallen down in this regard, he believed. Former Chancellor Adenauer was apparently thinking along somewhat the same lines when he urged the German press to stress common values and to assist in the education of the population for the duties of citizenship.[14]

The mass media reinforce democracy not only by acquainting different groups with each other, but by facilitating the membership of a single person in more than one group. Democracies would be even more rent by factionalism than is the case if it were not possible (1) for an individual to be simultaneously a member of several organizations whose aims did not completely coincide, and (2) for large political groups, especially, to include people with a variety of interests, so that party policies rarely go so far in the direction desired by one element in the party as to alienate other elements. If membership in major organizations and groups does not overlap with membership in others, and if the members of these groups have identical regional, religious, economic, and political affiliations, then the danger that a democracy will split up is ever present.[15] For example, the homogeneity of group membership poses a problem for democracy in India.[16] In so far as they enable both formal and informal associations to recruit members in different areas and from among different strata of the population, the media of communication serve as a powerful cement in the democratic fabric.

Popular Influences on Government

Channels of communication from the citizenry to the government make it possible for those outside the governmental structure to influence official actions and policies. In democracies one channel is established constitutionally, in that all citizens are, in theory at least, assured of access to their representatives in the legislature. This channel is supplemented, and indeed usually overshadowed, by other mechanisms through which the citizen can influence officials: the public media, pressure groups, lobbies, communications to administrative agencies, and public opinion. Public-opinion polls offer a relatively new device through which popular views on a large range of issues can be made known to policy-makers.

Many of the mechanisms for reaching a government depend for their effectiveness on lateral communication facilities *within* the population.

Lobbies and pressure groups require an organizational base, which can be maintained only if the individuals concerned can keep in touch with each other. Letters and petitions to the government, to be effective, ordinarily must reflect widely held opinions. Otherwise they will not occur in sufficient quantities or with sufficient concentration in a given time period to make an impression.*

The relationship between patterns of communication and government in a democracy is indicated by a diagram suggested by Hans Speier (Figure A). In this, the national structure is represented by a triangle, with the government and other decision-makers in the apex and the public in the larger space below. Communications within the state are represented by arrows. The larger arrows at the top represent instructions and other messages from the government to the public, and the pressure of public opinion on the government. The smaller arrows at the base of the triangle indicate communications at various levels within the public. Without this intercommunication among citizens, messages directed to the decision-makers would be relatively few in number and would have less impact.

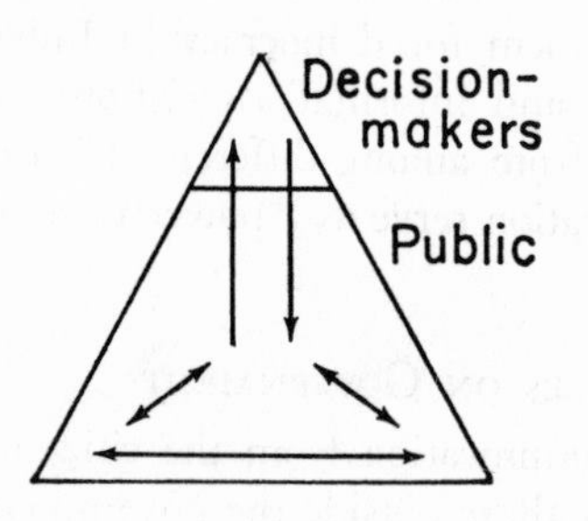

FIGURE A
LINES OF COMMUNICATION IN A DEMOCRACY

Although it is generally accepted that in a democracy communications to the government from the public do have an effect, it is difficult to ascertain just how great this effect is. In reviewing the literature on lobbies and pressure groups concerned with United States foreign pol-

* The exception to this rule occurs when individuals are so influential that a word from one of them, or from a very few of them, will be sufficient to influence policy. These individuals could, however, be thought of as part of the effective government, even if they have no official positions.

icy, Bernard Cohen notes that most studies have merely described the activities of these groups without inquiring into the actual results achieved. The equation of activity with influence is often simply assumed.[17] It is even more difficult to relate mass attitudes toward a given issue to government policy. One reason for this is that people often hold inconsistent opinions on related issues, and the effects of these opinions may cancel each other out. For instance, a University of Michigan survey in 1956 found that more than half of those who clearly favored the U.S. foreign-aid program also thought that taxes should be cut. Similarly, it was found that taxation to finance welfare programs was opposed more frequently by those favoring welfare programs than by those who were against them.[18] Instances where it seems almost certain that pressure brought by interested minorities affected governmental policy, such as recognition of Israel by the United States in 1948, can be found, but in most cases one cannot confidently say just how much pressure groups influenced a given action.[19]

In the United States, a few particularly successful lobbies and pressure groups in the foreign-policy arena have been identified. One is the shipping lobby, supported by both management and labor. Another is the West Coast fishing industry, which played a major part in the negotiation of a fisheries settlement with Japan after World War II. A third is the United States Beet Sugar Association.[20]

Groups that have had a marked impact on U.S. governmental actions have certain common characteristics. First, they are concerned with a specific aspect of policy that is directly related to their vital interests. Groups with a broad range of interests are less likely to be successful. Second, they are most likely to be influential when the issues in which they are interested are not in the public eye, or at least when there is no organized opposition to the policies they are advocating. Third, policy-makers usually share the general position or outlook of those groups whose recommendations they support. That is, government officials seldom agree to the demands of those with whom they are in basic ideological or political conflict. Fourth, those who are likely to be successful in influencing government policy usually have to be recognized by the government officials concerned as having the right to speak on the subject—for example, as being spokesmen for a group that will be affected or as possessing special expertness.[21] Very similar observations were made in a study of political influence in France during the early 1950's. There, the Association of Wine Growers, for example, was found to have a major voice in any policy affecting wine, but was not likely to be heeded on matters of foreign policy in general.[22]

It is characteristic of political communications in democracies that a large proportion of them are of a critical nature. Indeed, criticism is an important component in the working definition of news used by the mass media. When some institution or government agency is functioning as it should, this ordinarily remains unreported; a malfunction, however, usually merits headlines. The 999 honest government officials receive little attention; the one who proves to be corrupt may be at the center of the news for days. This pattern can also be observed in relation to racial integration in the United States: orderly integration is reported perfunctorily or not at all, while the names of the relatively few cities that have experienced disorders have become household words. When newspaper editors in a large Southern city were asked why they had not published reports about integration of the city's restaurants in 1961, they replied that since there had been no disorders there had been nothing to report. The accent on criticism is particularly noticeable with respect to government policies—both foreign and domestic. In reviewing a volume of twenty essays on U.S. foreign relations and diplomacy, a historian noted that only one of the contributors stressed the positive aspects of American foreign policy. That author, significantly, was a foreigner.[23]

Public opinion, especially, is likely to crystallize around an actual or potential grievance and to oppose something: corruption, segregation, integration, or inflation. Government officials may act or may be restrained from acting on an issue when they anticipate that their behavior is likely to mobilize a hostile public opinion.[24] This is not to say that public opinion does not also form around positive issues—better schools, a chicken in every pot, and so on. Many such examples could be cited, but they tend to be less noticeable than those that represent opposition.

The prevalence of critical communications in a democracy is often deplored. Nevertheless, criticism of things as they are, or as they might be, is vital to the functioning of a democratic order. Without them, organizations and opinions advocating change could not take shape, and an orderly transition of power from one government to another would be impossible. Even successful maintenance of an existing administration would be difficult unless malfunctions in need of correction were highlighted. While a certain ratio between expressions of approval and disapproval is necessary for stability, a preponderance of critical communications appears to be necessary to the functioning of a democracy, even when the opinions of a majority favor things substantially as they are. Whether attention given to real or imagined malfunctioning is justified on the basis of newsworthiness or for some other reason, information media are playing a necessary role when they give an opportunity for critical voices to be heard. The status quo, if it is to be stable, must continuously be tested against possible alternatives.

Not all citizens in any democracy take an intelligent or continuous interest in the affairs of government; the circle of those interested in public affairs, and informed about them, may be relatively small. Political scientists sometimes differentiate among the general public, the "attentive public," and policy and opinion elites. The elites take the most active interest in governmental affairs, and the attentive public, which constitutes the audience for discussion among the elites, is sometimes mobilized to act with regard to one or another political issue. The general public, which may include far more than half the population, rarely communicates to policy-makers. Congressional mail in the United States, for instance, usually comes from relatively few sources.[25]

The dangers inherent in this situation have been noted. Without adequate citizen participation in the affairs of government, it is difficult for a democracy to find a solid basis for policy.[26] The nation may be dominated by demagogues or by selfish minorities, or its stability may be threatened as important elements become aware of their interests and power, and demand special privileges. When any group combines political interest and activity with selfishness and ignorance, the results can be disastrous, unless its influence is countered by other groups. A minor, but disturbing, example of such a threat could be observed in the United States when Army reserve personnel, mobilized during the Berlin crisis of 1961, accused the Kennedy Administration of having created the crisis for political purposes and threatened revenge at the polls.[27] More serious examples can be found in some of the economically less developed democracies where influential minorities—for example, the armed forces or civilian government employees—have made use of their power to demand policies that have undermined the stability of the state.

Yet there are also dangers in overpoliticization. If everybody feels an intense interest in all questions, and seeks to make his influence felt, orderly government is almost impossible. A social scientist, writing on behalf of a group devoted to finding ways to assure peace, noted that if everyone held as strong views as did the members of the group in question, the result would more likely be civil war than a stable democratic process. The large majority who do not feel strongly about most questions, and who do not seek to make their influence felt, are important in assuring stability.[28]

Where the optimum division lies between participation and nonparticipation in political affairs has not been determined. It would appear that democracies have the best prospects for success when the circle of those actively interested in and informed about political questions is expanded gradually, when they are ordered in relatively stable groupings, and when overlapping membership and communication among these groups is encouraged. Whether democratic development along these lines can be achieved depends heavily on the structure and quality of the media of public communication. If the media can assist in building an increasingly large and informed segment of the citizenry, if they provide the information needed by the diverse groups that arise among those interested, and if they provide facilities for the exchange of ideas among these groups, then the prospects for democracy would seem to be good.

Governmental Dependence on Suasion

It is axiomatic that, in a democracy, laws cannot be enforced unless they enjoy the support, or at least the acquiescence, of a large majority. Indeed, the degree of compliance with some laws has been documented statistically, and it can be shown that enforcement agencies usually have to concern themselves with only a limited segment of the population.[29] If more than a small minority resists compliance, a law is likely to become a dead letter. Although most decisions are made by a few men, these usually decide on a given course of action only if they feel fairly certain that the public will support them. For they will hold power only as long as a sufficient number of citizens approve of the way it is being exercised.[30]

To secure compliance, a government therefore requires not only the means of reaching the population with instructions and orders, but also an opportunity to explain these, to justify them, and to defend them. One of the major functions of the press is to make this possible. An analysis of the tasks faced by the Office of War Information in addressing the American population during World War II found that these included both informing and motivating the public. Informational tasks included telling people what to do and what not to do—e.g., that they should buy war bonds but should not waste food. The motivational tasks included educating the public with respect to such matters as the issues involved in the war, the nature of the adversary, and the necessity to sacrifice in order to support the fighting forces.[31] Although the Domestic Branch of the Office of War Information was soon dissolved, these two tasks remained, and were undertaken by public officials and patriotic groups, using primarily nongovernmental channels. Similar problems of informing and motivating were faced by the British Government following the war, when it was necessary to persuade the citizenry to tighten their belts and simultaneously to produce more. In this case a combination of government and private information services was employed.[32]

Communications from a government, like other communications, are subject to serious limitations when it comes to changing strongly held individual attitudes, but they are particularly important as a means of encouraging pro-government groups and rallying public opinion behind specific measures. Indeed, an official in a democracy who is unable to reach the public through the mass media and must rely on personal or official channels is deprived of a large measure of his influence. This became apparent in England during the transition to a greater measure of democracy that took place in the eighteenth and nineteenth centuries. At that time, lawmakers who had previously regarded attention by the press as unjustified interference in the affairs of government began to realize that newspapers had a certain value. The House of Commons gave up attempting to prohibit reports of debates in 1771, and the Lords followed suit in 1775.[33] In 1810, a Member of Parliament, William Windham, apparently still operating under assumptions more appropriate to the previous century, launched a savage attack on the press. He criticized the publication of reports of Parliamentary debates, questioned the right of constituents to know what had happened in the House, and asked whether it was right that "bankrupts, lottery-office keepers, stockbrokers, footmen and decayed tradesmen" should make a business out of eavesdropping from the public gallery. Reporters retaliated by ceasing to report Mr. Windham's speeches, thereby probably doing him more harm than by criticism.[34]

In the present century, leadership in democracies has usually been associated with the ability to use the mass media to influence public opinion. Franklin D. Roosevelt and Sir Winston Churchill have both been frequently cited as two outstanding practitioners of the art. During his first ten months in office, President Roosevelt spoke over the radio 20 times, Mrs. Roosevelt spoke 17 times, and members of the cabinet spoke 107 times.[35] Even more extensive use of the mass media was made by the Kennedy Administration. As one political observer noted, not only was President Kennedy able to dominate the political news on national television during his first year in office, but his only serious competition in the national magazine press seemed to come from his wife.[36] A similar trend has been observed in other democracies. The strong presidential regime in France became possible in part because the top authorities of the state were able to approach the people directly and personally through television.[37]

When government is not able, or does not take the trouble, to inform politically attentive segments of the public about the basis for its policies, it is likely to be weakened. The instability of French governments in the years following World War II has been ascribed in part to poor communication from the authorities to the public. Many of these governments, says a French expert, possibly with some exaggeration, "did not even take the trouble or the pains to give a truthful explanation of the reasons for their actions." In contrast, he notes, the British Government of the same period was in constant communication with public opinion through the Treasury's information service and was able to solve exceptionally difficult economic problems.[38] Other students, also, have remarked on the extraordinarily self-centered behavior of the French Assembly during the years of the Fourth Republic.[39]

Government information programs in a democracy often give rise to fears that democratic processes will be weakened. Yet there are also grave dangers in not maintaining facilities that enable a government to present its case and appeal for support. Journalists have occasionally observed that the private information media would flounder helplessly in Washington without the assistance of government public information personnel.[40] As with so many problems of democracy, the solution appears to lie in a proper balance—in this case between government publicity and private criticism.

Controversy Over Access to the Media

Because communications play such an important role in the functioning of groups that compete for power in a democracy, one feature of democratic life is pressure on the part of some groups for preferential access to the media of public communication, and counterpressure from others that seek greater access for themselves or for all members of the society.

The most obvious group seeking preferential access to the media is government. Indeed, many of the earliest newspapers served as official organs. The first newspaper to appear in France, Renaudot's *Gazette*, was founded with the assistance of the court, and Louis XIV himself frequently wrote for it. In most countries of Europe during the eighteenth and much of the nineteenth centuries, media expressing views contrary to those of the government were either suppressed or were subject to serious disabilities. Even in England the press did not achieve complete freedom from government control until about 1860.[41]

As soon as formal government controls are removed from communication media, most governments attempt to secure preferential access to them by other means. In Prussia, for instance, a "Royal Control Office for Press Affairs" was set up in 1850-51, with duties that included directing two state-owned newspapers, subsidizing others overtly or covertly, cultivating good relations with uncontrolled domestic and foreign papers, granting reporters interviews with the Prime Minister and some other ministers, and coordinating police measures affecting the press.[42] Most states maintained similar bodies for influencing the mass media, although they were not always so well organized, and controversy has continued up to the present time about the extent to which government ought to try to influence the press and the means it should use. A French authority on law has observed that to find out whether the press of any country is free, one should look not at the country's constitution but at police regulations, economic provisions governing the purchase of paper, and so on.[43]

In the United States, the government has sought to gain a measure of preferential access by controlling information at its source, releasing it to favored media, or not releasing it at all. A Congressman who was attempting to liberalize access to governmental news sources once remarked that fighting official secrecy was like stepping on a balloon: as soon as you put your foot on one part it pops out somewhere else.[44] During the 1962 crisis over Soviet missiles in Cuba, government officials withheld some news items from the press, issued others that were misleading, and attempted to regulate the interviews of newsmen with officials more closely. This provoked a vigorous controversy over management of the news. Official spokesmen maintained that in time of national crisis a government was entitled to manipulate public information, while most spokesmen for the press pointed to the dangers of government controls that would keep the public from being informed.

Private interests, no less than governments, seek preferential access to the media of communication. In many democracies, labor and business, as well as political, religious, and social groups, support extensive public-relations programs, one of the principal purposes of which is to influence the content of the mass media. Indeed, the proportion of news in the daily and weekly press of the United States that is originated by public relations sources has been estimated to run between 40 per cent and 60 per cent. In addition, certain organs, although not officially spokesmen for economic interest groups, are believed to enjoy hidden subsidies or otherwise to be dominated by a particular point of view. Thus, the pre-Hitler *Frankfurter Zeitung,* one of the great newspapers of Europe, was considered to represent the views of a liberal industrial group that supported it.

As a matter of practice, no democracy has found a way of ensuring that communication facilities are open to all groups equally. Nevertheless, various formulas for equalizing access have been developed, and these are reflected in the laws and customs of each democracy. Many countries provide for the control of broadcasting by mixed commissions, representing both public and private bodies. Persons or groups who feel that they have been unfairly treated in the press are entitled under the laws of some states to demand space for a reply. A number of countries discourage press-radio combinations or limit the right of publishers to be involved in other businesses also.

The degree to which wide access to the public media can or should be assured by law and the extent to which preferential access of any group should be discouraged are both highly controversial questions. Certainly no one solution is the only correct one. Democracy can function (assuming its other requirements are fulfilled) as long as competing groups and interests are assured adequate use of communication media to satisfy their internal and external requirements, even though all do not have complete equality of access. A degree of preferential access for some groups is far less dangerous than the complete exclusion of others. If a government can suppress media serving other groups contending for political power, and pre-empt a major share of the communication spectrum for itself, then the threat of tyranny is imminent. Alternatively, if opposition groups enjoy a vastly preferred position, and no government is able to mobilize a favorable public opinion, then anarchy or instability is assured. American concern about the threat posed by government domination of communication channels may be explained in part by the fact that the ability of governmental leaders to reach their supporters, put their case before the country, and rally public opinion has never been seriously in doubt. Other democracies, in which political communications are primarily along tribal lines or are fragmented among splinter parties or social groups, may require a far higher degree of preferential access to the communication system on the part of government if stability is to be assured.

In states that have not yet become nations, or where the practice of democracy has only recently been attempted, the temptation for the government to impose restrictions on the media is particularly strong. The Director of the Institute of the Science of the Press at Amsterdam University has reported a large number of inquiries from emerging countries asking whether there are ways that irresponsible attacks and other misuses of press freedom can be curtailed without destroying the basically democratic character of the state. To all these inquiries he has replied that there have been many attempts to combine such restrictions with democracy but that none on record in European history has succeeded, and has concluded that "there is really no middle ground between press freedom and unchecked tyranny." He has also cited an observation made in the English upper house when it voted in favor of lifting censorship regulations toward the end of the eighteenth century—namely, that to enforce these regulations effectively the government sooner or later would have to make searches in the House of Lords itself.[45] The cure for an irresponsible, divisive press appears to lie less in imposing restrictions than in encouraging a responsible, national press as a counterweight and ensuring that the government has adequate facilities for reaching the public.

Implications for International Communication

A democratic form of government implies freedom of two-way international communication as well as domestic freedom of information. Many of the groups that contend and interact in a democracy require ideas and information from abroad if they are to form and function, and individuals no less frequently seek information from other countries to satisfy personal needs. Any person who wishes to take an intelligent interest in the foreign policy of his own nation must have access to foreign news and opinions. If the democratic process is to function, the right of individuals to incoming information must be assured.

When it comes to the right of private individuals and organizations to transmit communications to foreign audiences, the requirements of democracy are less clear. Perhaps a democratic state could exist without allowing private communication to other countries as long as domestic freedom of communication and freedom for incoming information were assured. Foreign commerce, missionary activity, and travel would be ruled out except under government auspices, but domestic groups and individuals could still obtain all the information they required, and the internal democratic process might be able to function. This is, however, pure speculation, since in practice all democracies allow private citizens a wide range of opportunity to communicate with citizens of other countries. Furthermore, if all democracies restricted the *outflow* of information, this would mean that for each the range of *incoming* information would be greatly narrowed, a situation that might be expected to lead to the gradual undermining of democracy everywhere.*

The hospitality of democracies to ideas from abroad means that democratic governments can be influenced indirectly by international communications that are given attention by important domestic groups. Dictatorships, by way of contrast, seek to exclude some categories of foreign ideas and are far less responsive to pressures from their own population. Consequently, a government in a totalitarian country, while it may be affected directly by diplomatic communications and propaganda from abroad, is less likely to be responsive to domestic pressures generated by ideas from outside the country. Although democracies do, in fact, attempt to influence mass opinion in dictatorships through propaganda, the paucity of upward communication channels in the latter makes it more difficult to affect their policies in this way.

Most democracies permit, and even encourage, a wide range of activities on the part of foreign publicists. In the United States, foreign advertisers, representatives of religious groups, and cultural salesmen of all kinds are usually welcomed. Foreign political spokesmen also are likely

* Speculation will be abandoned at this point. Nevertheless, the dependence of each democracy on a free flow of information from other countries is a fascinating area for inquiry, suggesting, as it does, the importance of an international democratic community. It also suggests that alliances and other combinations among democratic states that facilitate multilateral international communication, such as NATO and the Common Market, may have side effects that tend to strengthen the democratic process in each of the participating countries.

to be well received when they state their aims openly, and when they do not attempt to exert a direct influence on elections, legislation, or other political processes that are regarded as the prerogatives of citizens only. Thus, a foreign diplomat who presents his country's position on a tariff question is regarded as playing a legitimate political role, although he may actually influence future elections. If, however, he actively works for one candidate or against another, his activities will probably be resented. Even spokesmen from unfriendly countries are permitted if they make it clear for whom they are speaking and do not engage in covert activities.[46] Opposition to allowing free rein to foreign Communist propagandists is based in part on the feeling that Communism is conspiratorial in nature.

As is the case with some domestic groups, foreign interests may seek preferential access to channels of American public communication. Many of the groups registered with the Department of Justice as agents of foreign principals are engaged in distributing information to the American press on behalf of their clients. Public-relations personnel representing the government of former Dominican dictator Trujillo were particularly active when it came to planting unattributed material in the American press. Some of this was sent out through the facilities of the International News Service and some through an organization known as the U. S. Press Association that provided subscribing newspapers with "canned" editorials.[47] Most of the 419 individuals and groups registered under the Foreign Agents Registration Act as of the end of 1962 were considerably more aboveboard, and distributed material that was clear as to its point of origin. In the course of a Senatorial inquiry into the activities of foreign agents, a State Department official noted that, while there were abuses that should be corrected, spokesmen on behalf of foreign interests could play a useful role in bridging the gap between nations as long as they made it clear for whom they were speaking.[48]

Communications from abroad, if they are to have an effect, must find users among the population of the receiving country. Furthermore, if these ideas are to be politically influential, the users ordinarily must be organized in some way—in political parties, industrial enterprises, or groups sharing a public opinion. In economically developed democracies, the range of interests represented by organized groups is very wide; therefore, a great variety of domestic organizations are in the market for ideas they can use to achieve their purposes. In view of the intense competition for the attention of people in industrialized democracies, however, any communication from abroad that does not fill an important need is likely to be submerged in the sea of competing domestic and international communications.

This intense competition for attention tends to protect industrial democracies from some irrelevant and hostile ideas from other countries. There is a limited mass market for foreign media in the United States, for example, because most Americans feel that the domestic media serve their needs adequately. A wartime survey found that 35 per cent of a national cross-section had radios that could receive short-wave broadcasts, but only 7 per cent of the respondents had listened to a short-wave news broadcast from Europe during the week preceding the survey. The principal reason given for not listening to more material directly from Europe was: "Our papers give us both sides of the story, so why go to the trouble of listening?" [49] The lack of American organizations interested in giving resonance to Nazi propaganda seems to have been one of the principal reasons why extensive Nazi efforts to influence elections in the United States failed so completely.[50] Communist communications, likewise, have fallen on infertile soil.

On the other hand, if a communication from abroad helps to fill some important need of any population segment in a democracy, it is likely to be repeated and given wide dissemination by domestic media. It may also be seized upon by domestic organizations that find it useful. During a Presidential election campaign in the United States, for instance, ideas originating in other countries are frequently picked up and given extensive publicity by one or the other of the major political parties. The impact achieved by foreign communications in a democracy thus depends largely on the degree to which they are carried in domestic channels and are found useful by important organizations.

Another set of implications for international communication arises from the fact that democracies impose few restrictions on messages that leave the country. Anything that is publicly said or done in a democracy may become known abroad. Foreign newsmen are accepted as a matter of course, and are permitted a wide latitude in their activities. Critical communications, which are necessary for the functioning of the democratic order, are especially likely to find their way into international channels and to be given wide currency by hostile media.

Furthermore, because democratic states allow freedom for outbound communications, the information about these states that reaches foreign audiences is likely to contain contradictions and inconsistencies. Just as the numerous domestic groups competing for power and influence require different kinds of incoming information for their own functioning, they also will have different things to say to other peoples, and their actions that become known abroad will reflect the divergences in their values and goals. Communications from or about a democracy are likely to highlight the contradictions implicit in a pluralistic society.

VI

Communication in Communist States

In contrast to democratic nations, where communications enable a wide variety of groups to form, function, and compete for power, communications in Communist states are devoted mainly to supporting the power of the rulers. They are used to convey instructions from the political leaders to the population, to provide information required by organizations carrying out governmental plans, to mobilize the masses to perform officially designated tasks, and to indoctrinate the citizenry in the ideology of the ruling group.

At the same time, those who oppose the government are prevented from expressing their views publicly and maintaining an organized existence. Unauthorized public opinion is discouraged, and ideas coming from outside the country are carefully screened. The leadership is not content to suppress opposing views, but seeks to ensure that everyone contributes to spreading ideas that are officially endorsed and that everyone pays attention to official communications.

The way information media and channels are used and controlled by the rulers differs slightly from one Communist state to another. Nevertheless, the underlying pattern is substantially the same. In this chapter, primary attention will be given to the Soviet Union, as the major Communist power, although illustrations from other Communist countries will also be included.

Tasks Assigned Public Communications

The power of Communist leaders rests on a network of hierarchically controlled political organizations, on an economic system that is mobilized in the service of the central authority, and on the instruments of violence—the police and the military establishment. Each of these pillars of the regime is supported and supplemented by a massive information program. In addition, the press and radio help the rulers keep in touch with the thinking of the people, and provide a supplementary means of checking on the bureaucracy, by stimulating letters from their readers and listeners and by maintaining an unusually large number of part-time reporters.

A major part of the content of Communist communications consists of material that gives the "line" to be followed by functionaries at all levels, even though instructions are often so interlarded with polemics that pronouncements dealing with ideology and long-range goals are likely to be a confusing mixture of propaganda and policy content.[1] Lengthy statements by high officials are carried by the press and radio with great frequency, and are used throughout the apparatus as guidance by those who act and as teaching materials by those engaged in indoctrination and education. These statements are supplemented by articles and editorials, and by numerous specialized publications that are devoted to providing political information and instructions to all echelons. Much of the press in all Communist states can thus be regarded as a combination of trade journal and house organ for the government and party.[2]

Guidance given to functionaries through the information media is often of a rather subtle character, and may be presented in this way so as to be less apparent to those who are not directly concerned. Non-Communist journalists have noted, for instance, that major developments in Soviet policy are sometimes announced almost casually in the body of lengthy statements about a number of subjects. This was the case with a revolutionary change in Moscow's attitude toward collective farms, which occurred shortly after World War II. In the course of a 10,000-word statement, a Soviet official included a few remarks which indicated that the whole collective system was about to be turned upside down. Detection of this policy change required a close reading of the speech by an informed observer.[3]

Similarly, changes in the status of Soviet leaders have frequently been made known by the order in which their names were cited, or by their relative position in photographs. During the period when Malenkov was being built up as successor to Stalin, a photograph was published in the Soviet press showing Malenkov standing together with Stalin and Mao. Investigation showed that this was actually an adaptation of a picture taken three years earlier, in which Malenkov had been standing some distance away from the other two leaders. Further research revealed that even the earlier picture had been a composograph.[4]

While public channels thus provide the Communist organizational network with a valuable means of internal communication, they only supplement and do not supplant the flow of reports and memoranda that one would expect to find in any large bureaucracy. When Beria was removed from the top Soviet leadership in the fall of 1953, for example, a secret circular was sent to all Communist Party activists in the Soviet Union explaining why the action had been taken.[5] One advantage of using the mass media to provide political guidance, however, is that through this mechanism the top leadership can communicate efficiently and cheaply with subordinate officials in all organizations and at all echelons without fear that messages will be altered in emphasis while passing through administrative channels. In this way, the mass media help to prevent the growth of separate agency or geographic points of view.

Another advantage is that mass media also reach individuals who are outside the direct chain of command. The Communist concept of "positive loyalty" requires that people be able to say the "right" thing about leading issues of the day. In some cases, not knowing the current line may imperil a job or compromise chances for promotion. Most Soviet citizens in responsible positions therefore try to keep themselves informed of current official thinking by glancing at headlines and slogans each day. They do not, however, ordinarily read the incredibly boring pronouncements with the attention that is required of officials. Those in some occupations have to look at certain sections of the press more carefully. A former Russian librarian, for instance, told interviewers that she had had to read *Pravda* and a number of professional journals in order to know which books to remove from the shelves when their authors fell from favor.[6]

In addition to providing political guidance, Communist communications support all organizations engaged in carrying out officially designated tasks by furnishing specialized and technical information. Much of this function is performed by periodicals specifically designed for certain groups—engineers, scientists, farmers, teachers, and so on, although media intended for the general public also play a part.[7] For instance, a great deal of attention is devoted by the press and radio to improving working methods in industry and agriculture. New techniques that have been tried out in one factory or farm are reported to others, as are suggestions and criticisms made by workers and management. Some of these reports are carried by national media, while small newspapers and periodicals, each serving an individual area, collective farm, or factory, give detailed attention to the work of individual enterprises. In Bulgaria alone, 212 different factory journals with a circulation of over 225,000 were being published in the late 1950's. The specificity sometimes achieved by small "house organs" is illustrated by headlines such as "Follow Ivan Matyuschek's Example: Yesterday He Plowed *N* Hectares." [8]

Perhaps the most important example of a mechanism through which the communication network provides a specialized group with vital information is the news summary compiled for high Soviet officials by the news agency Tass. Throughout the world Tass gathers news about important developments and transmits this to Moscow in as accurate a form as it can achieve. Much of the news from the United States comes from *The New York Times, The Washington Post,* and a few other newspapers. These reports are not, however, distributed to the Soviet public, or even to the Soviet press. Instead, they are used as the basis for a secret daily news summary, which is circulated to the highest members of the Soviet hierarchy. Lower officials of the Party and state receive a less complete file which, nevertheless, has a higher level of objectivity than the one used by the press.[9]

A third task of Communist media is to whip up enthusiasm among the masses for specific policies, to mobilize them to perform certain projects, and to indoctrinate them with the official philosophy. Almost any Communist journalist, when asked to define his work, will cite a phrase from Lenin that describes the press as "not only collective propagandist and collective agitator, but collective organizer." In this assignment, the press and radio are joined by books, periodicals, films, and any army of oral "agitators." * The goal of "agitation" is to communicate a given policy to the masses and to mobilize them for action that will support this policy. Agitation frequently involves mass meetings,

* The Communists distinguish between "propaganda" and "agitation," the former consisting of theoretical education directed toward Party and government functionaries and intellectuals, while the latter is less theoretical and is directed toward the masses. Propaganda has been called "many ideas for few heads," while agitation is "few ideas for many heads." Another distinction is offered by an expert on the Communist press, who notes that propaganda usually appeals to the intellect, while agitation appeals to sentiment. (Antony Buzek, *How the Communist Press Works* [New York: Frederick A. Praeger, 1964], p. 26.)

waves of letter-writing, and "spontaneous" resolutions adopted by factory or farm workers.

Since many of the specific policies supported by Communist communications lie in the economic sector, both the content and the structure of the press are likely to reflect the economic goals being pushed by the regime at any one time. When industrialization was the key goal of the first Soviet Five-Year Plan, the media were full of material treating economic and technical subjects, recounting the achievements of Stakhanovites, and so on. During this period, the newspaper *For Industrialization* was given a tremendous circulation, only to disappear from sight when its work was done. Later, when emphasis was placed on agriculture, the publication of the Ministry of Agriculture was given enough newsprint for a circulation of 1 million, placing it among the top five papers in the country. At the same time, the rest of the Soviet press was mobilized in the service of agriculture. In the spring of 1955, when the goal of the regime was to popularize planting of corn, even city dwellers were barraged with articles on corn for a period of several weeks.[10]

The mass media also have a broader mission in support of political and economic organization. Together with the educational system, they have the task of molding a "new man"—one who will be sober, punctual, highly motivated, and completely responsive to the desires of authority. He should guard the property of the state more carefully than his own. He should continually criticize his own thoughts and behavior to ensure that both are in accord with the goals of the Party and state. Indeed, his own personal needs, desires, hopes, and dreams should be identical with those of the regime. He should have a kind of "dynamic obedience."[11] Efforts to create this "new man" have been particularly great in societies—such as Russia and China—that were close to feudalism when the Communists seized power, but they can be seen in other Communist states as well.

All communication channels are used in the attempt to produce this "new man." The press and radio offer examples of ideal workers and leaders, criticize those who fall short of the approved standards, and exhort everyone to greater efforts. Agitation meetings emphasize the need for better care of machinery, more frugality, and higher motivation. Heroes in plays and films are of course men and women of the "new type." Every effort is made to mold personalities that will be both highly obedient and highly productive.

The consensus of observers is that some character changes have indeed taken place among Soviet citizens since 1917. They are more practical and less contemplative than before. Rationality is more prominent and emotion less so. In short, they are better adapted to living in an industrialized and tightly controlled society.[12] There is, however, no way of establishing the extent to which Soviet education and communication policies have been responsible for these changes and the extent to which they reflect the ability of the people concerned to adapt to a new situation.

In addition to possessing character traits that facilitate his adaptation to a Communist society, the citizen of a Communist state should have a mental picture of the world that is in accord with the doctrines of his rulers. All communication media and educational institutions are pressed into service to inculcate this mental picture. The Communist system is consistently presented as the one that can best achieve all those values that people hold dear: peace, prosperity, democracy, dignity, and a high cultural level. All other political and economic systems are represented not only as less able to achieve these values, but as antithetical to them. Current events, at home and abroad, are interpreted in such a way as to conform to the approved picture, and even science, mathematics, and modern-language texts are used to instill the desired image. Laboratory experiments, for instance, should not only illustrate a particular scientific theory, but should also drive home a political doctrine —e.g., that socialism makes it possible for man to dominate nature.[13] History is rewritten so as to show the virtue and strength of Communist states and the immorality and weakness of non-Communist countries. On the twentieth anniversary of the Nazi invasion of Russia, the East German Communist press noted that Germany had already lost the war by the time Anglo-American forces opened a second front in Europe, and that the only reason they did so was fear that the Red Army would reach the Rhine. A massive two-volume history, published in Moscow in 1960, stresses American leadership of the forces that intervened against the Soviet Government in 1918 and 1919, and alleges that American imperialists expected to dominate the world with the help of the atomic bomb after World War II.[14]

As the most powerful nation of the non-Communist world, the United States receives special attention in education and propaganda systems of Communist countries, although the picture of all capitalist countries is substantially the same. In the Soviet Union the effort to develop an unfavorable picture of the United States starts in the fourth grade. Here ten-year-olds study a book entitled *The Little Boy from a Negro District,* which describes the unfair treatment given the colored minority. They also have class sessions on "Conditions of Workers in Capitalist Countries" and on "The Struggle of the World Masses Against the Imperialist Warmongers." In later grades, further attention is given to discrimination against minorities in the United States, to efforts of American capitalists to achieve world domination, to the exploitation of American workers by cynical monopolies, and to the misery, unemployment, and crime generated by the American system. Neither Soviet textbooks nor the information media describe how democracy in the free world actually functions; it is simply dismissed as "a dictatorship of the wealthy bourgeoisie." [15]

The press in non-Communist nations is portrayed as an instrument that helps exploit the masses. The U. S. press, in particular, is presented at best as a money-making device for its wealthy owners, and at worst as a venal instrument through which capitalists seek to promote war. One of the most frequently performed Soviet plays of the postwar era, Konstantin Simonov's *The Russian Question,* featured an attack on American newspapers for their alleged distortions, venality, and warmongering tendencies. In a passage that is often quoted by Soviet publicists, Lenin describes freedom of the press under capitalism as freedom to buy the newspapers and bribe the writers.

Even minor lapses, or imaginary lapses, of the press are used to justify this image. When, in 1947, *The New York Times* published the official texts of agreements made at Teheran, Yalta, and Potsdam, it received a letter from a Russian resident in the United States charging that it had omitted an important paragraph from the Potsdam Agreement to the effect that the German people could not escape responsibility for Nazi war crimes. *The Times* then inquired from the State Department why this paragraph had been omitted from the release distributed to the press and learned that this was not part of the official agreement, but had been inserted by a press officer at Potsdam to clarify some of the decisions taken. It forwarded this explanation to the reader who had complained, and no other letters from readers were received. Nevertheless, a few weeks later, a Tass report broadcast over Radio Moscow cited this correspondence, denounced *The New York Times* for forgery, and said that the editors in New York had been showered with protests from angry readers.[16] During this same period, Stalin gave an interview to Harold Stassen in which the Soviet Premier criticized

American correspondents for sending false news from Russia and making the Soviet Government look like a "zoological garden." When Stassen protested that any correspondent who filed an intentionally inaccurate report would be recalled, Stalin smilingly observed that the newspapers would publish such stories, make money on them, and then fire the writers.

Public opinion in non-Communist states is represented by Soviet spokesmen as being controlled by sinister powers. One Russian writer, in denouncing the theory of James Bryce that public opinion develops spontaneously and matures gradually, asserts that public opinion in the United States is made daily by the National Association of Manufacturers, the Chambers of Commerce, the news agencies, and the political organizations of the bourgeoisie. Only the views of official circles are presented as public opinion in capitalist countries, according to this interpretation, since the mass media are all in the hands of the bourgeoisie.[17]

In their mission of indoctrinating, persuading, mobilizing, and directing the population, communications are closely integrated with other instruments of state and Party influence. Communist writers have specified that persuasion is not enough—that it must be combined with other means of pressure.[18] Behind the exhortations of the press stands the power of administrative organs and the police, the mass organizations and labor unions. A former Soviet editor has noted that people were afraid of being mentioned critically in the press because they knew that other action was likely to follow.[19] The small factory and farm papers are especially important in this regard. They are able to identify by name those who fail to achieve their assigned output or violate work discipline. Information media are thus integrated into a larger coercive system.

A Soviet play produced shortly after the war illustrates the way the power of the press may be brought to bear on deviant individuals. In this play, Ilya Golovin, a modern composer, is shown as living in a bourgeois style, surrounded by flatterers, and praised by the Voice of America. A copy of *Pravda,* containing bitter criticism of the composer, is brought in. Immediately, his admirers desert him, his wife goes on a holiday to soothe her nerves, and only the Voice of America continues to support him.[20]

The mass media in Communist countries also help the rulers keep informed of what people are thinking and serve as a check on the performance of the bureaucracy. They do this primarily by encouraging letters from their readers and listeners. These appear to be studied carefully, and provide the leadership with the sampling of opinions (even if a very biased one). Writing to the editor became popular in the Soviet Union during the 1920's, when the Communist Party instructed the press to seek out and publicize shortcomings of the state administrative apparatus. Almost instinctively, newspapermen began to use complaints from readers for this purpose. People saw that their letters received attention, and the flow increased. Among the letter-writers were some who wrote fairly regularly, and these came to be called "worker correspondents" or "peasant correspondents." In several instances, bureaucrats became so infuriated by the criticisms of these amateur reporters that they sought out and murdered their tormentors.[21]

Since then, letters to the press and radio have played an important part in providing Communist rulers with a picture of what is going on at lower levels. The principal newspapers in Russia handle some million letters each year, and have to maintain large staffs to investigate and deal with the complaints and suggestions received, although only a small fraction of the letters are ever printed.[22] The picture of public opinion given by these letters is probably a very partial one, however, since writers must be careful not to criticize policy, but only the implementation of policy. Furthermore, many of the most active correspondents are Communist Party members, and it is doubtful that they would want to paint an unduly black picture of their districts.

Letter-writing to the mass media is common in other Communist countries also. *Rudo Pravo,* the largest Czech paper, receives an average of 2,200 letters monthly from readers, while smaller dailies receive between 200 and 300. Every editorial board endeavors to persuade as many readers as possible to act as amateur correspondents. In Communist China, the *Fukien Daily* claimed to have 5,000 correspondents in 1950, and the *Labor Daily* claimed 7,000.[23]

Other methods of keeping in touch with public responses are less commonly used by the mass media. The Soviet radio has arranged conferences of radio listeners at which people are urged to express their opinions, and has sent visitors to places where group listening is taking place. Some use has been made of "listeners' councils," panels, and polls, to ensure contact between radio stations and audiences. *Komsomolskaya Pravda,* the newspaper of the Young Communist League, has recently conducted rudimentary public-opinion polls on political questions.

Noticeably absent from the list of functions performed by communication media is that of keeping the public informed. Ideas that do not help to advance the purposes of the rulers are given little attention, and news that works against these purposes is usually suppressed, or held up until its effects can be negated. A former director of Tass has stated that news must not merely throw light on this or that fact or event, but must pursue a definite purpose. Journalists should therefore realize that not all facts or events should be reported, and should select facts and events that help the Soviet people to build Communism. "Information is agitation by facts."[24]

That these injunctions are followed is demonstrated almost every day by the Soviet press and radio. For instance, President Kennedy's warning in April 1961 that the United States would resist outside intervention in the Cuban situation was not reported, and several of Khrushchev's threats of nuclear attack on other nations have been edited out of news dispatches. Information about fighting on the Chinese-Indian border in 1962 was suppressed for five days after both Peking and New Delhi had disclosed the outbreak of hostilities. On the sixth day, an enigmatic Chinese statement was carried in *Pravda* and *Izvestia,* but not in other papers. Then silence descended again. Later in the year, American charges that there were Soviet missiles in Cuba were first ignored by Soviet media, then denied, and finally tacitly admitted.[25]

Sometimes direct distortions are involved. During a visit of American editors to Moscow in 1962, Premier Khrushchev asked them if they had been restricted in any way during their tour of the Soviet Union. With one voice, they roared "Yes!" only to find later that the version of the interview for publication in Moscow had them responding "No." They also complained that their questions had been changed in the record so as to conform better to the Communist line.[26]

In spite of news practices such as these, Communist officials have insisted that their people are kept thoroughly informed, and appear to be sensitive to charges that they are not. When U.N. Secretary General U Thant complained that the Soviet people had not been told about both sides of the Congo situation, this portion of his remarks was edited out by the Moscow press and domestic radio. And when the United States sent a note to the Soviet Union protesting that the Soviet people had not been given an adequate opportunity to study the American viewpoint on the Berlin question, Moscow replied that public opinion in the Soviet Union was widely informed on all questions of international life, and that "all basic documents, notes and statements of the Government of the U.S.A. on the German problem as a whole, including the Berlin problem as well, are regularly published in the Soviet press." [27]

Structure and Control of Information Media

The structure of Communist communications reflects the political and economic tasks they are expected to perform. Emphasis is given to the development of channels that can be used to indoctrinate or to disseminate material that is useful to the organizations forming the basis of Communist power. Those that are considered primarily purveyors of entertainment remain less developed. A partial exception is made in the case of media that can be used to improve cultural standards, such as theatre and books. These also receive emphasis, even when their content is not overtly political. Consequently, the citizen who is in search of entertainment often finds that the only material available is of a fairly high level.

Since the press is regarded as the basis for propaganda and agitation, great efforts are made to ensure that it penetrates to all sectors of society. In the Soviet Union, as of 1962, there were reported to be 457 daily newspapers, with a total circulation of nearly 40 million; about 4,300 papers published less often than daily, with a combined circulation of 66 million; and some 4,000 periodicals with a circulation of 872 million.[28] In 1960, Soviet book publishers produced 76,000 titles, far more than were published in any other country. Of these, about half were in the applied sciences. The total number of copies printed amounted to about 1 billion.[29]

Radio is also emphasized. As of 1962, the Soviet Union was reported to have 44 million radio receivers, of which over 30 million were wired sets that could receive only those programs piped to them from a central exchange. There was thus one receiver for each five inhabitants of the country.[30] This left the Soviet Union far behind the United States, where there are almost as many receivers as there are people, but approximately equaled the standards of most Western European countries.

Television has received less attention, and the number of receivers and transmitting stations has increased slowly. By about 1962, there were some 7 million sets, although more had been called for in economic development plans. Soviet authorities have apparently regarded TV as primarily an entertainment medium and less suited than the press or radio for the political purposes of the regime.[31]

Films occupy a more prominent place in the Soviet Union than does television. In 1960, the Soviets produced 140 feature films, and in the following year reported over 90,000 theatres and an annual attendance of almost 4 billion.[32] A large proportion of Soviet feature films are devoted to themes such as the reorganization of the management of industry, the struggle of farmers to surpass United States milk production, and so on. In Communist China, projection units jumped from some 600 in 1949 to about 14,500 by the end of 1959. Audiences increased from an annual total of about 50 million in 1949 to 1.4 billion in 1956.[33]

The degree to which films are used for purposes other than entertainment in Communist states is indicated by a West German analysis of East German feature-film production from 1946 to 1960. Of the 190 films released during this period, 30 were classified as "nonpolitical," 52 as "politically, historically, or socially educational," 83 as "Communist propaganda for 'the new life' " and 25 as "pure agitation." An "agitational film" released in 1960, entitled *At Any Time,* is typical of this class of production. It tells the story of a young border policeman in East Germany who foils the attempt of a peasant to flee to West Germany. He is also able to arrest the son of the peasant, who had set the farm on fire at the instigation of a wicked count. A happier film, *An Old Love,* classified as "propaganda for 'the new life,' " also deals with a peasant. In this case, the protagonist's wife is chairman of a collective farm, although he wishes to remain an independent farmer. This leads to tensions in the family that are resolved when he finally sees the light and joins the collective farm himself.[34]

Communist mass media are closely integrated with oral propaganda and agitation. Official slogans and pronouncements carried by the press and radio, or dramatized in films, are echoed by an army of propagandists and agitators. In the Soviet Union between 1945 and 1956, Communist Party schools trained more than 100,000 propagandists, many of whom took a three- or four-year part-time course. The system of Party schools is supplemented by the All-Union Society for the Dissemination of Political and Scientific Information, whose 400,000 members gave over 2 million lectures in 1956 alone. Agitators, who receive less training, are even more numerous. One authority places the total number of agitators usually active at about 2 million, but noted that this number may rise to as many as 7 million during special campaigns. This amounts to one agitator for every thirty people.[35]

In addition, most Soviet citizens are members of some variety of "mass organization" that conducts political education. Among the principal associations of this type are the Young Pioneers, an organization for children between nine and fourteen; the Komsomol, for older youth; labor unions; farm clubs; and, of course, the Communist Party itself.[36] In mainland China, everybody has to belong to some kind of "mass organization." One investigator identified well over 1,000 groups of various kinds that devoted at least part of their activities to political propaganda in a Chinese commune of 21,000 people.[37]

Supplementary means of communication, such as loudspeakers, posters, placards, leaflets, banners, and painted slogans, are everywhere in evidence in Communist countries. In 1953-54, 130 million copies of 5,000 posters were produced in the Soviet Union alone. Communist China seems to have used posters even more extensively. During a 1958 campaign against extravagance, the "masses and cadres" in Shanghai were reported to have produced over 100 million of them. Wired radio loudspeakers are now so prevalent in some areas that it is almost impossible to escape the din. An Indian traveler in China found that he had to feign illness so that he could pull the plug of the loudspeaker in his railway carriage and enjoy a few hours of quiet. In Bulgaria the blare of loudspeakers has caused complaints by workers who claim that it keeps them awake at night, or that they have to sleep with a blanket around their heads.[38]

Centralized control and direction of this gigantic mechanism is maintained by top leaders of the Communist Party, although administration of many sectors of it is left to the state. The most important Soviet control organ is the Department of Propaganda and Agitation of the Party. This department has been frequently reorganized, but the inclusiveness of its interests is indicated by a listing of its subordinate sections as of 1949:[39] (1) Party propaganda; (2) mass propaganda; (3) agitation; (4) cultural work; (5) the central press; (6) the press of the republics, districts, and territories; (7) the local press; (8) radio; (9) schools; (10) science; (11) book publishing; (12) fiction; (13) art; (14) films; and (15) sports and exercise. The Department of Propaganda of the Chinese Communist Party, operating directly under the

Political Bureau of the Party's Central Committee, maintains similar control of communication channels in mainland China.

Communist rulers direct the communication media primarily through careful selection and training of journalists and other personnel concerned with the spreading of ideas, general directives, and a series of mechanisms for supervision and guidance. In the Soviet Union, editors of leading newspapers and key personnel in other media are trained and appointed by the Party. The Party also issues detailed directives on a wide variety of subjects, extending down to such matters as handling letters from readers; a special network of journals for agitators is also published. In 1956, the 176 "agitator's guides" had a combined circulation of 50 million issues per year, and accounted for 13 per cent of total journal circulation. All media are kept under the supervision of Communist Party committees at various levels. These and other Party organizations criticize journals, dismiss film directors, evaluate the work of theaters, and even specify the content of specific newspaper issues.[40]

In providing guidance for the handling of day-to-day news, and also on many long-term policy matters, *Pravda,* the organ of the Central Committee of the Soviet Communist Party, plays a decisive role. It covers the major centers of the Soviet Union, flying matrices to more than a dozen cities where local editions appear, and its circulation is far larger than that of any other Soviet newspaper. Material from *Pravda* is often broadcast over the radio, and its principal editorial is wired or radioed in full to all other papers in the country each day. As guardian of the Party line, *Pravda* takes a position on all questions of public life, and other media fall in behind it. Its editorials and articles also provide material for propagandists and agitators, the less imaginative of whom discharge their responsibilities by reading this in a droning voice to their captive audiences.[41]

Radio is even more centralized than is the press. Radio Moscow serves as the basic station of origination for the whole Soviet Union, broadcasting four simultaneous programs totaling about 550 hours a week, which are relayed throughout the country.[42] Local stations supplement this fare with programs of interest to the areas in which they are located, but principal political themes are determined in Moscow. A similar situation prevails with regard to television. Although there are 92 centers capable of programing, the Moscow center originates the bulk of the transmissions.[43]

There are, of course, differences in the structure and control of communications in various Communist countries. Some of these differences are occasioned by geography and history; some by such factors as degree of literacy. Nevertheless, the similarities outweigh the differences. A study of the pattern of communications that North Korea sought to impose on conquered areas during the Korean War found it to be substantially the same as the blueprint that had already been observed in other Communist states.[44] In each country, a specialized Party instrumentality exercises over-all control; in each country, there is a central newspaper organ, and so on. Indeed, the organ of the Central Committee of the Socialist Unity Party in East Germany, *Neues Deutschland,* is known by its critics as the "German *Pravda.*"

Policies Toward Foreign Communications

For media in Communist countries to achieve maximum success in supporting the regime, it is necessary that the population be shielded against competing ideas from abroad. Nevertheless, it is impossible to shut out all foreign communications, since some penetrate even the most rigorous control systems and some are desirable from the point of view of the regime. Communist states therefore admit those ideas from abroad that their rulers find useful, endeavor to exclude those that are considered harmful, and try to discredit potentially disruptive ideas that are likely to come to the attention of the population in spite of the control system.

One category of ideas from abroad that Communist rulers find it useful to admit consists of those that reflect adversely on non-Communist countries. For instance, American criticisms of racial discrimination in the United States are widely circulated, admissions of mistakes or defeats by free-world leaders are publicized, and selected statements by non-Communist officials are reprinted in order to be attacked and demolished. Communist media in the free world are cited, often without identification of their political affiliation, as representing public opinion in non-Communist nations. In addition, Western classical novels, some nonpolitical writings (especially science fiction and detective stories), and works of social criticism are not only admitted, but in many cases are translated and achieve wide attention. The selection of American books offered to readers in Communist states gives them, however, an image of a sick and highly explosive society, and a very inaccurate picture of American political life. The America that the Russian reader knows from American books is predominantly the land of

Simon Legree, the sharecropper, the sweatshop, and the bloated billionaire.[45]

A special situation prevails with regard to scientific and technical literature from the Western world. Not only is this admitted to Communist states, but such extensive measures have been adopted to make it widely available that Communist scientists are often better informed about the work of their opposite numbers in the free world than are the latter about the work of the former. In 1952, an Institute of Scientific Information of the Academy of Sciences of the U.S.S.R. was formed to translate and summarize foreign scientific works. It soon had a regular staff of about 2,500, and 11,000 to 13,000 corresponding collaborators. The Institute issues more than a dozen publications in various scientific fields, and a great many mimeographed bulletins on specialized subjects.[46]

Another special category consists of information that is admitted as a result of exchange agreements. While this may not always serve the purposes of the regime, it is tolerated as the price necessary to obtain other advantages.

Methods used by Communist states to shield their citizens from disruptive ideas from abroad are sometimes ingenious and sometimes crude. When Turkey officially switched to the Latin alphabet in the 1930's, the Soviet Union changed the written language of its Turkic minority, which at that time was using Latin characters, to Cyrillic, thus making it more difficult for the two Turkic elements to communicate.[47] A more direct approach was used by Polish censors at the Poznan trade fair in 1961. They went through the Western pavilions at the fair and removed literature to which they objected. The British Broadcasting Corporation closed its exhibit in protest. The most comprehensive methods of exclusion are controls over imports and foreign visitors, and radio jamming.

Jamming of Voice of America and many other foreign broadcasts to the Soviet Union was started in 1948, and was gradually extended to Eastern Europe. U.S. officials estimate that Russia has operated as many as 1,500 jamming transmitters and that an additional 750 are located in the Communist states of Eastern Europe.[48] Nevertheless, English-language transmissions to the Soviet Union have rarely been jammed. Indeed, a Moscow professor of English once remarked to a foreign ambassador that Soviet students learned the American pronunciation by listening to the Voice of America.[49] Sometimes the Voice of America has been jammed and the British Broadcasting Corporation has not. Jamming of the Voice was relaxed for a time in 1959 and then resumed on a selective basis in 1960. In June 1963 Voice of America Russian-language broadcasts were again allowed to enter the Soviet Union without interference, and most East European states reduced or eliminated their interference with the Voice during 1963 and 1964, but jamming of Radio Free Europe continued. Cuba has attempted to jam American stations beaming Spanish-language news to the Caribbean.

Most Communist states have stopped short of making it a crime to expose oneself to non-Communist communications, but cases of jail sentences imposed primarily for this reason are not unknown. Thus, in 1961, an East German court sentenced a fifty-six-year-old woman to a year's confinement for listening to Western broadcasts and reading newspapers that she received from her sister in Bavaria.[50] The arrest of Yale professor Frederick Barghoorn on charges of espionage while he was visiting Moscow in 1963 was widely interpreted as an effort by Soviet authorities to let Russians know that contacts with Westerners were still dangerous.

The Communists have given particular attention to avoiding spreading hostile ideas through their own propaganda. When it becomes necessary to refer to something that opposing groups or nations have said or done, several devices are used to reduce the danger that this information will work against the purposes of the rulers. These devices were elaborated by Bolshevik leaders, primarily Lenin, prior to the time that they came to power in the Soviet Union, but have characterized Communist political communications to the present time. Quotations from unfriendly sources are replaced by paraphrases, which themselves may be distorted. The opposing political position is referred to only by a few ambiguous words (often ending in "ism") and interpreted in such a manner as to indicate its disreputable nature and the evil intent of those who espouse it. For instance, a proposal for arms-control inspection may be dismissed as an attempt to engage in "professional espionage." Dissent within the Soviet camp should usually be passed over in silence; if this is not possible it may be described as counter-revolutionary conspiracy, terrorism, wrecking, espionage, or defeatism.[51]

The degree to which Communist countries are able to exclude unwelcome foreign communications differs. The Soviet Union and Communist China are probably the most successful in exercising this kind of control. The Eastern European states find it much more difficult, because of their proximity to countries of the free world and the strong cultural ties their populations have with the West. A survey of refugees who fled Hungary following the uprising of 1956 found that nine out of ten respondents named foreign broadcasts as a source of news, and four out of five said they had relied on these broadcasts for reliable news of events *within* Hungary. Foreign broadcasts are probably even more popular in East Germany. A survey of East German refugees in 1958 found that 93 per cent of them had tuned in on Western stations, and 78 per cent described themselves as frequent listeners. During the height of the Berlin crisis in 1959, the American-operated station in West Berlin (RIAS) received more than 75,000 letters a month from East German listeners, in spite of the danger of Communist postal inspection.[52] Even during the period when short-wave broadcasts to the Soviet Union were being jammed most intensively, checks by diplomatic personnel, reports from listeners, and engineering studies showed that some broadcasts were breaking through.

In addition, there is always a trickle of other communications that even the most thorough-going authoritarian state cannot exclude. Visitors from abroad bring in some ideas, as do travelers returning from foreign countries. Their reports—to a limited extent—pass from mouth to mouth. Tourists and students from Western Europe and Poland, as well as occasional copies of *Time, Life,* or *Vogue* that they have brought with them, have served to transmit Western fashions and fads to Russian youth, greatly to the distress of Soviet authorities.[53] A few illegal books and pamphlets also circulate, and occasional leaflets from underground organizations turn up.

The result of this partial exclusion of ideas from abroad is that politically interested sectors of the public in Communist states are usually acquainted with a large range of facts in some areas, but display almost complete ignorance in others. A Soviet chemist who amazed an American traveler with his knowledge of chemical research in the Boston area asked the American: "Why can't Negroes publish works in their native language?"[54] The disjointed character of the information that Soviet citizens have about the outside world, and their frequently bizarre interpretations of it, may be explained in part by the fact that there are few circles in which one can discuss things that do not appear in *Pravda.* Each person tends to keep his knowledge of these things to himself unless he is among close friends or is assured of anonymity. Nevertheless, those who are intensely interested often show an amazing ability to piece together bits of information to form a fairly accurate picture of world events.[55]

Since not all undesirable information from abroad can be excluded, Communist authorities attempt to discredit those unauthorized sources to which their people may be exposed. This is particularly true with regard to foreign radio. In 1955, for instance, a long article appeared in a leading Soviet theoretical journal, *Kommunist,* denouncing the Voice of America as well as other radio networks broadcasting to Communist areas. These were all labeled as instruments of American imperialists, who were said to be fomenting a new war in order to achieve world domination. "Facts show," said the article, "that the ruling circles of the United States consider the systematic deception and misinforming of the peoples to be one of their most important tasks." Readers were warned particularly against such "emotional" forms of appeal as religion and corrupt bourgeois art, and the World Council of Churches and the Vatican were denounced as agents of American imperialism.[56] This article was presumably intended as a guide to propagandists and agitators who found it necessary to discuss Western radio broadcasts.

Similar warnings are frequently issued in more specialized contexts. In 1956, a Communist periodical for journalists presented a rather extensive summary of the operations of Radio Free Europe and labeled its staff as "people who were Nazis or collaborators during the war and fled the wrath of their countrymen."[57] When an East German Communist was murdered in 1961, the local Communist newspaper explained that the murderer was an unscrupulous opponent of socialism, whose mind had been poisoned by reading Western books and listening to Western broadcasts. The same explanation has been given by Soviet media when referring to attempts of young people to flee to the West. East German media have complained about the popularity of the light music broadcast over Radio Luxembourg, especially among the youth. Those who listen to this station, objects one Communist writer, are distracted from thinking about the great socialist perspective and about active cooperation in building socialism. Another complains that the atmosphere of hula girls, coconut islands, and love-making created by the radio makes the listener forget what is behind this musical façade—namely, cold and merciless atomic warfare.[58]

The mental picture of the non-Communist world that is inculcated by the Communist media and educational system helps to exclude disruptive ideas by predisposing the individual to doubt or reinterpret information he receives from nonapproved sources. Once this picture is accepted, it is possible to interpret practically all events in such a way that they support the official image, or at least do not conflict with it. Communist spokesmen provide constant examples of the way this should be done, and even such seemingly unambiguous phenomena as the erection of a wall to stop the mass flight of East Germans to West Berlin have been interpreted so as to conform to the approved picture. In this case, East German media asserted that the wicked capitalists in the West needed more slave labor for their miserable enterprises and were luring and blackmailing East Germans into leaving their happy country. The wall was therefore erected to prevent this "trapping of humans." This theme was expressed in a song that was frequently rendered in East Berlin, allegedly at popular request: "We have fenced off the human traps of the cold warriors on the Rhine, and have sealed the bars with red wax. . . ."[59] When an East German Communist returned from a visit to West Germany in 1957 and reported that there was real democracy there, because he had seen pacifists parading with a placard denouncing the West German Defense Minister, *Neues Deutschland* upbraided the traveler, saying that he should have interpreted this incident as a sign that opposition to Chancellor Adenauer was growing, and not as an indication of democracy.

The governments of some Communist countries may have concluded that their people have been sufficiently indoctrinated so as automatically to interpret information from the free world in accordance with the official line. This is suggested by the slightly increased exposure to non-Communist ideas that has been permitted in recent years. For instance, Soviet media have carried a larger number of Western statements than was formerly the case, and since 1956 the East European press has made extensive use of the news files of Western agencies. Nevertheless, when *Izvestia* published a verbatim interview with President Kennedy in 1961, the Soviets apparently did not feel sufficiently secure to leave the interpretation of the interview to individual readers, and five days later *Izvestia* published a 3,500-word critique of the President's remarks.

That the indoctrination process can achieve the goal of establishing internal defenses against discordant ideas is illustrated by the observations of a former Communist official. This man reported that he had resisted and suppressed his doubts about the Soviet system for some time, because they did not fit in with the picture of the world that had been inculcated in him. Only after several years was he forced to conclude that they were justified.[60]

While providing their people with a set of images about the non-Communist world against which information coming from the outside should be interpreted, Communist governments have also attempted—with a considerable measure of success—to alter the meanings of key words. Once the new meanings are accepted, communication with the outside world becomes increasingly difficult. Translation from one language to another no longer serves to facilitate an exchange of ideas, because the very concepts represented by the words differ. Some of the principal words that have suffered alteration are "democracy," "peace," "freedom," and even "socialism." In the new lexicon of the Soviet Union and other Communist states, democracy is a system whereby a Communist Party represents the interests of all workers and therefore deserves unquestioning obedience; it has nothing to do with majority rule or civil rights. Peace is a situation in which there is no resistance to Communist objectives. Freedom is sometimes defined as the recognition of necessity, sometimes as the right and duty of every citizen to obey the orders of the Party and state. At least until recently, socialism has been defined as the doctrine espoused by the rulers, any other doctrines stemming from the thinking of Karl Marx and other socialist theoreticians being corruptions or deviations.[61]

The "model" press law promulgated in Communist North Viet-Nam in 1957 illustrates some of these revised conceptions. According to this decree, "all the press shall enjoy freedom of expression and will not be subject to censorship before publication." At the same time, the law lays down five principles "which will preserve the press and its freedom from abuse." The press may not be used for propaganda against the people, their interests, or the people's democratic regime; it may not carry propaganda against peace, the national unification of Viet-Nam, and independence and democracy in the country; it may not propagate national chauvinism, imperialism, and war; it may not disclose state secrets; and it may not support prostitution or degenerate culture. According to a Communist journal, the new press law was warmly greeted by journalists and the public in North Viet-Nam, who expressed their satisfaction that the freedom of the press was now fully guaranteed by law and that the ignominious censor had been done away with.[62]

The North Vietnamese method for teaching new words and new

meanings for old words during the war against French rule has been described by an American Foreign Service officer. In North Viet-Nam, villagers usually walk to the market once a week, carrying their produce for sale. On the path to the market they might find a "teacher" with a blackboard on which had been written the words "Enemy, Friend, Fatherland." Each family would then be stopped and questioned. If all family members could not identify France as the enemy, Communist China as the friend, and Viet Minh as the fatherland, they would be sent to a nearby schoolhouse. When they had mastered the answers to the questions, they would be given passes to proceed. In the following months the questions would become more complicated, and the peasants would be asked to identify the "colonial exploiters," the "Wall Street capitalists," and the "struggle of the people." In this way the desired meanings could be fixed in the minds of even the most simple people.[63]

Much the same process can be seen at work in all of the newer Communist states, although other means of instruction are used. A West German writer complains that so many words are being given new meanings in Soviet-occupied Germany that reading East German publications is somewhat like reading middle-high German texts of 700 years ago. The same expressions are there, but their significance is different. He concludes that soon Germans from East and West will scarcely be able to converse, even though they speak the same language.[64]

Control and Direction of Public Opinion

Since public opinion is a form of organization, Communist rulers seek to control it just as they control formal organizations. Public opinion favorable to the purposes of the regime is encouraged; in so far as possible, unfavorable public opinion is prevented from forming; public opinion on nonpolitical subjects is sometimes tolerated.

The direction that Communist states exercise over domestic media simplifies their task of inhibiting the formation of public opinion that would interfere with their policies. For public opinion to take shape, one requirement is that people know what others are thinking about given issues, and since Communist media are allowed to acquaint the public only with ideas that serve the purposes of the regime, the range of subjects around which public opinion can form tends to be limited. Indeed, there are many subjects that may not be mentioned at all. At one time, for instance, directives to the Soviet press provided that silence should ordinarily be maintained about strikes, protest demonstrations among students or farmers, concentration camps, the flight of Soviet citizens, attempts to assassinate officials, and other events of a similar character.[65] These regulations have since been only slightly relaxed.

The degree to which silence can be maintained on a controversial subject is indicated by the experience of a former Soviet newsman from Odessa. In 1929, he learned from a chance remark of a friendly editor that 74 per cent of peasant holdings around the city had already been collectivized and that the wealthier farmers had been deported to the far north. Not a word had been said or written about this anywhere, although it had been taking place in close proximity to the city.[66] The Soviet practice of shifting journalists from one post to another at fairly short intervals may be based on the idea that if a journalist establishes roots in a community he may express the ideas of his fellow citizens rather than those of the regime. As of 1956, a journalist's average period of employment on a given local newspaper was about two years. In some regions the turnover was even more rapid.[67]

Public opinion is not, of course, entirely dependent on the mass media. It may form through word-of-mouth communication, although more slowly and with more difficulty. Authoritarian states therefore usually try to cut person-to-person channels at their base by a system of informers, which has often been highly successful. During the siege of Leningrad in World War II, a large proportion (although not a majority) of the population was disaffected and favored surrender to the Germans. The disaffected Leningraders, however, did not conceive of themselves as members of a like-minded group, but as isolated individuals confronting an all-powerful state. The Stalinist terror system had created such mutual distrust among them that they did not communicate effectively with each other on political matters; instead, each looked to someone else to bring about a change in the situation. The distrust was reinforced by the authorities, who assigned political organizers to every apartment house, campaigned against rumor-mongers in the press, and made examples of a number of people who had been convicted of loose talk.[68] No new local leaders arose, in part because no potential leader could be assured that he had a following.

A very similar situation seems to have prevailed in Odessa prior to its capture by the Wehrmacht, and in Nazi Germany during periods of heavy Allied bombing toward the end of the war. In both cases, disgruntlement was widespread but had little bearing on the overt behavior of the population, in part because the control system prevented the degree of intercommunication that would have produced an effective public opinion and local leadership.[69] Residents of Cuba noted that following consolidation of power by Premier Castro the formation of "bloc committees" representing the regime at the community level greatly inhibited free discussion of political issues, since nobody knew when his opinions would be reported to the authorities.

The system can never succeed in eliminating discussion of nonapproved ideas entirely, even though it can restrict this to fairly small groups. In all totalitarian societies people learn that there are certain other individuals with whom they can talk freely. As a former member of an East German publishing house noted, those with a high degree of skepticism toward the official philosophy tended to drift together spontaneously, and within these circles people were free from the climate of terror that prevailed in the larger organization. He added that without membership in such "informal" groups the hardships of collective life would become unendurable.[70]

At the same time that they seek to prevent the formation of public opinion that might interfere with their goals, Communist leaders both stimulate and simulate supporting public opinion. This has been done most extensively in the Soviet Union and Communist China. Sometimes genuine support movements seem to have been created; in other cases, only some of the outward manifestations of public opinion have resulted. Mass gatherings, demonstrations, letter-writing campaigns, and so on, do not necessarily represent a consensus of individual attitudes. A Soviet writer reports that public opinion in the Soviet Union has been *directed* to oppose remnants of the old social morality, and to fight against irresponsibility in work, careless handling of state property, drunkenness, hooliganism, and the pursuit of individual goals that are contrary to the interests of the society. As examples of changes brought about in part by public opinion he cites reorganization of industrial management and secondary education, and the tightening of provisions governing the release of convicted criminals.[71] He also asserts that public opinion is expressed through the election of members of the various representative organs of the state. That these are single-list elections is irrelevant, in his view, since "socialist societies are characterized by a homogeneous public opinion—a phenomenon that bourgeois scientists refuse to recognize."

Effects of Communist Communication Policies

The rigid control of communication media in Communist states leads to a uniformity and dullness that has frequently been commented on by both Communist and foreign observers. A Soviet periodical reported in 1960 that on a given day 100 different newspapers were found to have identical headlines, and former Soviet citizens who have worked within the Russian communication system confirm that the regime is aware that the media are tendentious and boring.[72] In the press of nearly all Communist countries one finds periodic injunctions to writers to show more sparkle. Nevertheless, this seems difficult to achieve under a completely controlled system.

If the mass media lack verve, the frequent "agitation meetings" are positively deadening. They have been described as generating boredom on a national scale; the tendency of Soviet citizens is to avoid them when possible. Their dullness may be due in part to the fact that the ability to speak in an interesting and persuasive manner is no longer a valuable talent in Soviet society, and Party schools now give less attention than formerly to the art of oratory. Russian Communists had good speakers when they were struggling for power, but now the road to political advancement is through the bureaucracy rather than through ability to persuade the masses. In addition, agitators are given a script they must follow and know that people cannot argue with them. Therefore they lack the motivation to put on an exciting performance. Few agitators in the Soviet Union and Eastern Europe are volunteers; most have to be dragooned for the task.[73]

Communist communications are also hampered by the fact that many people give them a low credibility rating. The disparity between life as it really is and as it is officially presented is often glaringly obvious to domestic audiences. Refugees who fled Hungary following the uprising of 1956 frequently mentioned that the contrast between "promise" and "reality" was one of the principal causes of their loss of faith in the system.[74]

Sometimes a particular incident causes a person to be skeptical of a broad range of reports. A former Soviet citizen mentioned that he began to doubt what he read in the papers when the Soviets issued a denial about troop movements in 1940. He lived right next to the railroad tracks and could see the troops being transported. A Polish newspaperman who was sent to Italy was shocked by the contrast between what he saw and the picture of capitalism that had been presented in the Polish press. Commenting on this case, the organ of the Polish Communist Party remarked that the newsman in question required intensive ideological treatment.[75]

The perpetual nagging of propaganda induces pronounced symptoms of apathy in all but the stoutest and most patient spirits. Soviet citizens, in particular, appear to be thoroughly fed up with politics and propaganda, and just don't want to hear any more political slogans. This tendency toward depoliticization is especially marked among the youth, and is one reason so many of them flee into the technical occupations where they are exposed to a minimum of indoctrination.[76] A Russian-born traveler who visited the Soviet Union during a period of intense ideological disputation with Communist China, reported that he heard nobody mention the controversy. Most conversation was about housing or about other domestic problems. Periodic drives to promote greater interest in politics, especially among young people, are announced by the Communist press and radio, but they have limited success. A study of East German films has found that those with a high political content are simply ignored by most movie-goers.[77]

A footnote to the dullness of Communist media is that citizens of Eastern Europe who visit Western Europe or the United States tend to be fascinated by the informal style of reporting in the Western press, and especially by stories portraying politicians in human terms. Frequently, however, they assume that Western newspapers are subject to substantially the same controls as is their press back home. The leader of one Soviet delegation to the United States, having visited a small Midwestern city where he met the editor of the local paper, was shocked to find the next morning that this paper had made a rather serious typographical error in a story involving the American President. "What will happen to the poor editor!" gasped the Russian. "Such a nice man, too."

People who do not withdraw within an apolitical shell and disregard as much of the political content of the information media as they can, often try to interpret official reports in a manner that will give them a more accurate or more complete picture. One refugee told interviewers that when he read about an event in the paper he would try to determine what was missing from the account. Then he would know what was needed to fill the gap. Reading between the lines has become a highly developed art in Communist countries, where newspapers are often treated as a decipherable code.[78]

Most of those who retain an interest in political matters try to develop sources of information to supplement official reports. These sources include foreign broadcasts and publications, but by far the most important one is word of mouth. When a sample of over 300 former Soviet citizens was asked to mention sources of all kinds from which they had obtained most of their information about what was going on while in Russia, half of them said "word of mouth," while 89 per cent mentioned newspapers, 50 per cent said "radio," and 19 per cent said "meetings." When asked which source was most important, 35 per cent chose word of mouth and 44 per cent newspapers.[79]

Heavy reliance on word of mouth as a supplementary source of information causes rumors to be more prevalent and more widely believed in Communist countries than in nations where there is a free press. In the Soviet Union, the authorities have conducted frequent and vigorous campaigns against "rumor-mongers." U.S. officials in postwar Bucharest noted that the content of Voice of America broadcasts was communicated to large numbers by a very efficient oral news service. More recently, the Hungarian Government has been repeatedly bedeviled by rumors that Soviet troops were to be withdrawn. As a correspondent reported from Budapest: "Government control of all information media makes people listen all the more carefully to the whispered word." The same correspondent noted in Warsaw that the willingness to believe any report, as long as it is not official, could be described as almost a Polish national trait.[80]

Among many citizens of Communist countries there develops a feeling of being cut off from the outside world—and a consequent hunger for more information. Travelers to the Soviet Union, in particular, have found that they are showered with questions about life in their own countries.[81] Crowds, composed largely of young people, are likely to form around a visitor, who may then be questioned for long periods. This same hunger for information was indicated by a study of television viewers in East Germany, which found that they differed from their opposite numbers in West Germany in two respects. First, they would leave no stone unturned to get better reception, particularly of Western programs. In this, they resembled the radio amateurs of the 1920's. Second, they had a greater hunger to be informed, and gave more attention to topical reporting and to features describing everyday life in West Germany. "The Schölermann Family," a show describing the personal experiences and problems of "average" West Germans, was among the most popular programs.[82]

The rigid controls applied to Communist information media also have a deadening effect on journalists and others who make a career in communications. The situation is especially difficult for creative writers and for those who seek to identify themselves with their audiences. On the one hand they are artists, and on the other hand they are functionaries who have to follow instructions; either role in the long run can be performed only at the expense of the other. A Soviet writer complained in 1952 that before plays could be presented everything true to life was combed out by the officials who controlled the theater. An important cause of the Hungarian uprising was that Hungarian writers and artists had found that they could not follow all the twists and turns of the Party line without losing both their self-respect and their readers. They felt that they had to develop their own standards and to write about things as they saw them. This path led, in stages, to outright rebellion. A study of 463 writers whose work was published in Czechoslovakia between 1945 and 1956 provided indirect evidence of similar frustration. After the Communist take-over, fewer writers tended to experiment creatively, fewer of the younger generation entered the writing professions, and older writers often turned to editing or to producing specialized material that was unlikely to be criticized on political grounds.[83] Thus, dullness in Communist media appears to be ensured by a circular process: dull media breed dull writers, who then add to the general monotony.

In view of the widespread passivity and skepticism with which officially approved communications are greeted in Communist countries, one might expect that they have largely failed in the task of indoctrination to which they have been assigned by the regimes. This is probably true in some of the Eastern European states. A Polish newspaper commented wryly in 1962: "Thinking is something even we can't get people out of the habit of doing." [84]

Some observers believe that indoctrination has been a failure in the Soviet Union also. A Soviet intellectual who left Russia in the late 1950's maintains that strong currents of independent and dissident thought have continued to flow and will go on doing so, short of a major purge.[85] This, however, is a minority view. Most students of the

Soviet scene conclude that indoctrination has been highly effective in shaping general patterns of thought about public issues. Thus it is widely accepted that Soviet economic accomplishments are superior to those of the free world, that a nation requires firm central direction by a single party, and that the state must assume reponsibility for all aspects of the welfare of its people. The basic values and premises of the regime have been adopted by all but a small minority, although complaints about the way officially endorsed principles are applied in practice are more widespread.[86] Even Soviet citizens who are avowedly anti-Communist tend to use Communist terms such as "First Imperialist War" and "Second Imperialist War" when referring to the two world wars. The image of the outside world presented by the mass media is usually accepted in its broad outlines, although "corrections" are made with respect to details and a hunger for more information remains.

The success of indoctrination naturally differs from one social group to another. In the Soviet Union the impact of propaganda is usually seen as greatest among the well-paid middle and upper classes, who owe their success to the regime and are identified with it, and among the youth.[87] These conclusions may seem, superficially at least, to conflict with other observations to the effect that the greatest interest in foreign communications is to be found among substantially the same groups: the better-educated and the young people. A large proportion of Soviet youth have proved hospitable to foreign ideas, fads, and fashions, in spite of frequent indications of official disapproval. They make a point of using foreign terms and dressing in Western styles, and even take anti-Western movies and "turn them upside down," admiring those aspects of Western society that the pictures are assailing. Higher-status Soviet citizens, including those who are members of the Communist Party, tend to listen more to the foreign radio and to hear more rumors than do those farther down the scale.[88]

This apparent conflict may be explained by the fact that interest in ideas from abroad is not the same thing as ideological disaffection. The better-educated and higher-status groups are likely to expose themselves more to all types of communications and to analyze these more critically than are other elements of the population. Thus, they pay more attention not only to rumors and foreign broadcasts but also to the official media. Less-educated members of the public, on the other hand, are likely to withdraw their attention from all sources of information that do not help them in their daily activities. Furthermore, "interpretation" of official information and "reading between the lines" may not indicate opposition to the regime but may reflect the need of some groups to know more about what is going on in order to do their jobs better. The youth and intelligentsia may rebel against indoctrination meetings and adopt certain Western forms, but this is no indication that they are striving toward a democratic form of government.

Some Indications of Change

The Communist communication system, substantially as we know it today, was developed under Lenin and Stalin. Since Stalin's death there have been some changes, mostly in the direction of liberalization. These have not taken place steadily, but in waves; periods of greater freedom have been followed by periods of increased restrictions. Nevertheless, the long-term trend appears to be toward relaxation of some controls and the correction of those features of the system that are most objected to by the public.

These changes are of three principal types. Most Communist regimes now allow slightly greater contacts with the outside world, they permit a little more freedom of expression, and they are making some efforts to appeal to the public taste.

Increased contact with the outside world has been the most noticeable of these changes. The Soviet press, for example, has somewhat improved its coverage of events outside the Communist bloc, and has more frequently reported the remarks of foreign figures who are opposed to Communism. Some recent newspaper articles have omitted the black-and-white picture of non-Communist countries that previously was characteristic of Soviet reporting, and a well-known Soviet novelist, Victor P. Nekrasov, has been able to publish a reasonably objective account of his trip to the United States.[89] Greater numbers of foreign visitors are allowed in the Soviet Union than before, and the number of Soviet citizens traveling to non-Communist countries has also increased, although the total in absolute numbers is still very small. Jamming of foreign broadcasts has decreased in frequency and intensity, although it still occurs. These changes have been mirrored in most other Communist countries, although China and Albania have been exceptions, and East Germany a partial exception. The Polish press has been allowed the greatest latitude in informing its readers, and has even criticized the lack of objective reporting in other Communist states.[90] During 1964, Czechoslovakia began to allow newsstand sale of leading

Western newspapers and magazines, and it was expected that other East European countries would follow suit.

Increased freedom of expression, at least in Russia and most of the East European states, can be noted primarily in the broader latitude given writers and intellectuals to express themselves and in the greater willingness of private citizens to voice their opinions in political discussions. Books, plays, and films have been able to comment on aspects of the system in ways that would not have been possible before, although the treatment accorded Boris Pasternak in the Soviet Union and subsequent official criticism of such writers as Ehrenburg and Yevtushenko indicate that the limits of expression are still rather narrow. A period of relaxation in 1962 was followed by a tightening in 1963, when Moscow established a State Publications Committee and several East European states also reimposed controls.[91] Nevertheless, during this period when the reins were being drawn tighter, the Soviet press published several articles and letters defending the writers who had been the target of official criticism—a phenomenon that would have been impossible under Stalin. In addition, people in the Soviet Union have for several years been willing to talk to each other and to foreign visitors in a manner that would have been very risky several years earlier, although there is the general feeling that "they" (the secret police) are still there, observing everything and taking notes, even though they are not arresting many people now.

Greater freedom of expression has occasionally made possible the formation of spontaneous public opinion within limited spheres. A former Soviet student reported that before 1955 he had confined his critical views to a small circle of friends, and sometimes had thought that he was completely isolated—"a real white raven among the flock of good and orderly black crows." Then, when the "thaw" came in 1955 and 1956, he was surprised to discover that there were many other small groups thinking much the way he and his friends did. This coalescence of opinion was stopped before any power center sufficient to exercise pressure on the regime could be formed, but not before one friend of the student had hung a picture of Trotsky on his wall.[92]

Efforts to appeal more to public taste are evident in somewhat livelier press and radio reporting, and the occasional inclusion of human interest material. Readability of at least some Soviet newspapers has improved; makeup is more imaginative, and Soviet journalism schools are placing more stress on learning to write in an interesting manner.

Khrushchev's son-in-law, Alexei Adzhubai, was able to make first *Komsomolskaya Pravda* and then *Izvestia* somewhat more readable. The Soviet television network has begun to stress on-the-spot coverage of news and "personality reporters." More material frankly intended for entertainment has been included in the Communist media in recent years, although whenever possible this is made to serve a political purpose at the same time, and it still occupies a very modest place when compared with material serving agitation, propaganda, and organizational functions.[93]

Some observers feel that liberalization of Communist policies governing communication is a surface indication of deep changes in Soviet society. It is probably too much to say, however, that this liberal trend reflects a major move toward democracy. The information media in Communist countries continue to perform the same basic functions as in Stalin's time: they serve as house organs for the various organizations that carry out the policies of the authorities, they communicate the line to all who need to know it, they provide technical information necessary for the performance of economic and political tasks, and they continue their efforts to mold people so that they will be efficient cogs in the system. Only if at least some of the media were allowed to provide facilities for political or economic groups that were not under the domination of the regime could one be sure that a substantial progress in the direction of democracy had been made.

Attention to International Communications in Communist Societies

Ideas from abroad do penetrate Communist countries, but most of them are overshadowed by domestic communications of great volume and high intensity that affect the daily life of the citizen at many points. Although he may try to escape the more boring aspects of political indoctrination, his job and his security make it necessary for him to pay attention to the official line. His freedom of action and choice is sharply limited; therefore the range of information from abroad that is relevant to his needs is also limited.

Nor can direct communications from abroad be expected to be of major importance for the formation or functioning of organizations within Communist states. There are few organizations, either political or nonpolitical, that are not part of the official establishment. In so far as existing organizations require ideas from or about the outside world in order to function, these ideas are sifted and interpreted in accordance with the purposes of the regime.

Nevertheless, some needs, both organizational and personal, remain. Among organizational needs that are only partially satisfied by the official communication system, the most obvious is for technical and scientific information from abroad. Communist states have never cut off this flow, and in recent years have taken steps to augment it. The fact that scientists and technicians are so often sent abroad by the Soviet Union and East European countries reflects this requirement.

Another largely unsatisfied organizational requirement is for information about developments, both domestic and foreign, that may lead to significant political changes. The tendency of the leadership, since it is intent on the most vigorous possible implementation of a particular line of action, is to restrict information about anything that might suggest a future change of policy. This is one reason why even convinced Communists find it necessary to supplement the official media by consulting rumor, foreign radio broadcasts, and other unofficial sources. This supplementary information is necessary if they are to look ahead. News about possible changes in top-ranking personnel, about the domestic and world economy, and about developments of all kinds within the Communist bloc is likely to be relevant to the behavior of many functionaries. For those in satellite and former satellite countries, indications of the probable future course in the Soviet Union and Communist China are likely to be of the very highest importance. It is difficult for foreign sources to gather such information, but to the extent that they do so and make it available to audiences behind the Iron Curtain, they receive close attention. In this respect, ideas from abroad serve a very different function in totalitarian countries than in democratic states, where foreign sources ordinarily cannot be expected to provide a significant increment of information about what is going on domestically.

As far as accurate information about international affairs is concerned, the need at the very top of the Communist pyramids in Moscow and Peking is particularly great. It is satisfied mainly by sources, such as the special Tass file in the case of the Soviet leaders, which are not available beyond a narrow circle. There are also indications that the highest authorities supplement the information about what is going on abroad that they receive through their own channels by consulting free-world publications. A number of Western newspapers, including *The*

Wall Street Journal, were observed by foreign visitors to the Kremlin in both Stalin's and Khrushchev's time. The increased frequency with which Communist leaders have traveled abroad in recent years may be due in part to a desire for more information about the non-Communist world.

On an individual level, ideas from abroad help to keep alive values that are cherished by many people but are not nourished by domestic media, and to satisfy at least some of the curiosity and hunger for news that censorship seems to have stimulated in certain population groups. Foreign communications also remind citizens of Communist countries that there are viable alternatives to the system under which they are living. Except in regard to such relatively apolitical matters as fashions in dress and taste in popular music, these alternatives do not appeal to Communist audiences as suggesting feasible courses of action, at least not at the present time. This information does, however, help make it possible for the individual to criticize in his own mind and among his close friends some aspects of the Communist system that cannot be criticized in public. Ideas from abroad thus help the individual to take advantage of and adjust to any tendencies toward liberalization that may appear in his own nation. They strengthen the capacity for future change.

VII

Communication in Developing Nations

More than two-thirds of the earth's population live in countries that are usually classified as "emerging," "modernizing," or "underdeveloped." As in other areas, the impact of ideas from abroad on emerging nations depends in large measure on the characteristics of the existing domestic communication networks and the functions they serve. In view of the different stages of development of the nations concerned, these networks are highly diverse, even if Communist states are excluded. Some of the newer countries, such as India and the Philippines, are already modern nations in many respects. Others have taken only a few steps toward modernization.

Nevertheless, the communication networks in most of these nations share certain important characteristics. Modern media are thinly spread, and a large proportion of the population rely for information on face-to-face conversation, usually supplemented by assemblies of various kinds, folk plays, or such traditional means of communication as, for example, drums. These channels are adequate for those who live as their forefathers did on the land or in small villages, and whose principal allegiance is to the family, tribe, or community, rather than to the nation, but they cannot fulfill the political and economic requirements of a modern state.

None of the emerging nations comes up to the "minimum" standards for communication media suggested by UNESCO: namely, for each 100 inhabitants at least 10 copies of daily newspapers, 5 radio receivers, 2 movie seats, and 2 television receivers. As of 1961, as many as 100 states and dependencies in Africa, Asia, and Latin America fell below this minimum in all 4 categories. An additional 19 countries fell below in 3 categories. Thus, a large proportion of the world's inhabitants lack adequate means of being informed about their own lands, let alone others.[1]

Characteristics of the Modern Media

Modern media in emerging areas naturally reflect the difficulties with which they have to contend, and the daily press is faced with particularly thorny problems. While there are several outstanding newspapers in developing countries, especially in India and Latin America, the overwhelming majority are small and unstable, providing very indifferent news coverage. This weakness is caused in part by lack of money. Few newspapers can afford to maintain foreign correspondents, and most find even the cost of subscribing to one of the international news agencies burdensome. Their mechanical equipment is usually obsolete.

The financial plight of the press is caused mainly by the difficulty of finding adequate advertising support in countries that lack a broad industrial base, and by the poverty of potential subscribers. Poverty often makes it impossible for the press to reach even those who are literate. India's dailies, with a combined circulation of about 5 million, are not read by more than a fraction of the approximately 100 million literate people in the country. In the Philippines, where literacy is about 70 per cent, the total circulation of the daily press is only about 350,000 in a population of more than 27 million. In some countries of Africa, a subscription to a daily paper would require about 20 per cent of the average family's annual income.[2]

A further cause of newspaper weakness is fragmentation: there tend to be many weak papers instead of a few strong ones. Language differences are responsible for some of this multiplicity. As of 1956, 8 languages were represented among the 36 newspapers serving the Congo, and a survey 4 years later found that the confusion of tongues had, if anything, increased.[3] In Burma, Rangoon's 32 dailies include 3 in English, 6 in Chinese, and 7 in various languages of India and Pakistan; the rest are in Burmese. India has an even greater multiplicity of languages, and, as of 1960, daily newspapers were published in at least 15 of them.[4]

Language differences are probably not the major reason for newspaper fragmentation, however, since it occurs even in those emerging countries where one tongue is clearly dominant. An expert on Latin American journalism noted in 1956 that Havana, with a population of about 1 million, could have supported 5 dailies adequately, but was saddled with 21. As of 1962, Istanbul had 24 daily papers.[5]

Closely related to the phenomenon of fragmentation are one-sidedness and subsidization. All but a very few of the 21 Havana dailies in 1956 were believed to be supported by subsidies that were given for the purpose of promoting a particular point of view. In Liberia, government financing appears to be involved in keeping alive a number of papers that otherwise would be unable to support themselves.[6] Whether because of subsidization or for other reasons, very few of the plethora of dailies published in the capitals of emerging nations escape a narrowly partisan outlook. The number of readers that each can attract therefore tends to be limited.

The press in the new nations is hampered further by a lack of professionalism among journalists, the majority of whom are intellectuals who have spent much of their lives in the struggle for national liberation from foreign domination. They therefore tend to be either critical of whatever government is in power or else completely submissive to the views of the party with which they are identified. Few have assimilated professional standards that make them mindful of the interests of a broader public and motivate them to dig for news that would be of use to their readers. They are also hampered by the lack of specialized training, the absence of a tradition of news-gathering, and the low status of correspondents in relation to government officials.[7] Finally, most journalists are so poorly paid that they cannot devote the necessary care to their work, since they ordinarily have to hold several jobs at once in order to make ends meet.

In view of these characteristics of journalists and of the press in general, it is not surprising that most newspapers in emerging countries are not highly regarded. Not only is the prestige of the press low, particularly in comparison with that of government, but people tend to be skeptical of the truthfulness of what they read. Under these conditions it is difficult to find public support for the creation of a strong, independent press.

Simple news sheets have sometimes proved more successful than full-size newspapers. Daily bulletins that have relatively big circulations are already being published by national news agencies in several states of Africa. These are read by a large proportion of the leaders in their respective countries and serve as a substitute for the conventional press; some of them may later develop into small newspapers.[8] In Liberia, representatives of the United Lutheran Church started a mimeographed weekly to serve 30,000 people in the 32 villages of the Loma tribe. It gained such a good reputation for its reliable coverage of local events that it soon undercut word of mouth as a principal source of information.[9] The possibilities for extending small papers of this type appear to be good. A UNESCO body has advised Asian news agencies to consider the publication of mimeographed news bulletins to supplement their incomes.[10]

Because of the difficulties besetting newspapers, the importance of radio in emerging nations is relatively greater. The radio listener does not have to be literate. National radio systems are for the most part operated by governments and are thus freed from many of the financial problems of the press. Radio is also spared transportation and distribution problems. The prestige, persuasiveness, and credibility of radio tend to be high, especially in cultures with a strong oral tradition, where respect for the spoken word is higher than for the written word.[11] The possibility of using radio broadcasting in conjunction with loudspeakers can make it widely available even in very poor areas. A key recommendation emerging from a series of UNESCO-sponsored meetings on information media in underdeveloped countries was that extension of radio broadcasting merited a high priority.

The principal difficulty standing in the way of extending radio coverage is that of providing low-cost, reliable, battery-operated receivers. Most radio sets today are far beyond the means of the masses in emerging countries, and in any case operate poorly in tropical climates. This impediment may, however, soon be overcome. The International Telecommunication Union has been studying the problem, and some manufacturers in industrialized nations believe that a suitable set could be mass-produced for as little as $5.[12]

A multiplicity of languages creates difficulties for radio, just as it does for the press, in many of the emerging areas. Experts convened by UNESCO have suggested that governments of multilingual states should decide on a limited number of languages for use over the radio and then stick to these over a period of years, rather than trying to satisfy the requirements of all language groups. A French authority on broadcasting in Africa, taking a less hopeful view, sees the language problem as the last one that will be solved by radio stations in this area. He found so little agreement on the subject among Africans that he concluded there was no alternative but to continue placing primary reliance on English and French.[13]

Both radio and press are hampered in their coverage of news by the difficulty of securing an adequate news file from their own countries as well as from abroad, even when they can afford it. Telecommunication facilities are usually antiquated, when they exist at all. A recent survey found that Central American telecommunications were at a stage characteristic of industrialized countries 100 years ago.[14] Facilities in Africa and some countries of South Asia and the Far East are still more rudimentary. A great many of the emerging countries have not yet developed national news agencies, and are dependent on international services for both domestic and world news. Those national agencies that do exist experience the same problems of obtaining adequate equipment and finding or training suitable personnel as does the press.

Motion pictures enjoy certain important advantages in emerging areas of the world. Literacy is not necessary for their enjoyment, and they are well adapted to the dramatic heritage that exists in many traditional societies. Mobile projectors can be used to bring films to areas with no theaters and no electricity, assuming that these areas can be reached by road or river transportation. Performances often can be held outdoors in warm climates, and admission costs are usually very low. A person who cannot read and is too poor to buy a radio receiver can still save up the few pennies necessary to attend a movie once or twice a month. In a Thai village, researchers found that only one person out of ten had never seen a motion picture, while a larger number had never listened to the radio. Among middle- and upper-class urban Thai 74 per cent go to the movies twice a month or more.[15]

The production and use of films in underdeveloped countries are impressive. India, the Republic of Korea, the United Arab Republic, the Philippines, and Mexico are among the major feature film producers of the world. In 1961, government agencies in a dozen countries of Africa were producing newsreels and documentaries, and at least as many were in the process of organizing units that could produce such films. Ghana has a fleet of 40-60 cinema vans that are used in connection with educational and development programs. To solve the language problem, these vans are accompanied by a commentator, who provides a "live" soundtrack in the local language.[16]

Book and magazine publishing is far less developed in emerging areas, due to the lack of a large, educated class of readers, the expense of modern printing machinery, and the poverty even of those who are literate. When people with very limited means have to choose among the printed media, they buy newspapers first, magazines second, and books last. This militates against the establishment of local publishing houses, and most emerging countries have to rely largely on foreign imports. Nevertheless, some domestic publishing is found in most of the developing nations. In Arabic-speaking countries, the American-based Franklin Publications, working in cooperation with local publishers, has had a hand in the publication of a significant proportion of serious books. Foreign missionaries are important publishers in many areas, and foreign governments often sponsor a number of locally produced publications. National government ministries or bureaus are, however, usually the largest publishers of books that are entirely locally produced, a large proportion of these being texts.

Regular television programs were available as of 1963 in only a few of the emerging countries, but others had started experimental service. The All India Radio began experimental transmissions for viewers in the Delhi region in September 1959. In October 1960 Nigeria became the first of the new African states south of the Sahara with television service. Brazzaville inaugurated experimental service in November 1962, although only about 50 receivers were available in the area served. Nearly all of the developing states are working on plans for the introduction of TV or for its extension to additional areas. In 1963, Nepal started construction of a television station to serve about 500 receivers within 50 miles of Katmandu. Seven African countries introduced television during 1963, although the total number of receivers they served was still very small.[17]

In spite of the relatively thin coverage of most mass media in developing countries, they reach more people than might be expected. A student of the press in Pakistan notes that the vernacular press, in particular, is often read aloud for the benefit of those who cannot read it themselves. In the evening it is a common sight in the villages to see a literate man reading a newspaper to his less-educated friends. Many Africans value a copy of a newspaper as a "possession" and share it with many people. In Thailand, where literacy is relatively high, group oral reading is less important, but pass-along readership chains for newspapers are common. A single one of these chains was found in a recent study to consist of twenty people. In South Viet-Nam, one can "rent" a newspaper at a kiosk, read it on the spot, and then return it.[18]

In the case of radio, group participation appears to be even more important. Studies in nearly all the emerging areas have found that when radio receivers are scarce, people tend to gather around them. Listening at the homes of notables or relatively wealthy persons, or in common rooms and coffee houses, is common. Where warm climates encourage outdoor listening, as is the case in the tropical African countries, 100 or more people may be seen gathered around the village radio set. In the typical Egyptian village the radio in the grocery store is played constantly, not only to entertain the proprietor, but as a service to his friends and customers.[19]

While the mass media in emerging countries thus reach a substantial number of people, it is striking how little information those operating the media have about their audiences. The pressing need for reader and listener surveys is frequently mentioned at meetings of newspaper and radio specialists. A seminar on journalism training in Asia, held in Manila in 1961, concluded that unless investigations were carried out among media audiences it would be impossible to answer such questions as "Who are the readers?," "Who are the listeners?," "What do they listen to?" The International Press Institute has also recognized the need for intensive readership surveys in Asia to learn more about the tastes and motivations of new newspaper readers, and a Senegalese official has pointed out that information about the behavior and reactions of radio listeners in Africa south of the Sahara would be of particular value.[20] With the encouragement of UNESCO, an International Association for Mass Communication Research has been formed to advance the study of questions of this type.

The Role of Organized Groups and Government

A more basic problem than lack of audience information is the paucity of organized groups that support and use the mass media in emerging nations. Family, tribe, and community, the characteristic organizations of traditional society, are well served by oral channels of communication and do not require the mass media for their functioning. The formal and informal organizations that are major users of comunications are usually few and far between. Except in one-party states, political parties tend to resemble cliques; organizations seeking to unite major elements behind broad national values are often weak or nonexistent. The intellectuals, civil servants, and industrial managers who might form the basis for a national public opinion are not drawn together in informal or formal associations, but remain isolated and out of touch with each other.[21] The mass of the population, long accustomed to having others make political decisions for them, do not feel the need to participate in opinion formation on national issues.[22] For all these reasons the developing nations lack the fairly dense infrastructure of private and voluntary associations characteristic of industrialized democracies.

The relationship between organizations and the media in emerging countries is a circular one. Because organized consumers are few, it is more difficult to build vigorous instruments of communication. At the same time, efforts to form both organizations and public opinion are hampered by the lack of media to keep people in touch with one another.

Nevertheless, those nontraditional groups that have managed to come into being serve as an important basis for whatever press there is, and provide a foundation on which further organizations and additional media can be built. As of 1958, for instance, Senegal had fifty-five publications, of which the great majority were sponsored by some formal organization. The table below provides a breakdown of these publications. A listing such as this does not, of course, give any indications about informal groupings, the extent or effectiveness of public opinion, and so on; but it does suggest the close relationship between the press and various forms of association.

PUBLICATIONS IN SENEGAL AS OF 1958[23]

Publications of general information	10
Government or semigovernment publications	5
Organs of political parties	6
Trade-union bulletins	5
Bulletins of private associations	7
Denominational publications	15
Journals of business concerns	7

In the absence of strong private groups, governments have played a large role in developing and supporting modern media. This is partly a matter of cost. Most emerging nations are eager for the establishment of media that will assist in education and economic growth, but the expense of introducing modern equipment and techniques is often beyond the reach of private enterprisers. Therefore public funds have been required. In addition, some governments see the information services as instruments for strengthening their own power, and therefore have restricted private initiative.

For these reasons, governments of emerging countries often end up by operating the major channels of communication themselves. Guinea has devoted a large portion of its Soviet economic aid to purchasing a powerful 100-kilowatt radio transmitter, a high-speed printing plant that can turn out 40,000 papers an hour, and a new outdoor theater. In the Republic of Senegal, the Ministry of Information not only operates Radio Senegal, the Senegalese Press Agency, and a Tourist Information Office, but also publishes two monthly illustrated magazines, a monthly illustrated wall newspaper, a review of the daily and weekly African press, and various pamphlets and specialized bulletins. Its film branch puts out two monthly newsreels and produces films on current events as well as educational films. Moreover, the Ministry has organized regional information centers throughout the country that have audio-visual materials at their disposal and also "stimulate and inspect" private media.[24] Some governments have provided professional training for journalists—in certain cases only for radio personnel who are employed by the government broadcasting service, but in other cases for newspapermen also.

The substantial expense involved in expanding the information services is indicated by a UNESCO estimate for Africa. To achieve even the minimum coverage suggested by UNESCO (excluding television), an initial outlay of at least $360 million would be necessary. This does not include recurring expenses or the cost of training personnel.[25] Nevertheless, the amounts of money invested by emerging countries in the information services are small when compared with sums devoted to other aspects of development. The media tend to draw the short end of the stick when they are competing for scarce funds against schools, roads, or basic industries. In no case does the amount of investment appear to be adequate. Furthermore, those countries that are tending toward democracy usually spend a far smaller amount on the information services than do Communist nations or countries leaning toward Communism. Since in the Communist scheme the mass media play an integral part in maintaining the power of the regime, they are given higher priority than in those countries where government is based on the consent of the governed, even though, in the long run, the democratic states are more dependent on adequate communication networks.

Directions of Media Development

In spite of the problem of finding capital, the future development of mass media in the emerging countries is likely to be rapid. A UNESCO group has estimated that the demand for information services in Asia,

Latin America (excluding Argentina), the Near and Middle East, and the Far East (excluding Japan and Communist China) is likely to be three and a half times as great by 1975 as it was in 1955. This is a far more rapid increase than could be expected on the basis of rising population alone.[26]

Existing trends support this forecast of rapid growth. An Indian Government report notes that during 1960 daily newspaper circulation rose at least 9.6 per cent and fifty-three new newspapers were started; newspaper experts in India believe that daily circulation will increase from about 5 million in 1962 to 20 million in 1973.[27] In 1948 radio sets at common meeting places in Indian villages numbered only 2,000. With government support, the number increased to nearly 30,000 by 1959, and was expected to reach almost 100,000 by 1961.[28] In 1950, only 3 African countries had national news agencies. By 1961, the number was reported to be 14; and by 1962, there were more than 20.[29] The development of television will probably be particularly rapid. A U.S.I.A. survey noted in 1962 that Manila had as many channels as Washington, D.C., and that Malaya, Singapore, Indonesia, and Cambodia were all about to introduce television service.[30]

Rapid expansion of the media in emerging countries will probably be assisted by new techniques for information handling. Having only a relatively thin coverage of conventional media, new nations may be able to jump from oral communication systems to the most recent ones. Communication satellites can bring them television from all parts of the world, teleprinter and teletype setting techniques will make possible simultaneous publication of newspaper editions throughout whole regions, projectors using the sun as a source of power may be used to present film strips in nonelectrified areas, and so on.[31]

Another obvious trend is for media in emerging countries to come more and more under governmental control, and for freedom of information to be restricted. It is far more difficult for a country in the early stages of economic growth to have a completely free press than for an industrialized country.[32] Not only are governments in these areas involved with the media financially, but they also are less able to tolerate criticism. Many are faced with threats of subversion, which could be fanned by hostile propaganda. Others have yet to mold their countries into nations, and fear divisive tendencies. In all of them the scarcity of resources and the necessity for unity of effort tend to produce a feeling that all media should promote goals defined by the government.[33] This feeling is nourished by Communist states, several of which are active in helping developing countries to build communication networks. The amount of freedom allowed by India and a handful of other emerging countries is highly unusual.

In addition, the leaders in many new countries are suspicious of media that are a holdover from colonial days, and are intolerant of criticism from any quarter. In Kenya, Jomo Kenyatta has been reported to regard the publication of opposing views as inspired by enmity. Tom Mboya has expressed support for a free press in theory, but has specified that it must be a national press and must make a constructive contribution to the national effort. The African journalist, he feels, cannot write as though he were in London, Paris, or New York.[34] In most Arabic-speaking countries, the regimes discourage critical and analytical tendencies and force the mass media to be promoters of political and cultural orthodoxy.[35] All of the sixteen dailies and a variety of other publications in Afghanistan are controlled by the Royal Afghan Department of the Press, which also controls the national news agency, Radio Kabul, the drama, the cinema, and tourism. President Sukarno has ordered the Indonesian press to publish only "constructive" material, on pain of being seized or destroyed; newspapers and magazines should become "the tool to mobilize the masses to consummate the Indonesian revolution."[36]

Several forces may be expected to work against the trend toward government domination of the media in the emerging countries and to help preserve at least some freedom of expression. One of these is the organization of information personnel into press councils, editors' guilds, and other professional associations. Most of the developing nations already have some kind of organization of mass media personnel, and others are being formed. Although the influence and activity of these associations varies greatly from country to country, they usually put the media in a slightly better position to bargain with the government, and by upholding professional standards they help to avoid journalistic excesses that might trigger official action to impose more extensive controls. Where governments are not basically authoritarian, a professional code is one of the best safeguards of freedom, since people will come to the defense of a press that they respect.

The heavy involvement of industrialized democracies and international organizations in the development of media in emerging countries also tends to support freedom of information. The United States and several West European countries are providing major assistance in building communication systems, as are UNESCO, the International Telecommunication Union, the Universal Postal Union, the Food and Agriculture Organization, and the International Labor Organization—as well as regional agencies and professional associations. Much of this assistance is technical and not concerned with content. Nevertheless, the fact that both the United Nations and the industrialized democracies are on record as favoring freedom of information would make it seem probable that governments receiving aid from these sources would be more restrained in imposing their will on the mass media than would otherwise be the case. Involvement of the International Press Institute and other international professional bodies in media development also makes it more difficult for governments to impose strangling controls without raising an outcry in other countries. Since officials in emerging areas are often sensitive to foreign criticism, this form of pressure has been successful in some cases.

Much of the outside assistance given emerging countries involves training personnel to operate the information services, and it is to be hoped that these personnel will absorb to at least some degree professional standards of objective reporting, critical independence, and impartiality in treating varying viewpoints. International centers for higher training in journalism, primarily for students from underdeveloped areas, have already been established in Strasbourg and Quito, and further centers are projected.[37] World news agencies have provided practical, on-the-job training to staff men of the newer national agencies.[38] The West German Radio and the German Foundation for Developing Countries have been active in training African and Asian press, radio, and television personnel. In addition, a substantial number of media personnel from developing countries are enrolled in training programs of universities in the industrialized nations, and others are aided by economic development and exchange-of-persons programs, such as those of the United States and the Colombo Plan nations. Information officials from the democracies often serve as informal teachers and advisers to media personnel in the countries where they are stationed.

Further pressures, even though gentle ones, favoring greater independence for the media are exercised by such gatherings as the seminar on freedom of information sponsored by the Commission on Human Rights of the U.N. Economic and Social Council which met in New

Delhi in February 1962. One of the recommendations of this meeting was that, since involvement of governments in broadcasting appears inevitable in view of the capital expenditures required, ways should be found to preserve a high degree of impartiality and to assure that the national radio does not merely become the voice of the party in power.[39]

Perhaps the most important question with respect to the development of modern communications in emerging countries is the extent to which the new media will become tied in with traditional channels. There is now little relationship between the two systems in many areas: a relatively small urban minority is served by the modern media, while the mass of the population relies mainly on older forms of communication. Indian villagers in Peru, for instance, although increasingly linked with the rest of the country by roads, still pay little attention to messages from the government and exchange few ideas with the inhabitants of nearby towns. In Burma, the lack of a unified communication system makes it impossible for the numerically preponderant rural elements to mobilize their strength and enforce their demands on the government. Instead, the villages have their own separate political processes.[40] If a sense of national identity is to be achieved, and if the masses are to be reached for purposes of education, economic development, and political mobilization, some way must be found to ensure that ideas transmitted through the modern media are relayed by the traditional system, and in general that the two complement each other rather than existing as parallel but unconnected channels.

Efforts to tie the two systems together or, more accurately, to supplement the mass media by using older styles of communication have been made in a number of developing nations. The Director-General of the All India Radio has urged that traditional art forms be adapted to broadcasting in such a way that they will help convey the information needed in the modern world.[41] Indian film producers have made effective use of mythological and religious subject matter that has been handed down through generations of oral tradition. Folk plays have been enlisted in the educational campaigns of a number of countries. One such play, used in a new African nation, deals with a bachelor who chooses the plain rather than the beautiful sister for a wife because she is literate. The good-looking sister thereupon joins a literacy class.[42] Similar techniques have been employed in connection with social and economic programs in Southeast Asia and the Caribbean, where *jongleurs* have been hired to carry messages about hygiene or modern farming methods through songs and recitations. Needless to say, in these dramatic episodes it is always the wise farmer who adopts the new methods. Communist propagandists in a number of emerging countries have made use of various forms of folk entertainment and traveling medicine vendors to dispense their ideas. In some countries, discussion leaders have been sent into the villages to help radio listening groups find and explore the significance of broadcast programs. By stimulating face-to-face conversation they ensure that the themes of the broadcasts are relayed through oral channels.

Person-to-person communication is important in giving wide currency to ideas disseminated through mass media in emerging areas, as it is in industrialized states also. It plays a larger role in the developing nations, however, because of the limited coverage of the media and because many people have not learned to rely on modern communications even when these are available to them. A 1952 survey, for example, found that over one-third of a sample of Arab radio listeners still depended heavily on word of mouth for news. A later study of an Egyptian village found that only eighteen out of a group of fifty-seven literate villagers had obtained their information about an important event (the death of the King of Morocco) from the newspapers.[43] Those who do not have access to the media naturally are even more dependent on oral channels.

Establishing a satisfactory relationship between the two communication systems is not always a simple process. Sometimes people in traditional societies do not want to pay attention to modern media, or are hostile to them. A Turkish horsewagon driver, when asked by Columbia University researchers if he missed anything by ignoring newspapers and the radio, replied: "I lose nothing because I am not interested in things which do not concern me." The same survey found that many Bedouins actively opposed the mass media, both because these were associated with the decadent city and because they were seen as contrary to God's commandments: "Radio? By God if I see one I will destroy it. This is from the devil." Lebanese villagers reported that they did not listen to the radio because they did not understand "what the talking was."[44]

A study of several traditional African societies, on the other hand, found little resistance to the use of modern communications. Most people seemed to have a tremendous interest in the mass media although they still relied mainly on oral systems. Shouts of joy could be heard in the villages when a mobile cinema van arrived; some very primitive people expressed an interest in having a radio receiver and even knew how much it cost; others reported having heard news that had appeared in newspapers within the past few days. "They themselves wish to open Pandora's box."[45]

Even when there is no resistance to introduction of the mass media, people still have to learn how to use them; they have to develop good communication habits and standards of judgment. If modern communications in emerging countries are to be fully effective in transmitting ideas, their introduction must be accompanied by measures to teach people how to select, criticize, and supplement the ideas contained in them—processes that are learned at least partially by citizens of industrialized societies as they grow up. Numerous reports from areas where mass media have been newly introduced stress that audiences frequently give their attention in an undifferentiated manner to everything offered by the media.[46] The sheer novelty of the experience is enough to make all messages interesting, but the relevance of some of these messages to the needs of daily life is not necessarily perceived; therefore they are not relayed through the traditional channels, or they are relayed in a distorted form. Sometimes the ideas expressed through the mass media are understood poorly, or not at all, even when they are given close attention.* On other occasions, information received through the mass media is accepted uncritically and the audience has little protection against one-sided presentations.

Students of non-Western cultures seem to delight in pointing out the difficulties that traditional peoples have in comprehending Western communications: those from some cultures can't understand line drawings, others are confused by perspective, and others cannot recognize a scene shown in black and white but can when it is shown in color. Nigerians are often unaware of color when it is used in films. In South Africa, conventional line drawings of faces were seen as representing people who had been mutilated or blinded. Enlarged pictures of lice in a public-health film were believed by Peruvian villagers to portray some

* An extreme example was mentioned to the author by the operator of a mobile projector unit. He took his projector into an area that had not previously been exposed to motion pictures, where the showing of educational films was watched attentively by enthusiastic audiences. Being somewhat skeptical of the degree of comprehension he was achieving, he experimented by running some of the films backward. They were greeted with the same attention and enthusiasm.

new and strange animal. Comprehension of voice commentaries likewise differs sharply according to cultural background. Many societies do not subscribe to Western logic: the same statement may be true or false depending on who says it or who hears it.[47]

Since people have to learn how to use Western communications, those from traditional societies who have already been exposed to Western patterns of thought usually learn more from the mass media than those who have not been so exposed. An unlettered Egyptian observed that his friends who had learned to read could see something in motion pictures that he could not see, and Africans who had had some contact with European ways were found to recall more material from newspapers than those who had not.[48]

Until its modern and traditional systems are satisfactorily linked, each of the emerging countries is likely to contain at least two separate societies for many years to come, and mobilization of its citizens for a national effort will be difficult. The formation of public opinion on current issues, which depends heavily on interaction of the two systems, will also be inhibited. It is not that the traditional systems should be eliminated, or even overshadowed; rather, the two systems should be so constituted that they will work together in bringing individuals and groups the information that they need while on the road to modernization.

The fact that there are always at least two cultures in emerging countries has often been ignored. In Russia, for instance, the cities and villages shared a single national culture until about the middle of the seventeenth century. Then, as the modernization process began, the urban and rural areas tended to develop separately. Thereafter, Russia had two histories, but only the one that concerned the small upper class received adequate attention.[49] A related observation has been made in several UNESCO reports, which note that there are two or more almost completely different audiences for radio in emerging countries, and that at least two program services of differing character are therefore required. One service should be addressed to the fairly literate urban minority and the other to the traditional majority, which requires not only programs but also the means of listening to them. Furthermore, the traditional majority is often made up of a staggering number of very diverse groups. Modernization has not been rapid enough to enable uniform tastes to develop. How, asks an Indian radio expert, can a single radio system satisfy a clientele with such diverse traditions?[50]

Integration of the two or more systems of communication in each developing country involves certain adaptations on the part of the modern media, as well as education of the audiences. The media have to take into account the traditional communication habits and psychological characteristics of the people. At the same time, opinion leaders from the traditional systems have to be involved in the operation and interpretation of mass communications, and representatives of the media must be brought into direct contact with the traditional systems at the grass roots. Recruiting and training village-level reporters and developing local opinion leaders on new subjects are fully as important as assuring an adequate supply of technicians and journalists who are versed in modern techniques.

Uses of Modern Media

Mass communications provide one of the principal avenues through which people in emerging countries learn new ways of thinking and behaving, and are closely associated with what has been called the revolution of rising expectations. They have also been used by existing leaders to consolidate their power, but more often are associated with the rise of new leaders and the breakdown of old political forms.

When people are first exposed to modern media, they usually have little interest in acquiring factual information or news of the outside world. Instead, they are fascinated by the pictures on the movie screen or the sounds coming from the radio receiver. They use the media first for entertainment.[51]

The results of exposure may, however, be a desire for new ways, new surroundings, and new experiences. Columbia University researchers encountered a seventeen-year-old Arab shepherd who had become restless after seeing an American movie. He missed the opportunity to watch "good things," such as beautiful girls, fine horses, and exciting battles. They also found women in Lebanon who were disenchanted with their traditional lot as a result of media exposure. Another observer of the Arab world reports that in Iraqi villages there is talk about progress because people hear references to it on the radio. They don't really understand what it is, but nevertheless are attracted by some of the new ways of living with which they are acquainted by the mass media. The ideas diffused by modern communications help people to imagine themselves as strange persons in new situations, and those who formerly accepted their lot without protest often become aware of new horizons.[52]

Awakened desires to live in a new world, in turn, may lead people to make new uses of media. Instead of being regarded primarily as sources of entertainment, modern communications may be seen as instruments for education and advancement—for achieving particular goals. The U.S. Information Agency has reported that libraries maintained by the Agency in Africa find only limited demands for fiction and light reading, but that works on government, economics, education, and history seldom remain long on the shelves. American authorities in Africa have been almost swamped by letters and visits from young men and women wanting to study in the United States. Newly literate Egyptian workers told interviewers that they preferred newspapers that gave news about labor. They wanted to see good coverage of strikes and attention to labor grievances. To them, information media were instruments for economic advance via class solidarity.[53]

Those who have money or position in traditional societies often have access to the new media before they become available to the masses. When this is the case, members of an existing elite may use mass communication facilities to strengthen their position. The first newspaper in Turkish functioned as an official gazette for the Sultan. In Thailand, the police and military officers have been the most active users of radio and newspapers. Tribal chiefs in Iran have found that radio is the best way to keep informed about the activities of the Shah and his Chief of Staff—information that sometimes has military significance for them, and the first newspapers and radio receivers introduced into Samoa went almost exclusively to the local chiefs.[54]

Introduction of modern communications may also strengthen existing social and cultural patterns. Some Jordanian farmers like the radio because it brings them readings from the Koran. Thus they incorporate it into their traditional way of life. Tribalism and localism may be encouraged when members of extended families are able to keep in touch with each other more easily than before, and when local feelings are stimulated by the use of the vernacular in the mass media.[55] In Thailand the new media contribute in some ways to social stability and political conservatism, since the Thai has traditionally regarded himself as a spectator rather than a participant, and the press and radio enable him to play this role even more easily than before. In such cases, information media may tend to delay the learning of new ways of behaving. Communications can be used as a tranquilizer, as well as for purposes of stimulation.[56]

The mass media are, however, more likely to promote change than to support existing patterns. Indeed, the examples that have been cited above are of interest more because they are exceptions to the rule than because they are indicative of a prevailing tendency. Modern communications help to bring about political change by involving wider circles in political life, by facilitating the emergence of new leaders, and by enabling these leaders to establish contact with others who are dissatisfied with things as they are.

Radio has been the greatest single instrument for involving people in emerging countries in political activity. Matters that traditionally were almost exclusively the province of a very small group have become the subject of mass attention. In some areas, political diatribes over the radio have caused politics to replace traditional village rites as the occasion for emotional outbursts. People have opinions on issues that did not previously concern them, and the media offer them a range of opinions among which they can choose. Government corruption, for instance, may become a subject around which public opinion forms, whereas in previous times it probably would have been accepted as normal behavior, or would have passed unnoticed.[57]

Modern communications also make it simpler for new leaders to emerge at all levels of traditional societies. The elders no longer receive the respect to which they were previously accustomed; their experience may be regarded as less valuable than the knowledge of younger people who can read newspapers and books, or who listen to the radio. If educated men are excluded from positions of power by the old elite, they may use the channels of public communication to build a following. In the early stages of modernization, writer-journalist-politicians are frequent, as exemplified by Keita Fodeiba in Guinea, Davidson Nicol in Sierra Leone, and Léopold Senghor in Senegal.[58] Juan Bosch, former President of the Dominican Republic, is a novelist and political scientist. Abdul Rahman Pazhwak of Afghanistan is a journalist and poet, as well as a diplomat, and the President of Nigeria is a former newsman. The influence of leaders such as these is based in part on their ability to use modern information media. The notables who previously were able to know everything that was going on and stamp out any dissident idea before it could take root have seen their power undermined by the psychic mobility that is encouraged by the mass media as well as the physical mobility made possible by modern transportation.

The important role that radio, in particular, plays in political disturbances in emerging countries has often been noted, since this is practically the only instrument through which a leader aspiring to power can establish contact with a mass following in a state with rudimentary political organization. An offical history of the first year of the Iraqi Republic calls the radio the "midwife by whose hands the republic came to life." [59] The radio station was the first target in the Iranian coup against Premier Mossadegh, since without it his opponents reasoned that he would be powerless to whip up support among the masses. When the Congo was torn by disorders during 1960, the Léopoldville radio was one of the principal prizes for which the rival elements contended.

In addition to playing an important role in the acquisition and maintenance of political power, communications are a vital link in the three processes that are most vital to the transformation of an emerging country into a modern state: education, economic development, and creation of a sense of nationhood.*

Especially close relationships exist between communications and education in emerging countries: there is little of the distinction between the two that is made in industrialized nations. Discussions of education immediately involve the mass media, and plans for developing the media are ordinarily tied to plans for education. A meeting of educators convened by UNESCO in 1962, for example, recommended that emerging countries planning educational programs emphasize the development of radio and TV, and organize demonstration projects using both the mass media and other methods. It suggested further that research on ways of combining the resources of the mass media with other educational tools be exchanged among the governments involved. Another international conference, this one on information services in Latin America, concluded that the media should be used on a coordinated basis in the service of education—for example, radio could channel news to school newspapers, and television viewing could be combined with community discussions of current topics.[60] An American expert has observed that for many years to come the mass media must bear

* The most complete single treatment of these subjects is found in Wilbur Schramm, *Mass Media and National Development: The Role of Information in the Developing Countries* (Stanford, Calif.: Stanford University Press; Paris UNESCO, 1964).

most of the burden of teaching in emerging countries, since it will be a long time before adequate school systems can be developed: there must be a "single strategy for education and information." A French authority suggests that there are great advantages in having responsibility for both education and radio centralized in a single government ministry.[61]

While the mass media are beginning to be used in conjunction with school programs for children in some of the developing nations—for example, in Ghana and Senegal—the importance of public communications in adult education has been even more widely recognized. By 1960, the Indian Government had supplied about 58,000 community radio sets for installation in rural areas, and 800 or 900 Rural Radio Forums had been set up throughout the country. Broadcasts covered all aspects of rural life, including agriculture, health, and hygiene. The All India Radio established its experimental television service primarily for adult education purposes, and installed 20 TV receivers at selected community centers in and around New Delhi in 1959. Teleclubs were formed at these centers, each of which was able to accommodate a regular viewing audience of from 150 to 200 persons. The educational activities of Radio Senegal have been concerned mainly with basic instruction in subjects of interest to the agricultural population. Its projects for 1962 included programs on local water supply, house improvements, and septic systems.[62]

Use of communications to raise the general educational level in regard to health, housing, or agriculture contributes to economic development also. Some programs, are, however, more directly focused on the economy than others. Mass education teams in Ghana, for instance, have employed visual aids to instruct farmers in the treatment of certain cacao-tree diseases and in the inoculation of cattle against rinderpest; and films, filmstrips, and radio broadcasts in almost all underdeveloped countries have attempted to raise agricultural output. UNESCO-sponsored conferences have repeatedly advocated increased use of the mass media to spread improved farming and industrial techniques.

Persuading people to adopt new techniques, however, is often a difficult task. A villager is reluctant to exchange a technique that works, even if poorly, for one that he is not sure will work at all. Sometimes adopting new techniques involves changing a way of life, or overcoming deep-seated resistance. Attitudes in most traditional cultures tend to be hostile to change. For example, one study found that most Indian farmers believed that mechanical farming methods tended to destroy the richness of the product grown.[63]

A basic function of information campaigns in economic development is therefore not only to teach new techniques but to activate and reinforce *desires* for change—to prepare the ground for the adoption of improved techniques and to focus attention on the desirability of new ways of behaving. A French authority speaks of the media in the emerging countries as having the task of "animation," which he defines as "helping the country to gather the impetus necessary for its full development." [64] India has made use of a field publicity organization in an attempt to "awake the capabilities" of the public in connection with its economic plans. During 1960, 76 mobile cinema units took part in a campaign in which over 20 million people in more than 17,000 places attended some 20,000 film showings and took part in 25,000 discussions. The slogan of this campaign was "Help the plan, help yourself." [65] The mass media can contribute to economic development by mobilizing public support for development programs and by helping to give people hope for a better life.

A third major function of the information media in developing areas is to help build nations out of geographical entities. They do this in many ways: by informing people of the same country about each other, by enabling them to cooperate in groups and organizations that cut across family and ethnic ties, by giving whole populations a common body of knowledge and a common focus of attention, and by cultivating a sense of national identity among people whose primary loyalties have been tribal and communal. The domestic information programs of nearly all the emerging countries place great emphasis on material with patriotic content and on communications that tie different population elements to each other and to the government.[66]

Countries whose populations share a single language are able to make more effective use of the media in cultivating a national feeling than those with a variety of local tongues. Language has been called the principal factor in contemporary Arab nationalism and Cairo's Voice of the Arabs the most impressive unifying force in the Arab world. "The modern press, radio and cinema are doing more in forming an Arab nation than all other factors put together." [67]

In nations where several languages are spoken, emphasis is placed on other unifying factors. Malayan newspapers, according to an official of that country's Information Department, formerly catered to communal or commercial interests. Now, whether they are published in English, Chinese, Malay, or Tamil, they must cultivate a national outlook and help to make citizens of various racial origins into a single entity. Several Asian countries have a requirement that all theaters showing entertainment films must also show a government-approved documentary film. States made up of different ethnic groups often seek to prevent the media from being used to widen the gulf among the various communities. Pakistan, for instance, has laws forbidding the incitement of hatred among classes and communities.[68]

In spite of the general recognition that the mass media can play an important part in cultivating cohesion and a sense of nationhood among the peoples of emerging countries, relatively little attention has been given to just how this is to be accomplished. Most observations about the subject remain on a rather general and hortatory level, at least as far as the non-Communist states are concerned. The way that communications should be patterned in order to create a stable and peaceful nation out of a series of traditionally discrete ethnic groups is a question that deserves a great deal of additional exploration. Research on this question might still help to reduce the intensity of communal strife in many areas of the world.

The Importance of Communications from Abroad for the Modern Sector

Every emerging country has a modern sector, even though this sector may be very tiny in the case of nations just starting on the path to modernization. The personnel who operate this sector use information in much the same way as their opposite numbers in industrialized countries. Since their own communication network is less developed, however, they pay relatively more attention to communications originating abroad. The international network helps to satisfy some of the requirements that would be taken care of by the domestic network in a more developed country, as well as those requirements that are normally filled by communications to and from other countries.

The extent to which urban, educated minorities use information from foreign sources is impressive. In Lebanon, two-thirds of those classified as "moderns" told interviewers that they listened to foreign broadcasts. Some of these people occasionally read foreign periodicals as well, including *Time, Life,* and *True Story*. A similar picture with regard to radio was found in Syria, where many listeners said they could receive London more easily than Damascus. A survey conducted among middle- and upper-class urban Thai found that more than half of them listened to one or more foreign stations (45 per cent mentioned the Voice of America, 41 per cent the British Broadcasting Corporation, and 9 per cent Radio Peking), about one out of five read American magazines, and nearly all had seen an American motion picture. (Almost half thought that these films gave a correct impression of life in the United States.)[69] Latin Americans who read English rely heavily on foreign publications—especially the London *Times, The Economist,* and *The New York Times*—for news analysis. In tropical Africa, foreign publications are read by many government officials and intellectuals, including some foreign publications that deal mainly with African affairs, such as the weekly *West Africa,* which is edited in London.[70]

The educated minority in developing nations is also likely to have extensive personal contacts with people from the developed areas of the world. Especially in capital cities of emerging countries, the relatively few modern men are thrown into far closer contact with diplomats, aid personnel, newspapermen and others from abroad than is the case with intellectuals in industrialized states. In 1955 it was found that 63 per cent of middle- and upper-class urban Thai had had some contact with Americans during the preceding year, and 41 per cent mentioned contacts with Britishers. In 1959, about half of a sample of Thai leaders in Bangkok reported that they had lived abroad at one time or another, for the most part in Western nations, and 14 per cent said they currently came in contact with Americans almost every day.[71]

Contacts with foreigners are especially likely to occur in connection with education. While adequate statistics showing the extent to which this is the case are not available, the figures that do exist suggest that in many emerging countries more than half of those with a college education or better have received at least part of their training abroad. In several cases, UNESCO surveys have indicated that the number of students from a given country pursuing a higher education abroad was greater than the total number of those already having a college degree.[72] Although the proportion of foreign-educated in emerging countries may be expected to decline as their own institutions are built up, the role of foreign teaching personnel and foreign-trained teachers in these institutions will probably be important for many years.

Foreign education affects mainly urban residents and those in the highest income and status levels. Nearly all the students from emerging countries who were studying in West Germany in 1961 came from cities (and 61 per cent from cities of over 100,000), although in these countries 80 to 90 per cent of the population lived on the land, and members of the students' families had already visited or had other contacts with one or more industrialized countries in about 75 per cent of the cases.[73]

Most important of all is that the leaders of most emerging countries are eager for ideas from any source that may be helpful to them in coping with the crushing problems they are facing. Their attitudes toward many vital political and economic questions have not yet become firmly established, and the ability of the international communication network to provide them with useful ideas will help to determine the direction taken by their nations in coming years.

PART TWO

The Use of Communications to Advance Policy

VIII

The Structure of International Communication Programs*

From very early times, political leaders have supplemented diplomacy and force with communications addressed to peoples of other nations. Most of these have been appeals made in wartime to win over or subvert an enemy, although some were intended to avoid conflict, to encourage friends, or to bring about cooperation. Thucydides tells how Athenian spokesmen made eloquent public speeches in neighboring city-states in an effort to prevent them from allying with the enemies of Athens, Herodotus recounts the efforts of Themistocles to subvert Ionian sailors by carving messages on rocks near a watering place, and Julius Caesar's *Gallic Wars* cites several instances in which the Romans gained military advantage by spreading rumors in the enemy camp, or in which equally damaging rumors were planted among the Romans.[1]

American governmental experience with using communication as an instrument of foreign policy has likewise been largely in situations of conflict. Benjamin Franklin's pamphleteering in favor of the American Revolutionary cause in Europe is well known. Less familiar, but equally fascinating, is the story of the psychological warfare used by the American colonists against Hessian mercenaries serving the British crown.[2] In this case, German-language leaflets promising free land to Hessian deserters were distributed by a number of ingenious means. Also during the American Revolution Thomas Paine proposed a daring scheme to

* This chapter is a revision and expansion of an article co-authored by Alexander L. George: "An Outline for the Study of International Political Communications," *Public Opinion Quarterly,* Winter 1952-53. It leans heavily on analytical concepts outlined in various writings of Harold D. Lasswell. See especially Lasswell's essay on "The Study and Practice of Propaganda," in Bruce L. Smith, Harold D. Lasswell, and Ralph D. Casey, *Propaganda and Promotional Activities* (Minneapolis, Minn.: University of Minnesota Press, 1935).

undermine British resolve to continue the war against the colonists by insinuating pro-American articles into London newspapers. Paine's plan was never put into effect, but during the Civil War the brilliant Confederate propagandist Henry Hotze was able to arrange publication in the London press of some very effective editorials favoring the cause of the South.[3]

All these were fairly small ventures, involving few people. It was during World War I that the United States first set up a large organization to make use of communications in support of foreign policy. The Committee on Public Information, in the course of its "fight for the mind of mankind," built up a world-wide network of agents to keep foreign countries supplied with a steady stream of material from the United States.[4] This tradition was revived with World War II, when the U. S. Office of War Information and related agencies again engaged in a campaign to sway foreign viewpoints. The OWI defined its mission as that of undermining morale in enemy countries, keeping alive the hope of liberation in enemy-occupied territories, winning the moral support of people in neutral countries, and countering enemy propaganda, promoting morale, and fostering better understanding of the United States in Allied nations. Even before the start of the war, Nazi subversion in Latin America had sparked a small educational and cultural exchange program with our neighbors to the south.[5]

American suspicions of peacetime propaganda almost snuffed out overseas information activities at the end of the war. They were saved at the last minute by Soviet aggressive behavior, which persuaded large numbers of Americans in and out of Congress that such an operation was necessary, even if distasteful. The Smith-Mundt Act, passed in 1948, called for an information and cultural program to "promote a better understanding of the United States in other countries, and to increase mutual understanding between the people of the United States and the people in other countries." Continuing Communist pressure, which reached a high point with the invasion of South Korea in 1950, led to a sharpening in the program's tone. It became a "campaign of truth" to fight world Communism, and its budget was expanded.[6] With modifications, improvements, and reorganizations, it has developed into the program we know today.

Private organizations, as well as governments, frequently make use of international communications to advance their policies. Many of these organizations are concerned with economic matters: promoting trade, investment, or tourism. Others are concerned with humanitarian, educational, or religious affairs. A substantial number have political aims: encouraging world peace, supporting resistance or liberation movements, or advocating a political ideology. While private organizations are important as sponsors of international communication programs that have political goals, their role relative to that of governments probably has declined in recent years. Of the some 400 agents of foreign principals registered with the U. S. Department of Justice at the end of 1962, most of whom were engaged in some form of propaganda activity, almost 75 per cent represented instrumentalities of foreign governments.[7]

Major international communication programs, whether public or private, are administered by large bureaucracies; but the processes involved in these programs closely resemble the thought and action of individuals who use communications to satisfy their personal requirements. "Please pass the salt," a humble but necessary persuasive phrase, is the observable part of an operation that takes place in several stages. First, we taste the spinach and find it flat; so we decide that salt should be added. With this decision, our goal has been defined. Next, we wonder how we should go about achieving our goal—whether to use the "boardinghouse reach" or to ask our neighbor to pass the salt. We decide that it would be more polite to ask. With that, the policy-making and planning stages for our personal communication program are complete.

Then comes the verbal stage. We proceed to make the request.

This leads to a fourth stage, in which we expect to receive the salt. It may be, however, that our expectations prove to be incorrect. Nothing at all may happen; or our neighbor may smile amiably and hand us the sugar. Evaluation thus discloses that our communication has been ineffective and suggests the need for research. Is it that our neighbor doesn't understand English, is he hard of hearing, or is he absorbed in conversation with the lady on his right? The results of our research may indicate that we should repeat the request in louder tones, that we should tap our neighbor on the shoulder and then point to the salt, or that we should do without salt or without spinach.

Organizations using public communications to advance their policies go through a very similar series of procedures. They define their goals, and decide whether communications can help bring about the desired results. Then they determine what ideas should be transmitted, and to whom, and how these ideas can be conveyed as effectively as possible. Finally, they attempt to evaluate the results.

In the case of foreign information and cultural programs conducted by major nations, all these stages are obscured and complicated by the size of the governmental machinery, the number of considerations involved in policy formulation, the problem of coordinating the activities of professional communication staffs with other actions of the executive, the availability of a large variety of media, the almost infinite amount of information that is required about audiences throughout the world, and the great difficulty of observing and explaining effects. No two nations follow exactly the same procedures when it comes to using communications as a foreign-policy instrument. Nevertheless, the basic process remains substantially the same in all cases.

Formulation of Foreign Information and Cultural Policy

The foreign information and cultural policy of a nation determines how it will use communications to help achieve foreign-policy goals. An adequate statement of this policy can be formulated only after a detailed analysis of two questions: What is national policy, and how can communications be used to help achieve this? Obviously, there are some national goals to the attainment of which communications can contribute very little, and there also are potential effects of communications that will not serve national goals. Information and cultural policy must therefore be designed to use the capabilities of available instruments in such a way as to advance national policy to the greatest extent possible.

A policy governing the use of international communications can be formulated best when national policy is clear and specific. Very general national goals, such as the achievement of a community of free and prosperous nations, provide some guidance, but they do not define the many intermediate steps that have to be taken before these ultimate goals can be attained. Since the effects of communications depend on the uses to which they can be put by individuals and organizations, national policy has to be traced all the way down to its implications for specific people or groups of people if it is to provide an adequate basis for communication policy. For instance, in an emerging area, should one concentrate on persuading local officials to introduce health measures, should one encourage farmers to raise more food, or should one do a little of both? Or, to take a problem that has often been faced by

Communist spokesmen, is it more advantageous to urge the non-Communist left to make common cause with the Communists, or would it be better to assail social democrats as agents of the bourgeoisie and betrayers of the working class?

While policy specificity is clearly desirable, it is difficult to achieve, especially for democracies. It requires decisions about contingencies that are hard to foresee, and a great deal of detailed information about many areas of the world. National decision-makers often prefer to restrict their advance planning to general outlines, on the assumption that this course allows them greater flexibility in dealing with each situation as it arises. Furthermore, machinery often does not exist for gathering and processing information about the implications of alternative policies for small areas and population segments.

Most countries try to assure specificity and realism in their policy-planning by delegating a part of this function to their overseas missions. Diplomatic, economic, information, and other specialized personnel at each mission are asked to recommend policies that will be appropriate for the area in which they are stationed. These recommendations are then harmonized with each other and are sent to the national capital, where they are reconciled with recommendations from other sources. The resulting amalgam becomes national policy. Decentralization is not a guarantee that plans will be specific, however. The overseas missions themselves may take refuge behind generalities.

For purposes of formulating information and cultural policy it is also desirable that national policy have a long-range time perspective. Many of the effects that can be achieved by communications require months or years to come to fruition. Even the so-called fast media—press, radio, and TV—depend for a large part of their effectiveness on cumulative impact over a period of time. Reinforcing attitudes, imparting factual information, and building new attitudes is likely to be a gradual process. The desirability of an extended perspective is still greater in the case of "slow" channels—books, exchange of persons, and films. In the case of educational programs, it may be a long time before those who have taken part in them are able to make use of what they have learned. Western-trained specialists in India, for instance, have often had to wait several years before becoming established in positions where they could employ their skills.[8]

Even if national policy toward a given area is specific and looks as far as possible into the future, the communicator may not have adequate access to it. This may be due to faulty coordination, or may occur because the policy-makers regard their decisions as so secret that they think information personnel should not be privy to them. As Hans Speier has pointed out, the propagandist is a professional talker—and who likes to entrust secrets to a professional talker? The history of foreign information programs is full of instances in which problems have arisen because communication personnel were not adequately informed about policy.* Nevertheless, most countries with large foreign information and cultural programs have made efforts to deal with this problem by including those in charge of communications in high-level discussions of national policy, or by appointing liaison officials to link agencies concerned primarily with policy formulation with those responsible for communication.

Sometimes, however, official channels don't seem to provide those involved in international communication with adequate policy guidance, especially when decisions have to be made very rapidly or under conditions of great secrecy. Informal channels may then become relatively more important. Many observers who felt that British propaganda during World War II was more effective than American attributed this in part to the fact that the British Political Warfare Executive had better informal channels to the British Foreign Office than the U. S. Office of War Information had to the Department of State and the White House. Sir Robert Bruce Lockhart, director of British psychological warfare during much of the war, was able to consult with the Foreign Minister at almost any time, as well as with old friends in the Ministry.[9] By way of contrast, President Roosevelt never seemed to be fully aware of what the Office of War Information was doing, and Secretary of State Hull ignored it.[10]

The public press and radio provide another vital link between policy and information officials. During World War II, since other channels furnished insufficient policy guidance, American communication personnel tended to rely in large part on reports of speeches by national leaders and on columnists with good access to decision-makers to sup-

* Commenting on the difficulties that information officials had in keeping informed about U.S. policy during the early postwar period, Charles A. H. Thomson observes: "The main objective has been current correctness [in output], with only a hope of using information to prepare the way for future action." (*Overseas Information Service of the United States Government* [Washington, D.C.: Brookings Institution, 1948], p. 335.)

ply them with details they needed to plan information programs. Formal channels now provide American communication agencies with more adequate information about national policy than was the case in the days of the OWI, but commercial news media remain an important auxiliary source.

Gauging the Potentialities of Available Media

National policy furnishes only one coordinate for the formulation of information and cultural policy. The other coordinate is provided by the capabilities of the instruments at the disposal of the communicator and the characteristics of the audiences he wishes to address. Communication policy should be a synthesis based both on national goals and on an estimate of what is possible to accomplish by disseminating ideas. An imbalance in either direction may make communications ineffective or counterproductive. At the outset of World War II, for instance, Allied propagandists called on the Germans to overthrow Hitler and end the war. This exhortation was in accord with the national policies of the Allies, but mere words were obviously insufficient to bring about the desired action. Later in the war, it was within the power of British and American spokesmen to spark revolts, or at least sabotage, in almost any of the German-occupied territories, but Allied policy restrained the propagandists when premature revolts would merely have led to the extermination of people with whom the Allies hoped to cooperate later on.

In formulating his plans, then, the communicator can take two approaches. He can consider each specific aim of national policy and ask whether, through the use of instruments at his disposal, he can help achieve it. Or, he can first ask what politically significant effects are within his power to achieve and then inquire whether these would advance national policy. In practice, an approach is usually made from both ends, with planning personnel at national capitals giving emphasis to deduction from national policy, and personnel in the field giving attention to what might be accomplished locally through the use of communications.

Whichever approach is used, an enormous amount of information about audiences is required. Various attempts have been made to list categories of data that are useful in planning and executing communication programs, but no such effort has been completely successful. The experience of several leading researchers at the Voice of America illustrates the problem. They started out one day to inventory all the kinds of data that were relevant to international communications research. The list became longer and longer, and finally one of them exclaimed: "Do you realize that we have branched out into practically the whole sphere of human knowledge?" [11]

In spite of the difficulty of defining in advance exactly what information will be required about each audience, the most relevant categories can be described in general terms:

1. *The power and influence structure of the society in question.* Who makes the important decisions? Where are the centers of political influence located, and how do they work? Which individuals or groups are likely to be of increasing significance in the future, and which ones of decreasing significance?

2. *Relevant political interests and attitudes among those who are politically significant.* Once the groups that are politically important, or are likely to become important, have been identified, information about the interests and attitudes of leaders and members of these groups is desirable. What subjects are in the focus of their attention, and what attitudes are prevalent? How intensely are these attitudes held? What utility have they for those who hold them? How were they developed? Answers to these (frequently complex) questions help planners to decide which attitudes might be reinforced or activated, whether new attitudes might be encouraged, and whether it is possible to modify existing attitudes.

3. *The ways information is used by potential audiences.* Ideally, the planner would like to know what functions a broad range of ideas have, or might have, for all the politically significant individuals or organizations in the society he is studying. What is the existing level of information on specific topics? Where does this information come from? What additional information is desired or could be used? How will people use the information that the communicator is able to provide them? What actions will it enable them to take?

Even this brief outline indicates the difficulty of knowing enough about an audience to make realistic planning possible. The area of inquiry is greatly narrowed, however, when political objectives are specified precisely. Careful definition of goals focuses attention on certain groups, attitudes, and actions, and rules others out. If a propagandist's primary task is to stimulate trade, he can concentrate on gathering data on the economic behavior of the relevant groups; if his task is to encourage support for an alliance, he will seek to become acquainted with official and unofficial groups concerned with foreign policy; and so on. The Swiss National Tourist Office in the United States, for instance, since its interests are clearly defined, is able to focus its attention on travel bureaus and certain other key organizations.[12] If it had to spread its efforts over a wider range of American audiences it might not be able to become sufficiently acquainted with any of them.

Similarly, psychological-warfare staffs that are charged with influencing an enemy's will to fight have been advised to identify and study those groups that are most essential to the opposing nation's war effort.[13] Not everybody in a nation at war is really fighting: it is the political leaders, the military leaders, the armed forces, and the labor force that are most critical. Furthermore, each one of these groups has different interests, and consequently can make use of different kinds of information. Thus, the more clearly one can identify those whose behavior is relevant to a specific policy, the more likely it is that one will be able to determine whether, or how much, they can be influenced by the available instruments of communication.

While the task of learning enough about an audience to make a reasonably good prediction about the way it will use information may seem formidable, most people do this quite successfully and almost instinctively in their personal relations. One role of audience research in international communication programs is to give the communicator something of the same insight into the behavior of individuals and groups abroad that he enjoys with respect to people with whom he interacts in his home environment.

Taking Foreign Reactions to Policy into Account

"Should the psychological warriors wear spurs?" asked Walter Lippmann rhetorically several years ago. He went on to observe that many people favored this because otherwise how could the warriors keep their feet from sliding off the mantelpiece![14]

This testy observation by the dean of American foreign-policy columnists, and even more disparaging remarks by less urbane commentators, reflect a tension that not infrequently arises between those concerned with the content of foreign policy and those concerned with communication. The policy-makers feel that communication personnel are prone to meddle in matters that do not concern them and about which they are ignorant, while the latter are convinced that they have an essential contribution to make to policy formulation.

One reason communicators feel that they have something important to contribute to policy-planning discussions is that their work forces them to develop an awareness of the effects that policies or actions are likely to have on various audiences that are exposed to them or hear about them. Those who conduct information or cultural programs usually come in contact with foreign groups with which the diplomat is not equally familiar, and accumulate a great deal of information about these groups—their role in the larger society, their reaction to previous events, and so on. This information not only is useful in planning, implementing, and evaluating a communication program, but can also be used in policy-making. An action or policy nearly always has the effect of imparting ideas (unless it is kept completely secret), and those who are primarily concerned with communications can often be helpful in predicting what the impact of these ideas will be. The U.S. satellite program was delayed several years because the psychological effects of allowing the Soviets to be first in this field were not taken into account in policy discussions on the subject.[15]

Furthermore, since his attention is focused on his audience, the communicator is aware that what his government (or other sponsoring organization) does is more likely to influence attitudes and behavior than even the most skillful propaganda. If his principal pursues a policy that is unpopular with an audience there is often little that the communicator can do to prevent negative reactions. As American observers have frequently noted, what the Secretary of State says to the press is usually much more important than what he says to U.S.I.A. The point of view of the propagandist might therefore be defined as: "Before you complicate my life by antagonizing my audience, at least give me my day in court."

In the commercial world, and to some extent in American domestic politics, it has become a widely accepted principle that probable audience or customer reactions should be taken into account during the process of policy formulation. Market research is used by manufacturers to determine what sort of product the public is most likely to buy. Public-relations advisers often make suggestions about policy as well as publicity. For instance, when California chain stores hired a public-relations firm to help them defeat proposed state legislation that would have adversely affected their interests, one of the first things the firm suggested was that the chain raise the pay of its employees.[16] Political campaigns and platforms have increasingly been shaped by the findings of public-opinion researchers. In all these cases, study of the audience by those concerned with popular reactions has contributed heavily to policy-making, and it is frequently reasoned that international communication personnel should make a similar input to foreign policy.

A related point is that communicators are frequently called upon to explain or justify a policy, especially when something goes wrong. If they participate in the planning process, they are much more likely to be able to give a satisfactory explanation than if they are called in at the last minute, or after the fact. In the case of the flights of U-2 aircraft over the Soviet Union, for instance, U.S. information personnel were not informed at all until one of the planes was shot down. As a result, a number of conflicting statements were made, and the United States damaged its own credibility. This incident could probably have been handled more satisfactorily if the public-relations problems of a misadventure had been faced during the planning process.

Even when a policy is bound to be unpopular with some audiences, advance planning can sometimes minimize negative effects. In one such instance a U.S. chief of mission abroad was faced with the prospect that an American decision, when it became known, would cause widespread dissatisfaction in the country where he was stationed. Indeed, it was expected that there might be hostile demonstrations, and that cooperation with the United States in military and economic matters might be prejudiced. Local U.S.I.A. staff members therefore prepared a comprehensive statement describing the exhaustive consideration that had gone into the decision and giving a full account of the arguments pro and con. They then compiled a list of several thousand persons in the country concerned who were believed to be the most important political-opinion leaders and mailed the statement to these persons, along with a letter from the chief of mission admitting that the policy would be unpopular and asking for an understanding attitude. On the following day a public announcement of the decision was released to the local press and radio.[17]

After the announcement, not only were there no mass protests or disorders but the United States received plaudits for having faced a very difficult situation squarely. Exactly how much credit for this should be given to the information program cannot, of course, be established precisely, but those concerned felt that the combination of personal letters and releases to the mass media had been largely responsible for the lack of unfavorable reaction.

Another reason why information officials feel that they should participate in policy-making is that they can often be of assistance in formulating and timing the announcement of a policy. Unless the policy is stated in such a way that its significance can be easily understood, and unless careful preparations have been made for releasing news about it, much of the force of the policy itself may be lost. For instance, the first news release announcing the Alliance for Progress, in July 1960, was a vague and rambling statement that gave little hint of the importance of the policy. No dollar figure was mentioned, so that there was no way of knowing whether this represented a major effort or a gesture. Latin American countries had not been consulted in advance, and their leaders tended to be confused or even hostile when asked by newsmen for comments.[18] Similarly, announcement of the Marshall Plan in 1947 was blanketed by two major Presidential statements made on the same day, and material supporting the plan was issued as a document of 150 pages just as Congress was recessing for Christmas and press wires were already loaded with dispatches about new legislation.[19]

President Eisenhower's Atoms-for-Peace plan was handled better. News about the plan was released only after full staff discussions in which information officials were included. The first public announcement was made by the President at a major forum—the United Nations General Assembly. His statement was couched in language that was easily understood, and the plan had already been discussed with the leaders of England and France. The U. S. Information Agency was prepared in advance to make the President's words known to audiences around the world.

Many nations and organizations have become aware of the contribution that communication personnel can make to policy, even though they don't always practice what they preach. In large industries it has been found that the public-relations office is most effective if it acts directly as adviser to top management.[20] That is, it is not considered one of the functional divisions of the industrial structure, but rather as an advisory service that can assist the executive in judgments affecting all functional subdivisions. A somewhat similar arrangement prevails in the Soviet Union, where information and cultural policy originates along with other forms of policy at the very highest level.

The United States, and democratic nations in general, have been somewhat less successful in taking the psychological impact of policy into account, in part because the responsibility for ensuring that this is done has rarely been clearly fixed. The specialized staffs entrusted with communications have been treated as functional units on a level with—or a notch below—the staffs responsible for economic, military, diplomatic, and other branches of policy. They have therefore not been in as good a position to help mold decisions that could be expected to influence the thinking of foreign publics. Other policy-forming staffs, jealous of their prerogatives, have been reluctant to solicit the advice of communication personnel. Various coordinating committees and other mechanisms for injecting the psychological dimension into policy considerations have been experimented with, but without outstanding success. Some diplomatic personnel of the old school have resolutely denied that a psychological dimension exists. When the Soviets launched their first satellite, a high American official remarked that this was simply a stunt with little political significance.[21]

By and large, however, those concerned with foreign policy today agree that it is necessary to take probable foreign reactions into account when deciding what should be done and what national leaders should say. The principal questions still at issue are two: How much weight should be ascribed to these foreign reactions, and who should have the task of introducing them into the policy-formulation process?

An answer to the question with regard to the weight that should be given to reactions in other countries is largely a matter of judgment. Some diplomatists, while agreeing in principle that foreign public opinion is important, feel that a nation should do what is "right," regardless of the probable foreign response. Other officials believe that expected psychological reactions should be weighed in the same way that economic, military, and other factors are taken into account when foreign policy is being determined. This does not mean that governmental actions and statements should be decided upon purely in the light of their advisability from a public relations viewpoint, but merely that this is an essential component in policy-making and should receive consideration.

Even though this second view is widely held, the question of whose responsibility it is to gauge probable foreign reactions and to represent these in policy discussions is not settled. One approach holds that the communication specialist is best equipped for the task. According to this way of thinking, the principal personnel of any government information agency wear two hats: they are in charge of communication operations, and they serve as policy advisers to their government. A White House memorandum defining the responsibility of the U. S. Information Agency in 1963 took substantially this position.*

The other approach is that taking account of foreign opinion is a normal part of the work of the policy-maker, and that there is no reason for another specialist to mix into the process of determining what action should be taken. If communication personnel were to familiarize themselves with the complexities of each foreign-policy question so thoroughly that their advice would be valuable, this would amount to a serious duplication of function—one would have, in effect, two foreign offices instead of one. Instead, all personnel concerned with foreign policy should be trained to evaluate foreign public opinion and the effects of communications.

There probably is no single optimum solution to this problem in a democracy, especially since both policy-making and communication functions are likely to be decentralized. The most that can be expected is a gradual broadening of view and increase in competence on the part of both policy and communication staffs and a more fruitful dialogue between them. Reshuffling of organization charts may lead to better mechanisms for this exchange, but cannot be counted on to improve its quality.

Directives and Guidances

In a large bureaucratic structure extending from a national capital to points all over the world, there are a great many different individuals and staffs who have some part in carrying out information and cultural policy. Those who man international broadcasting facilities, prepare news and feature material for the press, operate libraries and cultural centers, or arrange exchanges of persons all have to know what the policy is, or at least must be familiar with that part of it that applies to their activities. A number of techniques have been worked out to ensure that this is the case.

One of the principal means of guiding the activities of those engaged in communication operations is through written or verbal periodic in-

* This memorandum states that the mission of U.S.I.A. includes: "advising the President, his representatives abroad, and the various departments and agencies on the implications of foreign opinion for present and contemplated United States policies. . . ." ("U.S.I.A. Mission Redefined by President Kennedy," *Department of State Newsletter*, October 1963, p. 9.)

structions. Of the major nations conducting information and cultural programs, the United States probably relies most heavily on formal papers to instruct operating personnel. These include "country plans," long-term directives, and short-term guidances. They are supplemented by direct personal contacts between policy officials and operators. British information services rely more heavily on informal contacts and less on written directives. The Soviets appear to make extensive use of the practice of presenting local propagandists with "model" treatments that they are to follow. The most important of these are the *Pravda* editorials that are given world-wide circulation by Radio Moscow.

Periodic instructions to operating personnel are often on three levels of specificity. They outline general tasks that should be accomplished in the furtherance of foreign-policy goals, mention specific objectives that should be pursued through the information media, and prescribe particular ideas that should be stressed in output. For instance, if a general task is to assist a given country in its economic development, one subordinate objective might be to promote better farming methods, and the ideas to be presented in the attainment of this objective might be those relating to specific agricultural techniques. It would then be up to the operator to find ways of communicating these ideas to his audience most effectively.

For convenience in giving individual operating personnel the guidance they need, policy instructions are often subdivided on the basis of geographical area, communication medium, or time-period. Country plans and regional plans are prepared to inform officials who are responsible for communications in a particular country or region. Other personnel, who are concerned only with press or radio or films, receive plans and directives that are drawn up to apply specifically to these media. Guidances may cover varying time ranges: some deal with day-to-day treatment of events by press or radio, while others are concerned with long-range cultural policy. A single policy paper may, of course, combine two or more approaches.

Policy instructions also vary according to the specificity of the actions they prescribe for operating personnel. In some cases they may outline a very general course and leave day-to-day decisions in the hands of those responsible for the conduct of operations. This is usually the case with regard to libraries and exchange of persons. When "fast" media such as press and radio are concerned, day-to-day or even hour-by-hour guidances may suggest how individual news items are to be handled.

If national policy is poorly defined, or if those in charge of an information program do not know what it is, directives cannot be specific, and operators are hampered in their work. This situation was encountered frequently by the U. S. Office of War Information in World War II, when the OWI "basic central directive" often had to counsel information personnel to avoid certain subjects or to deal in generalities until policy could be more clearly defined. For instance, during the period when the French Government was installed at Vichy, we find passages such as the following in the OWI "basic central directive":

> Until we receive new instructions from the State Department, we should ignore both Vichy and the Free French in our broadcasts as much as possible. We should neither praise Vichy for resistance nor blame Vichy for weakness; in fact, we should not even let the French listener realize that we are aware of any special problem in the relations of Vichy with the Germans on the one hand and ourselves on the other.

Or again:

> To overcome our lack of a clear political attitude toward the problems of Europe and Asia: Continue to use all available statements by United Nations' leaders which indicate that such an attitude is in the making, and emphasize particularly such actions as demonstrate that we mean what we say. Give the greatest possible encouragement to all liberal anti-Fascist, anti-Nazi and anti-Japanese militarist movements, and identify our interests with theirs to the extent permitted by present policy.[22]

Communication of policy to operating personnel is rarely perfect. Indeed, in a large organization tension often develops between those who are responsible for drawing up plans and directives and those who are charged with carrying them out. One reason for this is that the plan writers usually are closer to national policy requirements, while the media operators tend to focus their attention more on audiences. Immediately following World War II, for instance, Allied directive-writers kept emphasizing that collective guilt should be stressed in communications to Germany. Allied press and radio personnel showed little enthusiasm for this policy, pointing out that Germans were likely to put down the newspaper or turn off the radio as soon as the subject of collective guilt was broached. Another cause of tension is time lag. One of England's leading propagandists during World War II observed caustically that directives were either so general as to be valueless or so detailed that they were invalidated by events before they could reach the operators.[23]

Furthermore, policy instructions can never anticipate all the contingencies that will arise. The success of any international communication program depends heavily on the knowledge, sensitivity, and good judgment of operating personnel throughout the world. Their ability to interpret directives wisely in the light of their own nation's interests and the interests of their audiences will determine in large measure the degree to which communications are able to advance national policy.

Coordination

Within most governments there are several agencies that communicate with foreign audiences, either directly or indirectly. It therefore not infrequently happens that two spokesmen for the same government will make inconsistent statements, or that the actions of one agency will conflict with the statements of another. Some mechanism for government-wide coordination is thus necessary.

Coordination problems have never ceased to cause furrows in the brows of those concerned with the foreign information and cultural programs of the United States. These problems are especially difficult to solve when they are rooted in substantive policy differences. An outstanding example came following World War II, when President Truman and Secretary of Commerce Henry Wallace differed publicly on the course to be followed in the face of Soviet expansionism. Military leaders have on occasion made speeches that conflicted with State Department pronouncements. In 1962 differences between military officers and civilian authorities led to a Senatorial inquiry to find whether the White House was "muzzling" the Pentagon. Serious differences of opinion on policy matters between Congressmen and Senators on the one hand and the Executive on the other occur frequently and noticeably.

Even when there are no substantive policy differences, and information output alone is concerned, coordination is difficult enough. During the Korean War, for instance, the Voice of America (then operated by the State Department) and the Voice of the U.N. Command in Korea (operated by the U. S. Army) sometimes showed remarkable inconsistency in their handling of important news. The entry of the Chinese Communists into the war was reported by the Voice of America on

November 2, 1950, but the Voice of the U.N. Command did not explicitly mention Chinese Communist intervention until November 12. This divergence was due in part to the fact that the two radios had no established mechanism for keeping in touch with each other, except through liaison between the Army and the State Department in Washington.[24]

In order to achieve harmony among the ideas expressed by two or more spokesmen, it is necessary that coordination be achieved at three levels. There should be agreement on substantive policies, the communication policies of the agencies concerned should not conflict, and their day-to-day output should be basically consistent. If coordination is thorough, the activities of various agencies engaged in international communication will not only be harmonious, but will be mutually reinforcing or complementary. This ideal situation is difficult to achieve in a governmental structure such as that of the United States. As one expert in political communication has observed, "a single propaganda agency with authority to coordinate government propaganda is too powerful. If there is not this coordination, it is ineffective." [25]

Closely related to coordination is the necessity of taking account of "eavesdropping audiences." Since ideas directed toward one audience are likely to reach others as well, communications have to be scrutinized from the point of view of the effect they may have on third parties. The United States has frequently experienced difficulties in that statements intended primarily for NATO allies have caused unfavorable repercussions in new nations, and vice versa. Thus, when former Secretary of State Dulles and the Portuguese Foreign Minister signed a joint communiqué referring to Goa as a Portuguese province, it stirred up a storm in India. Similarly, statements made by the leaders of emerging countries to placate leftist or neutralist forces at home have frequently returned to plague them in their relations with the United States and Western Europe.

The necessity for taking unintended audiences into account is constantly increasing, as improved communication facilities make it possible for reports to be circulated quickly to almost any place in the world. Furthermore, since improvement in technical facilities has been accompanied by a growth in the propaganda activities of most nations, the probability has increased that statements intended for one audience will be picked up by unfriendly sources and relayed to those audiences whose reactions are most likely to be adverse.

In governments and large organizations engaged in international communication, efforts are usually made to take unintended audiences into account by circulating plans and policy papers among subdivisions concerned with different parts of the world, and amending these documents when appropriate. This does not, however, eliminate the need for sensitivity on the part of all those engaged in framing the actual output as well.

Reaching the Audience

Communication policy is able to tell an operator (who in some cases plays a role in the formation of this policy) what ideas he is to transmit and, in general, to whom. Sometimes the policy will also make clear which medium is to be used. The operator then faces the problem of how to deliver these ideas so that they will be most likely to achieve the desired effect.

This leads him to a number of rather specialized questions. How can he secure the attention of his audience? What is the best way of expressing the ideas? Are there conflicting events or communications he should take into account? Answers to these questions require a body of knowledge similar to that required in the formation of communication policy, but on a more detailed level: knowledge about the capacities of available media, about the audience, about semantics, and about local circumstances that are likely to hinder or to favor the policies in question.

The problem of securing attention for an idea differs with each society and with each audience in a society. In some areas the leaders are the easiest to reach, since they are among the few who have access to the mass media; in other cases the more important citizens are so deluged with communications that they restrict themselves to a few key sources. In trying to secure the attention of certain people, therefore, the communicator usually tries to find out as much as he can about the channels of information to which they give attention and the subjects in which they are interested.

Sometimes these questions can be answered with considerable precision. An American advertiser who wishes to sell something to middle-income women who shop in supermarkets knows he should buy space in Magazine X, but if the product is principally of interest to plumbers, he will use Trade Journal Y. For a few dollars per thousand names, those engaged in direct-mail selling can even buy lists of American executives with tax-free expense accounts. Ordinarily, however, such detailed information about audiences is not readily available, and the communicator has to compile it through research and observation.

In theory, it would be possible to dispense with the difficult tasks of channel and interest analysis if one could reach a whole population with a message. Then, the interested audience would select itself out of the mass of those exposed. Sometimes this can be done, as in the United States when the President makes an important statement that is carried by several media and is extensively discussed. Blanket coverage can be achieved only rarely, however, and on a limited range of subjects. To be sure of securing adequate sustained attention by a relevant audience, it appears to be indispensable to make an analysis of communication habits and interests.

Problems of Presentation

American soldiers during World War II frequently chuckled when they read enemy leaflets that were directed to them. Sometimes the chuckle was caused by poor English usage: either the messages were too formal and stilted, or the opposing propagandists tried unsuccessfully to make use of G.I. slang. On other occasions the messages looked or sounded strange because their format was unfamiliar or the type face had a foreign appearance.

We may be sure that Axis troops also had occasion to be amused when they read American leaflets or heard American broadcasts. Indeed, Allied psychological-warfare personnel in Europe were instructed to be on the lookout for "recent German army lingo," so that their communications would sound natural and authoritative to the German Landser, rather than corresponding more to the taste of the Kaiser's Imperial Army. Such vital words as *Spiess* for top sergeant and *Tross* for rear echelon did not appear in German dictionaries. British specialists succeeded in finding a printer who had made a lifelong study of German typography and was able to produce publications that looked completely natural to readers in Germany.[26]

Yet there were also times when communication personnel on both sides *intentionally* made mistakes. One of the British Broadcasting Corporation's principal spokesmen to Germany, Lindley Fraser, was regarded as particularly reliable by German listeners partly because he spoke with a slight British accent. This, in effect, was his legitimation to speak on behalf of England. Allied personnel whose German was perfect sometimes found it necessary to introduce grammatical errors to remind their audiences that they were speaking for the Allies.

As these examples suggest, there are no firm rules for presentation of communications so as to achieve the greatest effectiveness with all audiences. Even such simple maxims as "state your ideas clearly" or "don't have too many ideas in a single message" may prove misleading. There are numerous cultures and subcultures where unduly clear presentation may be a hindrance to effective communication, or where an audience may be insulted by a direct approach or by a message that seems to be suited to a person of less sophistication. A Japanese executive once observed that a great deal of preliminary social contact with foreign businessmen was necessary before concluding an agreement because without this neither party would know whether to say what he meant or whether the other party meant what he said.[27] The difficulties of translation from one language to another are, of course, a constant problem.

Techniques of presentation that will help achieve the aims of any given program must therefore be worked out separately for each audience and will vary according to the effects that are desired. The communicator usually wants his message to be believed and understood, but even here there are exceptions. The transmission of gibberish has its uses on occasion, as for instance when alleged coded instructions were beamed to nonexistent underground organizations by Allied radio stations during World War II.[28]

There are several related methods of ensuring that messages are presented so as to convey the desired meaning. The simplest of these is to find a representative member of the audience you wish to address, or a person who has made it his business to obtain a thorough understanding of that audience, explain to him the idea to be transmitted, and then get him to compose the communication. This technique was used by both sides in World War II and in the Korean War.[29] Essentially the same procedure is used by foreign governments that hire American advertising or public-relations firms to help them promote tourist travel, private investment, or political objectives.

Another method of ensuring adequate presentation is to test the message to be transmitted on a group that is representative of the larger audience to be reached later. This approach is used constantly by advertising firms and other large-scale communicators in the United States and is an important step in the preparation of public-opinion polls. The

Lazarsfeld-Stanton program analyzer for radio broadcasts was a pioneering application of this technique and has given rise to many variants.[30] During World War II, the Allies formed groups of prisoners of war to pretest messages designed for enemy soldiers.* More recently, groups of persons formerly resident behind the iron curtain have been formed to pretest themes and messages for possible dissemination in Soviet-controlled areas.[31]

Nevertheless, time, expense, and technical difficulties usually make it impossible to pretest more than a small proportion of the messages used in any large program, and it is thus always necessary for the communicator to familiarize himself to the greatest extent possible with the political and cultural factors that are likely to affect the reaction of his audience to various ideas and the way they are presented. Many of these factors have been studied and assembled in central files in universities and elsewhere.[32] In addition, periodic efforts have been made to ascertain the reactions of audiences throughout the world to key words and symbols.†

The range of research and experience that communicators can draw on in framing material for presentation to foreign audiences is enormous. For instance, studies of election campaigns frequently disclose a "political vocabulary" characteristic of a given nation. A French researcher found that the election of 1956 was characterized by "words of the left" ("capitalism," "people," "reaction," "workers"), "words of the center" ("democracy," "equality," "justice"), and "words of the right"

* One story that circulated during the war, possibly apochryphal, was that early in 1942 only one Japanese prisoner of war was in American hands in the Pacific. Unaware of this, authorities in Washington frequently sent propaganda materials to psychological-warfare personnel in Hawaii, asking for a pretest. The materials would thereupon be shown to the lone Japanese, and on the basis of his opinion word would go back to Washington: "The Japanese reaction to this is . . ."

† Edward W. Barrett reports that when he was Assistant Secretary of State for Public Affairs, he prepared a list of words expressing positive concepts ("peace," "liberty," "independence," etc.) and sent them to U. S. Public Affairs officers throughout the world with the request that each rank the words according to their propaganda effectiveness in his area. No single word scored highest in all areas. "Truth" scored high in Europe but low in the Far East. "Progress" was highest in Africa and the Near East, while Europe was less enthusiastic. "Independence," "freedom," and "education" were relatively popular everywhere. (*Truth Is Our Weapon* [New York: Funk and Wagnalls, 1953], pp. 144ff.) A great many cross-cultural value studies have been reported in social-science journals. Most of these have focused on one, or a few, areas, and have been based on ratings by personnel native to the areas in question.

("civilization," "nation," "stability").[33] Economic-aid personnel have struggled with the problem of adapting texts and other materials to local conditions. In Arab countries it has been found, for example, that boy-girl relationships mentioned in texts must be interpreted as brother-sister relationships. Advertisers have learned to avoid using sex appeal to sell products in Pakistan, and to emphasize logic in Scandinavia.[34] One could continue almost indefinitely. Nevertheless, however much prior research and experience is available, it is rarely enough. The communicator is likely to face new problems with each new message.

The enormous body of research done on American audiences can be useful to the specialist in international communications, even though principles of presentation are ordinarily not transferable from audience to audience. Some of this research has been assembled and partially codified, and raises a large number of questions that a communicator should ask himself about other audiences.[35] It also suggests experimental procedures that will answer some of these questions; once an experiment has been done in one culture, it is usually much simpler to replicate it in another.

Research on American society, which discloses a great many subaudiences with varying characteristics, likewise serves as a reminder of the dangers of generalizing about other nations. The tendency to ascribe common characteristics to a whole people just because they speak a common language or live under the same flag is one against which the communicator has to fight constantly. One cure for this tendency is for him to gain some understanding of the diversity within his own nation.

Cultural differences, linguistic peculiarities, and the varying reactions of subaudiences are fascinating matters, and therein lies a danger that occasionally limits the effectiveness of communication programs. It is true that one should use the proper idiom in presenting a message and should take account of the communication habits of the audience to the greatest possible degree. But this should never be allowed to obscure the fact that *what* is said is usually more important than *how* it is said. One can break a great many presentational rules and still be highly successful if the message is of sufficient interest and importance to those who hear it.

Propaganda of the Deed

In November 1940, during the period of the Soviet-Nazi *rapprochement,* Soviet Foreign Minister Molotov traveled to Berlin to confer with Joachim Ribbentrop, chief of the German Foreign Office. The British got wind of this meeting and sent planes to bomb Berlin. As Churchill learned later from Stalin, the planes arrived as the conference started. Ribbentrop thereupon took his Soviet guest down to a luxurious air-raid shelter and suggested that it was now time to decide on a division of the spoils of the war between Germany and Russia. Molotov asked what the British would say to this, and Ribbentrop replied that England was already defeated and was no longer a great power.

"If that is so," Molotov is said to have observed, "why are we in this shelter, and whose are these bombs which fall?"[36]

The tactic of the British in sending planes to Berlin at the time that they did and for the reason they did is an example of using an action, rather than verbal or pictorial symbols, to transmit an idea. This technique of communication is sometimes known as propaganda of the deed. Presumably, the British hoped that the attack would interfere with the German war effort, but their main concern was to show that England was still a force to be reckoned with. The message seems to have been received.

A similar British air attack on Berlin came on January 31, 1943, timed for the precise moment when Reich Marshal Hermann Goering was to begin a broadcast speech in connection with the tenth anniversary observance of the Hitler regime. Since Goering had previously boasted about the strength of Berlin's air defenses, the sounds of bombing and anti-aircraft fire that interfered with his speech (and were carried over a radio hookup to which the Nazis forced millions of people in occupied Europe to listen) had special political significance. This incident provides an example of international coordination as well as of the use of propaganda of the deed. The timing of the attack was suggested to the British Political Warfare Executive by Leo Rosten, then Deputy Director of the U. S. Office of War Information. David Bowes-Lyon, representative of the PWE in Washington, took the idea to London, where he was able to persuade British authorities to give it a try. Subsequent interviews with workers in occupied France disclosed that they had been greatly encouraged by the incident.

Churchill engaged in propaganda of the deed on quite a few occasions during the war, sometimes with success and sometimes without. Perhaps his most notable use of this method of communication was in September 1940, when he concluded an arrangement whereby fifty overage American destroyers were exchanged for a number of British West

Indian bases. Churchill wrote in his memoirs that there was another reason for the exchange, more compelling than either the British need for destroyers or the American need for bases. This was to show that the United States was not truly neutral but was actively on the side of Britain in the war. "Although Hitler could not afford to resent it," Churchill observed with regard to this exchange, "all the world . . . understood the significance of the gesture." [37]

The Nazis and Japanese also made use of military gestures to transmit ideas. In the lightning attack on Denmark and Norway in 1940, the Germans put on a demonstration of military air power over Copenhagen to convince the Danish Government that it would be wise to capitulate. Shelling of the American West Coast by a Japanese submarine on February 23, 1942, just as President Roosevelt finished a fireside chat, was primarily a symbolic action, but it took precedence over the President's speech in most information media: by the expenditure of a few shells the Japanese made the front pages of 42 million newspapers.[38]

Nonmilitary actions for purposes of international communication have also become common. Sports have been used by both the Nazis and the Soviets, and to a lesser extent by the democracies, as a means of conveying political ideas.[39] On occasion, the Soviets have employed symbolic economic measures to indicate that they were interested in assisting other nations. For example, a token shipment of grain arrived in France from Russia just prior to the start of massive Marshall Plan shipments. The largest efforts in the realm of international propaganda of the deed in recent times, however, have been in science, and particularly in space.

Propaganda of the deed often encounters three closely related hazards: imprecision, ambiguity, and misinterpretation. When one seeks to convey an idea through an action or gesture, the danger is often great that some meaning other than the one intended will be perceived by the audience. Those using this form of communication are therefore well advised to define in advance exactly what it is they wish to convey, and to whom, and to be prepared to supplement propaganda of the deed with other communications if the intended idea does not seem to be getting through.

For example, even though the Soviets may have known fairly exactly what ideas they wished to convey when they orbited their first satellite, the action was still interpreted in a variety of ways by different people. Norwegian Gallup Poll interviewers, who asked respondents what meaning they attached to the Soviet achievement, found that three principal interpretations were mentioned. Some Norwegians said they were impressed by Soviet leadership in science. Others saw the event as signifying that wars would now be even more terrible than before. A third group said that they anticipated an improvement in the world-wide standard of living because of new scientific discoveries.[40] Similarly, military demonstrations may be subject to a variety of interpretations: a naval or air visit, for instance, may be seen as a gesture of solidarity and goodwill, or as a veiled threat.

In view of the dangers of ambiguity and misinterpretation, most communication programs that make use of propaganda of the deed take steps to make sure that the "correct" interpretation of an action is specifically stated and publicized. Following the orbiting of the first Soviet satellite, Khrushchev personally formulated one of the implications that the Soviets wished to have attached to it. Some people sought to minimize the achievements of socialist science, he said, and his answer to these people was: "Just look in the sky." He later made frequent references to the performance of Soviet satellites to prove that Russian military rockets could reach any part of the globe and had changed the world balance of power.[41]

Another use of action in connection with communications appears to be similar to propaganda of the deed, but is actually very different in character. An action or event may be used to collect an audience, which is then exposed to the ideas to be communicated, although these ideas may be unrelated or only partially related to the action. This technique is frequently used by public-relations practitioners and advertisers in the commercial world, who draw a crowd with a fashion show or a spaghetti-eating contest and then use the occasion to promote a given product. The travels or meetings of political leaders frequently accomplish the same results on the international scene. The encounters of Hitler and Mussolini at the Brenner Pass before and during World War II could always be counted on to attract attention to their joint pronouncements, and the visit of Khrushchev to the United States in 1960 provided the Soviet Premier with an exceptionally large American audience.

The usefulness of both propaganda of the deed and action as an audience-gathering device underlines the desirability of maintaining close liaison between communicators and policy-makers. Unless the communicator has access to other instruments besides the information media he will be unable to employ either of these tactics.

Propaganda Techniques

Since the time of Aristotle there have been efforts to formulate propaganda techniques, but these have in almost all cases proved to be rules of thumb that are applicable only to certain audiences or to certain situations. The rules of argumentation laid down in Aristotle's "Rhetoric" have not been substantially improved upon, as far as Western European society is concerned, but they are less reliable as a guide for international information programs and may be quite misleading in societies that share a different cultural heritage. Prior to World War II, the Institute for Propaganda Analysis described seven characteristics by which one could recognize propaganda. These included name-calling, the use of glittering generalities, the "plain folks" approach, the bandwagon or "everybody's doing it" approach, and several others.[42] An analysis of Goebbel's diary after World War II gave rise to a set of formulations that covered propaganda planning and coordination as well as presentation of material. Goebbels used the criterion of credibility alone to determine whether propaganda should consist of truth or falsehoods, he resorted to repetition up to the point where maximum learning was achieved, and placed great emphasis on phrases and slogans.[43]

Several efforts have been made to distill techniques from the experience of Allied propagandists during and after World War II. Some of these note, for instance, that the propagandist should keep in mind the varying interpretations that will be placed on a single message by the different audiences that receive it, and that the more a message deals with problems of immediate concern to members of an audience the more likely it is to have an effect. Or the propagandist is advised to try to "get inside the skin" of his audience in order to visualize the effect the incoming message will have on people who receive it. A senior official of U.S.I.A. has derived a series of "ten commandments" from American experience: good propaganda is purposeful, dignified, straightforward, factual, credible, meaningful, locally oriented, tailored to a specific audience, positive, and directive.[44]

One of the most commonly cited rules arising out of the recent experience of the democracies is that the propagandist should always tell the truth; not only is it better morality, but in the long run it is better business.[45] At the same time, it is noted that there are cases when the truth is simply incredible: German soldiers during World War II were unable to believe that American shipyards could build a ship in five days, or that prisoners of war were given eggs for breakfast.[46] Consequently, a wartime manual for psychological warfare counseled: "Half the truth believed is better than the whole truth disbelieved. . . . It is not profitable in practice to bring up matters that meet German resistance head-on." Similarly, Voice of America researchers have found that many women in the Soviet Union cannot be persuaded that frozen foods and other conveniences make it possible for an American housewife to prepare dinner in half an hour: they dismiss such statements as obvious capitalist lies.

Then there are cases where an out-and-out untruth seems to be required: for instance, when military security or espionage is involved, or when a state is about to devalue its currency. Should the propagandist adopt a higher standard of truthfulness than the diplomat or financial spokesman? There is no easy answer to this question. Nevertheless, there is a broad spectrum between the whole truth and a direct lie. Silence or partial truth is usually less damaging than falsehood. In particular, the head of state and the foreign minister of a democracy should never be involved in outright prevarication except in cases of extreme danger to their nation. Whether or not a propagandist for a democracy can always tell the whole truth, he should certainly be a person of integrity, one in whom his audience can have confidence.[47]

Another general principle that was observed by most propagandists on both sides during World War II was: don't become involved in a debate with spokesmen for the other side or you will lose sight of your audience. A closely related maxim was: never answer an opponent's charge directly; you will only give it further currency. Both these rules seem to apply in a large number of cases, but there are also important exceptions. For instance, members of the French underground reported that they longed to hear refutations of the Nazi propaganda with which France was flooded, and since it was unsafe for Frenchmen to speak out in public they relied on the BBC and other Allied radio stations to give them assurance that Nazi arguments were not going unopposed.[48] Similarly, some of the West Berlin radio commentators who discuss conditions in the Soviet Zone of Germany for the benefit of East German listeners have reported that their audiences are eager to hear refutations of Soviet propaganda themes.

A great many other general principles of propaganda strategy could be mentioned: always assume the truth of the proposition you are advancing, never debate it; attack, don't defend; don't arouse expectations that cannot be fulfilled; appeal to the emotions; repeat something often enough and it will be believed. All these maxims have proved to be useful in many cases, although they have been found inapplicable in some.

It would appear that there are no general principles or specific techniques that can safely be applied without exception. Instead, all kinds of techniques—whether they concern rules of debate, devices for attracting an audience, or standards of conduct, have to be tested against the particular audience and situation the communicator faces, the goals he wishes to achieve, and the media at his disposal. What are usually regarded as propaganda techniques are actually rules of thumb derived from prior experience. As such, they can be useful as sources for ideas and hypotheses, but are rarely algorithms.

Evaluation

Even the best-executed communication programs may not achieve the desired effects. Their goals may be too ambitious and beyond the capabilities of the available instruments, erroneous decisions may have been made during the planning or implementation phases of the programs, or critically important information may not have been available. Communications may inadvertently achieve negative results or positive results that were unanticipated. Any program therefore requires continuous evaluation to determine what effects, if any, have been achieved, and whether these are in accord with national policy.

Evaluation can be used in several ways. It may make possible the modification of a program in midstream so as to achieve better comprehension or acceptance: ideas that are not understood can be rephrased, and ideas that are resented can be modified. Evaluation may also help to improve planning for future activities. For instance, participants in exchange-of-persons programs are frequently asked what aspects of their experience abroad they found most useful, least useful, and so on, in order that the next exchange can be carried through more effectively. Experts on certain areas may be asked to read or listen to material that has been disseminated to these areas, in order to suggest improvements.[49] Evaluation of communication programs may even lead to recommendations affecting the policies on which the communications are based. Some of the Allied psychological-warfare personnel in Europe toward the end of World War II concluded that the "unconditional surrender" policy toward Germany was tending to stiffen German resistance and urged, unsuccessfully, that it be softened. On the other hand, analysts of the Office of War Information played a part in persuading policy-makers that it would be inadvisable to insist that the Emperor of Japan be deposed following the end of fighting in the Pacific.[50]

A very different use of evaluation, which sometimes takes precedence over all the others, is to justify a budget. In order to secure funds, communicators have to convince those who hold the purse strings that they are achieving desirable effects. Members of Congress usually ask U.S.I.A. officials to give examples of their accomplishments, and similar questions are asked of communicators for private organizations, who have to convince donors, trustees, or directors that their activities are effective.

Finally, evaluation programs may contribute to scientific knowledge that has implications far beyond the immediate interests of the communicators. A substantial number of scholarly works draw heavily on studies originally undertaken in part for purposes of propaganda evaluation.[51]

Evaluation is ordinarily not a simple process. It is often difficult to prove satisfactorily whether or not a communication program is achieving the goals prescribed for it, since the goals themselves may not have been defined with sufficient precision, or there may be technical research problems. For instance, if planners limit themselves to saying that they are aiming to present "a full and fair picture of the United States," it is unlikely that an adequate assessment of the achievements of the program can be made. If they go on to state that they wish to promote better understanding of the American economic system among politically active elements in Country A, then it is likely that at least a rough determination of the success or failure of the program will be possible.

A large number of research problems are encountered in evaluation efforts. How are the effects of a specific program to be disentangled from the effects of the total stream of international communications? When effects can be observed or inferred, to what extent are they to be credited to the communication program itself and to what extent to the policies or actions the communicators are talking about? This is the same problem faced by the manufacturer who wonders whether his sales are due mainly to advertising or to the virtues of his product. How is one to evaluate communications when they are only one element of a multifaceted attack on a problem? What is to be done when the audience is not accessible to the researcher, or when funds for adequate evaluation studies are not available?

The difficulties of evaluating performance are illustrated almost every year when officials of the U. S. Information Agency appear before a subcommittee on appropriations of the House of Representatives. The following dialogue is not atypical:[52]

> WITNESS: Also, we like to feel that in the recent election in one neutral country that our output has helped the results of this election. In the previous parliament in this particular country the Communists had forty seats through their front organizations, and in the election just concluded they won only two. . . .
>
> CONGRESSMAN: Do you think the U.S.I.A. had anything to do with that?
>
> WITNESS: Well, the general output; yes, I would say so.
>
> CONGRESSMAN: You would?
>
> WITNESS: Well, the general output . . .
>
> CONGRESSMAN: How would you attribute that to U.S.I.A.?
>
> WITNESS: Our pamphlet output stresses the United States and the free world, its advantages, and our output contains certain anti-Communist materials. This is true of our whole media output, including motion pictures, which reach a great many people in these countries. . . .
>
> CONGRESSMAN: We have been doing the same thing in Cuba, have we not?

In spite of the difficulties standing in the way of evaluation, all propagandists must attempt it—if only on a completely subjective basis—in order to decide whether to continue operations as they are or to try something else.

The most elementary level of evaluation is to determine whether a communication is accessible to its intended audience. If it is not, then there is no point in investigating its effects further. Those who distribute material to the press are always interested in knowing how many publications use their releases, and the total circulation of these publications. In the case of radio it is important to determine the quality of reception. This is relatively simple when broadcasts are beamed to areas that are not closed to outside observers. When broadcasts are directed to points at which it is impossible to check signal reception directly, various indirect methods can be used. For instance, Radio Liberty, a spokesman for non-Communist elements in the Soviet Union, has its engineers make predictions of what reception will be for a number of different areas, some behind the iron curtain and some outside. If the predictions prove to be consistently correct for the areas just outside the target area then one can assume with fair confidence that they are correct within the target area also. This technique can be used even when broadcasts are being jammed, since the degree of jamming effectiveness in any given area can also be predicted. Such technical estimates are, of course, checked and supplemented by reports from travelers and refugees who have recently been in the area at which the broadcasts are aimed, as well as by comments in listener mail.[53]

Evaluation must also establish that people have the means to receive a message directed toward the area where they live. For a newspaper story to reach an audience a sufficient proportion of the population must be literate; for a radio signal to be heard there must be radio receivers. Most large organizations engaging in international communication make periodic checks of literacy statistics and of the numbers, type, and geographical distribution of radio receivers in the areas with which they are concerned. In the case of films, libraries, lectures, exhibitions, and exchange of persons, the approximate number of persons exposed to certain types of communications can usually be established in the course of operational activities.

Even more important is to ascertain whether communications receive the attention of the intended audience and whether they are understood and believed. How many people tune their radios to a given program? How many read the press releases that are reprinted in their local papers? What do they learn from their visits to information centers, or from the films they see? Furthermore, what sort of people give their attention to which media? A communication may enjoy a wide audience and still not fulfill its purposes if this is not the audience that was intended.

It is fairly simple to answer these questions with a high degree of accuracy in most free-world countries if research funds are available. Where systematic surveys cannot be made, either because of lack of funds or because the government of the country in question will not allow them, a variety of other techniques for establishing attention can be employed. Embassy personnel, travelers, refugees, and knowledgeable people of all kinds can be asked to give their impressions, and a fairly accurate composite estimate can sometimes be compiled.

Researchers have worked out a number of ingenious ways to improve the accuracy of information that may be obtained from biased samples in cases where it is impossible to approach a cross-section directly. One of these is the "most like" approach, where respondents (e.g., from among refugees) are selected in such a manner that they will resemble a cross-section of the audience proper. Another is the "qualified judge" approach, where special attention is given to respondents who satisfy certain criteria that establish them as especially competent observers.[54]

Many communication programs are able to obtain additional insight into audience response through the analysis of mail they receive. People who write to a publication or radio station are thereby showing a somewhat higher degree of interest than those who don't. Their letters may contain expressions of approval or condemnation, or other comments, as well as some indication of the type of person who is writing. Sometimes listener or reader mail is deliberately stimulated by prize contests or special appeals, and radio stations broadcasting to audiences behind the iron curtain have occasionally provided their listeners with a number of innocent-sounding addresses in free areas, to which they can write. When Radio Liberty increased its signal power, in 1960, the volume of listener mail reaching it increased sharply.[55]

Critics and students of communication programs are often unsatisfied by all the available indications of attention, interest, belief, or even approval. They reply that this is all very well, but they want to see specific evidence that program objectives are being achieved. What actions have been taken, and what attitudes changed, they ask, as a result of the ideas to which the audience has been exposed.

When questions of this sort are asked, it is small comfort to those engaged in international communication that their opposite numbers on the domestic scene also have difficulty finding satisfactory answers, and that Congress itself is sometimes berated by the press for inability to prove the effectiveness of its activities. In justifying the work of his subcommittee on juvenile delinquency, for example, a Senator noted that approximately 10,000 copies of reports had been distributed and over 6,000 pieces of correspondence handled, and that appearances had been requested in a large number of cities. To which a hard-bitten columnist replied that he would like to know if the subcommittee had turned a single juvenile from a life of crime.[56]

While it is very difficult to trace specific actions or psychological effects to international communication programs, this can be done in some cases, especially when the objectives of the programs are precisely defined. In propaganda operations against military forces, for instance, one objective is to encourage surrenders, and the number of surrenders can sometimes be correlated with the use of leaflets or loudspeaker appeals.[57] Certain other situations permit controlled experiments, as was the case in two Greek cities, where it was found that newspaper advertisements were able significantly to affect the level of information about the U.N. Declaration of Human Rights, although attitudes did not seem to be affected.[58] The number of situations in which it is possible to make quantitative observations about the effects of communications to another country is, however, limited.

Difficulties are particularly great in iron-curtain areas, where some very indirect methods of measuring effectiveness have been experimented with. It has been assumed, for instance, that if a Communist government resorts to jamming or attacking communications from outside the country, then these must be having some effect on attitudes or behavior. If they were having no such effect, according to this line of thinking, they would simply be ignored. Thus, the Voice of America has on occasion kept a count of the number of angry references to itself coming from Moscow, and has interpreted an increase in such references as an indication of increased effectiveness. Radio Liberty has also been gratified by Communist attacks and observes in one of its publications that the Soviet authorities admit the impact of Radio Liberation (the former name for this station) by going all-out after it.[59]

Some spokesmen for the Voice of America and other broadcasting operations do not interpret unfriendly attacks as necessarily indicating effects on attitudes and behavior, and instead prefer the more modest interpretation that the signal is getting through and receiving attention. At the very least, they point out, official attacks are a strong indication that the output is being monitored, and that it thus gets to key government officials.

A very different indication that programs are effective comes from the fact that, in friendly countries, there is often an outcry when they are stopped. Discontinuation of some U.S. information activities in

Australia, South Africa, and several other nations during a budget cutback in 1947 brought widespread expressions of regret, and sometimes indignation, from newspapers, citizens, and government officials in the countries affected. Ten years later, when budget cuts made it necessary to discontinue support for joint Anglo-American television productions in England (60 per cent of the cost was borne by the United States and 40 per cent by the British Broadcasting Corporation), even sectors of the London press that are usually critical of the United States protested the discontinuation, and described the series as "outstanding." Similar outcries were heard from West Germany when a number of "America Houses" were about to be closed in the early 1960's.

From some points of view, evaluation of exchange-of-persons programs is simpler than is the case with other kinds of international communication. Those directly involved are usually accessible and cooperative, and studies are often able to identify a number of the effects that occur as a result of the exchange experience. It is, however, difficult to determine the long-range impact of the programs and effects that involve others than the exchanges themselves—e.g., people in the host communities and the families and friends of the exchanges.

On occasion, it is possible to gain impressions about the effectiveness of communications by examining events that have already taken place and inquiring into the role that information or cultural programs played in these. After World War II, for instance, a broadcaster who had been speaking to Bulgaria over the BBC was able to interview one of his wartime listeners, a former Bulgarian resistance fighter, and reproached him for having cooperated with the Communists. "You're telling me!" exclaimed the Bulgarian. "The first time *I* heard . . . of the desirability that all Bulgarians should join the Resistance was on the BBC in one of *your* broadcasts." [60] Such testimony as this, while unequivocal, is also rare. Ordinarily, communicators must be content with less dramatic indications that they are achieving results.

Even though evaluation has remained an inexact procedure for the most part, one can usually determine whether a program is going in the right direction by adding together research results of varying kinds, and supplementing this mixture with the judgments of informed observers. If the evaluation effort is not made, or is severely limited, prospects for program improvement are poor. In particular, adequate evaluation helps to guard against the danger of consistently setting goals that are beyond the capacity of communications to achieve. It thus contributes to the planning stage, as well as the implementation stage of the communication process.

Research and evaluation also help to make international information and cultural programs into a two-way street. By studying foreign attitudes and reactions to communications, and reporting on these to policymakers, researchers and observers provide a mechanism through which foreign audiences can talk back to those who are seeking to influence them. As a former American Public Affairs officer in India has noted, to open Indian minds to American viewpoints it is first necessary that we open our minds to theirs.[61] In a sense, it can be said that every successful program is the result of a collaborative effort between the communicator and his audience.

IX

Communist International Communication

Communist states have traditionally made use of vigorous international propaganda. When they came to power in Russia, the Bolsheviks immediately turned to the mass media to advance their policies. During peace negotiations with Germany at Brest-Litovsk, Trotsky insisted that news about the conference be broadcast, so as to expose the annexations aspired to by the Central Powers and to incite German workers and soldiers to revolt. World revolutionary propaganda by the Soviets was sporadic during the following decade, although the Comintern used it to intervene in crises such as the general strike in England; but in the 1930's the Communists greatly increased their attention to this instrument, employing a wider range of communication channels.[1] Since then it has occupied an important place in Soviet foreign policy. As Khrushchev phrased it: "The press and radio, literature and art, music, the cinema, and the theater are sharp ideological weapons of our Party. The Party concerns itself to see that these weapons are always in combat readiness and hit the enemy accurately."[2]

As Communists came to power in other states, they assigned a similar role to communications, and, at least until recently, most of these states have accepted a broad measure of policy direction from the Soviet Union in their foreign propaganda activities. In a few cases—notably Yugoslavia, Albania, China, and China's Asian satellites—they have not.

The Relationship of Communications to Policy

The very close relationship in Communist states between communications and other instruments of policy, between what is said and what is done, derives in part from the fact that Communist leaders found information and cultural instruments to be among the few political tools available to them before they came to power. They explored the potentialities of communications thoroughly and developed a body of doctrine regarding their use, devoting endless hours of discussion to what "line" should be taken in addressing both friends and enemies, and how each event should be treated so as to enhance the power of the Party. Indeed, to leave any possible advantage unexploited came to be regarded as a major error.[3] Continued use of the instruments of communication in the domestic and foreign fields after coming to power increased their skillfulness. Many of those who achieved the highest positions of power thus were already expert in the use of ideas as political weapons.

One cannot fail to be impressed by the degree to which Soviet and Communist Chinese leaders take an active part in international information and cultural affairs. Not only do they personally work behind the scenes in setting policy for foreign propaganda activities, but through their public pronouncements they provide guidelines to personnel at lower echelons and take an active part in disseminating ideas to foreign audiences. Speeches and articles of Khrushchev and Mao have constituted a very important part of recent Communist propaganda. Furthermore, they are adept at capturing world headlines by creating news. Soviet achievements in space have frequently been timed to reinforce political moves, disarmament proposals have been advanced as a part of propaganda campaigns, and offers to negotiate have been used to delay Western actions.[4]

Top-level attention to information and cultural matters in Communist states, combined with a totalitarian form of government, makes it relatively easy to adjust communication policy as national policy or the international situation changes. A hard line and a soft line can be alternated, and attention can be switched rapidly from one area of the world to another. Communist China, for instance, sharply increased its exchanges of delegations with Arab countries at the time of the Suez crisis in 1956. These exchanges then slackened, and visiting groups of Arabs were replaced by delegations of Burmese at the time of border negotiations with Burma.[5]

While Communist leaders are skillful in their use of communications, they do not hesitate to flout world opinion when they believe this is to their over-all political advantage. An outstanding example is Soviet military intervention in the Hungarian uprising. Another is the resumption of atmospheric testing in 1961. Indeed, it became known that the Soviets would resume testing only the day before an antinuclear demonstration was scheduled to take place at the Communist-dominated World Youth Festival in Helsinki. Some delegates attempted to demonstrate anyway, but were physically restrained by Party stalwarts. Later that year, Soviet military pressure on Finland dealt a serious blow to Moscow's contention that small, uncommitted nations could trust Moscow to respect their neutrality.[6]

Each major Communist Party throughout the world is organized in such a way as to provide central direction for international communication. Policy control is maintained by the highest Party authorities, but administration of the various media and channels is entrusted in some cases to government agencies, in other cases to Party units, and in still others to organizations that ostensibly report neither to the Party nor to the government. Thus, in the Soviet Union, Tass is officially a government agency, reporting to the Council of Ministers; the Ministry of Culture operates publishing and film enterprises; a committee of the Council of Ministers is responsible for radio and TV broadcasting; the Communist Party supervises the activities of Communist parties and front organizations in non-Communist countries; and the Union of Soviet Societies for Friendship and Cultural Relations With Foreign Countries is ostensibly independent. The Chinese Communist apparatus for external communication is similarly fragmented at the operational level; and a typical satellite Party ordinarily has half a dozen or more departments and sections concerned with such activities. In all cases, however, centralized Party control is maintained.[7]

International Communication Channels and Programs

An international news service has been recognized as an important political tool by the Soviet Union since its earliest days. The principal Soviet instrument for servicing the world press and electronic media today is Tass, which has bureaus and about 300 permanent correspondents in 65 countries. In many areas, the Tass service is given away free. Thus it often is able to place its material in media that cannot afford to subscribe to one of the international commercial agencies.[8]

Tass provides a selective picture of Soviet society and world events to foreign media, just as it does to media in the Soviet Union. It also disseminates manufactured expressions of opinion from outside the Soviet Union. One of its devices is to plant a specially prepared article in a foreign organ, and then quote this back to the Soviet Union or a third country as a viewpoint current in the country where the article was planted. An explanation of how this "farming-out" technique works has been given by a former member of the Soviet Embassy staff in Rangoon. He reported that microfilmed articles prepared in Moscow were received by the Soviet Embassy through intelligence channels, translated into English and Burmese, and inserted in local newspapers by trusted agents. Tass then picked up the stories from Rangoon and sent them back to Moscow (after a check was made to see that the sense of the original Russian had not been distorted by local editors), from where they were redistributed all over the world.[9]

In 1961, a new Soviet press service, Novosti, was launched. In contrast to Tass, which is overtly attached to the government, Novosti was presented as unofficial. Its aims were defined as the "wide dissemination abroad of truthful information about the Soviet Union and informing the Soviet public of the life of the peoples of other countries." In addition to providing background and feature material to the press, it publishes some thirty magazines abroad, including fourteen in languages used in India. Novosti's daily information bulletin, *News from the Soviet Union,* is transmitted by wire to forty countries.[10]

Moscow depends heavily on free-world news media, both to provide material for Tass and to carry stories from the Soviet Union that are provided by Soviet sources. For instance, riots in the Panama Canal Zone during 1959 were covered by Tass in a story taken from *The New York Times*. This was picked up by the Soviet news agency in New York, transmitted to Moscow, rewritten to conform to the Soviet version of anticolonialism, and retransmitted abroad—still credited to the *Times*.[11] When the Soviets were attempting to whip up a war scare in the Middle East in October 1957, *Pravda* and *Izvestia* complained that American newspapers and radio stations, on orders from the State Department, were not giving sufficient attention to Soviet charges that Turkey was about to attack Syria with American support. The most specific complaint was that no American newspaper had carried the full text of a 5,000-word statement on the subject distributed by Tass, although *The New York Times* had carried 3,000 words of verbatim excerpts from the Tass text.[12] This complaint may in itself have been a move to gain more publicity for the Communist charges.

In the past few years there have been signs that Hsin Hua, the Chinese Communist news agency, is attempting to compete with Tass in some parts of the world. It has built up strong bureaus in Southeast Asia and the Middle East, and has established footholds in Africa and

Latin America. As of 1961 it had a staff of forty in Iran (where Tass had a staff of three or four), and it was issuing a free twenty-page daily news bulletin to the press in the United Arab Republic. By 1962 Hsin Hua had 22 foreign bureaus, and offered its clientele a daily radio-teletype service of some 12,000 words in English and 10,000 in Russian.[13]

Communist states have made extensive use of political advertising to insert material into the free-world press. Khrushchev's speech to the World Congress for General Disarmament and Peace in July 1962 was published as a full-page advertisement in such papers as the *New York Herald Tribune, The Manchester Guardian,* and the *Winnipeg Free Press.* The Chinese Communists have bought space in the West German press, and several Communist states have placed political advertising in the press of various African and South Asian countries.

International radio broadcasting by the Communist powers has grown steadily. Toward the end of 1962, the Soviet Union was reported by BBC monitors to be transmitting 1,072 hours a week to overseas audiences (as opposed to 767 hours by the Voice of America); Communist China was broadcasting 732 hours (as compared with 598 by the BBC); and seven Communist nations of Eastern Europe accounted for an average total of 1,222 hours each week. Since much of the American and British short-wave programing is directed to iron-curtain areas, the imbalance in favor of the Communists in the uncommitted nations is even greater than the above figures would suggest. For instance, Communist states (including China, East Germany, and Cuba) broadcast over 500 hours per week to Latin America, in 1963, while Voice of America programs totaled less than 100 hours.[14]

Comparisons of this sort are not always meaningful, however, since one must take into account broadcasting by democracies other than the United States and Great Britain, and also the use of programs from both the democracies and the Communist powers by domestic radio stations in other countries. As of the beginning of 1963, the U. S. Information Agency estimated that total non-Communist international broadcasting was some 7,400 hours per week, as opposed to the Communist total of 3,900 hours. When it comes to providing programs to foreign radio stations, the Voice of America leads the field, placing an average of 14,000 hours a week as of the beginning of 1963.[15] Exact figures on Communist placement are not available, but they do not add up to more than a fraction of this.

Communist broadcasters make use of a wide range of devices to build audience interest, indicate audience size, and provide program content. Radio Prague promised transistor receivers to Africans who could answer questions asked on its programs, and offered North American listeners portable typewriters and other manufactures for writing 50-word essays on what they liked about the Czech broadcasts. A prize contest run by the Sofia radio offered Arab listeners tourist trips to Bulgaria. Many Communist stations mail elaborate brochures to listeners who write for them, and Soviet stations advertise their schedules widely in local papers. In 1956, Radio Moscow asked a number of prominent Americans to record their opinions on how to promote friendship between the United States and the Soviet Union. A few complied, but most did not. Walter Lippmann cabled: "Thanks. Sorry. Not available." [16]

Attempts of Communist states to use television to reach foreign audiences have not been extensive, most of them having only rudimentary TV networks of their own. The principal efforts have been made in border areas, where viewers in non-Communist countries can receive broadcasts directly from the sending stations. East Germany, especially, has tried to attract a West German viewing audience, which was estimated in 1961 to number from 600,000 to 800,000.[17] Television will probably become a more important medium for Communist propaganda in the future, especially now that the Soviet-bloc television organization (Intervision) is linked with the West European network (Eurovision).

In the field of publications, Communist international activities are generally thought to surpass those of the free world. As of 1961, the bloc was publishing about 140 periodicals for distribution in other countries. These ranged from specialized journals to mass-circulation magazines. The number and variety of Communist pamphlets and serial publications for export have grown rapidly in recent years. The Soviet Union alone printed 55 Spanish-language pamphlets in editions of about 275,000 during 1962, and in the previous year it was estimated that more than 100 Sino-Soviet bloc periodicals were circulating in Latin America, including such standard publications as *Pravda, New Times,* and *China Reconstructs.*[18]

Total Communist activity in book publishing is enormous and is growing rapidly.* The Soviet book industry increased the number of

* More recent figures on Soviet publishing (as well as on some other media) can be found in the publications of the Comcom Project of the Center for Inter-

languages on its lists from 16 in 1958 to 34 in 1961, and total book output in non-Soviet languages reached some 40 million copies. In the following year, Soviet book publishing for Latin America increased by over 30 per cent. As of 1960, the Chinese Communists were publishing about 500 titles a year for export to non-Communist countries in editions averaging 20,000 copies per title. North Korea, Czechoslovakia, and other Communist states were also active.[19]

In many countries, Communist materials are published by local firms under contract with Soviet publishers. As of 1960, the Soviets claimed to be publishing some 100 million books in more than 70 foreign countries. In Buenos Aires alone, Spanish editions of 500 titles, in quantities of 10,000 copies each, were scheduled for publication in 1961 at a total cost of about $1 million. This was roughly the equivalent of the total yearly outlay of U.S.I.A. for its world-wide book-translation program at that time.[20] In the United States a number of publishing firms are registered with the Justice Department as agents of foreign Communist principals.

Some of the books exported by the Communists or produced locally under contract are overtly political in character: works of Marx, Lenin, Mao, and other Communist leaders; manuals on how to organize demonstrations and conduct political activities; and volumes attacking the United States and other Western nations. Other titles include "Communist classics" by recent authors, as well as a few classics by older masters. Increases have been noted in texts and in books intended for juveniles. The Soviet textbook production schedule for 1961 called for publication of over thirty texts in English alone, most of these apparently for use in the developing nations. A final category includes books about life and culture in Communist countries, such as *Soviet Music* and *The Bolshoi Ballet*.[21]

For the distribution of foreign-language publications manufactured behind the iron curtain, Communist states rely heavily on direct mail. In February 1962 the U. S. Customs Bureau counted 715,671 pieces of Communist printed matter entering the country at New York. Of this amount, 292,127 pieces were judged to be "substantial pro-Communist or anti-American propaganda." Another 120,605 pieces were found to be

---

national Studies, MIT. The first in this new series was scheduled for publication in the summer of 1965.

technical, scientific, or other "non-propaganda" material. According to U.S.I.A., air-freight charges for Communist publications sent to Uruguay alone each week during 1960 were greater than the Information Agency's total budget for operations in that country.[22]

Some publications are shipped by diplomatic pouch to the embassies of bloc countries for further distribution. When Mexican authorities seized Communist pouch shipments in 1961, they found four tons of Soviet, Cuban, and Communist Chinese propaganda materials destined for Guatemala, Honduras, Costa Rica, and Panama.

During 1961 Communist countries sponsored major exhibitions at seventy international trade fairs and industrial exhibitions throughout the world. Communist China entered forty-three of these; Czechoslovakia was the next most active, participating in forty-two; these were followed by Poland, with twenty-eight, and the U.S.S.R., with twenty-six.[23] Participation of the Soviet Union and other Communist states in such events has increased steadily since World War II, and has been characterized by considerable virtuosity in the use of exhibits to hammer home politically significant ideas.

Two channels of communication that are used extensively by the United States are given much less attention by the Soviet Union and other Communist countries: libraries and information centers, and films. While a few libraries and reading rooms are maintained by the Soviets, particularly in the underdeveloped countries, these are not numerous or large. Soviet libraries in Addis Ababa and Accra, for instance, had book holdings of only 2,000-3,000 as of 1961. The reason for this apparent neglect is probably that the Communist states do not need these outlets to achieve their purposes, since local Communist parties and other organizations under Communist control serve as distributing points for literature and centers for those interested in learning more about Communist countries.

In the case of films, it appears that Communist backwardness is less voluntary. The Soviets and Chinese have both participated vigorously in international film festivals, and have made efforts to stimulate the circulation of their films abroad. These efforts have been only partially successful, probably because they produce few good entertainment features. Even the prize-winning films at international festivals have in many cases been designed to reinforce global propaganda themes.[24] It may be expected, however, that Communist states will give the free world stiff competition in the field of documentaries and instructional films in the future. Some excellent industrial training films made in Czechoslovakia and East Germany have been reported.

If Communist countries are not fully exploiting the potentialities of films, they are doing so when it comes to the exchange of delegations and cultural attractions with other nations. In about 1953, the Soviets apparently decided that they could gain from displaying selected aspects of Soviet life and culture to foreigners, and that it was safe to send a number of carefully chosen Soviet citizens abroad. Other Communist states followed suit. By 1959, the Soviets had concluded some ninety cultural-exchange agreements with foreign countries, including France, Great Britain, and the United States. Although they permitted some visits to the Soviet Union outside the framework of these agreements, they made it clear that the only type of cultural exchange they regarded as satisfactory was that which proceeded through channels approved by the Kremlin. The preferred form of exchange was through "cultural delegations," with carefully planned itineraries and schedules.[25]

No comprehensive figures on exchanges between Communist and non-Communist countries are available, but partial figures give an indication of the orders of magnitude involved. During the first 8 months of 1959, some 1,500 Soviet artists and other cultural leaders traveled to non-Communist foreign countries, and nearly 500 foreigners in the same categories came to the Soviet Union from these countries. Between 1954 and 1958, more than 1,000 Soviet sports delegations visited 38 countries, while about the same number of foreign athletic groups from 46 countries came to Russia. In 1958 alone, Soviet representatives took part in more than 500 international congresses, conferences, and competitions. The Soviets have conducted more exchanges with the industrialized democracies than with the emerging countries, although Moscow has given greater publicity to the latter. From 1954 to 1957, for example, 196 delegations from India visited the Soviet Union, as against 348 from France and 368 from Great Britain.[26]

In the case of China, between 75,000 and 100,000 foreigners came on visits in the 1949-59 period, while more than 400 groups of Chinese traveled abroad to participate in international sports, cultural, and other events. A large proportion of the visitors to China during this period came from Communist-bloc nations, but more were from Japan than any other single country.[27] In 1960 and 1961, Communist China received more than 800 delegations from non-Communist countries, mainly in the Far East, Latin America, and Africa, and sent some 250 in return.[28]

Numbers do not, however, give an adequate picture of the significance of the Soviet and Chinese cultural programs. Delegations to and from the non-Communist world have included a high proportion of leaders in politics, education, science, and the arts. Indeed, few notables in emerging countries have not been invited to visit one or both of the great Communist powers. Although the Communists have not been able to involve such a high proportion of the elite from the industrialized democracies, they have succeeded in attracting influential groups, and have sent an excellent selection of their own leaders and artists in return.

Visits of foreigners to Communist countries are handled by a network of official and ostensibly nonofficial organizations, all of them ultimately under Party control. These organizations maintain a huge apparatus of interpreters, guides, and "welcomers" who are capable of supervising almost every move of almost every visitor in mainland China and the Soviet Union. Several East European Communist countries appear to exercise less supervision. In Russia, Intourist, which had a staff of about 5,000 in 1957, is the principal agency for assisting, as well as observing, foreign visitors. Travelers to the Soviet Union usually find that Intourist guides stick to them like burrs, although there have been many exceptions. The supervision of visitors in Communist China seems to be even closer. A British visitor, eager to have a few minutes by himself, resorted to the device of challenging his guides to a race and then outrunning them. Japanese have reported that to elude their Chinese mentors they have been forced to disappear into crowds or pretend to go shopping.[29]

The most powerful Soviet agency involved in exchanges is the State Committee for Cultural Relations with Foreign Countries, which is attached directly to the U.S.S.R. Council of Ministers.[30] Working closely with the State Committee is the Union of Soviet Societies for Friendship and Cultural Relations with Foreign Countries, which coordinates the activities of 38 societies and associations for friendship and cultural relations with specific foreign countries or areas. The Union is said to derive its funds from "subscriptions from Soviet friendship and cultural relations organizations, publications, economic undertakings, subsidies and donations." It maintains relations with scientific and cultural organizations in 112 countries, conducts exchanges of delegations and individuals, and helps arrange professional meetings, discussions, and interviews for foreign tourists in the U.S.S.R.[31] The Chinese People's Association for Cultural Relations with Foreign Countries seems to occupy an analogous position within China. The "nonofficial" status of these organizations is presumably to facilitate their dealings with private individuals and organizations abroad.

A great many other groups also take an active part in sending and receiving travelers. Professional societies and educational institutions in the Soviet Union are particularly active. The Academy of Sciences, the Union of Soviet Composers, the Union of Soviet Writers, and so on, often play host to visiting delegations and send delegations of their own abroad. The same is true of numerous government departments. It must be assumed, however, that the work of all these bodies is coordinated by the Party.

The Soviet Union and Communist China, and in varying degrees most other Communist states, have made strenuous efforts to shield their own citizens from "contamination" by foreign visitors. The Experiment in International Living discontinued sending groups of American students to the Soviet Union in 1962 because the Soviets were unwilling to allow meaningful contacts with Russian young people.[32] Travelers to Communist countries frequently find it difficult to talk with ordinary citizens unless a guide or interpreter is present. Even in private conversations with foreigners, Soviet and Chinese citizens are often reluctant to express themselves freely, for fear that their remarks might be overheard or that the visitor might reveal what had been said. A Chinese who has spoken with a foreigner can expect a security official to interrogate him later about what went on. One anti-Communist Chinese reported an incident in which a bluff Britisher tried to persuade him to speak frankly. The Chinese, annoyed by the indiscreet approach, responded that he loved the Communist Party and government.[33] Soviet citizens, although sometimes more communicative than the Chinese, are restrained by the Law on Criminal Liability for State Crimes, published on December 26, 1958, according to which "fabrications defaming the Soviet state and social system" can bring exile or lengthy imprisonment.

While foreign visitors are screened from those who are critical of the regime, they are given ample opportunity to converse with the most persuasive advocates of the Communist system. They are also restrained from seeing what the Communist government does not want them to see, and instead are led into "model" prisons, factories, schools, and collective farms. Pro-Communist visitors, and those from emerging countries, are frequently allowed greater latitude than others, but even this is a matter of degree.

The effectiveness of Chinese controls over visitors is illustrated by the fact that few foreigners in China during the "hundred flowers" period and the antirightist campaign that followed were able to learn that anything out of the ordinary was going on. An Australian labor delegation returned with glowing reports about Chinese popular satisfaction, even though some of its members were in one city when serious riots and attacks on the local Communist Party headquarters occurred in another part of town. Some students have maintained that more information about Communist China is available in Hong Kong than on the mainland. Nevertheless, "no screen can be completely impervious," and an expert who is able to see through the stage-managing will be able to increase his understanding by a visit.[34] On the other hand, a naïve or prejudiced foreigner may return with more misinformation than enlightenment. A Senate Internal Security Subcommittee study has suggested that visitors to the Soviet Union should strive for a reasonable balance of homework and footwork.[35]

Two potent instruments for influencing foreign visitors to Communist countries are hospitality and flattery. Delegations and prominent individuals—even some not so prominent—are frequently impressed by the cordiality of their reception and the lavish entertainment given them. By Western standards, the funds allocated for the entertainment of foreigners in Communist countries must be enormous.

Flattery is even more important. Because they control so many aspects of their own societies, Communist authorities can immerse a visitor in an environment prepared especially for him. A writer who feels unappreciated at home may learn that his works have been translated into Russian, Czech, or Chinese, and are "being eagerly read." Cultural delegations may find that festivals or exhibits have been organized to celebrate some cultural achievement in their own countries. Prominent guests are flattered by highly favorable articles about themselves in the Communist press. Travelers of only medium rank are likely to find the doors of the very highest officials open to them.* When President Sukarno of Indonesia visited Peking, he was given a book containing

* Deception may sometimes be involved. Herbert Passin has reported a case in which a Chinese claimed to have had the duty of impersonating a prominent public figure for the benefit of foreign visitors. (*China's Cultural Diplomacy* [New York: Frederick A. Praeger, 1962], p. 9.)

hand-painted color reproductions of his personal art collection that would have cost $200,000 to produce at American prices.[36]

Just as visitors to Communist countries are carefully "managed," bloc authorities attempt to shield their own citizens who travel abroad from infection by unorthodox ideas. At the same time, these travelers are expected to act as apologists, and occasionally as salesmen, for Communism. Both of these objectives are served by very careful selection. Soviet students who have visited the United States under exchange programs have ordinarily been older than the average, and often seem to have been chosen in part for their skill in advocacy; some have stated that they were briefed on how to react to conditions abroad before they left Russia.[37] East European bloc countries appear to be more liberal about allowing citizens who are not "100 per cent" Communists to visit the free world.

In addition to being carefully chosen and briefed, Soviet citizens who travel abroad are subject to strict discipline, enforced sometimes by Soviet embassy officials and sometimes by accompanying Party workers, who "interpret" the environment for the travelers, shield them from intimate contacts with foreigners, and reassure them that what they see has been selected by their hosts. A Soviet writer who visited the United States in 1962 complained that his group had been fenced off from contacts with Americans by the accompanying political official, who was described as "a nice man, but evidently one frightened from birth."[38]

In spite of the selection and control of Communist nationals who travel in the free world, they apparently do take some disturbing ideas back with them. These may have to do with the standard of living, freedom of movement, the variety of publications, or the right to disagree with the authorities. Ordinarily, such ideas are expressed only in private after the traveler returns home, but visitors from Eastern Europe, in particular, have been known to publish relatively objective reports about what they have seen.[39] On the other hand, most Soviet travelers have described their visits to America in terms that support the current Communist line, emphasizing unemployment, crime, and general misery. As a Soviet dancer wrote of Chicago in 1959: "We saw here the hunched backs and the sullen faces of men and they told us much more even than the run-down houses and dirty sidewalks." An American reviewer, commenting on the gloomy distortions in a book by two Soviet visitors to the United States, notes that they seemed to be more interested in feeding their preconceptions than in looking for the truth.[40]

The education of foreign students plays an important role in the international cultural programs of Communist states. As of 1960, some 12,000 students from more then 70 countries were reported by the Soviets to be studying in the Soviet Union. By 1963, according to a Tass dispatch, the number had grown to 29,000. There are more than 1,000 foreign students at Chinese universities, most of them coming from the neighboring Communist states of Asia which, in comparison with China, have less developed educational systems. Substantial numbers of foreign students, especially from the developing countries, have been reported in European satellite countries also. As of 1960, these included 1,166 students from Africa alone.[41]

Moscow's major venture in education for students from emerging countries is the Patrice Lumumba Friendship University. This institution, nominally sponsored by three nongovernmental organizations, was started in 1960 with some 300 students, and planned to expand to a capacity of 3,000-4,000. Scholars at Friendship University are given free tuition, room, and medical care, funds for food and personal needs, a special clothing allowance, and transportation to and from Moscow. As of the end of 1961, most of the 1,500 students in residence were pursuing technical or scientific subjects, but all received intensive Russian-language training, apparently with a heavy dose of ideology mixed in.[42]

Educational programs of Communist states for students from emerging countries have not had smooth sailing. From the beginning, many of the young people have resisted and resented ideological indoctrination, and some have bridled at being asked to join political demonstrations or to take part in "voluntary" labor projects. A Liberian was expelled from the University of Leipzig (East Germany) for refusing to carry a banner in a Communist May Day parade. Incidents of racial discrimination—primarily directed against Africans—have been reported, and a feeling of being watched and hemmed in is apparently quite common. A Nigerian who studied at Friendship University complained that to build a segregated university for Asians, Africans, and Latin Americans was insulting, violated the concept of a university as an institution open to all who wished to learn, and represented an "attempt to insulate the Soviet people from contact with foreigners." [43] In recent years, well over 200 African students are known to have transferred from institutions in Communist countries to West European universities. As of 1963, all 350 African students in Bulgaria allegedly wanted to leave.[44] Indeed, study in one of the bloc countries often seems to give young people from emerging countries a sense of identity with Western values.

Disenchantment with Communism is not limited to students from the new nations. During the first few years of Franco-Soviet educational exchange, most French students were reported to have moved toward the political right after studying in Russia. Members of a group composed primarily of French Communists and sympathizers who studied in the Soviet Union in 1955-56 were said to have emerged as non-Communists, with one exception. The lone dissenter stated that, while he still considered himself a Communist, he did not think there were any real Communists in the Soviet Union.[45]

Such reports as these should not, however, be regarded as proving that Communist states are failing in their attempt to use education as a political instrument. There have been no indications that the Soviets, in particular, are having difficulty in recruiting all the young people from emerging countries that they can take care of. Furthermore, the Communists are likely to become more adept at handling non-Communist students as the years go on.

Communist cultural, educational, and information programs all have their counterparts in the programs of free-world nations. One very important channel that has no free-world counterpart is provided by Communist parties, front groups, and controlled organizations in other nations. Indeed, these parties and groups can be considered the major instrument for international communication at the disposal of the major Communist states.

Membership in Communist parties outside the iron and bamboo curtains is estimated at somewhat over 4 million. The Indonesian and Italian parties, with an estimated 1.9 and 1.3 million members, respectively, account for about three-quarters of this total. France, with about 260,000 members, India with 120,000, Japan with 115,000, Mexico with 50,000, Argentina with 45,000, and Finland with 40,000 account for most of the rest. The Party is suppressed or prevented from operating in 43 countries.[46]

The influence of Communist parties is larger than the number of their members would suggest. The French Communist Party received almost 4 million votes in the elections of 1962, and the Communist Party of India received 11.4 million votes in the same year. In British Guiana, which has no organized Communist Party at all, local Communists have apparently gained control of the largest political party.

Front organizations and other controlled groups are even more widespread than Communist parties. A survey of Communist propaganda activities in 1956 listed the following as the principal international front organizations:[47]

World Peace Council
World Federation of Trade Unions
International Union of Students
World Federation of Democratic Youth
Women's International Democratic Federation
International Association of Democratic Lawyers
World Federation of Scientific Workers
World Federation of Teachers' Unions
International Organization of Journalists
International Broadcasting Organization
International Federation of Resistance Fighters, of Victims and Prisoners of Fascism
Committee for the Promotion of International Trade
World Congress of Doctors

A later survey added several other names to the roster of major front organizations, including the Afro-Asian People's Solidarity Organization.[48]

These organizations have branches throughout the world, especially in the major uncommitted countries. In addition, there are numerous specialized front groups appealing to certain population sectors: professional people, youth, women, businessmen, artists, farmers, and others. A survey in 1961 found fifty-two major front groups in India, thirty-two in Japan, thirteen in Argentina, a "multitude" in Western Europe, and so on. In a slightly different category are the "friendship societies," most of which have direct ties with corresponding societies in one of the Communist countries. These have been organized not only by the Soviet Union and Communist China but also by some of the East European satellites. There is, for instance, a Mexican-Czechoslovak Cultural Exchange in Mexico City, a Colombian Association of Friends of China in Bogotá, and a Nigerian-Soviet Friendship Society with branches in Lagos and five other cities. The Australia-China Society has been called a "holding company" for formal relations between the two countries, in the absence of official recognition of Communist China by Australia.[49]

Controlled organizations, such as labor unions that have been "captured," are ordinarily run by a minority of Communist Party members organized into a "fraction" within the larger group. This fraction, through careful planning and hard work, elects key officers and guides the policy of the organization as a whole. Before important organizational gatherings the fraction meets secretly to assign each person his role, to formulate texts that are to be approved, and to prepare measures for discrediting or neutralizing the opposition. An early manual on the organization of the Communist Party in the United States specified that fractions responsible for carrying out the decisions of higher Party authorities must be formed within all organizations where there are at least three Party members.[50]

Communist parties, front groups, friendship societies, and controlled organizations serve as important channels through which Moscow and Peking can reach audiences in foreign countries. Most of them sponsor one or more publications, conduct innumerable meetings and rallies, and distribute material prepared behind the iron curtain. They also assist in Communist educational exchange programs by facilitating study and travel in bloc nations. In some countries—for example, Mexico and Ghana—students to be sent to Friendship University in Moscow have been selected by pro-Communist trade unions or cultural organizations.

Pro-Communist organizations are able significantly to enlarge the audience for Communist ideas, since through them person-to-person contacts can be established with people who are not already Communists or even inclined toward Communism. An American government official who studied the composition of a world congress of the Communist-led Women's International Democratic Federation concluded that many of the delegates from underdeveloped nations were ladies who if they lived in Scarsdale would be members of the League of Women Voters. Organizational contacts thus help to overcome the self-selection process that operates in the case of mass media, where most people read or listen to opinions with which they already are in substantial agreement.

The trade and aid programs of Communist nations provide a supplementary vehicle for communicating with peoples in other countries. In 1962, the bloc traded with virtually every country in the free world to a total value of over $10 billion—almost $1 billion more than in the previous year. To facilitate these commercial relations, Communist countries made use of trade agreements, high-level government delegations, exhibits, grants, and technical assistance. Trade agreements were in force with about 50 free-world countries, and economic delegations visited at least 25 of the emerging nations of Africa and the Near East. From 1954 to 1962, the bloc extended more than $4.5 billion in economic aid, mostly to emerging countries, with the Soviet Union accounting for two-thirds of this amount. Technical assistance was being given to 28 developing nations in 1961. About 7,000 students received technical training in bloc schools and industries from 1956 to 1961, and the Communist countries furnished more than 8,000 technicians and skilled workers for temporary duty in developing countries, two-thirds of these coming from the Soviet Union. Bloc technicians were active mainly in Guinea, Yemen, the United Arab Republic, Cuba, India, Iraq, and Syria.[51]

Through their aid programs, Communist countries have been active in providing communication facilities and training communication personnel for new nations. East Germany has presented a printing plant to Ghana's Trade Union Congress, and Czechoslovakia has provided technicians for Ghana's government film unit, as well as training for indigenous technicians. The Soviet Union and Czechoslovakia have played an important part in establishing news agencies in Kenya and Tanganyika. Schools for training journalists for emerging nations have been reported in several Communist countries.

Emphasis on Organization

The popular stereotype of Communist international propaganda is that it represents a massive effort to persuade people throughout the world to adopt the Communist ideology. In actuality, the information and cultural programs of Communist states are only secondarily ideological in character. Indeed, persuading a person to adopt the ideology may be downright dangerous, from the point of view of Communist leaders, unless he has already acknowledged the authority of these leaders and been incorporated in an approved organization. Free-floating conversions may lead a person to decide for himself what correct Marxist conduct is, and thus create additional confusion in the Communist camp.[52] A person is usually recruited for a local Party or other controlled organization because he has a grievance against the existing political structure, because he wants to own land, or because he thinks this is the way to get ahead in the world.[53] Only after he is safely aboard is he given systematic ideological indoctrination.

In their efforts to seize and retain power, Communist leaders thus work largely through organized groups, and one of the principal uses to which they put communications is that of helping to form these organizations, to sustain them, and to give them direction. In this they are following Lenin, who saw propaganda as a helping hand to organization. As one authority describes the relationship: "Propaganda only spreads the germs; it is the organization that maintains the epidemic. . . . Organization is to propaganda what the factory is to science." [54]

The importance of using mass communications in building organizations was recognized by Communists in and outside Russia at an early point in their struggle for power. Lenin saw that establishment of a newspaper would provide an excellent nucleus for a political machine. It would enable reporters to collect information of use to the Party, give jobs to otherwise idle supporters, provide a focus for activity, and in general act as a morale builder for those involved in what often seemed like a hopeless cause.[55] As Communist parties were established in other countries, they started publications both to provide internal strength to their organizations and also as a means of recruiting new supporters. Distribution of material received from bloc countries serves an analogous function. Numerous technical publications appear to be designed primarily for use by existing pro-Communist groups—for instance, political organization manuals and books on guerrilla tactics; Cuba has published and distributed in Latin America approximately 1 million copies of books on guerrilla warfare.[56]

Radio also appears to have been used as an organizing tool. Comintern congresses during the 1920's and 1930's passed resolutions calling for the formation of listening groups abroad, although little was done to implement these resolutions until after World War II. As of 1956, Japanese Communists were reported to be forming "listening circles" for broadcasts from Moscow, Peking, and Pyongyang.[57] "Pen friends clubs" have been sponsored by Moscow broadcasters in Africa, and "The Voice of the Soviet Afro-Asian Solidarity Committee" has invited listeners to get in touch with the Committee by writing to 10 Kropotkin Street, Moscow. A great deal of broadcasting time has been devoted to exhorting African workers to organize and to affiliate with "anti-imperialist" trade unions, and broadcasts from East Germany to Iran have attempted to assist the reconstitution of the Tudeh Party.[58]

Soviet educational and exchange-of-persons programs likewise play a part in building organizations and recruiting additional members for already functioning groups. In connection with the founding of Friendship University in Moscow, Premier Khrushchev noted that the task of education was to create national cadres that "will understand correctly the interests of their country." An official of the Institute of International Education who examined the records of 100 African students in Bulgaria concluded that only six could be considered qualified college students.[59] Most of them may have been selected for study in Bulgaria not according to educational criteria, but for the purpose of playing a role in Communist-led organizations on return to their own countries. If this hypothesis is correct, then the fact that some foreign students behind the iron curtain resist political indoctrination does not necessarily represent a net loss for the Communists. Educational programs may be part of a winnowing process: those students who are willing to put up with indoctrination and other unpleasant aspects of life behind the iron curtain are more likely to emerge as reliable tools for the local Communist parties and front organizations in their own countries. Moscow-sponsored exchanges have helped to create personal and organizational links between Soviet artistic, scientific, and academic institutions and their opposite numbers in other countries. Through an intensive program of inviting Japanese business leaders to China, the Communist Chinese have built up what amounts to a pressure group of businessmen in Japan who are active in advocating increased trade between the two countries.[60]

In addition to using communications to organize and sustain controlled or friendly groups in other countries, Communist states have given international broadcasting and publications an important role in guiding and coordinating the world-wide Communist apparatus. This use of the media on an international scale parallels the domestic practice in Communist countries, where Party personnel are kept informed of what they should say through central news services, radio broadcasts, and publications. The *World Marxist Review,* for instance, is a central theoretical clearing house for international Communism. Thus, after the breakdown of the Paris summit conference in 1960, the *Review* provided a specific set of instructions to Communist adherents as to the line they should take. Leaders in each country were required to prepare an adaptation of this line and circulate it to all local Communist Party groups and front organizations.[61] Both Moscow and Peking have made extensive use of short-wave broadcasts in Morse code at dictation speed. These clearly cannot be aimed at mass audiences, and one of their functions appears to be to provide guidance to local Communist cadres or sympathizers, who monitor the broadcasts with pencil in hand in order to determine what to do and say, and what to print in the publications they control.[62]

During international crises, this mechanism for providing guidance is particularly apparent. When the Hungarian uprising occurred in 1956, for instance, the Latin American Communist press at first ignored it or else interpreted it as a result of reforms inspired by the Twentieth Party Congress. As soon as Soviet media provided a firm line, however, the whole Communist press fell into step and denounced the revolt as a "brutal fascist attack" on the Hungarian Government.[63] A comparative study of news treatment by a number of leading world newspapers at the time of Soviet military intervention in Hungary showed that not only did Communist organs in various countries follow the same themes in commenting on the event, but even their basic allocation of space was similar; they clearly had some mechanism for centralized editorial decision-making.[64]

Until recently, at least, the central media of the Soviet Union and Communist China have played a part in guiding Communist activities in satellite countries as well. Following the Twentieth Party Congress, when the rapidly shifting official line was causing confusion in Communist ranks, state and Party officials in Czechoslovakia attempted strenuously to adjust their actions and words to the guidance received through Moscow's *Pravda* and the Soviet radio. The line changed so fast, however, that some Czech teachers, instead of adapting the Soviet materials to local conditions, resorted to giving their students direct translations from *Pravda* and other official Soviet sources, or even assigned these sources in the original. And when the Hungarian revolt of 1956 cut Moscow off from its local radio outlets in Hungary, the Soviets tripled their direct short-wave broadcasts in Hungarian, and Rumania introduced a Hungarian service.[65]

While general guidance is provided by the central organs of the major Communist countries, guidance on specialized questions is communicated through publications serving particular functional groups. *The Democratic Journalist,* for example, the organ of the International Organization of Journalists, helps to give the line on matters affecting journalists in their professional capacity. A large part of its content is devoted to describing the miserable working conditions of free-world newspapermen and restrictions on the freedom of the press in non-

Communist countries. It gives sympathetic attention to the problems of the press in emerging areas of the world, and praises the freedom and good working conditions afforded journalists in bloc countries. The Communist reader of *The Democratic Journalist* is thus informed as to the position he should take on major questions affecting journalism, as well as the Communist line in general, and is armed with arguments and factual material that will assist him in maintaining his position against all comers. It also may help him recruit new members for the International Organization, which as of 1957 claimed to have more than 60,000 journalists in its ranks.[66]

Similar functions are performed by the *Bulletin* of the International Radio Organization; *World Student News,* publication of the International Union of Students; and by the organs of other Communist-led international associations. *World Student News* not only presents the Communist line and material to support it, but sometimes issues very specific instructions. The issue for March 1961, which was devoted entirely to the situation in the Congo, included a box on the front page headed "ACT IMMEDIATELY," calling on all readers to: send cables to the United Nations protesting the U.N. plot against the Congo and the complicity of the Secretary General in this, and demanding the recall of U.N. forces; send deputations to the Belgian diplomatic missions in each country demanding the immediate recall of Belgian troops; organize solidarity rallies in universities, faculties, and schools; organize signature campaigns in solidarity with the Congolese people; and send messages of solidarity to the Central Congolese Government "now headed by Mr. Gizenga in Stanleyville." A later issue (November 1961) dealt with the Berlin situation and issued similar instructions.

Communist international communications thus devote substantial attention to creating, nourishing, and guiding organizations under Communist control. These organizations are the cutting edge of Communist power; information and cultural programs play an important part in making them effective instruments.

Goals of Persuasive Communications

Communist communications also have a number of objectives that involve persuasion. One of the most important of these is to weaken non-Communist political power. Particularly in areas where the organizational base of the Party is still weak, the information media are devoted to undermining trust in the United States (or other nations that stand in the way of Communist expansion), sowing confusion, and discrediting local leaders who cannot be won over. This is done by identifying dissatisfactions, frictions, and contradictions in each society and then using communications to accentuate these. An Indian Communist leader, for instance, predicted that his party would be able to take power by playing Bengali against Assamese, Hindi against regional languages, intellectuals against bourgeoisie, and so on. As a leading student of Soviet policy has phrased it, a basic Communist goal is to further social disorganization by harnessing traditional resentments and unrest, and thus to create a power vacuum into which Communist organizations can move.[67]

In emerging nations, Communist output appeals to anti-Western radicalism and ascribes all social ills to the West. Extensive use is made of real and alleged discrimination by peoples of European stock against those of other races. A Soviet bulletin distributed in Addis Ababa claimed that African diplomats using public conveyances in Washington had to enter special cars bearing signs "For Negroes," and that the State Department was considering issuing special uniforms for African diplomats. The Communist Chinese have shown great skill in appealing to Ghandians and anti-Western nationalists in India, as well as to racialism and pan-Asian sentiments. Communist output to Africa describes the West as seeking to reimpose imperial control through "neocolonial" measures, including economic and cultural aggression and the use of "stooge" governments. A favorite device of Communist spokesmen is to demand the immediate withdrawal of Western technical personnel from newly independent nations, in the knowledge that local personnel to replace them are not available and that serious confusion would result if the demand were carried out.

Communists have shown skill in exploiting frictions and resentments in other parts of the world as well. The Soviets and their East European allies have kept up a constant drum-fire of accusations that leading Nazis have returned to positions of power in West Germany. Radio Moscow has repeatedly alleged that the atom bomb was dropped on Japan at the end of World War II for political rather than military reasons, and Communist spokesmen have proved adept at exploiting the anti-Americanism prevalent among European intellectuals.

Because communications can activate and reinforce existing resentments and frictions, Communist information and cultural programs have frequently been successful in promoting essentially destructive policies. A former Assistant Secretary of State for Public Affairs has noted that comparisons of the effectiveness of American and Soviet programs may be misleading, since much of the Soviet effort is disruptive, while American information and cultural activities are aimed at building a stable world order. The United States could achieve more striking results if it, too, sought to tear things apart.[68]

A related aim of Communist programs is to disparage conditions in the free world, and especially in the United States. This is an easy game, since the self-critical emphasis in free-world communications provides abundant material that can be collected and played back to audiences outside the country of origin. Indeed, when the United States failed in its first attempt to orbit an earth satellite in 1957, American self-condemnation was so ample that Soviet agencies found it unnecessary to add criticisms of their own.[69] The same has been true of race relations in the United States; Communist spokesmen have relied mainly on a selection of material from American public sources, although they have occasionally added embellishments of their own. Efforts of free-world journalists' and publishers' organizations to mobilize public opinion against violations of press freedom have provided bloc agencies with copious examples to "prove" their thesis that the press outside of Communist countries is muzzled. While this stream of disparagement is unlikely to change the outlook of people who already have well-formed attitudes towards the democracies, it probably does reinforce existing negative stereotypes and influence those whose attitudes are in the process of formation.

Communist persuasive communications do, however, serve positive as well as negative goals by encouraging a favorable view of conditions under Communism, and by identifying the policies of Communist states with the principal aspirations of peoples throughout the world. Bloc countries are described as having the kind of society to which all nations should aspire and in which formerly oppressed classes are achieving freedom, prosperity, and a high cultural level. When there is general agreement throughout the world with regard to certain goals or values, such as peace, antifascism, or anticolonialism, the Communists use what has been called the "universalistic argument." The formal structure of this argument has been stated by Paul Kecskemeti as follows:

> There is a manifest evil in the world. All right-thinking people, regardless of party, abhor that evil. The main exponents of the evil are enemies of the Soviet Union or of the Communist Party. . . . Hence, all right-thinking people, regardless of party, must count the Soviet Union, or the Communist Party, as an ally, and act accordingly.[70]

Essentially the same tactic is followed on a national as well as on a world-wide basis. Communist spokesmen in Japan have attempted to exploit popular sentiment opposing nuclear weapons and rearmament, and favoring trade with Communist China and Asian solidarity, by identifying their Party as the leading advocate of these views. Similarly, the Soviets and Chinese have proved adept at representing themselves as the most appreciative of cultural and political values of emerging countries.

Probably the most important goal of Communist persuasive efforts is to convince audiences around the world that the triumph of Communism is inevitable. This has been stated explicitly many times by Soviet and other bloc leaders, who also frequently emphasize that the Communist camp enjoys overwhelming military might. The achievement of the specific foreign-policy goals of Communist states is treated as a foregone conclusion; the only question is when. Thus, one of the main themes of Chinese Communist propaganda has been that mainland China is "sure to liberate Formosa." East German spokesmen have consistently maintained that the Western powers cannot escape the necessity of recognizing East Germany; their only choice is with regard to timing.

Communist attempts to persuade the world that the Communist camp is stronger than the West, and that the disparity will grow, are based mainly on demonstrated Soviet military power and economic growth, and on advances in space science. Soviet achievements in space have been skillfully exploited and contrasted with Western failures.[71] Smaller powers associated with the West have been repeatedly warned that there is no area of the world that cannot be reached by Soviet missiles. Former Premier Khrushchev's confident statements that the grandchildren of the present generation of Americans would live under socialism, combined with his frequent allusions to Soviet rocket power, contributed to the picture of Communism as the wave of the future.

Warnings of nuclear terror or revolutionary cataclysm are often combined in Soviet communications with efforts to present Communism as a humanitarian and "cultured" way of life. Target audiences are told that the power of Communist states is irresistible, but at the same time are reassured that submission will not be onerous because of the generous nature of the conqueror. Threats that initially promise total destruction are later toned down into more moderate demands that seem reasonable by contrast. Various themes within Soviet persuasive communications thus are used to condition each other so as to secure maximum compliance.[72]

Campaigns, Covert Operations, and Wordmanship

A number of devices are particularly characteristic of Communist international communications. These include the staging of major campaigns to whip up popular sentiment and focus attention on specified issues, the use of "black" propaganda, and the assignment of special meanings to commonly used words.

A full-scale campaign involves not only a flood of persuasive communications on a particular theme, but mass demonstrations, petitions, conventions, resolutions by "front" groups or sympathetic organizations, and often official diplomatic action by bloc states. Such campaigns enable the entire apparatus to be trained on a single objective, they raise morale by providing a common activity for Party members and sympathizers, and they make it possible to enlist the cooperation of non-Communists who approve of the specific end in view. Campaigns are particularly important in recruiting new people for front organizations, or otherwise bringing them into sympathetic contact with Communist activists. If a person can be persuaded to sign a petition or take part in a mass demonstration, this is the first step toward bringing him into an organization.

Some of the most significant Communist campaigns have been based on causes with almost universal appeal. Of these, the best known is the "peace" campaign that started shortly after World War II.[73] The argument behind this campaign was that all right-thinking people were for peace, but that the Communists were the only ones working effectively for it, while capitalist leaders were plotting to start a new war. This theme was stated by Andrei Zhdanov at the founding meeting of the Cominform in September 1947 and was reflected in the title of the Cominform journal, *For a Lasting Peace, For a People's Democracy!*

The organization used as the nucleus of the peace movement was a French group known as Combattants de la Liberté, formed in France early in 1948. Later in the year an international base was provided when Polish Communists sponsored a World Congress of Intellectuals for Peace. This meeting attracted a number of prominent non-Communists from Western nations, and resulted in the establishment of an International Liaison Committee of Intellectuals for Peace, with headquarters in Paris and national committees in forty-six countries. Mass meetings followed, including a Cultural and Scientific Conference for World Peace in New York in March 1949 and a World Peace Conference in Paris in April. Culmination of the Peace campaign came following a meeting in Stockholm in 1950, at which a resolution was adopted calling for unconditional prohibition of atomic weapons and branding as criminal the first use of these weapons. The full energies of the movement were then concentrated on a signature-collecting campaign in support of the Stockholm appeal. Half a billion signatures were claimed by the end of the year. Although most of these came from bloc countries, some 15 million were said to be from France, 17 million from Italy, and 2.5 million from the United States.

The specific purposes for which the Soviets used the peace campaign varied at different times. During 1949, all adherents of peace were called upon to oppose formation of a "militaristic" West German state and the North Atlantic alliance. The campaign was also directed against United Nations resistance to North Korean aggression in South Korea. The Stockholm peace appeal apparently was intended to neutralize the West's nuclear superiority while the Soviets were accumulating an atomic stockpile.

Another world-wide Communist campaign, although on a smaller scale, was based on the widespread revulsion aroused by bacterial weapons.[74] North Korea had from time to time accused the United States of using such weapons in the Far East, but a full campaign was not organized until March 1952, when a mass meeting in Moscow protested their alleged use. Communist-controlled media and front groups then swung into action, and the United States responded by demanding that the International Red Cross investigate the charges. The Soviets refused to support such an investigation, charging that the International Red Cross was a Swiss organization, and in July vetoed a proposal advanced in the United Nations Security Council for an investigation by an impartial commission. Meanwhile, several "investigations" had been made by Communist-controlled bodies, such as the World Peace Council and the International Association of Democratic Lawyers. Alleged confessions by American prisoners of war were brought forth, but these were couched in such strange terms as to make them incredible to those familiar with American usage of English. This campaign was not as well coordinated as the peace campaign, and suffered from a number of internal contradictions, but it apparently did convince some people. When the General Assembly voted to institute its own commission of investigation, four Asian nations abstained.

Other Communist campaigns have been conducted in individual countries or regions. Whenever a prominent Communist leader was arrested in France, for instance, organized agitation in favor of his liberation often succeeded in mobilizing not only those already under Communist influence but also those who sincerely believed that the civil rights of the individual in question had been violated. The Rosenberg spy case in the United States in 1951-52 was the focus of a vigorous campaign in North America and Western Europe that served to unite Communists with others who felt either that the Rosenbergs were innocent or that the death penalty was too severe. More recent campaigns in favor of Soviet-style coexistence or opposing United States intervention in Cuba have provided vehicles for both persuasive and organizing efforts by the Communist apparatus.

A major element in Communist campaigns is the mass demonstration, although this also is used independently. Such demonstrations bring people who may be sincere adherents of a cause, or who may have a real grievance, into direct contact with Communist agitators and give them a sense of taking a specific action. In Communist countries mass demonstrations are relatively orderly affairs, with overt action confined to window-breaking and paint-smearing. When a protesting crowd gathered in front of the British Embassy in Moscow on the occasion of the Suez invasion, a British official pushed his way through to a Soviet policeman and asked how long the demonstration was to last. "Oh, about thirty more minutes," replied the officer, looking at his watch.

In non-Communist countries more extensive violence is likely. Instances have been reported where agitators have called for the plundering of hardware stores, police stations, and gunsmith shops in order to arm an existing or potential mob, as was the case during riots against the Inter-American Conference in Bogotá in 1948. When the Communists are interested in whipping up sentiment to riot temperature, this is usually done through publicity and meetings that start well before the demonstration is scheduled to take place. Such preparations were associated with the riots that occurred during the visit of Vice-President Nixon to Venezuela in 1958, as well as the Bogotá riots.[75]

In addition to campaigns and mass demonstrations, Communist international communication programs frequently employ techniques of "black" or "gray" propaganda. Indeed, the practice whereby the Soviet Union and Communist China reach audiences abroad largely through local Party organizations, front groups, or controlled publications could in itself be defined as a technique of "black" propaganda, since the source of the ideas disseminated is alleged to be domestic. The voice or organization transmitting slogans or calls to action is rarely identified as a foreign one.[76]

The Communist apparatus operates several "black" radio stations, most of which represent themselves as the voice of a resistance movement within some non-Communist nation, while actually broadcasting from bloc territory. "Freiheitssender 904" (Freedom Station 904), located in East Berlin, purports to be a secret station in West Germany. "Radio España Independiente," allegedly in the Pyrenees, is actually in Eastern Europe. Other clandestine Communist stations are "Oggi" broadcasting to Italy, "The Voice of Truth" to Greece, and "Our Radio" to Turkey.[77]

A rather unusual covert technique that has been extensively employed by Communist states is the dissemination of forged documents. Between 1957 and 1961 the U.S. Central Intelligence Agency identified thirty-two forged documents allegedly written by or sent to officials of the American Government, and several other possible forgeries were under investigation. The major purposes of these forgeries appeared to be to discredit the West generally and the United States in particular, to sow suspicion among the Western allies, and to drive a wedge between peoples of the free world and their governments by fostering the idea that these governments were puppets of the United States. One such document was an alleged memorandum from Secretary of State Dulles to the President saying that American policy toward the Middle East was to replace European colonialism with American hegemony. Another was represented as a letter from an Assistant Secretary of Defense in charge of Health and Medical Services to the Secretary of Defense, reporting that examination had shown 67.3 per cent of all flight personnel in the U. S. Air Force to be psychoneurotics, whose symptoms were phobias, unaccountable animosity, and generally irrational behavior.[78]

Forgeries are distributed and publicized in a number of different ways. Some are mailed anonymously to newspapers and other recipients. Some are played into the hands of intelligence services of third countries. Others are first published in controlled newspapers that have no overt connection with the Communist apparatus, and still others are unveiled by the official Communist press in bloc countries. When a forgery is reproduced by an ostensibly non-Communist paper, it then is often given wider dissemination by Communist media, which attribute it to the free-world source. Sometimes no mass publicity is necessary. When a forged letter insulting the Shah of Iran, allegedly from the U. S. Secretary of State, came into the hands of Iranian officials its work was done. Similarly, an insulting and vituperative leaflet, purportedly from the Ku Klux Klan but actually printed in East Germany, was mailed to African and Asian delegates at the United Nations.[79]

Another form of "black" activity is the harassment of individuals by poison-pen letters and malicious telephone calls. This has been noted primarily in West Berlin and West Germany. The wife of a German federal official in Berlin, for instance, received frequent telephone calls wrongly informing her that her husband had been killed in an automobile accident or threatening to remove her to an insane asylum. The East German Communists who conducted this campaign apparently hoped that the wife would refuse to stay in Berlin and that it would be difficult to replace her husband if he asked to be transferred.[80] Similarly, West Germans have received false reports of the death of relatives in the West German armed forces, or bogus induction notices. In 1958, the East German Ministry of State Security sent 500 identical perfumed love letters to the home addresses of married West German officers, on the assumption that in most cases these letters would be opened by the officers' wives. The assumption proved to be correct. In spite of efforts by the West German Defense Ministry to clear up the situation, the letters were not without effect.[81]

A third characteristic of Communist communication programs is a specialized vocabulary, and the ascription of new meanings to words that are used in a different sense in the free world. Communist "wordmanship" has already been discussed in connection with domestic information and education programs, but it plays a part in international communication as well. People in the free world who are not acquainted with the new definitions are frequently confused when they hear Communist leaders say they are in favor of peace, democracy, and freedom; and it appears probable that the redefinition of terms long associated with Western democracy has led some people in emerging countries, and even a few in the older democracies, to conclude that the aims of the Communists and those of major free-world nations are not far apart.

Assets and Liabilities of Communist Communications

Communist information and cultural programs enjoy certain advantages that are denied those of Western nations. One advantage is the consistency and focus that monolithic societies can give their communications. Few reports about contradictions within the society are allowed to reach audiences outside; all available media can be used to convey the same set of ideas. Tass World Service, for instance, presents a clear-cut picture of the actors on the world stage, dividing them into the "good guys" and "bad guys." Communist information-gathering personnel abroad send back ample material to support this picture. As an East German television correspondent who defected to West Germany reported, his instructions required him not only to violate the laws of the Federal Republic (presumably a reference to gathering of secret intelligence), but to supply only film footage that reflected adversely on West Germany in general and the Bonn Government in particular.[82]

At the same time that Communist communications are able to offer a fairly consistent and focused picture of world events at any one juncture, centralized controls make it possible to adjust rapidly to changed conditions and to coordinate words with actions to a degree that cannot be rivalled by the democracies. (The same control structure makes it possible to relax restrictions on communications and to permit exceptions in cases where this is judged advantageous.) Each human cog in the world-wide machine usually knows just what he should say or do to help achieve objectives defined by his superiors. Even when a local Party is put in an impossible position, as was the case with Israeli Communists when Moscow decided to back Arab goals in the Middle East, the local group is given a line of argument to advance—the best that can be worked out under the circumstances.

Local parties and front groups throughout the world constitute another great advantage. Through these organizations ideas from Moscow and Peking can be presented to audiences in most countries of the free world by indigenous rather than foreign spokesmen. Local organizations can help to circumvent restrictions on the import of political material by producing it themselves. In addition, they provide what amounts to an excellent research and intelligence service. Through their contact with grass-roots sentiments, and their close attention to local political developments, they can help frame specialized material for a wide variety of audiences.

The educational system in bloc countries offers another great advantage to Communist international communications. Large numbers of specialized personnel can be trained, as required. For instance, the Soviet Union has gone a long way toward meeting its requirements for an adequate pool of personnel speaking foreign languages by requiring that every high school student study a second language for six years. As of 1958, 10 million Soviet students were said to be learning English (as opposed to 8,000 students in the United States who were studying Russian). In addition, Soviet universities emphasize the languages of Africa or Asia, and further emphasis is given by special schools and institutes. At the World Youth Festival in Moscow in 1957 the Russians were able to provide top-quality interpreters and translators even for the dialects and lesser-known languages spoken by delegates. An Indian visitor was said to have felt very much at home when he learned that numerous Russian young people could speak Hindi, Urdu, or Bengali.[83]

Other specialized needs are met by schools that indoctrinate large numbers of personnel in methods of political organization and argumentation, communication techniques, and even the conduct of mass demonstrations and riots. Communist parties throughout the free world maintain facilities for political training, while higher schools are located in the Soviet Union, Communist China, and the satellites.[84]

Although the Communist apparatus for reaching and manipulating foreign audiences is extensive and efficient, it receives a major assist from those who credit it with doing more than it actually does. As James Baldwin and many others have pointed out, those who attribute all civil-rights disturbances in the United States to Communist agitation are strengthening the Communist hand.[85] The same is true with respect to nationalist movements in emerging areas of the world. Crediting Communist leaders with having inspired major social unrest helps to convince those who feel they have a legitimate grievance that the Communists are indeed their champions. Such misinterpretations also tend to obscure the real causes of social upheavals and to hamper formulation of policies to deal with them effectively.

Several of the advantages and strong points of Communist international communication do, however, have disadvantages built into them.

The consistency with which the Communists speak to foreign audiences, which contrasts so markedly with the inconsistency of Western expressions, leads to a uniformity and dullness that bores foreign audiences just as it does people within Communist states. Once one is familiar with the current line it is often possible to know what ideas will be expressed in a given article, speech, or motion picture without reference to the actual material, and the phonograph-like presentation of ideas by bloc spokesmen tends to alienate many foreign audiences. As a West German observer noted, Moscow's propaganda seems to produce an immunity in those who hear it, so that it often rolls off without effect.[86] Added to this is the use of untranslatable expressions in translation and a lack of frankness and humor, both in part the result of centralized control.[87] These characteristics often make Communist communications vulnerable to ridicule and satire.

Furthermore, a price must be paid for presenting a consistent picture, in that history is full of instances that do not fit easily into any one line of argumentation. Soviet spokesmen have frequently been embarrased by the Molotov-Ribbentrop Pact, Soviet intervention in Hungary, and Soviet resumption of atomic testing. Some phenomena can only laboriously be explained away.

The fact that Communist communications are so closely coordinated with other aspects of policy, usually viewed as one of the advantages enjoyed by totalitarian states, likewise carries with it certain liabilities. Audiences in foreign countries that have been favorably impressed by Soviet and Chinese cultural-relations activities can be alienated when they see that these programs fluctuate with the political temperature. The same has been true in the case of "peace" propaganda, which has been turned on and off in accordance with policy requirements.

The advantages offered by the network of local Communist parties and front organizations are also not unmixed. In some cases, the connection between the local organization and a foreign Communist power has been so obvious as to arouse resentment in the host country. This has been true in West Germany, where Communist spokesmen were reduced to impotence by their identification with the Soviet Union even before the Party was officially outlawed. Similarly, suspicion in some of the new African states that local Communists are meddling on behalf of foreign powers has tended to worsen relations with Moscow and Peking. The atmosphere of conspiracy and secrecy with which

Communists surround themselves does nothing to allay this suspicion.

Even the machinery for training and indoctrination can be a source of weakness. This is partly due to the increasing theoretical obsolescence of Marxism-Leninism. Personnel who are schooled in the Communist view of the world may be outstanding when it comes to argumentation, but may suffer from a trained incapacity to understand the real situation. The frequency with which Communists are led away from reality by their officially prescribed doctrines is unknown, but numerous individual instances can be found.[88] Some personnel may be able to argue on the level of official stereotypes and at the same time to reason on the level of objective observation, but this ability cannot be taken for granted. For instance, Communists frequently allege that officially inspired press campaigns are being conducted for one or another objective in countries where the press is uncontrolled. To the extent that they really believe this they are in danger of being misled by the views of an editor who may or may not agree with the thinking of his government.

One of the greatest liabilities of Communist doctrine is that it does not permit an objective view of public opinion. This has led to incorrect predictions about Western responses to such Communist moves as the Berlin blockade and the invasion of South Korea. In both cases, Communist authorities appeared to be convinced that the West would accept a *fait accompli;* they did not take into account the change in the political climate of the free world brought about by the aggression.

The division of the Communist world into two major blocs, one centered around the Soviet Union and the other around Communist China, and the greater independence of the East European states, may lessen some of the advantages that Communist international communications have previously enjoyed. Certainly, it will no longer be possible for all Communist information and cultural programs in the free world to be coordinated in all their aspects. On some questions there will be two major views; and two sets of international front organizations seem to be developing, especially in Asia, Africa, and Latin America.*

* A recent West German analysis adopts a more cautious view, concluding that "it is premature to speak of a division of world communism into two distinct movements, one Soviet and the other Chinese." (Robert Orth, *International Communist Front Organizations* [Pfaffenhofen/Ilm: Ilmgau Verlag, 1963], p. 6.) The author emphasizes that the dispute within the Communist bloc concerns only methods, and not goals.

To the extent that former satellite states are able to maintain a degree of independence in their foreign policy, even more shades of opinion may be represented. In some cases, this may lead to poor cooperation among various Communist factions abroad, and among the front organizations they control. Automatic acceptance of the guidance provided by Moscow and Peking can no longer be taken for granted.

X

Foreign Information and Cultural Activities of the United States

Because of their totalitarian structure, Communist states can assure that most of the politically significant communications that flow from their countries to the outside world serve a specific end—or at least do not conflict with it. Communist international communications are essentially of an orderly character.

The opposite is true in the case of democracies such as the United States. A survey of American communications to foreign audiences immediately reveals their disorderly, complicated, and kaleidoscopic character, thus reflecting the decentralization of our political, economic, and cultural life. Not only are our overseas communications in themselves a maze of independent and semi-independent actions and programs, but they often are by-products of activities that are directed primarily toward some other end than the transmission of ideas. The U. S. Information Agency makes great efforts through the mass media to disseminate a more accurate picture of life in the United States; but the American soldier, scholar, or trader in another country often spreads information or misinformation without thinking about it. In view of the variety and diversity of American international communications they cannot be inventoried completely, and only examples of current activities will be given in the following pages.[1]

It is difficult in the case of the United States to make a clear distinction between public and private activities. When an overseas audience reads a statement of the President as reported by a wire agency, it is the result of combined official and nonofficial efforts. The same is true of a news broadcast over the Voice of America that is based on commercial dispatches. A student-exchange program could not take place without the cooperation of colleges and universities over which the federal government has no control. Most important of all, people in other countries frequently fail to notice where an official program ends and a private one begins.

There is, however, a *de facto* division of labor that has grown up between the public and private sectors. Private initiative covers the lion's share of the cost of American communications to foreign audiences, it supplies most of the basic ideas and materials that are disseminated abroad, and it develops the specialists that are needed in both public and private activities. The government serves as formulator for official policy, and as a catalyst, encourager, and supplementer of private efforts. It also emphasizes communications to areas that cannot be reached efficiently through private channels, either because of official restrictions or economic problems. This still leaves a large area where the two sets of activities overlap.

The rate of increase of both official and nonofficial communications from the United States that reach foreign audiences has been very rapid, especially during the last few years. During the late 1950's and early 1960's, literacy and the communication network have expanded dramatically throughout the world, making American radio and TV programs, publications, and films accessible to new audiences. The volume of American books exported has more than doubled, the number of foreign students and other visitors to the United States has increased sharply, American business involvement overseas has been greatly augmented, and American universities have for the first time become massively involved in world affairs. At the same time, American community efforts to take an interest in foreign visitors have grown apace. It is striking in how many cases new international communication activities, public and private, date from the past decade. The significance of this expansion cannot yet be accurately gauged, since in most cases a generous passage of time is required before the full effects of communication become apparent, and the full impact of the American information and cultural activities of the past decade will be seen only in the next generation.

The Commercial Media

Of all the channels for reaching people in other countries of the free world, the commercial news and entertainment media are the most important. Dedicated to providing reliable information that is of interest to their audiences, and entertainment that will attract readers and viewers, these media are jealous of interference by either official or private groups. For them, audience interest is the primary factor in determining which ideas to disseminate. Daily readers of AP and UPI dispatches in foreign newspapers runs into the hundreds of millions. American films are seen by some 150 million persons a week in foreign countries. American television exports are viewed in nearly all non-Communist nations that have established TV service, and exchange agreements with Communist states make some programs available there as well. The daily audience for U.S.-produced television programs abroad is about 65 million. In 1960, U.S.I.A. researchers found that 70 per cent of a Japanese cross-section had seen American television shows. This was true of 67 per cent in Great Britain, 49 per cent in Italy, 24 per cent in West Germany, and 20 per cent in France.[2] American newspapers, books, and magazines are read by smaller, but influential, circles throughout the world.

American commercial radio has played a more modest part in international communications, largely because of the limited opportunities for supporting programs beamed overseas through advertising revenue. The only major commercial station in international operation is WRUL, operated by Radio New York Worldwide, and owned by the International Educational Broadcasting Corporation, with transmitters at Scituate, Massachusetts. WRUL broadcasts a full daily schedule (with advertising) to Latin America, Europe, and West Africa, and claims a daily audience of some 4.5 million.[3] Commercially prepared programs reach additional audiences abroad through indirect routes. Some, especially musical broadcasts and special features, are sold to foreign stations. Other programs are exchanged with networks abroad through arrangements made directly between American and foreign broadcasters, by educational or cultural bodies, or by U. S. Government agencies.

Although they are not intended to serve a political purpose, American commercial communications do have a powerful political effect abroad, and are among the most important influences shaping the picture that other peoples have of the United States. This has led to expressions of concern from both Americans and others. International news services and most books and magazines have drawn little criticism, but lurid entertainment material in American television, motion-picture, and comic-book exports has aroused numerous protests. The late Edward R. Murrow, a former U.S.I.A. Director, was of the opinion that our TV programs gave an inaccurate picture of the United States to those who lacked adequate background information; others have condemned them in even stronger terms. The British Committee on Broadcasting, headed by Sir Harry Pilkington, and the Director General of the British Broadcasting Corporation, Hugh Carleton Greene, have both deplored the crime and violence in exported American TV shows. The "cowboy menace" has attracted the attention of foreign humorists as well as critics. During the Chinese attack on India in 1962, a Cairo weekly carried a cartoon showing two Egyptian boys in cowboy costumes, one of whom was saying: "We cowboys must stick with the Chinese because they are fighting the Indians."

The TV industry has made a vigorous response to criticism of its exports. Frank Stanton, President of the Columbia Broadcasting System, has expressed the opinion that we ought not to conceal from the rest of the world that we are diverted by mysteries or Westerns, or that we have disturbing social problems. Robert W. Sarnoff, of the National Broadcasting Company, has pointed out that more than 15 per cent of the television product his network distributed abroad consists of news and informational programming, and that the popularity of entertainment shows scarcely supports the notion that they are creating ill-will toward the United States. He also cited a 1961 U.S.I.A. survey, which concluded that American commercial TV showings are more helpful than harmful in creating favorable attitudes toward the United States.[4]

The film industry has similarly responded to criticisms by noting that mass audiences abroad like American entertainment films as they are. Others have pointed out that it is difficult to predict just what effects various films will have. For example, a poll of Burmese movie-goers found that predominantly favorable reactions were aroused by such American films as *Man and Woman, Loving You, Rock Baby Rock, Beautiful but Bad,* and *Blackboard Jungle*.[5] Communist authorities who have distributed American films that they thought would give a poor impression of life in the West have frequently misjudged audience response. This was the case when Soviet movie-goers noted that even the poorest families in *The Grapes of Wrath* had cars, and that everybody in pictures showing life in urban slums was wearing sturdy shoes. An impressionistic survey made by U.S.I.A. in about 1960 seemed to indicate that American commercial films were doing slightly more good than harm as far as opinions about the United States were concerned, and this conclusion was borne out by a more extensive U.S.I.A. study of West European reactions in 1962. While movie-goers were unfavorably impressed by Hollywood's portrayal of crime, youth, and treatment of the American Negro, they liked what they saw of the American standard of living, the American workingman, and American women.[6]

The political effects of commercial exports result partly from the fact that many foreign audiences see private American communications as having an official role. Back in the 1930's a British observer argued that England required a government information program to compete with influences from across the Atlantic. "The Americans," he asserted, "have turned every cinema in the world into the equivalent of an American consulate."[7] In a similar vein, a prominent Swiss leftist more recently cited American news services, films, and magazines as vehicles for American propaganda in Switzerland.[8] Indeed, instances of confusion between official and nonofficial communications can be found in almost any part of the world.

Other Nongovernmental Activities

In addition to the commercial media, a large number of private bodies and individuals disseminate ideas abroad, sometimes intentionally and sometimes unintentionally. These may be grouped in four broad categories: organizations that use communications primarily to promote their own political goals; organizations whose activities supplement political programs that have been originated by others, or help individuals to achieve their personal objectives; organizations that are pursuing nonpolitical aims, but whose activities often have political side-effects; and individuals who are pursuing personal aims—tourists, students, letter-writers, and so on. While those who visit other countries in a private capacity, or who keep up contacts with friends abroad, are not often thought of as engaging in information or cultural activities, the effects of their communications are sometimes indistinguishable from those of organized bodies that are pursuing specific goals. A large-scale example of a propaganda campaign conducted by individuals occurred in 1948, when thousands of Americans of Italian extraction wrote to friends in Italy urging them to vote for one of the non-Communist parties in the Italian elections of that year.[9]

Of the nonofficial organizations using communications to promote specific political objectives abroad, perhaps the two best known are the

National Committee for a Free Europe and the American Committee for Liberation. The former operates Radio Free Europe, a voice for exiles from the Communist countries of Eastern Europe, publishes the magazine *East Europe,* and engages in a number of other educational and propagandistic activities.[10] The latter organization is devoted primarily to operating Radio Liberty, which broadcasts to the Soviet Union, and whose staff of more than 200 is composed mainly of former Soviet citizens.[11] Both Radio Free Europe and Radio Liberty have studios in New York and transmitters in Western Europe, and have built up substantial audiences. They seek to give their listeners behind the iron curtain a feeling of contact with the outside world, to acquaint them with news that is not reported by Communist domestic media, and to keep alive democratic values. They thus serve as an "opposition press." Other private organizations using foreign information programs to achieve specific political goals include the Cuban Freedom Committee, which buys time from U. S. Radio stations for broadcasts to Cuba and distributes literature in Latin America, and the Information Council of the Americas, which supplies "truth tapes" describing life in Communist countries to over 120 radio stations in Latin America.[12]

Most of the organizations that use international communications to further political goals (usually of a very general and long-range nature) conduct exchange-of-persons programs. One of the oldest of these is the Experiment in International Living, which helps American students learn to understand peoples of other countries by placing them in foreign homes for several weeks or months during the summer. It also arranges stays in U.S. homes for visitors from abroad. Its objective has been to "create understanding where misunderstanding is greatest." In the first twenty-nine years of the Experiment's activities more than 30,000 persons participated in this two-way traffic.[13]

Substantial programs are also conducted by Operation Crossroads Africa, which seeks to introduce Americans and Africans to each other by recruiting young Americans for work in African nations, and by the American Field Service, which between 1948 and 1963 brought 13,000 foreign high-school students to the United States for a year's study and sent 8,000 American young people abroad.[14] Operation Amigo, under which several hundred Latin American students have visited this country and groups from American high schools have traveled south, was initiated in 1962 by the *Miami Herald* and the Dade County school system, in cooperation with several Latin American organizations. A large number of religious, labor, business, civic, and professional organizations have sponsored exchange-of-persons programs of widely varying types, most of them with the aim of promoting international understanding, although some have no specified political purpose. One estimate is that there are about 3,400 private programs bringing foreign nationals to the United States for educational purposes.[15] If those not involving education and those that sponsor foreign travel by Americans were included, the total would probably be higher by several hundred. These programs are conducted by more than 2,000 nongovernment groups that have become involved in international education and cultural affairs, most of them in recent years.[16]

Among private efforts to promote better understanding through personal contacts, the Pugwash and Dartmouth Conferences deserve special mention. The former, started by an initiative of Bertrand Russell in 1955, had brought American, British, Soviet, and other scientists together on twelve occasions by 1964 to discuss arms control and other areas in which science impinges on world affairs. Although the Pugwash Conferences are an international undertaking, American scientists and intellectuals have played a prominent part in them, and they take their name from the site of the first meeting—the summer estate of American industrialist Cyrus Eaton, who has been one of the major financial supporters of the venture. The Dartmouth Conferences, stressing humanistic and political subjects, were organized in 1960 by Norman Cousins with the assistance of Philip E. Mosely, and have enabled American academicians and businessmen to meet with Soviet intellectuals on four occasions in a very informal atmosphere. Both sets of conferences seem to have succeeded in achieving fairly frank interchanges and in reducing the suspicion with which those from different political and economic systems tend to regard each other.

Other popular forms of private initiative in international communication include organized letter-writing, affiliations between towns in this country and foreign cities, and the collection of books for shipment overseas. Letter-writing crops up everywhere. In Huntington, Long Island, a group of thirty families arranged during 1962 to exchange letters with eight citizens of Sestroretsk, a town near Leningrad, with the aim of encouraging mutual understanding. Larger efforts to stimulate international correspondence have been sponsored by such organizations as Letters Abroad, Inc., by newspapers or periodicals such as the *Christian*

Science Monitor and *Scholastic Magazine,* and by numerous educational institutions.

Affiliations of towns are also numerous. According to U.S.I.A. officials, about 240 American municipalities had "sister cities" abroad as of 1962. Some of these were "really working at it" and had rather extensive programs. For example, a many-faceted program of cultural exchange was established in 1955 between Darien, Conn., and the town of Mercara in India. Since that time residents of the two communities have exchanged letters and gifts, entertained each other's nationals, and arranged for lecturers to tell each about the other.

Book collection has been organized in many localities. The Scarsdale, N.Y., Woman's Club organized a service known as Operation Bookshelf in the mid 1950's, and by 1962 had distributed some 130,000 books, many of them going to countries in Africa and Asia. In the same year the Workmen's Circle, a national Jewish fraternal organization, was awarded a distinguished service citation by the U. S. Information Agency for having collected more than 1 million books for distribution in emerging countries. "Books abroad" programs are also conducted by the Darien, Conn., Book Aid Plan, the African-American Institute, the United States Book Exchange in Washington, and many other organizations.[17]

Another vehicle for private international communications is the international cultural center. An example of a modest-sized center is the "Villa Jones" in Mexico City, where Mr. and Mrs. Robert C. Jones have made their large residence into a rooming house for tourists with professional interests, a meeting place for Mexicans and intellectuals from other countries, and an information center for researchers. A much larger establishment, providing residential and recreational facilities for scholars from India and abroad, was opened in New Delhi in 1962, with the aid of a $1 million grant from the Rockefeller Foundation. Somewhat similar International Houses are found in New York and several other major American cities.

One of the most ambitious private international communication operations aimed at achieving greater international understanding is the "People-to-People" program, which was started in 1956 as the result of initiative by President Eisenhower, and is supported mainly by the Hallmark Foundation of Kansas City. It coordinates the work of thirty-three committees that encourage exchanges between Americans and foreigners in the arts, sciences, and professions; help to establish ties between American and foreign cities and institutions; arrange for shipment overseas of books and periodicals; promote international sports events; and assist in the exchange of scientific information.

A second large category of private organizations includes those that do not originate international exchanges or information programs, but play a very important supporting role. Most of these provide hospitality for foreign students or other foreign visitors in the United States. How many such supporting groups exist would be difficult to determine, but they are legion, ranging from those that are national to those that are purely local in character. In the Washington, D.C., area alone, ninety organizations providing various services to foreign visitors were identified by a survey in 1961, and more than fifty such groups have been reported in the New York area.[18]

One of the principal organizations in this category is the National Association for Foreign Student Affairs (NAFSA), which includes foreign student advisers on more than 1,200 college and university campuses. Members of NAFSA not only assist foreign students with academic problems, but sometimes help to find housing and jobs, arrange social activities, and counsel on personal problems.[19] A newer organization, the National Council for Community Services to International Visitors (COSERV), helps to coordinate the activities of some seventy-five groups throughout the country, including hospitality committees, reception centers, and foreign-relations institutes. The Institute of International Education in New York is the principal center in the United States for assisting students in other countries to get in touch with American educational institutions, as well as for helping American students to establish contact with institutions abroad.

Most programs for providing aid to foreign students and other visitors have been started as a result of local initiative in communities or colleges. In the Riverdale section of New York City, 400 residents "adopted" ten East African students attending New York colleges, offering some financial assistance as well as hospitality. In Ithaca, N.Y., several such programs have been reported, including a Community Host Family Program for International Hospitality, the main objective of which is to make visiting students feel welcome. Ambassadors for Friendship, with headquarters at Macalester College in St. Paul, organizes annual tours of the United States for overseas students at American colleges. The Midtown International Center in New York is especially interested in foreign business and industrial trainees brought here under government auspices.

An elaborate program was started at the University of Kansas after a survey showed that relatively few of the 300 foreign students on the campus had American friends or a realistic picture of American society, and that many would not be able to continue their studies if they did not find summer jobs. This led to organization of six committees, with responsibility for such matters as student-to-student relationships, hospitality, forums, and job placement. One of these committees arranged for letters from Kansas University students to be sent to incoming foreign students even before they left their homes. Through the People-to-People Program similar projects were started at more than 600 colleges and universities in the United States, and by 1962 some 40,000 students were actively participating in University People-to-People activities.[20]

Other organizations focus their activities primarily on foreign diplomatic officials and their families. Most of these are privately sponsored, but some are supported by state or local governments. New York City and New York State maintain offices to assist U.N. delegates and other visitors. A New York organization called Private Entertainment for United Nations Delegations, Inc., arranged about 5,000 "occasions" for more than 8,800 guests from nearly all the U.N. member nations between 1955 and 1961. It was started by a small group of New York women, and by 1962 had expanded to a point where it kept a card file of 600 hostesses who were available to entertain delegates and their wives, take them around New York, and extend assistance to help them make a satisfactory adjustment to the community. A similar group in southern Connecticut conducts analogous activities. In 1961, a Hospitality Information Service for the United Nations, supported by the Carnegie Endowment for International Peace, was opened to help guide foreign visitors to the various organizations that are available to assist them. All these bodies rely largely on unpaid volunteers, so their expenses are relatively small. The budgets of those in and around New York total about $1 million a year.

Supporting organizations that are concerned primarily with foreign tourists are more rudimentary than those assisting students or diplomats, and for the most part are of recent origin. A newspaper survey in 1961, primarily of the New York area, found that a number of bodies were encouraging tourists to come to the United States, but that little effort was made to help them after they arrived. Groups of non-English-speaking visitors had spent hours waiting at airports because they could find nobody to tell them how to get into town, and even some of those with English had difficulty finding advice about places to visit or things to do. Two information bureaus for tourists were maintained in the city at that time, but neither of them had adequate language skills available. If a visitor who knew no English showed up, a call would be put through to a foreign-language newspaper that could handle his language. A newspaperman would then interpret by telephone between the tourist and the information official.[21] Problems of providing adequate services for foreign tourists have recently received attention from both official and commercial agencies, and it can be expected that the situation will improve rapidly.

Although nonofficial information and cultural programs and supporting activities, taken in the aggregate, are substantial in number and in total volume of effort, they are dwarfed by the activities of private organizations whose involvement in international communication is incidental to the pursuit of their main interests. These organizations fall primarily into three categories: economic (business and labor), educational, and religious.

A large proportion of the total exchange of ideas between the United States and other countries is occasioned by business activities. American private enterprise is found throughout the world, even behind the iron curtain, although about three-quarters of American private investment is in Europe, Canada, or Latin America. In the neighborhood of 3,300 American companies have branches, subsidiaries, or affiliates in other countries. These are staffed by 25,000-40,000 Americans (who thus outnumber total State Department personnel), as well as by more than 3 million local employees.[22] In addition, countless other Americans travel abroad in connection with their business interests. Indeed, it is an unusual American business executive who has not visited a foreign country. A recent survey found that even among smaller firms six out of seven executives had done so.[23]

American business has been harshly criticized for failing to devote sufficient attention to its public and political relations in foreign countries. Decisions have been made, it is alleged, almost exclusively on economic grounds, without taking other factors into account. Few companies have employed specialists for public-relations functions; most have entrusted them to "line executives." According to an international business consultant, most American companies appear to be neglecting public opinion in the countries where they have interests, or are paying only lip service to it.[24]

A number of efforts have been made to improve this situation—some by individual companies, and a few by business associations. Perhaps the most elaborate effort to promote greater sensitivity to local political and social conditions has been made by the Business Council for International Understanding. Founded in 1956, this organization is supported by more than fifty companies, most of them of substantial size. Its principal activity has been a training program for executives who are to be assigned abroad—a "Foreign Service Institute" for business. It has also sponsored conferences between American business executives and government officials, training and community relations projects in Latin America, and occasional radio broadcasts on foreign stations.

Numerous individual American companies have instituted programs to encourage good relations with the people of countries in which they are active. The Creole Petroleum Corporation, through the Creole Foundation in Caracas, has conducted a scholarship program for Venezuelan students since 1937, and by 1960 was assisting an average of forty Venezuelans to study outside their country, and another seventy-five in Venezuela itself. The Foundation has also provided aid to local universities, has established a training program for rural teachers, and has helped to found training programs and trade schools for less educated young people, who are thus enabled to progress to better-paying jobs.[25] The General Electric Company in Brazil works with local schools to improve technical training and provides opportunities for the educational advancement of its employees at all levels. Programs such as these have increased rapidly in number during recent years.[26]

Business enterprise abroad is stimulated by several privately sponsored foreign-aid schemes. Perhaps the most ambitious of these is the Executive Service Corps, formed in 1964 by a number of leading American businessmen to provide managerial talent and knowledge to enterprises in developing countries. Modeled on the Peace Corps, the organization hopes to recruit as many as 1,000 advisers for overseas service by 1967, primarily from among retired executives. Another business-supported aid program, Tools for Freedom, was formed in 1960 and has enlisted the cooperation of some 400 companies and trade associations. In 3 years it shipped mechanical equipment such as lathes and printing presses to 22 schools in 17 countries. A Development and Technical Aid

International Assistance Corps was founded in the previous year by a professor from Los Angeles State College, who enlisted a group of consultants to provide free technical advice to those requesting it from overseas. In the first 5 years of its existence it handled approximately 3,000 inquiries.[27]

Since World War II, American labor organizations have played an important part in assisting foreign trade unions. Much of this effort has been channeled through the International Confederation of Free Trade Unions, which sponsors training courses and conferences throughout the free world, supports colleges in India and Uganda for union leaders, and represents the interest of free labor in the United Nations and its specialized agencies. American unions have also helped to staff and support the International Trade Secretariats (federations of national trade unions in the same or related industries), several of which have been particularly active in organizing labor in emerging countries.[28]

American unions have also given substantial direct support to foreign labor, and have frequently played a large part in preventing unions overseas from coming under Communist control. In 1960, the AFL-CIO contributed $180,000 to establish the Afro-Asian Institute for Labor Studies in Israel, and has been influential in many areas through its traveling representatives. Between 1959 and 1961, the International Ladies' Garment Workers' Union spent over $1 million to assist non-Communist unions in Asia, Latin America, and Europe. The United Auto Workers has contributed heavily to a Free World Labor Fund, and several AFL-CIO unions have provided training aids, films, books, and other materials to new labor movements in the developing world. Through the American Institute for Free Labor Development, founded in 1960, American labor has cooperated with U.S. business and government in promoting welfare projects abroad, and in 1962-63 alone committed about $13 million in loans for workers' housing in Mexico, Peru, and El Salvador.[29] The *Free Trade Union News* is published monthly in four languages by the AFL-CIO Department of International Affairs, which distributes nearly 200,000 copies of this periodical throughout the world.

Educational institutions and foundations, as well as business and labor, have developed important activities that involve communication with foreign publics. A survey by the Institute of International Education showed that during the academic year 1962-63 there were nearly 78,000 foreign citizens on educational assignments in the United States, as opposed to some 40,000 in 1955. Of these, 64,000 were students, 6,000 were faculty members or advanced scholars, and more than 7,000 were hospital interns or residents. Every major area of the world was represented, with the largest number of visitors (37 per cent) coming from the Far East, 17 per cent from Latin America, 15 per cent from Europe, 13 per cent from the Near and Middle East, and 10 per cent from other North American countries. Africa showed the smallest number of any major region, 7 per cent, but this represented a 24 per cent increase over the previous year.[30] The number of foreign academic personnel at American universities is expected to continue to rise, and probably will reach the neighborhood of 120,000 by the end of the present decade.[31] By comparison, there were about 3,000 American faculty members on overseas assignments in 1962-63, and some 16,000 American students were at foreign educational institutions during the previous academic year. Somewhat fewer than half of the faculty members and 60 per cent of the students were in Western Europe, although Canada reported more American students (2,500) than any other single country.

Universities have taken an active part in promoting and guiding the international flow of academic personnel through a variety of educational-exchange programs. These are of two basic types: traditional educational exchange, in which scholars move among countries in the course of their individual intellectual pursuits; and developmental exchange, in which the flow of students, scholars, and educational materials takes place in the interest of improving social and economic conditions. The two types sometimes become blurred, with the result that scholarly and developmental objectives are sought through the same program. A recent survey found 382 international-exchange programs of both types at 184 American colleges and universities. These 184 institutions are a small proportion of the almost 2,000 in the country, leaving ample room for growth.[32]

The exchange and training programs sponsored by American educational institutions are of almost infinite variety, involving an enormous investment of time and money. In many cases, colleges provide free tuition or financial support for foreign students whose travel has been paid by government agencies. Several universities maintain foreign centers at which American students spend part of their academic time, or cooperate in Junior Year Abroad programs. Foreign study programs for American undergraduates increased from 22 in 1956 to more than 100 in 1963.[33] An example of a specialized program is that of the World

Press Institute of Macalester College, which offers groups of foreign newsmen opportunities for study and travel in the United States and seeks to awaken American interest in international affairs.

Several studies have emphasized the need for further examination of the role of American universities in world affairs. The Committee on the University and World Affairs, organized by the Ford Foundation, described the response of universities to the demands of the international situation as "largely sporadic and unplanned." Edward W. Weidner has concluded that by and large American university exchange programs have been improvisations, lacking a fundamental philosophy. H. Field Haviland of the Brookings Institution observes that "relatively few universities have done an adequate job of determining their long-range commitment to international education and designing comprehensive programs to support that commitment." [34] These critical observations are scarcely surprising, since most academic and technical-assistance programs are of very recent origin.

Other academic and professional bodies also play an extensive role in the international exchange of ideas. Nearly every professional association, whether concerned with education, law, medicine, or a specialized branch of science takes part in international congresses and exchanges of professional information and materials. The international scientific community, in particular, has built channels through which information flows almost without regard to national barriers.

Closely allied to the work of professional and educational organizations is that of the philanthropic foundations, which have supported many of the programs carried on by the universities, as well as international conferences, scientific institutes, technical training, educational radio and TV, and publications. A few examples may suggest the tremendous range of foundation activities in international communication. The Rockefeller Foundation, learning that the foreign ministries of some newer countries did not have even the most elementary reference materials available, offered to provide basic book collections to those ministries that requested them. As of 1964 it had assisted in building diplomatic reference libraries in thirty-five Asian and African countries. The Carnegie Endowment for International Peace has sponsored a series of training seminars for diplomats of newly independent nations. By 1964, the Ford Foundation had appropriated a total of $3,650,000 to promote educational and cultural contacts between the United States and the countries of Eastern Europe, including the Soviet Union.

Ford grants have also supported the development of American studies in Western Europe (through the American Council of Learned Societies), and have financed a number of orientation and English-language courses for foreign students in the United States.

Among enterprises that are partially foundation-supported, Franklin Book Programs (formerly Franklin Publications) deserves special mention. It is a nonprofit corporation, founded in 1952, that has worked in cooperation with American and foreign commercial publishers to arrange publication of American books in Arabic, Persian, Urdu, Bengali, Malay, Indonesian, and Pushtu, and in 1964 it started operations in Nigeria and Latin America. It operates with a small American staff in New York; actual publishing is carried out by foreign publishers in each of the areas concerned. In some cases, Franklin responds to requests by foreign leaders or educators that certain American titles be published in their local language, and seeks to find indigenous publishers who will undertake translation and publication. In other cases, local houses take the initiative in publishing titles on Franklin's list that they think have good commercial possibilities. By 1964, Franklin had assisted in the publication of some 41 million copies of 2,375 titles. The costs of its operations are partially covered by commercial sales, and it has received support from American publishers, individuals, and several governments (including that of the United States), as well as foundations.

Franklin Book Programs also contributes in a variety of ways to the formation of strong publishing houses in the countries where it operates. For example, personnel from New York assist local publishers in overcoming problems of production and distribution, and conduct a variety of training activities. In Iran, Franklin assisted in the establishment of a loan fund under which the Industrial Credit Bank of Iran advances credit to Iranian publishers. By working in countries where the publishing industry is not well developed, Franklin thus assists in building institutions that are capable of producing books of all kinds.[35]

Other programs that have important implications for international communication are conducted by American churches. In the 1950's about 65 U.S. religious bodies were operating some 1,360 schools, 120 hospitals and clinics, and 43 farms and agricultural extension programs in Latin America, involving a full-time staff of about 2,100 people. By 1961 American churches were spending nearly $225 million annually to support some 35,000 missionaries overseas, most of whom were teachers or medical personnel.[36] Of the 21,000 American Protestant missionaries reported in a recent survey, the largest groups were in Japan (1,736), India (1,636), and Brazil (1,450).[37] Of a total of about 7,000 Roman Catholic missionary personnel from the United States, approximately one-third are in Latin America, 2,000 are in Asia, and over 600 in Africa.[38] Nearly all major religious groups engaging in missionary activities make use of the mass media, and some sponsor exchanges of persons. A great many publish newspapers and magazines, as well as more specifically religious materials.

International radio broadcasting represents a newer undertaking of American religious bodies. Two stations were established in Korea following the end of the Korean War, and as of 1963 others were being constructed in the Philippines to reach Hong Kong, Thailand, Burma, Indonesia, and Malaya. A transmitter in Monrovia (ELWA) started long- and medium-wave broadcasts in 1954, and in 1960 added a short-wave signal that could reach the Middle East. The Trans World Radio, a missionary network with transmitters in Curaçao and Monte Carlo, broadcasts to the Soviet Union, as well as to Europe, the Middle East, and Africa. A survey by the President of the World Missionary Radio Fellowship found that there were twenty-three such stations on the air as of 1962, while a substantial number of local stations broadcasting to domestic audiences in a great many countries were being given support and technical advice by major American denominations. Programming on most religious stations includes news, educational broadcasts, and agricultural, health, and homemaking advice, as well as religious material.[39]

In addition to their roles in all these varied organizations, a great many individual Americans are engaged in communicating with foreign nationals in the course of travel or residence overseas, entertainment of foreign guests, or even casual conversations with visitors to this country. The 1960 census listed 1,374,421 Americans overseas. This figure included 609,720 members of the armed forces, 38,010 federal civilian employees, 506,393 dependents of military or civilian personnel, 32,464 crewmen of merchant ships at sea or in foreign ports at the time of the census, and 187,834 other Americans on extended residence abroad. To these should be added the millions of American travelers who visit foreign countries each year. Traffic in the other direction during 1961 included nearly 1.5 million foreigners who were admitted to the United States, some 750,000 of whom came for pleasure and 116,000 on business.

In the same year, somewhat more than 3 million aliens were listed as residing in the United States. Travel to the United States is increasing steadily; in fiscal year 1964 more than a million nonimmigrant visas were issued. The ideas that flow through this international network of individuals constitute an important part of all communications between the United States and other countries.

Government Agencies Involved in International Communication

Although nearly all federal agencies are involved in international communication in one way or another, for most of these the dissemination of ideas abroad is incidental to the pursuit of a specific activity or the achievement of a specific task. They do not think of themselves as conducting communication programs to help achieve foreign-policy goals, even though they may be doing this in practice.[40]

The largest program that supports American foreign policy directly is that of the U. S. Information Agency, which has some 10,000 employees, divided between Washington and more than 200 posts in 100 countries. More than half of these are foreign nationals, most of whom occupy custodial or administrative positions at overseas posts, although some are employed in important professional capacities. Appropriations for the operation of the Agency in the fiscal year 1964 were approximately $166 million.[41]

The functional subdivisions of the Agency headquarters in Washington include those that provide staff services (research and liaison), those concerned with particular information media (radio, television, motion pictures, information centers, and publications), and those responsible for specific geographic areas. Larger posts overseas reproduce in miniature the media divisions of the headquarters, and some of the staff services. Smaller posts may be limited to a handful of Americans, who function in many different capacities, or even to a single U.S.I.A. representative. Overseas posts operate under the designation "U. S. Information Service" (U.S.I.S.)—a label that fortunately has remained constant ever since World War II, although the official name and status of the headquarters organization in Washington has changed several times.

Other important international communication actitivies are conducted by the Department of State. These include exchange-of-persons and cultural programs, as well as a great many traditional functions that involve public information. Appropriations for State Department international educational and cultural programs increased by irregular jumps from $6 million in 1947 to approximately $50 million in the fiscal year 1964 (including $5 million for the Center for Cultural and Technical Interchange Between East and West at the University of Hawaii). These programs are the responsibility of an Assistant Secretary for Educational and Cultural Affairs, who also provides guidance for similar activities that are conducted by other departments and agencies, and tries to see that these complement one another and do not compete or overlap. The Office of the Assistant Secretary and the Bureau of Educational and Cultural Affairs, which operates under his direction, had about 400 employees as of 1964, most of them in Washington. Overseas administration of the educational and cultural programs is handled by the U. S. Information Agency, which is reimbursed by the Department of State for expenses incurred.

The State Department provides policy guidance to the U. S. Information Agency through a Policy Plans and Guidance Staff of about fifteen people in the Office of an Assistant Secretary for Public Affairs. This Assistant Secretary is also responsible for the State Department Office of News, which is the principal point of contact in the Department for both domestic and foreign newsmen. Other instrumentalities of the State Department play an extremely important part in international communication, although they are primarily concerned with quite different functions. Many of the duties of diplomats involve the dissemination of ideas to wide publics through speeches, social activities, and statements to the press. In Washington, State Department officials help to prepare public communications for the Secretary of State, the President, and other governmental officials. These include not only speeches and policy statements, but also such seemingly routine messages as greetings to heads of foreign states on important anniversaries and special occasions.

Although it is not directly engaged in conducting international information and cultural programs, the Agency for International Development sponsors several activities that involve international communication in the course of its efforts to promote economic progress in emerging areas. The most important of these are the training of foreign personnel in a variety of technical skills, including the operation of communication media; assisting foreign educational institutions; and providing communication equipment, including, in some cases, radio, film, and printing components, as well as books and technical publications.[42]

The Department of Defense engages in even more extensive activities that require communication with foreign audiences. Each year thousands of foreign military officers and men are brought to the United States for specialized training. The Armed Forces Radio and Television Service operates more than 200 radio stations and some 30 television transmitters overseas. Although its programs are designed specifically for American servicemen and their families, they have an "eavesdropping audience" of several million. Much of the material broadcast is contributed free of charge by U.S. commercial radio and television networks, and is "decommercialized" by military studios in New York and Los Angeles. Newspapers and other publications intended for U.S. military personnel overseas similarly find their way into non-American hands in large quantities.[43] U.S. military posts scattered throughout the world conduct extensive community-relations programs, which sometimes include dissemination of materials about American policy. Visits and demonstrations by air and naval units in foreign areas help to transmit ideas about American capabilities and intentions.

The greatest impact of the U.S. military establishment on foreign audiences comes, however, not as a result of special demonstrations or the use of information media, but as a result of its size and normal activities. The mere presence overseas of more than 1 million servicemen and their families, the movement of military equipment, maneuvers, and related activities automatically ensure a stream of communications to and from Americans, and about the United States.

Another agency with extensive overseas contacts is the Peace Corps. From a modest beginning in 1961, the Corps expanded rapidly, and received a budget of approximately $115 million for fiscal year 1965. By the end of 1963, it had 6,000 volunteers overseas in 46 countries, with 1,200 more in training. More than 2,000 were in Africa, and another 2,000 in Latin America. By 1965 it expected to have about 14,000 volunteers overseas in some 40 countries.[44]

Additional federally supported programs that involve overseas communications in one form or another are so numerous that only examples can be given. The National Science Foundation, the Department of Health, Education and Welfare, and the National Aeronautics and Space Administration receive Congressional appropriations for international exchange-of-persons or training programs, and at least seventeen other agencies play a supporting role in these activities. The U. S. Office of Education sponsors language institutes in the Soviet Union and West European countries. The Department of Commerce, besides arranging U.S. trade fairs abroad, maintains a U. S. Travel Service with offices in several foreign cities and engages in publicity to promote tourism to the United States. Visits of Congressmen and high executive officials to other countries usually involve discussions with leading citizens of foreign countries and generate news reports that are widely circulated. Indeed, there are few activities of either the executive or legislative branches of the government that do not result in the dissemination of ideas to foreign audiences.

The Government-Operated Network: News

Since most people in all countries depend on their local media for information and entertainment, an important part of the official U.S. information program is devoted to serving these media with news and feature material, radio and TV programs, and films. The major official U.S. news service is operated by the U. S. Information Agency, which sends 6,000-10,000 words of copy daily by radio-teletype to approximately 114 American embassies and other posts abroad. Some of this material is based on dispatches from the Associated Press and United Press International, or on stories or columns in American newspapers, and a large part consists of complete texts of official documents and important statements by American leaders. In addition, 16 full-time reporters and a large number of part-time correspondents throughout the United States cover stories that are not dealt with extensively by the commercial services: U.S. policies with respect to countries that are not in the news, displays of foreign art, or the activities of foreign students or other visitors in this country. These stories, while of less interest to American audiences, sometimes receive headlines abroad.

The content of the file sent to different areas varies, depending on the interests of the audience and American policies. When audience interests and U.S. policies conflict, local media are unlikely to carry the material. For instance, in 1955 Japanese editors complained that U.S.I.S. was emphasizing American-Soviet negotiations, while their readers wanted more news about U.S. business and industry.[45]

Once arrived in its country of destination, the file is put to a number of uses. Information officials circulate parts of it to the U.S. embassy staff in order to help them keep up with events back home; some items are translated and distributed to the local press; others are used in publications or in radio and TV programs that are produced locally by members of the U.S.I.S. staff. At some posts, especially where there are no local newspapers, news sheets are prepared in the local language and distributed to leading citizens. Many posts have "leadership distribution lists" of anywhere from several dozen to several thousand names of persons who receive U.S.I.S. materials.

The importance of the U.S.I.A. news service varies in different parts of the world. In highly industrialized countries that are well covered by international news services it usually plays a modest role. A survey of Japanese editors in 1955, for instance, found that only six of the sixty-two editors who replied placed the U.S.I.S. service among the three most reliable news sources, although nearly half said that they used the U.S.I.S. material to check the accuracy of stories received through commercial agencies.[46] In the Near East and South Asia, on the other hand, U.S.I.S. materials are used by some 1,200 daily papers, many of which rely heavily on the official service, in part because they cannot afford private ones. A U.S.I.S. press officer has reported that of the 400 stories he sent to local Greek newspapers in 1959, all but 15 were used.[47] In Western Europe the principal role of the U.S.I.S. service is to provide complete texts, which often are too expensive for commercial agencies to transmit in full, as well as background materials about American foreign policy.

U.S.I.A. news personnel abroad devote particular attention to becoming acquainted with local newsmen, and attempt to keep in touch with their interests, needs, and complaints. When a good relationship has been established, it is not infrequent for an editor to call up his acquaintance in the American embassy to check on the accuracy of a story or to request further background material.

Assistance is also given to foreign reporters in the United States. The White House, State Department, and U.S.I.A. jointly maintain a Foreign Press Center in New York, where some 550 correspondents from abroad have access to AP, UPI, and U.S.I.A. news tickers, as well as to a library containing current U. S. Government releases, periodicals, and newspapers from all parts of the country. The Center helps visiting newsmen overcome red tape and language difficulties, arranges interviews, sets up briefings by prominent Americans, and assists correspondents who wish to see other parts of the United States.[48] Many of these trips are arranged in cooperation with private organizations or state and local agencies. The State of Maine has launched a program of inviting two foreign correspondents and their wives to Maine every other weekend, and other states have indicated an interest in sponsoring similar visits.[49]

Unfortunately, no such arrangements have been worked out in the Washington area. Nevertheless, the State Department Office of Public Affairs has devoted increasing attention to answering queries from foreign newsmen, and occasional news conferences designed specifically for foreign reporters are held by the White House and the State Department.

Limited governmental assistance has been given to private American news services engaged in commercial operations abroad. Following World War II, diplomatic, information, and military officials overseas helped American wire agencies to become re-established in areas from which they had been excluded during the war, and in starting services to new areas. As late as 1961, U.S.I.A. found that the ten Chinese newspapers in Sarawak relied mainly on news monitored from the Peiping radio. When the commercial services were notified of this, they began supplying their news files to the Sarawak press. Despite the expansion of American news agencies, however, as of 1960 about two-thirds of all newspapers published overseas had no American commercial news source.[50]

U.S. Radio and Television Services

The Voice of America, which is usually thought of as the principal component of the U.S. foreign-information program, is in reality at least two operations. As of 1964, U.S.I.A. broadcast directly to foreign audiences in 37 languages from several domestic and foreign sites. Most broadcasts, totaling nearly 800 hours a week, were short-wave. About 40 per cent of these were directed to Communist areas, which are not easily accessible to other types of communications, although here jamming has sometimes interfered with reception. Nevertheless, this interference can apparently be overcome if a special effort is made. When the Soviets resumed nuclear testing in 1961, the Voice massed 52 transmitters on 80 frequencies for an 8-hour barrage to tell the Russian people of this, since they had not been informed by domestic media. Subsequent estimates indicated that these broadcasts broke through the jamming on more than half the frequencies used.[51] Soviet jamming of the Voice stopped in June 1963, after several periods of off-again-on-again interference and selective jamming.

Short-wave broadcasts are also useful in reaching certain free-world audiences. In emerging countries, where broadcasting services are rudimentary, many people rely on foreign short-wave programs. Even in areas with well-developed local radio it has been found that some listeners who are seriously interested in political matters like to tune in on distant countries directly.

Far larger audiences hear U.S.I.A. broadcasts over their local stations. Some of these stations pick up and relay Voice of America short-wave programs. In other cases, "package programs," consisting of tapes or discs of news features, music, special events, and interviews are sent to foreign stations. In still other cases, programs are prepared by U.S.I.S. overseas, usually in close cooperation with the local stations that use the programs. By 1964, American programs totaling some 14,000 hours per week were being placed on local stations throughout the world, about two-thirds of them in Latin America.

Voice of America broadcasts feature factual reporting of current news, with emphasis on matters of particular interest to the audiences being served. Newscasts are based principally on the files of the commercial agencies, although during the past few years the Voice has built up a small group of foreign correspondents. News analyses, commentaries, and features are usually prepared by staff members in Washington, but frequently cite opinions expressed by American columnists, editorial writers, or commentators. Summaries of American editorials and commentaries are also presented. The official government position is explained, using statements of the President, the Secretary of State, and other high officials. Special-events coverage provides recorded interviews in American homes, schools, farms, and factories. Other programs deal with economic conditions, science, agriculture, race relations, and religion. Music occupies an important place in the schedule. One of the most popular programs in all international broadcasting is "Music U.S.I.A.," which runs for two hours daily and is devoted to American popular music and the people who compose and perform it. Foreign visitors to the United States are frequently asked to speak over the Voice, usually to their own nations.

In recent years, the Voice has developed news and feature programs that use a simplified English vocabulary of about 1,000 words. These are beamed especially to areas where because of the profusion of local languages and dialects English is a lingua franca. A word list, giving the complete vocabulary required by listeners, is distributed through U.S.I.S. offices abroad. Simplified English broadcasts are spoken at a rate of 90 words a minute, as contrasted with the 150-200 words a minute that are customary on domestic radio stations.

On an average day, between 17 million and 26 million people listen to the Voice of America either on short-wave or via relays. In times of crisis or on special occasions—for instance, when American space flights have received minute-to-minute coverage—hundreds of millions of listeners may tune in. Audience size is estimated by occasional sample surveys, by the volume of correspondence received from listeners, and by the number of entries in prize contests that are sponsored by the Voice from time to time. In Korea, a contest that offered transistor radios as prizes drew 130,000 responses. A similar contest in Burma, where there were about 50,000 radio sets, drew 14,000 written entries.[52] Audiences behind the iron curtain are estimated on the basis of reports from U.S. diplomatic observers, or through surveys carried out among refugees.

Two official radio operations occupy a special position. RIAS (Radio in the American Sector of Berlin), although it comes under the supervision of U.S.I.A. and uses some material from Washington, broadcasts programs that are prepared mainly by escapees from East Germany. Only seven Americans are employed at RIAS. The Voice of the U.N. Command in Korea is a leftover from the Korean War. It is administered by the Department of the Army, and broadcasts daily to North China and North Korea in local languages. While it operates under the same general policy directives as the Voice of America, its programs are separately prepared.

The U. S. Information Agency did not make a serious effort in the television field until 1958, but then expanded its operations rapidly and by 1961 was producing over 550 programs per year for placement on foreign stations. In the same year it acquired (by purchase or gift) some 55 programs that had been produced by American commercial television enterprises, and adapted these for overseas use by dubbing in foreign-language sound tracks. In addition, it produced or acquired a number of program segments for integration in programs made overseas by foreign TV stations. During the calendar year 1961, U.S.I.S. posts were able to place over 2,500 hours of TV programming on local outlets in more than 50 countries. The following year saw an increase to more than 10,000 hours of local television time in more than 60 countries. By 1963, stations in 80 countries were using U.S.I.A. programs.

U.S.I.A. television programming includes coverage of news events, background treatments of current history, technical information, and portrayals of American life and culture. The Agency's TV series "Panorama Pan Americano" was being shown by stations in seventeen American Republics in 1963. Background features included coverage of the Cuban situation, the Berlin wall, the Alliance for Progress, and space explorations. Two important technical series, started in fiscal year 1962, were continued in 1963. One was a major effort in language teaching, entitled "Let's Learn English." The other was "Science Report," emphasizing the scientific progress of the free world. Special programs in all categories were prepared for distribution in specific countries or areas.

Much of the work of U.S.I.S. television personnel abroad consists of providing material that can be incorporated in live shows produced by local outlets. Several thousand such programs received U.S.I.S. assistance in 1960. Occasionally, American TV officers collaborate with local stations to originate new material. One such series, made in Caracas, was entitled "Venezuela Looks Toward Her Future." A similar weekly show was produced in Guatemala City.[53]

Private American TV interests assist U.S.I.A.'s television operations in several ways. In many cases, commercial networks make tapes available without cost—as when ABC-TV in Chicago contributed 18 hours of "Science Expedition" productions, valued at $108,000.[54] Advisers from the industry not only help to keep U.S.I.A up to date on technical matters, but also assist in obtaining rights to programs that the Agency would like to show abroad and in arranging practical experience for foreign TV personnel brought to this country under U.S.I.A. training programs.

Government Motion Pictures

The U. S. Information Agency operates a world-wide system for distributing and showing documentary films, of which it had more than 1,700 in its film libraries in 1963. More than half of these were produced or contracted for by U.S.I.A.; others were acquired from other government agencies, educational institutions, or industry.[55] U.S.I.A. films are shown in U.S. information centers throughout the world, loaned to foreign groups, rented to commercial theaters, or exhibited by mobile projection units, of which the Agency had 204 in 1964. In recent years the estimated annual audience for films distributed through U.S.I.A. auspices has been about 750 million persons. A film that is put into the 40 languages used by U.S.I.A. in its motion-picture program has a potential audience of about 50 million over a period of years.[56]

Motion pictures available for showing through U.S.I.A. facilities include newsreels especially prepared for Africa, Latin America, and other areas; documentaries such as *Architects of Space* and *Nigeria—A Salute to Independence;* films on technical subjects, such as *Fight Against Malaria* and *The Versatile Soybean;* and films giving background information about the United States, such as *An American Factory* and *All About New York*. Perhaps the best known of recent U.S.I.A. films is *Years of Lightning, Day of Drums,* telling the Kennedy story.

Special attention is given to producing and acquiring films dealing with issues of current importance to U.S. policy: for instance, the nuclear-test-ban treaty, Berlin, the United Nations, freedom of choice, modernization, scientific achievement, defense against Communism, and space activities. This emphasis on selected foreign-policy issues has led to an increase in the proportion of films that U.S.I.A. produces itself as opposed to the proportion it acquires from nonofficial sources. In the fiscal year ended June 30, 1964, U.S.I.A. produced 593 newsreels and documentaries, most of these overseas, and acquired only 32 films from other sources.

For many people in emerging countries, U.S.I.A. films are the first motion pictures they have seen, since the Agency's distribution system serves remote areas having no commercial theaters. Mobile projection units penetrate to villages that have previously been cut off from the world outside. When there are no roads, films and projectors are shipped by such means as mules, jeeps, riverboats, and small aircraft.

Extensive use of films is also made by the Agency for International Development. In 1963 it set up a film library of over 1,000 titles, including reels on agriculture, health, industry, and education. AID personnel overseas are able to borrow from this library, as required, on a 60-day basis.[57]

Books and Other Publications

Libraries and binational centers are the principal mechanisms used by the Information Agency to make American publications directly available to foreign audiences. As of 1963, some 260 libraries and reading rooms of varying sizes were operated throughout the world. Holdings averaged about 13,000 titles, and frequently represented the best collections freely available to the public in the local community. A survey in 1961 found that the 11 American libraries in Latin America contained a total of about 175,000 books, of which 50,000 were in translation. Annual attendance at these centers was close to 1,250,000; book circulation totaled about 500,000 per year.[58] Throughout the world, U.S.I.A. circulated more than 8 million books through its libraries in 1961; in 1962 visitors totaled 30 million.[59]

As distinct from the U.S.-operated libraries, binational centers are autonomous institutions, jointly sponsored by American residents in foreign areas and nationals of the host country. Their purpose is to foster cultural exchange and mutual understanding, and they maintain libraries as one means of achieving their goals. As of 1962, there were 160 binational centers, two-thirds of them in Latin America. These Latin American centers had holdings of some 275,000 volumes and an annual circulation of about 300,000. Expenses of binational centers are covered in large part by income-producing activities and local contributions, but the U. S. Government makes a relatively modest contribution toward the purchase of publications and supplies, and provides grants to cover operating expenses and to pay the salary of a full-time American staff member in some cases.

There are five other principal ways in which the U. S. Information Agency promotes the circulation of American books abroad. These are the encouragement and subsidization of works both in translation and in English, exhibition of books at fairs, facilitation of commercial sales in "soft-currency" countries, the distribution of privately donated publications, and the presentation of especially important books to key figures overseas as well as to libraries and other educational institutions.

During the fiscal year 1963, the Agency assisted American and foreign publishers in producing more than 10 million copies of 1,202 titles in English and 35 foreign languages. This assistance included outright subsidies to reduce prices in the case of export editions in English and certain low-priced foreign-language editions, agreements to purchase a number of copies after publication or to pay for translation costs, and the purchase of translation and English-reprint rights. In the same year, U.S.I.A. displayed book collections at 87 book fairs and other special events throughout the world, and encouraged U.S. publishers to participate in semicommercial book events such as the annual fairs in Warsaw and Belgrade.

Commercial sales of American books (as well as other publications and films that are consistent with U.S. foreign-policy objectives) in several countries where local currencies are not freely convertible into dollars have been assisted since 1948 by the Informational Media Guarantee Program, administered by the U.S.I.A. Under this program, foreign importers pay American exporters in the currency of the importing country, and the American firm then exchanges this currency for dollars through application to the Information Agency. Most of the foreign currencies thus acquired are later used to cover operating expenses of U.S. missions abroad. Since the start of the program, book publishers have accounted for more than half the dollar value of contracts signed under its terms, texts and technical literature being the most important categories of books involved. Magazine publishers and film producers have divided most of the remainder. Funds available for Informational Media Guarantee have declined in recent years, due to the reluctance of Congress to make new appropriations for it, and as of 1963 it was operating at a level of under $5 million and in only eight countries, including Poland, Yugoslavia, Turkey, Pakistan, and Korea.

During each of the past few years, U.S.I.A. has distributed abroad between 2 and 4 million books and magazines provided by private sources, most of these donated by publishers, school systems, or the Post Office Department Dead Letter Centers. American magazine publishers who sell in foreign markets have contributed overseas newsstand returns, so that U.S.I.S. has been able to supply readers in emerging countries with recent issues of periodicals. A few publishers donate current subscriptions. In 1963, six of the largest paperback book publishers were enlisted in a campaign to collect funds for sending abroad the best American literature in paperback form. Each of the volumes issued by these publishers for sale in the United States was to include a form in the back inviting the reader to send in $4 so that a collection of up to ten paperback books could be sent by U.S.I.A. to foreign libraries and schools.[60] As a result of bitter experience, government agencies are cautious about soliciting used-book donations from the public. Unless the kinds of publications needed are carefully specified in advance, good-hearted donors are inclined to clean out their attics and deluge the authorities with long-forgotten novels and out-of-date texts.

A small amount of money is available to U.S.I.A. for presentation of publications. In 1963 this amounted to about $145,000, some two-thirds of which went for books. Volumes given to foreign leaders and institutions have included more than 1,000 copies of the "New Frontier Bookshelf," a collection of the writings of officials of the Kennedy Administration; plays by Thornton Wilder and Tennessee Williams; and the Army, Navy, and Air Force blue books.

Other major distributors of American publications overseas are the Agency for International Development, the Peace Corps, and the Defense Department. AID uses large quantities of American texts and manuals in connection with educational and development projects. For the 1963 school year, it distributed more than 2 million readers to Latin American schoolchildren, and assisted in publishing Spanish translations of outstanding science books. In addition, it has conducted a "Little Library" program, through which small collections of American technical and scientific paperback books are made available to institutions in some 80 countries.[61] The Peace Corps also is a large-scale distributor of books in connection with its teaching activities. Most of these books are contributed by private sources. The Defense Department acts as a channel in several ways, both intended and unintended. Many of the magazines and books that are sent overseas for the use of American military personnel and their families end up in the hands of nationals of the host country, and some of the community-relations programs conducted by the armed forces overseas involve providing reading material to local employees or institutions. In Latin American countries the U. S. Defense Department is making available materials on Communism for use by these countries in their military information and education programs.

It is noteworthy that no U.S. agency emphasizes the writing of books, or having them written, especially for foreign publics. By and large, the volumes that are distributed are originally published for the American reader; foreign distribution is an afterthought. In some cases, texts are adapted to fit local requirements, language may be simplified, or translations may omit portions of little interest to the foreign reader, but such cases are exceptions to the general rule. The U. S. Information Agency commissions several book-length manuscripts each year and supports the publication of a few other books that otherwise would not appear, but the numbers are very small. In 1963, it commissioned five original manuscripts, and provided publication support for four other books and six booklets, at a total cost of about $62,000.

The close relationship between government efforts to promote the distribution of American books abroad and the American publishing industry has been recognized by the formation of a U. S. Advisory Committee on International Book Programs, composed of leaders in the industry. The purpose of this committee is to "determine the most effective means for increasing the number of readers abroad for American books." Among its first actions were to ask American publishers to cooperate in U.S.I.A.'s translation program for Latin America by letting translation rights at less than commercial rates, and to suggest a policy of investment guarantees that would enable more U.S. publishers to cooperate in strengthening the publishing industry in developing countries.[62]

In contrast to the field of books, where emphasis is placed on distribution of privately published works, the U. S. Government (through the U.S.I.A.) is one of the world's largest producers of magazines. Most of these are for circulation in emerging areas, but one is published for the Soviet Union, one for Poland, and several for West European countries.

Magazines published by U.S.I.A. for Western Europe are of a specialized nature. For instance, the French-language *Informations et Documents,* appearing 18 times a year in an edition of 115,000, contains important texts relating to U.S. foreign policy. *Labor News, American Economic Report, Science Horizons,* and the *American Review* are designed for specialized audiences in the United Kingdom.

In the emerging areas, U.S.I.A. magazines are more often intended for general readers—although in some cases limited literacy means that these audiences are still small. *Aneka Amerika,* produced by U.S.I.S. Djakarta, had the largest circulation of any magazine in Indonesia—approximately 175,000—at least until Indonesian authorities started interfering with its distribution. *Free World,* which appears in 10 languages used in 16 Asian countries, has an annual print run of 5.4 million and claims the widest circulation of any magazine in the Eastern Hemisphere. *Perspectives Americaines,* a monthly publication for French-speaking Africa, reached a monthly circulation of 60,000 in 1964.

There are an increasing number of intellectual journals being published for distribution in emerging countries. The *Nigerian-American Quarterly,* designed for Nigerians of college-level education, was started in 1961, and *Span,* a magazine for Indian intellectuals, began to appear in New Delhi slightly earlier.

Among U.S.I.A. publications oriented toward intellectuals, *Problems of Communism* deserves special mention. This journal, edited in Washington, contains sober, factual accounts of life and politics in the Soviet Union and other Communist countries, contributed by outstanding experts in the United States and abroad. It enjoys wide respect for its scholarly quality.

Most of the magazines published by U.S.I.A. are edited overseas, although much of their content is furnished from Washington. This includes stories on science, education, culture, economics, and American life in general, as well as material bearing on topics that the Agency wishes to emphasize at any one time. Some of this material is staff written, while some is specially commissioned or is taken from commercial magazines by permission. Publications are sold at a very low cost—in most cases for the equivalent of 5 or 10 cents—or are given away.

The Agency also distributes pamphlets and cartoon books on foreign-policy issues. For instance, in 1961-62, several million pamphlets on the Berlin situation, in thirteen languages, were provided to U.S.I.S. posts around the world for local distribution, and six cartoon books were printed for mass audiences in Latin America. These dealt with such subjects as Communism, the Alliance for Progress, and Puerto Rico. Three more cartoon books had been published by the middle of 1963, and the total distributed during the preceding two years came close to 20 million.

International Exhibitions and Promotion of Trade and Travel

In the course of promoting international trade and travel, government agencies have recently begun to reach large numbers of people in other nations with ideas about the United States. The U. S. Travel Service of the Department of Commerce is the principal official agency for the promotion of tourism. It was organized in 1961, and had opened eleven offices abroad by the end of 1962. The principal activities of these offices include placing advertising and distributing literature about travel in the United States, and maintaining contacts with foreign travel editors and travel agents. They also make use of films produced by industry and by U.S.I.A. Just how great the effect of travel propaganda has been is difficult to gauge, but the Travel Service has noted that visitors coming from areas covered by U.S.T.S. offices increased by 16 per cent between 1961 and 1962.[63]

The overseas trade centers of the Commerce Department are also commercial in character, although they have informational and cultural overtones. As of January 1964, these were located in London, Bangkok, Frankfurt, Tokyo, Stockholm, and Milan—the first office having been opened in 1961. The centers organize trade shows displaying U.S. manufactures, maintain commercial libraries, and assist American businessmen in making contacts. The one in Tokyo has a small theater for showing industrial films.[64]

American activities in connection with international exhibitions are of three types. The United States contributes commercial and cultural exhibits to trade fairs, it sends labor missions to them, and it organizes special exhibits for particular purposes. Participation in trade fairs is coordinated by an interagency committee, on which the Department of State, U.S.I.A., and the Department of Commerce are represented. The Office of International Trade Fairs of the Department of Commerce is responsible for preparing U.S. exhibits and negotiating with participating American firms, but the committee decides whether to take part in any given fair and determines the "theme" for the American exhibit as a whole. During the fiscal year 1962, the Office of International Trade Fairs organized 14 industry exhibits in which 1,100 American business firms participated. These exhibits were seen by an estimated 14 million persons.[65] Themes emphasized in past American displays have included "Marketing and Services in an Industrial Economy" (Zagreb), "Buy American with Confidence" (Vienna), "New Techniques in Science and Industry" (Tunis), and "Power to Produce for Peace" (Cairo).

Labor missions to international trade fairs are organized by the Department of Labor with trade-union assistance. During the fiscal year 1962, the Department sent small delegations of officials and American labor leaders to six fairs, and in three cases set up special labor exhibits. In New Delhi, for instance, the U.S. mission included officials of the Retail Clerks and Electrical Workers unions, and the exhibit dealt with the social-welfare mechanisms protecting American labor. Union representatives who take part in labor missions often speak the language of the host country and are able to establish close contacts with local labor leaders.

Special-purpose exhibitions are conducted in Eastern Europe by U.S.I.A. under exchange agreements between the United States and the countries concerned. A number have also been organized in Europe and Latin America. During 1962 and 1963, three American exhibits costing about $1.5 million were shown in cities of the Soviet Union, after which they were moved to other East European countries. These exhibits were "Plastics—U.S.A.," "Transportation—U.S.A.," and "Medicine—U.S.A." They were seen by nearly 3 million people during their first two years, and were followed by a graphic-arts exhibit in 1963 that attracted 700,000 persons in Moscow alone.[66] United States participation in the Venice and São Paulo biennial cultural expositions was financed and arranged by the Museum of Modern Art until 1963, when U.S.I.A. assumed this responsibility.

A particularly large American exhibition in Moscow during 1959 featured Edward Steichen's "Family of Man" photographic collection, color television, automobiles, a bookmobile, a model house, voting machines, and many other aspects of American life and culture. A special feature was the presence of 75 Russian-speaking Americans who served as guides and answered the many questions about the United States asked by the 2.7 million visitors. The demand for tickets to this exhibition was so great that it could not be satisfied during the six weeks the display was open.[67]

Exchange of Persons

A number of government agencies sponsor foreign travel by private American citizens. This may involve study, teaching, research, or participation in conferences. The largest of these programs is administered by the Department of State under the Fulbright-Hays Act of 1961, and legislation that preceded it. This has provided financial assistance to about 2,000 teachers and students in each of the last few years.[68] Americans who go abroad as Fulbright scholars are regarded as private persons and not as official spokesmen for the United States. They are, however, encouraged to cooperate with overseas information and cultural programs, for instance, by giving lectures in their field of specialization, although they are free to refuse. In many parts of the world American exchange teachers have been able to increase understanding of American life and culture among those who seldom come in contact with Americans.[69]

Another program administered by the State Department involves sending relatively small numbers of highly qualified Americans abroad for short visits of from thirty to ninety days, during which time they meet with selected groups to discuss important developments in American education, science, or culture. Between 1949, when the program was started, and 1961, some 3,300 U.S. specialists had been sent to foreign countries. Most of these appear to have demonstrated their effectiveness in promoting a broader and more accurate understanding of the United States.[70]

When it comes to bringing foreigners to the United States, an impressive array of official sponsors is involved.[71] The largest American educational program for foreign nationals is that of the Department of Defense. Under the Military Assistance Training Program, some 18,000 Allied officers and men come to the United States each year for instruction in a variety of military specialties, and about 10,000 more are trained in the United States under other Defense Department programs. This instruction is primarily in technical military matters, but it also involves English teaching and general orientation about the United States. Many trainees are given opportunities to visit various parts of the country, and are entertained in American homes. A few are sent to civilian institutions for further study. In addition to the thousands who visit the United States in connection with this massive training program, hundreds of thousands more are trained by American personnel overseas. While this phase of the program does not involve exposure to the United States, it does result in many close personal contacts between American and foreign military personnel.[72]

Another extensive training program is sponsored by the Agency for International Development. AID brings about 6,000 foreign nationals each year to the United States for instruction in a wide variety of specialties, ranging from administrative and teaching methods to the operation of many kinds of industries. The actual training is ordinarily carried out by private institutions or corporations. Most trainees also have an opportunity to travel in the United States and to attend orientation courses.

The third major set of programs for foreign visitors is conducted by the Department of State. These sometimes involve specialized training, but usually the objectives are more general. During the academic year 1961-62, some 2,300 foreign leaders and specialists, including editors, labor leaders, government officials, educators, and creative artists, were brought to this country for visits averaging about 60 days.[73] Students, professors, and researchers ordinarily stay for longer periods. In 1962, some 3,000 students and about 1,800 teachers and research scholars were in the United States in connection with these programs, most of them beneficiaries of Fulbright grants. During the fiscal year 1963, a total of about 5,800 foreign visitors were supported in whole or in part by State Department funds.[74]

A special example of an officially sponsored educational program is the East-West Center of the University of Hawaii. This was authorized by the Mutual Security Act of 1960, and is supported by funds appropriated to the Department of State. The Center is able to offer grants and fellowships to attract outstanding teachers and students from the United States and Asia, who live in a newly constructed international community on the University of Hawaii campus. As of 1963, the Center had about 500 students from more than 20 countries in residence, as well as 26 senior scholars. About 1,700 students are expected by 1968.[75]

The interrelationship between the public and private sector in educational activities is closer than in other branches of the U.S. international communication program. The exchanges sponsored by the State Department, and by most of the other agencies involved, would be impossible without the cooperation of many private individuals and educational institutions. At the same time, private activities in the field of international education are stimulated and assisted by the State Department, U.S.I.A., and other official bodies.[76]

One way in which private influences are brought to bear on government-sponsored educational exchanges is through advisory and supervisory bodies. A Board of Foreign Scholarships, composed largely of leading American educators, selects Americans to participate in exchanges under the Fulbright-Hays Act. The U. S. Advisory Commission on International Educational and Cultural Affairs, also established by the Fulbright-Hays Act to succeed an earlier body with similar functions, maintains a continuing review of the whole program. In addition, the State Department is advised by numerous private groups familiar with particular geographical or functional areas. For example, in 1963 it requested interested private educational agencies to form a group to advise on action for dealing with the needs of African students in the United States, noting that nobody knew the exact number of sub-Sahara Africans then studying here, and that there was no single body, either governmental or private, that was gathering information about their needs on a continuing basis. This group, known as the Council for Educational Cooperation with Africa, included among its members the African-American Student Foundation, the African-American Institute, the United Negro College Fund, the Phelps-Stokes Fund, the Institute of

International Education, and the African Scholarship Program of American Universities.

Furthermore, most phases of the officially supported exchange programs (with the exception of those of the Defense Department) are actually administered by universities or other nongovernmental institutions. Of these, one of the most important is the Institute of International Education in New York, which is supported primarily by foundation grants and corporate and individual donations.[77] Indeed, without the facilities of the Institute, which had been developed in the 1930's and 1940's through private idealism and initiative, it is doubtful whether government programs of the 1950's and 1960's could have expanded at the rate they did.[78] The Institute interviews many foreign exchangees abroad, helps them to find appropriate educational opportunities in the United States, and conducts orientation programs. To the activities of the Institute must be added the influence of numerous school and college administrations, foreign student advisors, American students, such bodies as the Committee on Friendly Relations Among Foreign Students, and the communities visited by foreign exchangees. The great majority of communications to which foreigners coming to this country under government programs are exposed thus emanate from private sources.

At the same time that official educational exchange programs are heavily dependent on cooperation from private individuals and bodies, the State Department, AID, the U. S. Information Agency, and other government agencies have increasingly assisted private efforts in this field. Part of this assistance is in financial form. As of 1963, the State Department budget provided for partial financial support to American-sponsored schools in thirty-two countries, and for grants to promote certain phases of the activities of such organizations as the 4-H Clubs, the American Field Service, and the Experiment in International Living. Additional assistance to American schools abroad, and to other bodies concerned with economic development has been provided by AID.[79] In some cases, financial responsibility for exchange programs that were initiated by private agencies has been taken over by the government: for example, in the case of students from Africa and Eastern Europe, who initially were brought to the United States under private auspices.

Fewer than 10 per cent of the foreign students in the United States are government grantees, but the State Department also attempts to assist the other 90 per cent. It helps to find private support and summer jobs for them, and in general seeks to assure that their total experience in the United States is a satisfactory one. A State Department Director of Foreign Student Affairs was appointed in 1961, and in 1962 the Department unsuccessfully sought funds to provide further services for students coming to the United States under private sponsorship, including additional counseling and orientation. The Department also helps to make arrangements for about 2,000 American and foreign leaders each year who travel at nongovernment expense, and assists many nonofficial visitors through reception centers for foreign visitors at seven American ports-of-entry.[80]

Exporting the Arts (and Sports)

Although the importance of art as an instrument of national policy has been recognized for many years by major European powers, especially France, the first major American move in this field came in 1951, when *Oklahoma!* was staged at the Berlin festival under State Department sponsorship. This was followed by *Porgy and Bess,* which toured Europe, including Moscow, and the Middle East in the following year. In 1954, Congress approved an administration proposal to provide partial support for overseas tours by American artists, and this support has been continued.[81]

A wide variety of cultural exports are now sponsored by the Department of State Cultural Presentations Program, which since 1959 has had an annual budget of about $2.5 million. Professional theatrical, musical, dance, and variety groups are sent to all parts of the world. In addition, tours by individual artists and performing groups from educational institutions receive official support. Academic groups taking part in this program in 1962 included the Eastman Philharmonica, the University of Maine Masque Theater, and the Berea College folk dancers. Nine athletic groups, including four basketball teams and a crew, were also sent abroad during 1962. The artists and athletes concerned were seen by some 4.5 million people in 84 countries. In 1962, following criticisms of this program, it was re-examined by the Advisory Commission on Cultural Presentations, which recommended several administrative changes, but affirmed that it had a record of inspiring achievement in the past and saw great challenges and opportunities for it in the future.[82]

While the major responsibility for official support of artistic and cultural exports rests with the Department of State, the U. S. Information

Agency and the Defense Department conduct related activities. U.S.I.S. information centers and binational centers often display American art collections or scientific exhibits, provide a location for smaller performances, and offer a meeting ground where American artists can associate with their opposite numbers and other interested persons. Many U.S.I.S. libraries include recordings of American music, as well as scores that are loaned to foreign musicians, and U.S.I.A.'s news and feature output emphasizes the work of American artists and musicians. American military units have sponsored a broad range of cultural activities in areas where U.S. forces are stationed. These have included concerts by military bands and symphony orchestras, displays of paintings and sculpture created by soldier artists, and performances by military theatrical troupes.

Educational and Cultural Exchanges with Communist Countries

Especially in the case of Communist countries, where international commercial channels function to a very limited extent, cultural and educational exchanges have been regulated by very detailed agreements. The cultural agreement with Rumania concluded in 1962, for example, provided for the showing of the American film *The Old Man and the Sea* in four Rumanian cities, while *Darclee,* a film based on the life of a famous Rumanian opera star, was to be shown in an equal number of cities in the United States.[83] This pact was enlarged the following year to include provisions for encouraging the interchange of books and translations, radio and TV programs, national exhibits, and tourists.

The United States began proposing exchanges with the Soviet Union shortly after World War II, but initially these approaches were not accepted; indeed, most of them were not acknowledged. The Soviets started to show more interest in 1954, when they suddenly granted visas to four American graduate students to visit the Soviet Union, and in January 1958, Soviet Ambassador Georgi N. Zaroubin and U.S. Ambassador William S. Lacy of the State Department concluded an agreement providing for limited exchanges. By the end of 1958, 38 American technical, academic, cultural, sports, and entertainment groups had visited the Soviet Union, while 33 Soviet groups had come to the United States. In addition, 22 American graduate students were enrolled at Moscow and Leningrad universities for the academic year 1958-59, and 17 Soviet students were at 5 American universities. Tourism expanded:

about 5,000 American tourists traveled in the Soviet Union, and a handful of Soviet tourists—the first since the war—arrived in this country. The Lacy-Zaroubin agreement also laid the groundwork for increased circulation of the U.S. magazine *Amerika* in the Soviet Union and the magazine *Soviet Life* (formerly, *USSR*), in the United States, for motion-picture and television exchanges, and for U.S. and Soviet national exhibitions in Moscow and New York. Under the terms of this agreement, further exchanges of personnel in the natural sciences and humanities were subsequently arranged through negotiations between the U. S. Academy of Sciences and the American Council of Learned Societies, on the one hand, and Soviet authorities on the other.[84]

The Lacy-Zaroubin agreement has been renewed at intervals since 1958 and has been slightly broadened, but always after hard bargaining. The basic difficulty has been that the Soviets have been interested primarily in using exchanges to gather scientific and technical information, while the United States has sought to penetrate Soviet censorship with more balanced information about life in this country, and American students have wanted to gain a better understanding of Soviet society. The bargaining situation has been uneven, since American society is much more open than is Russian society. For instance, the Soviets can easily introduce any material that has news value into the American commercial news network without difficulty, while Soviet media are under strict government control. Similarly, Soviet students at American universities have broader opportunities for research and travel than do American students at Soviet universities.

Since 1960, fulfillment of the exchange agreements has been most satisfactory in the scientific, technical, and industrial fields, where Soviet interest is greatest. Some success has also been achieved in the case of films. The Soviets had purchased twenty-two American films by the end of 1962, and American companies had bought twelve Russian films during the same period. Exchanges in the performing arts and athletics have also taken place, with two or more musical or theatrical groups, about the same number of athletic teams, and a few individual artists traveling each way every year. Some exchange of graduate students and professors has occurred, but the numbers involved continue to be very small. The implementation of agreements in the fields of radio, TV, publications, and tourism has been even more spotty. Although the Soviets have authorized exchanges in principle, negotiations have frequently broken down over the details.

In spite of the limitations of the cultural- and educational-exchange agreements with the Soviet Union, many observers feel that they are beneficial. While American scholars have found it difficult to obtain access to Soviet libraries and laboratories that are relevant to their work, and their opportunities for travel have been restricted, most of them have been satisfied that the time spent in Russia was worth while. Several Soviet visitors have indicated publicly that their ideas about the United States had changed as the result of a sojourn in this country.[85] A former Assistant Secretary of State for Public Affairs, after visiting the Soviet Union in 1962, concluded that the cultural exchanges were valuable, even though they provided for only a trickle of contacts, since through them more and more influential people on both sides were learning to understand one another better, although with painful slowness.[86]

Building International Communication Channels

Both governmental and private international information and cultural programs often have the effect of building new communication channels, although some of these are used for international communication only in part.

Equipment for printing plants, radio stations, and film projection has been furnished by AID in connection with economic and educational assistance projects. Press, radio, and film personnel, librarians, and others who are concerned with operating communication channels have been trained by a number of government and private agencies. The largest program for training foreign communication personnel is conducted by Indiana University, under a contract with AID: about forty citizens of emerging countries have come to Indiana each year during the past decade for intensive courses in the operation and use of modern media and techniques.[87] Seminars for communication personnel are conducted by AID in Latin America and elsewhere. In India alone, some thirty workshops were held in 1961 by the Communications Media Center of the AID Mission; they stressed simple visual aids: chalk boards, posters, pamphlets, filmstrips, and so on.

The United States promotes international communication more directly through educational and cultural agreements. By mid-1964, agreements providing for binational commissions to help administer exchanges under the Fulbright-Hays Act had been signed with forty-eight countries. Some of these agreements, for example, one with the United Arab Republic—provided in addition the creation of chairs in each country of the language and literature of the other, establishment of centers for cultural and technical interchange, and the encouragement of a two-way flow of cultural and scientific publications, films, newsreels, exhibits, and artists.[88]

Other diplomatic measures have sought to open channels for all kinds of international communications. In 1959, for example, the U.S. representative on the United Nations Economic and Social Council submitted a resolution providing for freedom of news-gathering within all countries and its unhindered transmission across frontiers. An effective international agreement on the flow of news has never been achieved, but limited gains have been made in more specialized areas, such as the elimination of import duties on some educational, scientific, and cultural materials.[89]

One of the most effective ways in which the U. S. Government helps to build international communication channels is through the teaching of English to foreigners. Several agencies are involved in this, among them U.S.I.A., the State Department, the Department of Defense, the Agency for International Development, and the Peace Corps. In 1962, Edward R. Murrow estimated that U.S.I.A was reaching about 250,000 persons through its English-teaching programs, and in the following year the number rose to nearly 265,000—a better than fourfold increase since 1955. In addition to teaching beginners, the Information Agency conducts seminars where foreign teachers of English brush up on modern teaching methods while also learning about the United States. A great many U.S. officials overseas, and their wives, have served as English-language instructors in their spare time.

English-teaching provides an opportunity to convey information about the United States in an informal, nonpropagandistic manner. The Information Agency's twenty-five-week TV English course, for instance, contains scenes of Americans shopping, engaging in recreation activities, and so on, and includes a sequence showing a newsstand that sells publications from around the world, including iron-curtain countries. English-teaching also helps to establish contacts between Americans and those abroad who are interested in international affairs, especially those in the newer nations. In one African state, the Acting Public Affairs Officer was teaching English to the country's president less than a month after he had arrived in the country. In another, the local government requested places in the U.S.I.S. language school for 1,100 of its employees.[90]

For a foreigner, learning English is similar to acquiring a radio transmitter or a printing press: it is a facility that can be used in a variety of ways in both domestic and international communication. He may employ his linguistic knowledge to read technical literature, to listen to foreign broadcasts, or to communicate with people in neighboring states for whom English is also a second language. (A substantial amount of creative writing in English is now done in countries where it is not the native tongue.[91]) Knowledge of English is, of course, no guarantee that a person will be sympathetic to the United States or to the West in general. He may use his knowledge to read some of the Communist literature that is distributed throughout the world in English.

Government and private agencies also help to build communication channels through the encouragement of American studies throughout the world. The Department of State spent over $1 million for this purpose in fiscal year 1962, mostly in the Far East, the Near East, and Southeast Asia, to support teaching chairs in universities, lectures, seminars, and discussions. Until recently, it was impossible for a student to do any advanced work on American civilization even at major European universities, and American literature and history were largely ignored. This situation is now changing, in part through the work of U.S.I.A., AID, the Department of State, the U. S. Office of Education, and private foundations. Visiting professors of American civilization have been supplied in hundreds of cases, and this area of study has become established as a part of the regular program in many foreign schools. One of the principal tasks of U.S.I.S. offices abroad is to cultivate interest in American studies on the part of local educational institutions, and also to help supply these institutions with materials that they can use in American study programs.[92]

International exchanges of persons often have the effect of setting up continuing channels of international communication. Personal contacts formed through study abroad may be maintained over a period of time, and former students may organize alumni groups that serve as channels of information between nations. In 1960, the Department of State reported that American agencies were giving assistance in 44 countries to 136 associations of persons who had studied in the United States, and that newsletters were being published by alumni associations in 23 of these countries. A later survey found more than 200 such alumni associations in 47 countries. One of the most active of these was the Association Amicale Universitaire France-Amérique, with 1,700 members, which conducted a social and lecture program and also assisted in the orientation of exchange students coming to the United States. The Philippine Fulbright Scholars Association, with 800 members in 1963, takes part in the screening of Fulbright applicants, conducts a radio forum, has worked for the abolition of a tax on imported books, and provides information about Philippine life and culture to foreign visitors. In addition, alumni clubs of graduates of specific American colleges or universities were active in several countries. In Japan alone there were 32 such groups in 1960.[93]

American public and private bodies have made some attempt to maintain and deepen the channels formed as a result of educational exchange-programs, but these have so far been limited. In the late 1950's, "Follow-Up Sections" were established at major U.S.I.A. posts to keep in touch with returned Fulbrighters. The Tokyo Follow-Up Section, for example, issues a directory of returned grantees, publishes a magazine, and arranges social and cultural events.[94] Most posts do not appear to have been so active. In 1963, then U.S.I.A. Director Edward R. Murrow reported that the Information Agency was planning to make increased efforts to keep in touch with students from other countries who had been in the United States, and to supply them with scholarly publications and other materials in their fields of special interest.[95]

Covert Activities

It is generally assumed that the United States, like other major powers, Communist and non-Communist, engages in some covert activities in the field of communications. During World War II, the Office of War Information, the Office of Strategic Services, and some military agencies operated "black" radio transmitters and produced leaflets and other publications that purported to emanate from a neutral or enemy source. Following the war, some of these activities were apparently continued by the Central Intelligence Agency, and possibly by other agencies.

In the absence of adequate sources, the extent and nature of covert American propaganda has remained a subject for speculation. Several accounts of the Central Intelligence Agency's operations have scarcely mentioned propaganda at all, implying that it is a very minor part of the Agency's activities.[96] Others have asserted or implied that the CIA has operated or had an interest in certain radio stations engaged in international broadcasting. During the abortive invasion of Cuba in 1961, for example, the CIA appears to have operated a "black" transmitter on

Swan Island in the Caribbean. In addition, it has been suggested that CIA agents overseas are engaged in strengthening certain selected newspapers, backing opposition parties, and so on. Nevertheless, most studies of the CIA are in agreement that its principal task is the collecting of intelligence.[97]

Communist sources make frequent references to "black" operations carried on by the United States, but they tend to extend these to cover almost any activities of which they do not approve (just as some Western sources attribute all anti-Western manifestations to the Communists). A recent Soviet article devoted primarily to CIA activities in Latin America, for example, asserted that generously financed special units of this agency engage in "black" propaganda and support local anti-Communist groups throughout the world.[98] No further discussion was devoted to the size of these "special units," or to the funds at their disposal.

It is reasonable to conclude that the United States does in fact engage in some "black" propaganda activities, and also that some of the communication programs that are carried on overtly may have covert counterparts. Since the sources of the overwhelming majority of the ideas from or about the United States that reach people in other countries can be satisfactorily identified, however, it also appears likely that covert operations account for a relatively modest portion of the total American activity in international communication.

Communications Under International or Multilateral Sponsorship

Many of the information and cultural programs conducted by American agencies benefit greatly from the cooperation and support of other governments. U.S.I.A. seminars for English teachers are usually co-sponsored by local ministries of education. Binational centers throughout the world are supported by both American and foreign contributions. In several cases, foreign countries, including West Germany, Austria, and Sweden, have agreed to share the cost of educational exchanges. West Germany has also helped out financially in the case of U.S. information centers. When it looked as though nine of the America Houses in the Federal Republic would have to close because of budgetary limitations, the host city governments indicated their willingness to foot up to 50 per cent of the bill to keep the centers open. In several cases, the German cities concerned declined an offer to share in the management of the centers, preferring to preserve their existing character by leaving them under exclusive American control. In Ethiopia, the Ministry of Education requested U.S.I.A. to open eleven additional reading rooms, offering to supply rent-free space and to pay the salary of one staff member in each reading room.[99]

On some occasions, U.S. information and cultural policies have been coordinated with those of friendly countries. After the erection of the Berlin wall, the Allied governments concerned worked together in hammering out an information policy to deal with the crisis. An informal attempt to synchronize the cultural policies of the Atlantic nations was made when cultural officers from the Washington embassies of thirteen friendly European countries started meeting with representatives of the State Department Bureau of Educational and Cultural Affairs in 1962. These meetings were, however, later discontinued.

A large number of informational and cultural programs are carried out by international organizations of which the United States is a member. In 1963, this country contributed nearly $70 million through the Department of State budget to thirty-one international organizations, including the United Nations and the U.N. specialized agencies, seven inter-American organizations, six additional multilateral organizations (including the North Atlantic Treaty Organization) and ten other organizations (including the International Atomic Energy Agency). Several of these organizations carry on programs ranging over almost the entire spectrum of informational and cultural activities. Most of them also engage in training and educational activities, and some have assisted in developing international communications systems.

The Peace Corps, which started as a purely American venture, has shown signs of developing into an international movement. After its first year of successful operation, other countries became interested in developing similar organizations. West Germany, Norway, and Denmark began studying the possibility of establishing their own Peace Corps. Colombia sent thirty social workers to be trained with American volunteers scheduled to do social rehabilitation work in Colombian cities.[100] The Netherlands, New Zealand, and Argentina initiated similar programs, and a dozen other countries were reported to be following suit. Italy offered a site for an International Peace Corps training center in Europe, and Argentina volunteered to send Spanish-language teachers to the United States. An International Peace Corps Secretariat has been established in Washington to help develop a "human consortium" of skilled manpower that could lead to joint projects in emerging areas. In 1963, the United States and El Salvador started the first joint Peace Corps project in a developing country.

Alongside government-supported international organizations that conduct informational or cultural programs are numerous bodies in which private Americans participate. These include the international religious, business, and labor organizations, as well as a number of civic organizations with international structures, such as the Rotary Internationals, and various professional and special-interest groups. An example of the latter is the Association of International Exchange Students in Economics and Commerce, which seeks to supplement the academic experience of its members by arranging practical training during the summer months with business concerns in the host countries.

A form of international organization that has received increased attention in recent years is the international school. In West Berlin, for example, Mayor Willy Brandt and the U.S. military commandant jointly sponsor a school where instruction is given in both German and English by bilingual teachers. A network of schools in Great Britain, the United States, West Germany, and Norway is planned by a group of citizens from Atlantic Community countries. One of these, a preparatory school in Wales, opened in 1962 with a group of sixty students from ten countries, including eight from the United States. A second is being organized in western Canada. An institution to train personnel for international careers has been proposed by the Committee for the Promotion of an International University in America, Inc., and a $3 million fund drive to establish an international college on Long Island was launched in 1963 by the Friends World College Committee. The college is expected to open its doors in 1965. Numerous proposals for schools and universities under United Nations sponsorship have been advanced, and UNESCO has made a start in this direction by helping to organize international courses at leading West European universities.

The extent to which international organizations, public and private, work toward goals that are shared by Americans depends largely on the degree of interest and the excellence of the ideas that Americans bring to them, the amount of money American sources contribute to their budgets being less important. The quality of American participation differs from organization to organization; in some it is high, and in others rather low. Efforts to raise this quality are made by the Bureau of

Educational and Cultural Affairs of the State Department, which keeps in touch with the activities of official international organizations, and some of the private ones. The total task, however, is too great for any single agency, and inevitably is fragmented among many public and private groups and individuals.

XI

Focusing Official American Communication Programs

Since U. S. Government programs account for a relatively small proportion of the ideas in international circulation, they have to be focused as precisely as possible if they are to have an appreciable effect. Aims must be carefully defined, audiences studied, government programs harmonized with each other, and the relationship between government and private activities taken into account. The various agencies concerned have in most cases been trying to do all these things. Their measures have not always been adequate, and sometimes have been feeble, but they are conscious of the problems and are making efforts to solve them.

Defining Objectives

At the present time the U.S. international communication program suffers from the lack of an adequate statement of aims and objectives. This is partly because information and cultural activities are conducted by a number of agencies, each with its own goals. Furthermore, since communications enter into so many processes in so many ways, any large program is likely to use them for a variety of purposes, some of which are difficult to define. When the pressure of justifying a budget, giving a speech, or issuing a directive forces an official to formulate a list of general objectives, these are often so vague that they shed little light on the aims being pursued in day-to-day operations. In some cases, statements of goals by high officials have little direct relationship to the activities of employees down the line. As a study of U.S.I.A.'s operating assumptions in 1955 noted, the day-to-day functioning of the organization involved many premises that were never set down in writing and never received an official stamp.[1] While considerable progress in defining the objectives of our major communication programs has been made since 1955, it is still necessary to look at what is actually being done, as well as at statements of purpose, to find what goals are being pursued. The two methods of approach do not reveal two completely different sets of aims, but rather two overlapping ranges of goals, some of which receive more emphasis from those at the top, while others are seen as more immediate by operating personnel.

Differences among geographic and functional areas cause further complications. A statement of aims applicable to one area is rarely completely applicable to another, unless the level of generality is so high as to make it almost meaningless. Nor should one ignore the role of faith: educational exchange and dissemination of information are often believed to be good things in themselves, requiring no further justification. This does not mean that they cannot be justified, but only that there is less pressure to do so.

Another factor inhibiting definition of aims is the belief that some objectives should be kept secret. To disclose what one wishes to do with communications is often thought to nullify the desired effects. This belief frequently rests on a confusion between goals and techniques. The concealment of techniques is sometimes necessary, but to hide goals is not only usually unnecessary, but it is also impossible for those who operate from within the glass house of a democracy. Since the propagandist has to explain himself in order to secure the cooperation of his own countrymen, he can scarcely hope to conceal his purposes from his audience.

For all these reasons, it is impossible to give a completely satisfactory statement of the goals of this country's official international communication activities. The following summary is only an approximation.

A basic aim of U.S. information and cultural programs since their inception has been the promotion of a free flow of ideas. In 1947, Secretary of State Byrnes told a House Appropriations Subcommittee that it was the policy of the State Department to work for the abolition of all barriers standing in the way of international freedom of the press and of communication in general. This goal has been reiterated in various forms many times since, often with the added statement that private channels will be encouraged to the maximum extent possible. In the words of Secretary Byrnes: "It is the policy of the Department . . . to assist and support private channels of communication in giving the world a correct understanding of America."[2] Government-supported channels are to be used only to supplement private channels—not to compete with or replace them. This policy, also, has frequently been reaffirmed although it can be argued that in some cases it has not been adhered to rigorously.

Behind the goal of promoting a free flow of ideas are several deep-seated assumptions: that those who come to know American society will appreciate that it is, by and large, rational and moral; that peoples will be more likely to live in peace and cooperate fruitfully if they are able to communicate freely; and that our own enlightened self-interest will be advanced by encouraging international communication. These assumptions are difficult to prove, but they have been basic to the conduct of our official information and cultural programs, and many private ones.

A closely related aim of U.S. programs is to provide a correct picture of the United States and of American policies. Secretary Byrnes defined this objective as follows:

> To assist in making clear to foreign peoples the nature and objectives of American foreign policy, in order to prevent misunderstandings of American aims and policies and to aid foreign peoples to arrive at a true understanding of American life; and to present a representative picture abroad of American opinion.[3]

Later statements have tended to place more emphasis on explaining U.S. policies and on countering distorted presentations of life in the United States. In its report for January 1961, for instance, the U. S. Advisory Commission on Information noted that one of the functions of U.S.I.A. was "to explain and interpret to people overseas the meaning and purpose of U.S. foreign policies" and "to present the full sweep of American life and culture to the people of the world in order to correct misconceptions and to combat false or distorted pictures of the United States."[4] Presenting an accurate picture of American life has also been one of the principal aims of most public and private cultural and educational exchange programs.

Occasional directives have prescribed that the United States should be depicted in a rosy hue. In 1963, U.S.I.A. was instructed to identify the United States as a strong, democratic, dynamic nation, qualified for its leadership of world efforts toward a peaceful community of free and independent states. A more sober description of U.S.I.A. treatment of the United States was given earlier in the same year by its Director, Edward R. Murrow: "We report the good as well as the bad. . . . If we do not report our faults ourselves, others will report them for us, and to our discredit." [5] At different times, both these approaches have been used by the U.S.I.A.

A third goal of United States official foreign information programs has been to counteract Communist propaganda and to show the true nature of Communist totalitarianism. The emphasis placed on this objective has varied with the temperature of the cold war, but it has always been present. Attacks on Communism were most intense in the early 1950's; in 1955, exposing international Communism was mentioned by an experienced observer as one of the three principal purposes of the U. S. Information Agency. This goal later receded somewhat as far as the industrialized areas of the world were concerned, but it continued to receive emphasis in programs directed to emerging countries. In Latin America, for instance, counteracting Communist efforts to defeat the Alliance for Progress, subvert labor organizations, and indoctrinate students was listed as one of the principal aims of the Information Agency in 1963.[6]

A fourth frequently enunciated aim of official communications programs is to support our current foreign policies, not merely by explaining them, but by persuading people of their merit and by providing information that will assist in their implementation. During the "psychological offensive" conducted by the State Department in the early 1950's, emphasis was placed on persuasion: the objectives of U.S. information activities were seen as encouraging confidence and a spirit of self-reliance and international cooperation among the free nations, convincing the Soviet and satellite peoples that we were friendly toward them but that their governments were war governments, and making the captive peoples realize that we still considered them a part of the free world.[7] This statement of objectives was modified in 1953: the aim of persuasion remained, but it was to be accomplished by more indirect means. According to a Presidential pronouncement, the purpose of the U. S. Information Agency was to "submit evidence to peoples of other nations . . . that the objectives and policies of the United States are in harmony with and will advance their legitimate aspirations for freedom, progress and peace." One of the ways this was to be done was "by depicting imaginatively the correlation between United States policies and the legitimate aspirations of other peoples of the world." Ten years later, another Presidential directive instructed U.S.I.A. to "emphasize the ways in which United States policies harmonize with those of other peoples and governments, and those aspects of American life and culture which facilitate sympathetic understanding of United States policies." [8]

The use of communications to support specific policies by providing technical (rather than persuasive) information has not often been stated in ringing terms, but it has quietly come to the fore. For instance, a 1963 U.S.I.A. exhibit on economic and social progress in Africa was intended to encourage economic and social development by showing Africans how their neighbors had solved certain development problems.[9] Feature articles, TV programs, and films on disease prevention, economic activities, science, and education further the U.S. policy of assisting emerging nations in the process of modernization. Training programs help to create strong economic institutions, efficient governmental administration, and the capacity for self-defense in these countries.

Policies that are supported by persuasive or technical communications change from year to year, and the emphasis given to any one of them may vary. The Director of the U. S. Information Agency defined the five objectives that had been given priority treatment during the fiscal year 1962 as: disarmament with adequate controls, preservation of a free Berlin, support for the United Nations, American determination to uphold freedom of choice over Communist totalitarianism, and assistance to the developing areas of the world. In the following year the same themes continued to receive emphasis, but additional attention was devoted to supporting the Alliance for Progress, alerting Latin America to the dangers of Castro's brand of Communism, and preparing world opinion for the resumption of atomic testing.[10]

A fifth general aim of U.S. communication programs is to promote good will and mutual understanding between the United States and other countries. This objective provides at least part of the basis for a wide range of actions: presenting publications to foreign institutions, arranging for exchanges of personnel, providing speakers to a wide variety of groups, and replying to requests for information. Indeed, many activities that have the effect of promoting good will are undertaken by personnel in the field without any specific objective in mind beyond that of being helpful. Most Americans abroad genuinely like the people among whom they are working, and when they see a need that they think they can fill they try to do so. Their actions may serve specific national objectives also, but these are not necessarily uppermost in their minds.

Exchange-of-persons and cultural programs are especially likely to be designed to promote general understanding and good will. One of the purposes of bringing young political leaders to the United States, for instance, is to let them see this country before their attitudes become set in traditional patterns. By sending athletic and performing-arts groups abroad, the State Department shows other peoples appealing aspects of life in the United States, in the hope that this will win good will and strengthen ties with the nations concerned.[11]

A sixth purpose of our overseas communication programs (one that is rarely stated specifically) is to provide a public-relations service for the United States. A Senate investigator who studied U.S.I.A. operations overseas in 1957 remarked laconically that information personnel spent a great deal of time drafting speeches for the Ambassador and giving counsel and advice on public relations.[12] Much of this is important and necessary, especially since ambassadors are among the most significant spokesmen for the United States. Nevertheless, some Public Affairs personnel complain that so much of their time is spent on short-range public-relations functions that they are unable to devote sufficient attention to long-range programs. A former Public Affairs officer in India has described the frantic efforts of the local U.S.I.A. staff to offset unfavorable public reaction when U.S. forces landed in Lebanon in 1958. The press officer went without sleep for two days, and his press section worked eighteen-hour shifts.[13]

Communication personnel in Washington, as well as overseas, frequently become involved in a variety of vitally necessary, but time-consuming, short-term public-relations tasks. When a prominent American makes a statement disparaging another country, when an American economic or military policy arouses resentment abroad, or when there is a racial incident in the United States, U.S. information officials in Washington will generally be asked to locate and disseminate material that will calm ruffled feelings and, if possible, repair the damage. The U.S.I.A. press and radio services are usually the ones called upon, but educational and cultural programs sometimes become involved. On one occasion, a well-known newspaper editor was sent to Africa to explain the background of race relations in the United States in an effort to offset the effect of racial incidents.

Finally, overseas communication programs assist in advancing education, the arts, and the sciences. This is usually done in the context of specific policies, but it is sometimes recognized as a legitimate function in itself—much as is the task of promoting good will and understanding. Programs that are specifically educational or cultural in nature are more likely to be devoted to this end than those involving current information, but the latter play a part as well. Exchange of scholars in the arts and sciences ultimately contributes to the development of art and science not only in the countries directly involved, but on a world-wide basis. The same may be true of exchange of current information about the arts and sciences. The advancement of education and cultural achievement for their own sake is a very immediate concern of many government personnel who administer official programs, and is of great interest to a large proportion of the private organizations that cooperate in these programs.

The weight that is given to each of these goals, and the way in which they are pursued, vary in each area of the world. According to Secretary of State Rusk, an important part of the work of U.S.I.A. is to ensure that people behind the iron curtain have more information than their own governments are willing to make available, in the hope that a better-informed public may be able to exercise a moderating influence on government policy. Educational and cultural programs have been given a similar task—that of seeing that Americans and peoples in Communist countries have better knowledge of each other. In developing nations, emphasis is usually placed on providing the necessary information for building modern institutions, on training personnel to run these, on establishing channels of communication with the emerging leadership, and on calling attention to Communism as the foe of freedom. Communications to Europe have the task of correcting misconceptions about the United States and fostering a sense of unity and common identification with the basic values shared by the Atlantic Community. In this way it is hoped that European support for the institutions of Atlantic cooperation will be increased, and that a continuing dialogue between Americans and Europeans will create conditions for a more stable Atlantic partnership.[14]

Statements of goals for individual countries are usually more down-to-earth than this. In some cases, the tasks assigned to communications are very specific: strengthening individual educational institutions, assisting democratic union leaders to frustrate Communist take-over attempts, and explaining U.S. policies to young people or to political leaders. Nevertheless, in many cases the problem of reducing broad goals to manageable tasks that can be pursued through the use of communications remains unsolved. Too often, education and information programs are justified on the grounds that they continue earlier programs, or that in some unspecified way they contribute to the attainment of general goals. The United States Advisory Commission on Information has suggested that U.S.I.A. has not been sufficiently tough-minded in weeding out programs and media that are no longer necessary.[15]

Research and Planning

All organizations that are engaged in international communication devote at least some effort to studying the audiences they wish to address and deciding how best to use the available media to reach these audiences with ideas that support foreign-policy goals. The former activity is usually referred to as "research"; the latter as "planning." Both are basic to the transformation of policy into action. They have to proceed hand in hand, since plans that do not take into account the nature of the audience are unlikely to lead to the desired results, and research that is carried on without reference to plans is likely to be at least partly wasted.

The principal formal communication-research activities within the government are maintained by U.S.I.A. This agency spent approximately $1.7 million on communication research in fiscal year 1962, and slightly more in 1963. About 20 per cent of each year's budget was devoted to maintaining a reference library in Washington. Overseas, during fiscal year 1963, some $70,000 was spent for contractual research in the Far East, $60,000 in Africa, $107,000 in the Near East and South Asia, $140,000 in Latin America, and $55,000 in Western Europe. Most of the balance went for staff salaries and travel.

U.S.I.A. has established five objectives in its research: to determine the basic attitudes and motivations of the peoples it wishes to reach; to analyze their current preoccupations; to define key audiences within societies; to determine the best ways of reaching these audiences; and to measure the impact of the Agency's programs.[16] In addition, U.S.I.A. research personnel analyze Communist propaganda and arrange for independent reviews of U.S.I.A. materials. This "self-study" is necessary to ensure that the Agency's vast output actually follows policy directives, and to assist in the evaluation process. An activity that borders on research, but which for the most part is carried on by units outside the formal research structure, is the collection of material for use in various media; for instance, the Agency maintains an office in Hong Kong to gather information on Communist China.

Most of U.S.I.A.'s audience studies are actually contracted for by private research organizations. During 1962-63, the Coordination Center for Southeast Asian Studies in Bangkok looked into the interests of readers of *Dawn* magazine; ROBOT Statistics in Manila evaluated the success of various media in projecting major themes; and a West German market research firm (DIVO) surveyed radio listening habits and program preferences of the West Berlin population, including recent refugees from the Soviet Zone. In addition, U.S.I.A. maintains a special unit to sift the reports of the Central Intelligence Agency, the State Department, and other government collecting services, and to cull the data that might be of use in its program. The same sifting process is performed in the case of studies made by universities and other private organizations. The Agency also has attempted to define some of the questions of particular interest to it and has tried to interest outside researchers in studying these questions.

Even with assistance from other government agencies and private sources, U.S.I.A.'s research office cannot adequately fulfill the tasks assigned to it. About $200,000 of the funds allotted to the Research and Reference Service in 1963 went for survey research; with this amount the Agency could only begin to explore the relevant characteristics of foreign audiences. U.S.I.A. estimates that about five times that amount would be necessary to do an adequate job.[17] In India, for instance, lack of research funds has hampered the Agency's efforts to define precisely which audiences it should be addressing. As of 1962, U.S.I.A. had conducted almost no audience research in Africa and, according to its Director, had to rely mainly on random comments, newspaper observations, and the reports of government officials to determine African opinions. The U. S. Advisory Commission on Information has repeatedly called for more research and better use of research in U.S.I.A., and as of March 1965 found "some evidence" of progress.[18]

Other government agencies have smaller communication research units. The office in the State Department that evaluates the effectiveness of the Department's educational and cultural programs has been able to sponsor only a few studies itself, but it does systematically collect relevant data and research reports from other government offices and private agencies. In addition, members of the U. S. Advisory Commission on International Educational and Cultural Affairs have made a number of independent evaluations of the Department's international cultural activities.[19] The Agency for International Development has embarked on more extensive efforts to measure the effectiveness of training given foreign personnel in the United States. These studies are, however, oriented primarily toward finding out whether training in particular specialities has actually been used, rather than toward determining the broader political effects of AID's programs.* AID has also contracted for a few studies specifically on communication—for example, to find out how well the typical Thai villager can read, and where he gets his news.[20] The Peace Corps has sponsored a number of research projects on the effectiveness of its operations, but as of 1964 results were only beginning to come in. The Defense Department has given very little systematic attention to the nonmilitary implications of its extensive training operations.

Planning, as in the case with research, takes place both in Washington and in the field. All government offices have to look several years into the future in order to prepare their annual budget estimates, and most draw up more detailed plans as well. U.S.I.A.'s formal country plans, worked out collaboratively by the Agency headquarters and field posts, are based on guidelines prepared by the Department of State after consultation with other agencies that may be concerned. These country plans are revised each year, and attempt to specify both general and specific objectives and the way they are to be attained through the presentation of certain themes to defined audiences. Even more detailed planning is done in U.S.I.A.'s media and geographical area offices. State Department officials in charge of educational and cultural programs go through a somewhat similar series of planning processes. Other Federal agencies, such as AID and the Defense Department, have given less consideration to planning how they will use ideas in support of U.S. foreign policy, largely because they have not faced up to the fact that they are in actuality engaged in large-scale international communication.

Nearly all government plans are classified documents not available for public inspection. Nevertheless, from such information as is avail-

* As of 1964, the Bureau of Social Science Research, Inc., in Washington, D.C., was completing a major three-year study under AID sponsorship of the effectiveness of training programs in twenty-three countries.

able, one cannot escape the impression that in most cases they fail to specify just how ideas are to be used in order to help achieve foreign-policy goals, and are largely statements of aspiration and intent. In part, this is because the necessary information about audiences is unavailable; but plans also suffer because political objectives are not spelled out in sufficient detail, and because most personnel, especially in the field, are so overburdened by the demands of day-to-day operations that they have little time to think about the future.

Coordination

Since U. S. Government activities in international communication began, it has been agreed that the words and actions of the various agencies involved should be harmonized with each other: the United States should speak with one voice. Contradictions should be avoided insofar as possible; duplication and overlap should be minimized. In spite of numerous efforts during the past twenty years, however, completely satisfactory harmonization has never been achieved.[21]

One major line of attack on the problem has been through interdepartmental boards and committees. A Psychological Strategy Board, representing the principal agencies engaged in international communication, was created in 1951. This achieved better coordination in some cases, but served mainly as a mechanism for exchanging views among the agencies concerned. In 1953, the Psychological Strategy Board was replaced by an Operations Coordinating Board, with a somewhat broader charter. This board was to be concerned not only with coordination of propaganda and psychological aspects of policies, but also with coordination of the policies themselves. It soon developed into a maze of working groups and committees, most of them chaired by State Department representatives. At one time there were some forty of these, each considering a specialized aspect of foreign affairs. The OCB also failed to give complete satisfaction, since it lacked the authority to enforce common policies even if these were agreed on by agency representatives on the board. As James Reston pointed out in 1957, it represented only moderate progress for U.S.I.A. to know in advance about conflicting foreign-policy statements of governmental leaders if they were going to make them anyway. A special Presidential committee to study U.S. overseas communication activities (the Sprague Committee) recommended in 1960 that the Operations Coordination Board be strengthened in order to deal more adequately with situations such as this. Instead, the board was abolished by the incoming administration, and some of its functions were taken over by *ad hoc* working groups. More recently, new interagency committees have been formed to coordinate various parts of government international communication activities, such as educational exchange and the teaching of English overseas.[22]

Further coordination of communications is achieved through the fact that the Secretary of State is concerned with the foreign-policy aspects of activities conducted by other government agencies, while overseas the U. S. Ambassador is responsible for all official programs carried on by personnel assigned to his embassy. The authority of the Secretary and the ambassador is, however, shadowy in the case of the armed services and difficult to enforce whenever other agencies make a strong stand against it. An advisory committee to the Department of State recommended in 1961 that "the authority of the Secretary of State for policy direction in the full range of educational and cultural affairs . . . be clearly affirmed and supported by the President," and advised further that the Secretary establish mechanisms for country and regional planning among all agencies responsible for international programs in education, science, culture, information, and the educational aspects of technical assistance. Repeated efforts have been made to ensure the authority of the ambassador over all U.S. official elements (except operational military forces) in the country where he is stationed, and both President Eisenhower and President Kennedy issued directives to this effect. The impression of several informed observers is that there has been considerable improvement in coordination at overseas posts in recent years. One noted that a situation such as existed in Greece after World War II, when the State Department was trying to bolster the Greek Government and another U.S. agency was trying to topple it, was no longer thinkable. Nevertheless, the U. S. Advisory Commission on International Educational and Cultural Affairs reported in 1963 that exchange-of-persons programs still had not been tied in adequately with broader "country plans," either in Washington or at most posts overseas.[23]

It is probable that improved coordination among the various agencies engaged in communication activities will be achieved gradually as a result of informal contacts among the personnel involved. Indeed, this has been apparent during the past few years. For instance, Public Affairs officers sometimes work informally with local stations of the

Armed Forces Radio and Television network, U.S.I.A. has lent books and exhibition materials to American military posts overseas, and military bands and athletic teams have cooperated in programs of civilian agencies. Cooperation of this sort depends, however, on the personalities of the officials concerned and on the way lines of authority are drawn.

A number of systematic efforts have been made to strengthen informal contacts, and to increase the ability of officials from different agencies to cooperate smoothly. Staff members of U.S.I.A. have been assigned to work in the Department of State, and vice versa. There is also an exchange of personnel between State and Defense. Training programs for government representatives going overseas have emphasized the "country team" approach, and have tried to familiarize each set of officials with the missions of the others. The long-term objective of these measures is to create a corps of specialists in communications and other fields dedicated to broadly national purposes rather than parochial agency programs.

A great deal remains to be done, however, before adequate coordination is assured. In 1962, Bureau of the Budget officials interviewed government personnel primarily concerned with exchange-of-persons programs, and found little consensus among them. Private organizations with exchange programs also showed a great disparity of views about aims and techniques. There are enough inconsistencies in U.S. information programs to provide observers with a basis for charges that one arm of the government often does not know what another is doing.[24] These inconsistencies are the exception rather than the rule, but they continue to detract from the effectiveness of U.S. overseas communications.

Information Versus Culture

The question of how to relate activities primarily involving current information to those devoted to educational, cultural, and scientific exchange has long bedeviled U.S. officials. At one pole of the controversy have been educators and artists, who have maintained that the two activities should be separated completely, and that education and culture should be kept free of "propaganda taint." When, in 1946, informational and educational activities were put under the direction of the same office of the State Department, leading American educators succeeded in having this office broken in two, although both activities remained under the direction of Public Affairs officers in U.S. embassies abroad. At the other pole are the "psychological warriors" who, while sometimes recognizing the desirability of educational and cultural activities, relegate these to a secondary place.[25]

The difficulties of harmonizing the two sets of programs were exacerbated in the years following World War II by conflicting definitions of aims. International educational and cultural activities were seen as ends in themselves, only vaguely related to current American policies. The less policy guidance they were given, their adherents felt, the more effective they would be. Former Assistant Secretary of State Howland H. Sargeant has characterized this approach as the belief that political values come as by-products of free cultural exchanges. In other words, "If you aim at it, you'll miss it."[26] Consequently, the role to be assigned to educational, scientific, and cultural factors within the broad framework of American foreign policy remained poorly defined for over a decade. By contrast, information programs were seen as being linked with specific political strategies.

During the second half of the 1950's, the definitions of purpose of the information and cultural programs moved closer together: the former was seen as involving more long-term goals than before, and the latter became more closely identified with specific objectives. In 1959, the Secretary of State's Special Assistant for Cultural Affairs defined part of his task in the same words that have been used to describe the Voice of America, namely, "to project the image of America abroad," and a Foreign Service officer observed that many embassies relied heavily on cultural-exchange programs to prove certain points, as well as to orient thinking about the United States in general. In 1961, Senator Fulbright called for a new rationale for cultural activities, one recognizing that educational exchange is "a positive instrument of foreign policy designed to mobilize human resources just as military and economic policies seek to mobilize physical resources." The U. S. Advisory Commission on International Educational and Cultural Affairs noted in 1963 that the educational-exchange program had a flexibility that enabled it to serve a multitude of purposes, both political and nonpolitical: to increase mutual understanding, assist in the modernization of emerging countries, and support many basic foreign-policy objectives, as well as to promote international cooperation for educational and cultural advancement.[27] During the same period, those in charge of U.S. foreign information activities began to place more emphasis on cultural activities and long-term aims, such as creating conditions for a free flow of information, and building international good will and understanding.[28] At the present time, the major information and cultural programs of the United States are being used to further substantially the same basic set of objectives.

In many cases, information and cultural programs are mutually reinforcing. Foreigners who visit the United States under exchange programs are frequently able to explain certain matters to their countrymen when the mass media cannot. For instance, U.S.I.A. researchers found that visitors from abroad who observe our social security and welfare programs, collective-bargaining procedures, graduated income tax, and so on, often conclude that the U.S. economic system largely meets the definition of what they understand by the word "socialism."[29] Foreign students frequently become interested in coming to the United States as a result of exposure to material distributed by U.S.I.A. The opportunities given foreigners to visit this country and see for themselves constitute one of the important guarantees of the accuracy of our foreign information program. In emerging countries, the two sets of activities tend to be even more closely linked than elsewhere. The mass media in these areas are important instruments of education, and both information and cultural programs are heavily devoted to the aims of promoting literacy, economic progress, communication systems, and the other aspects of modernization.

As the above examples suggest, it is frequently difficult to distinguish between informational and cultural activities. When a visiting scholar speaks to his own country over the Voice of America, is this a part of an information or an education program? When an American traveling abroad gives a talk about current U.S. policies, into which program does this fit? Are libraries instruments of culture or of information? Obviously, they are both, since the way that each reader uses the library resources is the determining factor. Magazines, radio and TV programs, and even news releases frequently contain material that can be defined as educational or cultural as well as merely informative. Books and exchanges of persons, while primarily long-term in their effect, also convey information that can be defined as news.

The heavily interlocking character of the two programs should not, however, be allowed to obscure the differences between them. Even though both serve the same basic set of policy objectives, their capabilities differ. The information program can be used more easily to support specific, short-range objectives, even though it also has long-range functions. Educational and cultural programs are able to give a deeper picture of American life and to provide a stronger impetus for development of the arts and sciences, even though their short-range importance should not be overlooked. By providing a training ground for Americans, and giving people in the United States an opportunity to become acquainted with foreign visitors, they also increase American capabilities to conduct successful international relations.

The nature of the two programs differs also in that educational exchange activities, at least, are more likely to involve a two-way influence and a broader range of thought. Americans traveling abroad and foreigners visiting the United States are simultaneously receivers and distributors of ideas. Information programs represent a two-way street to a lesser degree. While the reaction to what is distributed may influence policy as well as subsequent communications, the path of this reverse flow is tortuous and its impact diluted. Educational exchange and cultural activities deal with the whole range of human thought, while information materials can present only selected ideas to any given audience. A human source, a library, or even a dramatic presentation can convey thoughts that an information official might never think to express.

The skills needed to conduct the two sets of programs also differ appreciably. Knowledge of journalism and electronics is of relatively little importance to the cultural officer who is concerned with student exchanges or artistic presentations, while the press officer is rarely required to be an authority on modern American music or to be familiar with the degree requirements of major American colleges. Critics of our present cultural program have pointed out that it has proved very difficult to recruit a sufficient number of cultural officers who are real experts in their field. A smattering of teaching or administrative experience does not enable one to converse intelligently with foreign intellectuals on symbolism in modern American novels or the influence of Sartre on Tennessee Williams.[30] By the same token, reading the daily paper does not qualify an official who has come up the ladder by way of the cultural program to administer a news service.

There are thus compelling differences between information and cultural activities, at the same time that there are important policy and operational links between them. In order to make sure that both are conducted efficiently and are properly coordinated, it is necessary that each be administered by specialists but that planning be done jointly.

The present situation at American overseas embassies, in which the Public Affairs officer is responsible for the two sets of programs, offers a good basis for joint planning. If, as is sometimes charged, the Public Affairs officer does not appreciate the significance of educational and cultural activities, then he is simply not doing his job properly. To remove these activities from his jurisdiction would not be the solution, since a new official would then have to be appointed at a higher level to supervise the planning of both sets of programs. Adequate coordination in Washington is more difficult to achieve under present circumstances. Although the State Department provides policy direction to U.S.I.A., and also administers the domestic end of cultural and educational programs, there is no single office that views all government communication activities as a whole.

Government Versus Private Activities

Mention of the desirability of coordinating public and private communications conjures up the specter of censorship, thought control, and a ministry of propaganda. The subject is a delicate one, and has been approached gingerly. It is generally agreed within and outside the government that any restriction on freedom of speech is too high a price to pay for coordination. Nevertheless, both officials and private observers have felt that some effort should be made. As Walter H. C. Laves has noted:

> The impact of all these [private] influences upon the understanding which others have of us is clearly so great that by comparison the impact of governmental programs must often appear insignificant. The U. S. Government therefore cannot be unconcerned with them and must make an effort to increase the positive contributions which they make toward our larger national goals.[31]

The principal steps that government agencies have taken thus far to bring about better coordination between public and private communications have included establishing advisory groups of those who are active in the private sector, giving assistance to private activities that further national goals, engaging in cooperative programs with private organizations, and providing advice or guidance to individuals or organizations that are involved in international communications.

Private advisory groups to official information and cultural programs are legion, some of them of a formal and permanent nature, and others informal or *ad hoc*. The U. S. Information Agency receives the counsel of the U. S. Advisory Commission on Information, which was established by act of Congress, and is also assisted by advisory committees on broadcasting, music, and books. The State Department is advised by a Commission on International Educational and Cultural Affairs, and by groups specializing in the arts, UNESCO activities, and other aspects of the Department's educational and cultural programs. In 1961, eight working groups were organized by the Department to give advice on such subjects as the role of books and other published materials in international relations, the application of new technology to education in emerging countries, and long-range educational development in Africa and Asia.[32]

Advisory groups are of varying effectiveness in linking private activities and public policy. The fact that such a group exists on paper does not necessarily mean that its advice is used, or used properly. Members of some groups have reported that they feel themselves to be letterhead figures, retained by the government mainly to assist in its public relations. Others report the opposite. Furthermore, advisory groups are not chosen specifically with the aim of creating a two-way flow of information between the private and the public sector. That they do in fact perform such a function is often fortuitous. Nevertheless, they are potentially, at least, an important mechanism for increasing the harmony between public and private activities.

A great many nonofficial organizations engaged in international communication receive some kind of government assistance, direct or indirect. This assistance is usually based on the assumption that the private activities in question will further national goals. The most obvious form of assistance is financial, as in the Informational Media Guarantee Program. In other cases, government facilities are provided, as when a motion picture or TV program uses shots of equipment or personnel of the Defense Department. Both the State Department and U.S.I.A. have helped private groups that are interested in forming educational or cultural contacts in other countries.

Closely related to cases in which government agencies have assisted private efforts are those in which joint public-private programs have been conducted. A number of such cooperative activities have been worked out with American firms that have representatives overseas. As of 1963, U.S.I.A., through its Office of Private Cooperation, was distributing materials on such topics as nuclear testing, the Berlin Wall, and

Cuba to more than 400 American corporations. These then sent the materials to their representatives abroad, on the assumption that these representatives might have occasion to discuss American policies with their contacts in the host countries.[33] Similar materials are put in the hands of home office executives who travel frequently, and about 250 firms that have well-established contacts with Latin American business are helping U.S.I.A. distribute information about the Alliance for Progress.[34] U.S.I.A. also supplies articles on American foreign policy to company publications that circulate abroad in substantial numbers, and in one case cooperated with a business firm in an effort to ensure that the company's advertising overseas contributed to American national objectives as well as to commercial sales.

Other joint government-business efforts have resulted in arrangements for coordinating public and private activities abroad. In several capitals, committees made up of members of the resident American business community and U.S.I.A. representatives enable each group to benefit from the advice of the other. Sometimes joint programs are conducted. In one city, for instance, a group of American businessmen contributed funds sufficient to almost double U.S.I.A.'s local information output. In another, an American firm hired an economist and a public relations man to assist in conducting a seminar program sponsored by U.S.I.A. American missionaries have cooperated in showing U.S.I.A. films on such subjects as health and agriculture.[35]

The Information Agency has also explored the possibility of producing some materials jointly with American commercial enterprises. During the fiscal year 1964, for instance, it proposed to make ten television programs in conjunction with private producers, on a cost-shared basis.[36]

Collaborative arrangements between government and the private sector in educational and cultural affairs have been even more frequent, and almost all official educational, training, and cultural activities depend on the cooperation of private institutions. As a result, a corps of individuals has been built up in the private sector that is familiar with government programs, and many U.S. officials have been influenced by thinking in private organizations. In addition, efforts have been made to establish mechanisms through which the community of interest between government and higher education can be more effectively acted upon.[37] One of the purposes of an organization entitled Education and World Affairs, established in 1962 with the support of the Ford Foundation and the Carnegie Corporation, is to explore government-private cooperation in international education.

The aims of the various parties involved in public-private collaborative ventures do not necessarily have to be identical. When the government's objective in promoting educational exchanges with the Soviet Union was described in *The New York Times Magazine* as being "to punch holes through the Iron Curtain," officials of the Inter-University Committee on Travel Grants, which administers the exchanges, objected that this was not the purpose of the Committee, which aimed instead "to strengthen American education, to expand knowledge in all fields, and . . . to promote scholarly understanding." [38] In this instance, both kinds of aims appear to have been served by the same activities.

Government efforts to assist and to collaborate with the private sector in educational matters, with a few exceptions such as the one just described, are relatively noncontroversial. The opposite is likely to be the case where news or entertainment is concerned. Commercial news media have reacted violently to any whisper of a suggestion that they should be responsive to government advice about their content and when U.S.I.A. attempted to prevent a CBS documentary on migrant workers in the United States ("Harvest of Shame") from being shown abroad, protests were heard from Congress and the press, and the attempt was unsuccessful.[39] Entertainment media have been almost as sensitive, although in some cases motion picture and television films have been discussed informally with government officials before being made or released.

Government principally influences private expressions indirectly, through the policy explanations that are given to the American people in the normal course of conducting the nation's business. The statements of the President, the Secretary of State, and other public officials are likely to influence at least some of the private communications directed abroad. Government publications and "background briefings" for information media, community leaders, and representatives of organizations concerned with world affairs, many of which are engaged in some form of overseas communication activities, also play a role.[40] As long as advice is not directed specifically at any one organization or information medium, and pressure is not brought to bear, it does not appear to arouse adverse reactions, even though it may not be accepted.

Somewhat greater latitude appears to be possible when it comes to giving advice to individuals. At one time the State Department mailed a booklet along with each passport that was issued, advising the recipient on ways of conducting himself abroad. This booklet is still being distributed at passport offices, although budgetary restrictions do not allow it to be mailed.

In the case of military personnel and the dependents of American officials abroad, official guidance has been more vigorous. Military personnel are given orientation about ways of conducting themselves overseas, and a large proportion of them receive literature on how to answer questions most frequently asked about the United States. One pamphlet widely used by the Defense Department (published by the American Council for Nationalities Service in New York), entitled *Americans Abroad,* contains suggested answers to questions about the U.S. economy, racial discrimination, and foreign policy. Wives of Foreign Service officers are briefed by the Foreign Service Institute of the Department of State on opportunities for participating in civic and cultural activities in other countries, the problems of emerging nations, and how to answer questions about the United States. A few other agencies with large numbers of personnel abroad also have orientation programs for dependents. Overseas military personnel and dependents of officials cannot, of course, be considered in the same category as private citizens at home. Nevertheless, many of them soon return to assume a place in American society, presumably bringing their knowledge about foreign countries with them.

While there are thus important links between the public and private sectors, these affect a relatively small segment of private international communications. The numbers of commercial films, TV programs, and publications that represent a net liability rather than an asset for United States foreign relations are appreciable, and most individual Americans at home and abroad are still rather poor spokesmen for the United States. How to achieve more effective harmonization of public and private activities without compromising freedom of expression remains an unsolved problem.

Domestic Constraints

Even if it were possible to find a way to achieve greater harmony between public and private international communications, certain characteristics of American society would still make it difficult to utilize communications in support of foreign policy to their maximum effectiveness. Indeed, it is frequently asked whether a free society can hope to compete with the information and cultural programs of totalitarian states in view of domestic constraints in the democracies. These constraints apply more to government programs than to private ones, although the latter are not unaffected by them.

One characteristic of Western society that tends to make the task of those using international communications to achieve political purposes more difficult is that almost everyone considers himself an expert. There is some justice to this claim, since we all make extensive use of communications in our daily lives and therefore have to be familiar with certain aspects of them. Yet this widespread tendency to consider oneself an expert also ignores the extensive knowledge of foreign societies, foreign policy, and communication media that is needed by the successful international practitioner. As a former official of Radio Free Europe notes, people in Western societies agree that a plumber must be a trained specialist, but feel that everyone is qualified to engage in propaganda.[41] He might have added that most people therefore feel themselves qualified to criticize and evaluate international communication programs. An impressive number of travelers return from visits abroad to announce that the United States is losing the battle of ideas, and they often go on to say why they think this is the case. Some of their criticisms are undoubtedly correct; others are wide of the mark.

Criticism of information and cultural activities by nonspecialists is difficult to ignore when it comes from those in high administrative positions or with power over budgetary allocations. Officers of the First Radio Broadcasting and Leaflet Group, who were responsible for disseminating material to North Korean and Chinese Communist forces during the Korean War, soon realized that their output had to be designed for two different audiences: the staff colonels first, and the enemy only second.[42] Similarly, U.S.I.A. personnel producing material for specialized audiences have had to consider the effect it was likely to have on other executive officials and the U. S. Congress, as well as on the people for whom it was designed.

The supposedly wide diffusion of expertness with respect to international communications, which amounts to a denial of any special expertness to those who have had extensive experience in using them, opens the way for programs to be judged on the basis of clichés and assumptions that at best are valid only in certain circumstances. One of these is that the principal function of communications is to change attitudes and to persuade. Foreign students, it is frequently maintained, should be brought to this country so that they will develop more favorable attitudes toward the United States, our information program should cultivate a more positive image of America, and we should disseminate propaganda to hostile and uncommitted peoples to persuade them that democracy is preferable to Communism.* Another popularly held conception is that international communication is in the nature of a debate, and that the side winning the debate receives the prize. A third is that our social and economic system is so good that if it is described adequately to other peoples, or if they experience it by visiting this country, they will want to adopt it. Specialists who attempt to explain that such assumptions do not hold in all cases usually encounter a blank stare.

Another domestic factor that operates as a constraint on U.S. information and cultural programs is the complex of deep-seated prejudices and preconceptions that Americans have toward government communications. As Dean Acheson once remarked, State Department programs for giving out information are often criticized as propaganda, but if the information is not promptly made available the Department is accused of cynically denying the public its right to be informed: the Department is damned if it does and damned if it doesn't.

Similar contradictions can be observed in the case of international programs. U.S. communication activities have been criticized as inconsequential exercises and treated with disdain, while at the same time so much is demanded from them that their failure to achieve results beyond their powers is used to justify the original low opinion.[43] An extreme view of the efficacy of communications was exemplified in 1949, when a distinguished Senator suggested that a massive propaganda offensive might be an economical substitute for the Atlantic Pact.[44] The other end of the spectrum could be seen in 1947, when the House of Representatives favored abandonment of the U.S. information program. These extremes of overevaluation and underevaluation have become less pronounced during the past decade, but wide differences of

* A corollary of this view is that the United States does not require an information program in countries that are already friendly. (*Cf.* Eugene W. Castle, *Billions, Blunders and Baloney* [New York: Devin-Adair, 1955], pp. 67, 72.) The author objects that the U.S.I.A. is spending millions of dollars in countries "where we should not be spending one dollar for propaganda"—such as Turkey, Greece, Great Britain, and Spain.

opinion about the effectiveness of international communication programs remain.

U.S. foreign-information activities have also been hampered by the fact that since some of them can be classified as "propaganda," depending on how one uses the term, all of them encounter the American prejudice against this term. Largely as a result of its use by the Nazis and the Communists, propaganda is seen in our society as an attempt to deprive people of their ability to think independently through the use of lies, slanted presentation, and a variety of underhanded tricks. This, it is argued, is no business for a democracy to be in. Cultural and educational programs are less disadvantaged by associations with propaganda, although they do not emerge completely unscathed. Nazi misuse of German culture ("we shall proceed from Beethoven to Hitler") combined with Soviet and Communist Chinese emphasis on cultural attractions have bred suspicion in this field also. Most Americans are willing to accept propaganda when used in advertising, sermons, or domestic politics, but remain suspicious of its use on an international plane.[45]

As a result of the lack of agreement about how communications should be used and what they can accomplish, and the tendency to be suspicious of anything that can be called propaganda, those engaged in international communication have often received poor support from their superiors or from officials concerned with other instruments of policy. There has been a tendency, less pronounced now than previously, for professional diplomats to regard information and cultural programs as extraneous instruments, and to exclude those responsible for them from the mainstream of policy. As a Foreign Service officer wrote in 1953, the information service was regarded in the State Department as being on indefinite probation; its functions were never assumed, and its right to existence had to be justified over and over again. This is certainly not the case today, especially since U.S.I.A. personnel have recently been given the opportunity to become Foreign Service officers, but a residue of the old attitude remains. Those in charge of international cultural programs have frequently complained that personnel in this field are given less recognition and support than those performing comparable activities in other areas.[46]

The degree to which adverse attitudes inside and outside the government can hamper the conduct of overseas communication programs is enhanced by the lack of a powerful domestic constituency to support these programs in their claims for funds and recognition. Educational programs receive some backing from the academic community, cultural programs from the artistic community, and information programs from some sectors of the news media, public relations, and advertising industries. Nevertheless, these sources of support are weak in comparison with the farming constituency represented by the Agriculture Department, or the veterans organizations that take an interest in the armed services.

Several attempts have been made to organize a broader base of public support for U.S. international communications. One of the most ambitious of these was the National Committee for an Adequate Overseas Information Program, chaired by Edward L. Bernays. It took such steps as to solicit the reactions of U.S. ambassadors overseas to the information programs and then to publicize these reactions in the United States. It also organized a seminar of interested private citizens, discussed the program with President Eisenhower, and disseminated a number of statements backing it. In recent years, however, the committee has been relatively inactive.

The absence of a broad-based source of public support for information and cultural programs means that they are especially susceptible to budgetary cuts, and to other forms of pressure from Congress and administrative authorities. In 1954, for instance, the House of Representatives, without debate either in the Appropriations Committee or on the floor of the House, cut $6 million from the $15 million requested by the administration for exchange of persons. According to Senator Fulbright, this cut, if allowed to stand, would have virtually destroyed the Smith-Mundt program and seriously crippled the Fulbright program.[47] Appropriation requests for information and cultural programs have been heavily reduced by Congress in most years.

Because of their politically exposed position, both the State Department and the U.S.I.A. have been favorite targets for witch-hunters and have been forced to tolerate more interference with their day-to-day operations than is usually the case with government agencies. Not only have some employees been forced out, and others shifted, as a result of outside pressures, but cultural exhibits have been canceled and internal directives written and rescinded. At one point, an American history textbook was withdrawn from overseas libraries, in part because it included a picture of a "little red schoolhouse" that critics feared could be represented as typical of the American educational system.[48] The more egregious pressures on these programs have lessened in recent years, but the susceptibility of the programs to destructive interference remains high.

While most sectors of the American public have been relatively apathetic about our official international communications, this has not always been the case with citizens with family ties in other countries. Minority groups have provided tremendous assets to U.S. information and cultural activities, but they also have presented certain problems. Whenever the Voice of America reduces the time allotted a given language in overseas broadcasts, it is likely to receive vigorous protests from members of that language group in the United States. Minority groups sometimes campaign for greater representation on the Voice staff and more broadcast time, or try to involve the United States in the internal political affairs of their home countries. Nor have such efforts been limited to minority groups. Former U.S.I.A. Director George V. Allen has noted that pressures are frequently brought by those who would like the Voice of America to reflect their particular economic beliefs.[49]

All these constraints, while significant, appear minor when compared with the difficulties that information and cultural programs inevitably encounter in a society where each citizen has a wide latitude of speech and action. Carefully prepared visits of foreigners to the United States can have their good effects negated by a few unkind remarks or instances of uncivil behavior on the part of private American citizens. A survey conducted among African students who were in the United States during 1962 indicated that almost every African visitor to this country has at least one bad personal experience and sees or hears of many more.[50] Americans visiting other countries often make unfavorable generalizations about their hosts as a result of a few instances of discourtesy or inefficiency. Freedom of speech and of the press in the United States makes it possible for bizarre interpretations of American policy to be spread around the world, nullifying some of the effects of our overseas programs. An offhand opinion on how to solve the Berlin problem given by an administration official at a Washington cocktail party is certain to appear in the German press shortly thereafter.[51]

The occurrence and reporting of incidents that put the United States in a bad light, and the frequency of statements from both official and private sources that conflict with U.S. policy, certainly make the conduct of an effective overseas communication program more difficult. They do not, however, make it impossible. While the persuasiveness of official American efforts may suffer as a result of conflicting communications emanating from our society, persuasion is only one of several possible effects of communication. Those goals that can be achieved by providing information for people to use in their personal or professional lives, or by using communications to strengthen certain kinds of institutions in foreign countries, are scarcely affected at all. Furthermore, dissonant reports reaching foreign audiences can have a positive as well as a negative effect. One of our major aims is to convey a clear picture of American pluralism, and completely consistent communications could never do this. Self-critical statements, and a moderate quota of foolish ones, are a characteristic of our society. No one can claim to understand this country until he is able to take these in stride.

XII

Roles of the U. S. Government in International Communication

A major problem facing the United States as a participant in the international dialogue is how to find ways in which both public and private channels of communication will make a maximum contribution to the attainment of national foreign-policy goals. While the government conducts a number of important information and cultural programs, it is not the only spokesman for our democracy; part of the responsibility devolves on a myriad of private individuals and groups. Nevertheless, it is incumbent on the government to search for ways in which the total national potential can be used effectively. It cannot control private expressions, either at home or abroad, but it can try to promote conditions under which they will better serve the interests of a country as a whole.

The government thus has not one but at least four roles in international communication:

1. As administrator of the nation's foreign policy, it should do its utmost to create an international environment in which free and uncontrolled communications can contribute toward the development of the kind of world in which we want to live.

2. As an advocate and special pleader for official American foreign policies, it should make the best possible use of the extensive communication channels under its own control to further these policies.

3. As a servant of the public, it should try to bring about a harmonious relationship between official and nonofficial communications by adjusting its own activities to those of the private sector, and by offering assistance to private individuals and groups that are in touch with foreign audiences.

4. As an authority entrusted with domestic leadership, it should take

steps to improve the quality of the ideas and personnel on which both public and private international communication programs have to draw.

These governmental roles have been recognized in the past. It has not usually been recognized, however, that the success of the United States in using communications to advance its foreign policies is directly related to the excellence with which all four are performed. Nor have they all been given sufficient emphasis.

Encouraging Free International Communication

A basic foreign-policy goal of the United States should be to create an environment throughout the world in which full public discussion of important issues can take place on an international level, much as it takes place on a domestic level within each democracy. In such an environment, both uncontrolled private expressions and official government voices would have a constructive part to play in international communication. Instead of emulating totalitarian states by attempting to silence dissident voices (which we cannot do effectively anyway), we should vigorously urge the advantages of a free exchange. Private channels should be seen as a source of strength rather than weakness. A free flow of ideas cannot be achieved on a world-wide basis so long as some governments muzzle their citizens and shield them from foreign ideas, but each step in the direction of greater freedom tends to benefit the foreign policies of nations allowing full public discussion.

To suggest that the United States should encourage free international communication is scarcely to put forth a new, revolutionary proposal. Governmental spokesmen have frequently advocated world-wide freedom of information, official agencies have taken numerous steps to advance it, and most Americans assume that it is one of our national goals. Indeed, any position other than one of favoring a free flow of ideas across national boundaries would conflict with some of the basic principles and practices of American democracy, and would bring the government into head-on conflict with powerful private interests. In this area we really have no choice.

Nevertheless, while favoring free international communication in principle, we have been less than thorough in exploring its implications and ensuring that these find expression in our official actions at home and abroad: in international information and cultural programs, in assisting underdeveloped countries, in granting visas, and in determining the behavior of government officials toward newspapermen. Freedom of information and cultural exchange has been more than a slogan, but it has not attained the status of a well-developed and vigorously pursued policy.*

In order to show that we are serious about promoting freedom of information we should set our own house in order, and consider carefully whether certain self-imposed barriers to the exchange of ideas cannot be eliminated. For instance, the reintroduction in 1962 of censorship of unsealed mail from abroad that is designated as Communist propaganda appears to be a clear violation of our own principles.[1] Restrictions on American travel overseas and on foreign travel to this country should be re-examined. Cumbersome and humiliating regulations governing the entry of noncitizens to the United States have caused other countries to doubt our protestations that we believe in an international free trade in ideas, and have even led to the establishment of a direct airline route from Mexico City to Canada, so that Latin Americans can fly to Europe without the annoyance of having to obtain a transit visa from the United States.[2] A vigorous democracy has ample means to protect itself against subversive ideas without sporadic and ineffectual attempts to stop them at the border. Temporary restrictions on free international communication can sometimes be justified when their purpose is to increase ultimate freedom by insisting on reciprocity, as has been the case with regulations governing the travel of Communist diplomats in the United States, but even here frequent checks should be made to ensure that the restrictive measures are actually helping to achieve the intended goals.

American ventures into "black" propaganda also violate the spirit of free international communication, and tend to cast a shadow of doubt on all American information and cultural programs, public and private. Perhaps "black" activities cannot be abolished entirely, but at least they should be delimited in such a way as to apply only to certain areas and situations—for instance, in connection with military operations. It is probable that, with the exercise of a little ingenuity, ways could be found to pursue openly some of the programs that are now conducted

* A concerted effort to increase the free flow of information on a world-wide basis was started by Assistant Secretary of State William Benton in 1948. This led to a United Nations Conference on Freedom of Information. The emphasis given to advancing freedom of communication diminished, however, as the United States became more and more concerned with resisting Soviet expansionism.

on a covert basis. Other "black" activities, while possibly useful when judged by themselves, may prove to have a net unfavorable effect when their impact on American credibility is taken into account. The United States should not seek to maintain different standards for private activities, "overt" government communications, and covert activities; instead, official programs should adhere to the best traditions of the private sector.

Difficulties can be caused by even minor failures to conform to commonly accepted domestic practices. In 1964, vigorous protests were heard when it was revealed that the U. S. Information Agency had contributed $14,952 toward the editorial costs of compiling a manuscript on world Communist tactics which was later accepted and published by a private American firm. The objections were on two counts: that the U.S.I.A. had no right to pay even part of the costs of material that was distributed through domestic channels, and that the book itself carried no acknowledgment of a government subsidy. Yet critics generally agreed that the quality of the material was high and that it deserved publication on its own merits. Thus failure to comply with domestic standards tarnished the reputation of a small, but extremely important, book program, and one that should be expanded.[3] It can be argued that to have acknowledged partial government sponsorship would have diminished the book's effectiveness. Clearly, however, the cost of not doing so turned out to be considerable.

It is also disquieting to learn that in recent years the U. S. Information Agency has increased the volume of materials distributed abroad on an "unattributed" basis.[4] This would appear to be a trend in the wrong direction, insofar as efforts are made to conceal the source of the materials from those who would like to know it. There is, of course, no necessity that U.S.I.A. actively claim credit for all the factual information that is given further dissemination by local distributors who are aware of its origin, and it should be emphasized that the overwhelming proportion of government information and cultural programs abroad already attempt to observe standards that would be completely acceptable at home. A few do not, and these should be carefully re-examined.

Admittedly, there is a thin knife-edge that must be traversed here. For instance, is the United States engaging in "black" operations when it advises or subsidizes a prodemocratic group in another country, and thus enables this group to engage in propaganda? The rule of thumb suggested here is that such assistance may be in accord with the principle of free communication when no policy-control strings are attached —when the group in question is merely enabled to place before the public ideas that it already holds and for which it takes full responsibility. Nevertheless, each case must be examined in the light of the degree to which it conforms to or violates our own domestic standards, and often the way in which assistance is given determines whether or not it can be viewed as acceptable. Thus, it may be preferable in many cases to provide aid for information activities under international or multinational auspices, rather than unilaterally, and the greatest possible openness is always desirable.

In addition to ensuring that its own policies and actions do not violate the principle of free international communication, the United States should look for ways in which it can take positive action to encourage the exchange of ideas among nations. It should support private and multinational organizations that are working to eliminate barriers, and play an active role in helping to reduce high cable rates on news dispatches, tariffs on information and cultural materials, and restrictions on international travel. The government could also be of greater assistance in exploring overseas distribution and marketing possibilities for information and cultural materials produced under private auspices. Increased diplomatic activity in support of free international communication should be given consideration. It has been suggested, for example, that all treaties signed by the United States should include a clause providing for the unhindered flow of news among nations.[5] At the least, U.S. embassies overseas should use whatever influence they have to create conditions for unhampered news-gathering and dissemination in the host country; in the developing nations, they should try to encourage the growth of free and independent national mass media. The secrecy of totalitarian states, and their frequent distortions of information, should be exposed and attacked more vigorously.

If the United States is to benefit from a free flow of ideas, it must provide the background information that will enable people to evaluate and understand the significance of messages from abroad. In the case of ideas from or about the United States, this involves sufficiently acquainting audiences throughout the world with American society and the part that the American communication system plays in it to enable them to place in perspective the confusing and contradictory reports and impressions that come to them from a wide variety of sources. For example, background information about the problem of racial discrimination in the United States seems to have had a moderating effect on the reactions of African leaders to reports of racial disorders, and the full texts of important official statements which the U.S.I.A. provides to foreign editors often enable them to explain the meaning of brief news-agency dispatches to their readers more adequately. Most useful in interpreting information about the United States is recognition of the diversity of American society. As an Assistant Secretary of State noted when addressing a group of foreign visitors, this country does not have a "system." "The one essential thing about American democracy is this: that no individual or group ever gains the exclusive right to say authoritatively what American democracy is." [6]

Similarly, an understanding of the way the American communication system works, and especially how it serves a number of very different functions, often helps foreign audiences to evaluate the significance of American media to which they are exposed. This is illustrated by an experience of American anthropologists working in Samoa who were asked by local chiefs why Americans were so violent and lawless in films, while in Samoa they were generally friendly and orderly. The anthropologists replied by pointing out that Samoans enjoyed telling the tales of wars and adventure embodied in their own traditions, and that Americans also liked to be entertained by stories that were out of the ordinary—an explanation that seemed to satisfy their questioners.[7]

The task of intepreting American society and communications to foreign audiences is shared by government and private programs. Initially, however, the responsibility of government is the larger, since interpretation is most needed in areas where nongovernmental activities are poorly represented. In addition to assisting private media to enter new areas, therefore, the government should seek to prepare future audiences of these media to interpret them correctly and make the best use of them when they become available. Government information and cultural programs should supplement existing private activities in such a way as to ensure not only that adequate information is disseminated to other peoples, but that it is understood.

Freedom of international communication implies a two-way flow, yet to date the United States has made far greater efforts to send ideas abroad than to encourage other peoples to speak to us. The overwhelming emphasis of both official and private programs is on "outbound" ideas. Some foreign governments spend substantial sums in order to influence Americans, but there are others that can afford very limited information and cultural programs, or none at all. Since in most parts of the world private initiative has strictly limited resources, if an approximate balance of effort is to be achieved it must be through American action.

A two-way flow is as much in our own interest as in the interest of foreign peoples. In our person-to-person relationships the words and gestures of others give us a large part of the information we need in deciding how to speak to them and behave toward them in general. A similar relationship exists in international relations. An effective foreign-information program and a sound foreign policy both require an adequate reverse flow of communications. Until other nations can speak freely to us, and be understood, American foreign policies are likely to be less realistic, and domestic support for these policies in the United States will ordinarily be weaker. A two-way interchange with our friends and allies is particularly important in facilitating cooperation and the formation of common institutions.

Some encouraging steps have been taken to promote communication *to* the United States. Efforts are being made to increase the quantity and quality of foreign coverage in the American press; foreign films, radio broadcasts, and TV programs are encountered with increasing frequency; and foreign area study programs in American universities are being emphasized. Foundations have supported the translation into English of the great literature of other countries. Exchange-of-persons programs have a two-way flow of ideas built into them, and the lecturer from overseas has been an institution at American churches, clubs, and associations for several generations.

Nevertheless, the process of informing Americans about other societies has just begun. American universities have tended to regard foreign students as individuals to be educated rather than as a source of knowledge about other cultures.[8] Africans, Asians, and Latin Americans still complain, with considerable justice, that life on their continents is inadequately reported in American commercial media. Prominent Americans who think UNESCO is a "fine little country" can still be found. The Fulbright-Hays Act authorizes the government to support the presentation of foreign plays and other cultural works in the United States, but as of 1964 no funds for this purpose had been appropriated.

Since the American Government is unable to commit the principal domestic media and institutions in the United States to providing channels for communications from abroad, it can play only a limited role in promoting a reverse flow, but it could nevertheless take more vigorous action in a number of areas. It should be able to support foreign cultural presentations in the United States, and to encourage friendly nations to expand their information and cultural activities here. Howland H. Sargeant has suggested that reciprocal information programs might be arranged with other countries, leading eventually to a partnership between Americans and others for the welfare of both.[9] Perhaps the most important task that government agencies could undertake would be to help identify those areas from which a reverse flow of communications is most needed, to describe the form it might take, and to try to interest private bodies in providing the necessary channels.

While there is widespread agreement that it is desirable to encourage a two-way flow of ideas, as well as to promote freedom of international communication in other ways, no official or agency of the U. S. Government is specifically charged with seeing that this is done. Various offices within the U. S. Information Agency and the Department of State carry part of the responsibility, as do the U.S. delegations to UNESCO and the United Nations, and many other agencies are peripherally concerned. There is, however, no watch maintained over developments affecting world communications as a whole, as there is in the case of economic and military trends. Nor is there a systematic attempt to examine all governmental policies and actions from the point of view of the effect they will have on freedom of information. If we are to take seriously the task of promoting a free flow of ideas, a single office must be charged with the responsibility of monitoring the whole picture and making recommendations to the various governmental and private bodies involved.

Improving Government Programs

Although the communication facilities now available to the United States for supporting its foreign policy are considerable, they still need to be expanded in certain respects. Even more important is that existing facilities should be used more effectively. In general, increased effectiveness could be brought about by greater attention to ideas to achieve results that are within their power to attain, by more thorough research and planning, and by more careful coordination of the activities of various official agencies. These suggestions apply equally to persuasive propaganda programs focused on very specific objectives, to long-range programs designed to change a climate of opinion or build new institutions, and to the use of communications to inform and instruct, as in the case of development programs in emerging countries.

Most experienced officials in the U. S. Information Agency and the State Department, and in many private organizations, are familiar with existing research on the capabilities of communications.* That communications are likely to be most successful in influencing those who are already predisposed to heed them, and are less likely to influence hostile or indifferent audiences, hardly comes as a surprise to them. They are also aware that attentive audiences are usually self-selected, and that communications are more able to promote cooperation among friends than to win over enemies. Nevertheless, faced with the momentum of current activities and pressure from well-meaning domestic critics who feel that propaganda is a method of achieving difficult national goals at bargain-basement rates, many programs too often devote a part of their slender resources to deluging foreign audiences with ideas to which they are not receptive. Communications that are intended to exert a political influence would be more effective if they were persistently tested against the question: "How will members of the audience be able to use these ideas?"

American policy-makers have been less aware of the role that communications can play in creating and sustaining both formal organizations and public opinion. In this respect, the Communists have been way ahead of this country. Nevertheless, some beginnings have been made, largely through private efforts. For instance, since 1948 the 4-H Foundation has sent more than 1,500 American rural youths overseas to assist in organizing similar groups of young people, American unions have recognized the importance of strengthening free labor movements abroad, and the League of Women Voters, through its Overseas Education Fund, has made a promising start in helping to form civic organizations in other countries.[10] Government programs, too, should give greater emphasis to this aspect of communications. Foreign students from certain areas could be given training in the techniques of the democratic political process, greater use could be made of publications to link like-minded individuals and make it possible for them to organize and pursue common aims, and in general a sharp lookout should be maintained for opportunities to use communications in the formation

* Some of the literature on the effects of communications is summarized in Chapters III and IV.

or strengthening of organizations and public opinion that could contribute to peace and stability.

In short, it is important that all those engaged in information and cultural activities be aware of the full range of possibilities open to them. Too often, modest but useful effects are overlooked while more spectacular results, such as basic changes in attitudes, are vainly pursued.

Which of the various capabilities of public communication are likely to be politically relevant in any specific case depends in large measure on the characteristics of the society being addressed. This is one reason why detailed research and planning on a local level are necessary. As a leading authority on the Soviet Union has observed, we cannot cultivate those favorable predispositions that exist if we lack knowledge of them and are unable to establish rapport with the people possessing them.[11] Or, in the words of a former AID official, until we know more about communicating with people in emerging countries, we are working with half our brains tied behind our backs.[12] U.S.I.A. and the State Department have done a great deal with the slender research resources—both personnel and funds—that have been made available to them, but a far larger effort is needed if the potentialities of communications are to be realized. A major part of the research conducted thus far has been for the purpose of ensuring that our messages are in fact getting through to people in other countries. Greater efforts should be devoted to detailed analyses of the structure and functioning of individual societies in order to decide precisely how communication should be used in each locality.

The goal of research and planning should be to make it possible to state in advance exactly what each radio broadcast, magazine article, film sequence, or cultural-exchange activity is intended to achieve, and how this is to be accomplished. What individuals are to be reached, and how will they be able to use the communication? What are the politically relevant effects likely to be, given the political and social structure of the society in question? In view of the limitations of the behavioral sciences, and the tremendous investment of manpower that would be required, it is manifestly impossible to answer such questions fully. Nevertheless, if they are kept constantly in mind, the resulting increase in effectiveness will be appreciable. Incorrect hypotheses about effects can be corrected through experience; if no hypotheses are formed, the possibility of improvement is small.

It is at the level of research and planning in individual societies that a basis should be laid for stemming Communist encroachment. Purely negative anti-Communist propaganda, which has proved to be an ineffective method of defending threatened countries, has usually been based on the misconception that the United States and the Communist powers are fighting a duel for the impressionable minds of people in the emerging countries. The real battle is much more between the indigenous cultural systems and the Communist system.[13] Information and exchange programs can most effectively help to prevent other societies from falling under Communist domination by working for strong, local containing forces. If these can be identified and strengthened in each town and village, attempts at subversion will be nipped in the bud.

Education programs, the most vital component of communications to emerging nations, must be very carefully adapted to local needs. Too often, education programs emphasize knowledge and skills that, while important for industrialized countries, are of less relevance to the requirements of developing areas. In this connection it is worth recalling Benjamin Franklin's testimony with respect to education programs for the Indians of North America. After a conference with the Six Nations in 1774, during which a treaty was concluded, the commissioners from Virginia told the Indians that a fund for educating Indian youth had been established at the college at Williamsburg. If the Six Nations would send half a dozen of their young men to that college, continued the Commissioners, they would be well provided for and given a modern education. The Indians politely considered this proposal overnight, and in the morning expressed appreciation for the offer, but pointed out that their conception of education differed from that of the white man:

> We have had some Experience of it; several of our young people were formerly brought up at the Colleges of the Northern Provinces; they were instructed in all your Sciences; but when they came back to us, they were bad Runners, ignorant of every means of living in the Woods, unable to bear either Cold or Hunger; knew neither how to build a Cabin (or) take a Deer . . . spoke our Language imperfectly, were therefore neither fit for Hunters, Warriors, nor Counsellors; they were totally good for nothing. We are however not the less oblig'd by your kind Offer, tho' we decline accepting it; and, to show our grateful Sense of it, if the Gentlemen of Virginia will send us a Dozen of their Sons, we will take great Care of their Education, instruct them in all we know, and make Men of them.[14]

The lesson offered by the Six Nations has not been completely learned. Educational programs for students from emerging countries still occasionally result in turning out graduates who are misfits in their own societies. The U. S. Advisory Commission on International Educational and Cultural Affairs has suggested that greater thought be given to politically relevant considerations in selecting exchangees in general: From what area, class, professional group, or political sector should they be chosen, and what will be the effect of the revolutionary ideas to which they are exposed when they come to the United States? [15] Consideration should also be given to the way in which foreign audiences are likely to react to the ideas that Americans take abroad. All these questions can be answered only with detailed knowledge of other peoples and societies.

While the greatest improvements in government communication programs can be made by strengthening research and planning, and emphasizing quality rather than quantity, there are a few areas where a larger volume of output would be desirable. One of the most obvious of these is television. The remarkable increase in the numbers of television transmitters and receivers throughout the world has created a mass market for ideas that has outstripped the pace of U.S.I.A.'s television services.

Another area where expansion would be desirable is that of specialized books and publications. Once politically relevant needs have been identified in foreign countries, and they cannot be satisfied by using materials that have been produced privately, the government should have the means for seeing that such materials are written and published. At present, U.S.I.A. and AID are able to do this only to a very limited extent, with the result that texts sent abroad often do not explain their subject matter in terms the overseas reader can understand, and more specialized works do not answer the questions in which foreign audiences are particularly interested. It was only in 1963 that a brief history of the United States, in French translation, was placed in U.S.I.A. libraries in Africa.[16] When Harvard University was asked by the State Department to organize an orientation program for Brazilian student leaders, the participating professors found that existing books about American society were designed basically for Americans who already had considerable background knowledge about their country.[17] They therefore had to prepare new readings, which were later published in four volumes.[18] These are, however, among the very few serious books written in the United States especially for foreign readers. An irate publisher has remonstrated that there is not even an adequate guidebook to the United States for visitors from abroad.

Ideally, it would be desirable to arrange for publications that are designed for more specialized foreign audiences. For instance, a history of World War II and its aftermath, written for people in the newer states, would be a valuable tool for U.S. international communication programs. American diplomats have frequently complained that even high-level government officials of emerging countries have only the foggiest notions about recent history, and similar observations have been made by intellectuals from the developing nations themselves.[19]

A third area in which greater emphasis is required is that of person-to-person communication. Critics have often observed that government information personnel have been so bemused by the potentialities of the mass media that they have overlooked the importance of simple conversation. An American foreign correspondent, expressing the fear that U.S.I.A. personnel were failing to establish personal touch with the populations of host countries, suggested that a full team of U.S.I.A. media specialists was not necessary at each post. "Where the press does not exist for all practical purposes . . . I think we can safely ignore it." [20] Another observer, reporting from an emerging nation with an educated minority of at the most a few thousand, found it unreasonable for the U.S.I.A. to devote most of its efforts to mass-media activities, while ignoring the possibility of getting to know personally the very small group of local leaders.

Information and cultural programs can, of course, be strengthened by improving the organization and administration of the agencies that conduct them. Organizational questions affecting official agencies engaged in international communication will be given limited attention here, however, since they have already received both sustained and expert consideration. Karl Mannheim's observation that Americans tend to convert every problem into one of organization is nowhere more true than in this area. Since the so-called Macmahon Report on the constitution of an American international information program was issued in 1945, there has been a steady stream of public and confidential reports on the agencies concerned, many of them very thoughtful. Among the best of these are a study conducted by a subcommittee of the Senate Committee on Foreign Relations in 1952-53 (the so-called Hickenlooper Committee); an analysis by a special committee, under the chairmanship of William H. Jackson, appointed by President Eisenhower in 1953 to examine the whole range of government operations that affect public opinion abroad; and the report of another committee with a similar mission, under the chairmanship of Mansfield Sprague, appointed by President Eisenhower in 1960.[21] In addition, various advisory groups to the respective agencies have made a great many useful suggestions, and numerous studies of specialized aspects of government communication programs have been made by both official and private bodies of an *ad hoc* nature. Most important of all have been the continuing efforts of each agency to improve its own organization and operations.

How to organize government programs so that the activities of all the agencies concerned will form an integrated whole has proved to be a particularly stubborn problem. Observers agree that the U. S. Government should "speak with one voice," that all official communications should complement each other and should support a single range of foreign-policy goals, but no completely satisfactory way of achieving this has been found.

Improved coordination will require action both at overseas posts and in Washington. Overseas, greater emphasis should be placed on joint planning and research among representatives of all government instrumentalities at each embassy. Joint planning is now done in theory, but information and cultural programs in many countries still do not complement each other as they should, and the communications of AID, military agencies, and the Peace Corps have been even more poorly fitted into over-all plans. One reason for this is that the political side-effects of economic and military activities have remained largely unexplored. Thorough studies of the ideas that economic and military agencies disseminate to foreign audiences in the course of their activities would make it possible to frame plans that would take better account of the potentialities of all major U. S. Government communications.

More adequate machinery for coordination in Washington is also urgently needed. Since the abolition of the Operations Coordinating Board there has been no central mechanism for reviewing the information and cultural activities of all agencies. So much thought and effort has been devoted to the problem of central coordination in the past—and with so little effect—that one hesitates to suggest specific remedies. The danger of setting up merely another paper-producing mill is ever present. Nevertheless, several moves might be considered. One would be to strengthen the geographic bureaus of the State Department with additional public affairs personnel (some of whom could be drawn from economic and military agencies), giving them responsibility for central coordination of U.S. communication activities in each area. Another possibility would be to establish a Presidential Information and Cultural Policy Board, as advocated by Lloyd A. Free, to exercise central supervision of all official communication activities.[22] A permanent advisory body, along the lines of the Jackson and Sprague committees, might also be established to maintain a continuous review of all activities involving public communications. This could be done either by Presidential order or by act of Congress, preferably the latter. The greatest weakness of present advisory groups is that they advise individual agencies only. What is needed is a group able to concentrate on official international communications as a whole, without reference to agency responsibilities. The great value of analyses such as the one by Charles A. Thomson and Walter H. C. Laves is that they are able to look at problems without reference to bureaucratic divisions.[23]

Improved coordination among executive agencies would make it possible for the President and Secretary of State to take a more active part in speaking to foreign peoples than is presently the case. Their voices carry further than those of other Americans, but their ability to attract world-wide attention cannot be utilized to its greatest effectiveness until a government-wide information policy has been agreed upon.

By far the most difficult problem of coordination in Washington is that of achieving a satisfactory relationship between the executive branch and Congress. Perhaps coordination should not even be attempted here, since one function of Congress is to represent the diversity of the United States, and a single view should not be expected of it. Nevertheless, those executive agencies that are engaged in public communication overseas also reflect American diversity. They not only carry out policies of the administration, as other agencies do, but also reflect many different trends of thought in the United States. Therefore, their relationship with Congress should be different from that maintained by most other executive offices.

Just what this relationship should be remains an unsolved question. Certainly it should be characterized by a measure of partnership. Possibly Congress should be represented on various advisory groups at the highest level, and a joint Congressional committee on public communications might be able to achieve greater harmony between the executive and legislative branches. The greatest need, however, is for more Congressional interest in communication policy and a better understanding of the functions that can be performed by communication in support of foreign policy. The excellent work done by the House of Representatives Subcommittee on International Organizations and Movements, under the Chairmanship of Representative Dante B. Fascell, suggests how much a continuing intelligent interest by the Congress could mean.

Harmonizing Official and Private Communications

Official information and cultural programs are conducted against a background of a far larger volume of private communications. Some of these have a political intent; many more do not, although they may in fact have political effects. While any governmental attempt to control nonofficial communications would be out of place, government agencies can take account of these in their own programs, and in some cases can make it possible for private bodies to support national goals more effectively.

In particular, government agencies should be more active in acquainting the private sector with the goals of official programs and in providing private bodies with specialized information they need in order to make their overseas communications more effective. The majority of Americans who are concerned with international affairs support our principal foreign policies; when they do not, the policies are soon changed. Yet the citizen who wishes to acquaint himself with the objectives of official information and cultural activities in any country or area, or to learn how he might help support these, is faced with a frustrating quest. The U. S. Information Agency, the State Department's Bureau of Educational and Cultural Affairs, and the Peace Corps all issue periodic reports on some phases of their activities, but these are restricted by agency horizons and are written without reference to each other. The Agency for International Development and the Department of Defense make very little specific information available about what they are doing in the realm of ideas. To obtain even a partial picture of official overseas operations one must comb through a variety of sources, some of them very obscure, and even then many facets remain unexplored. There are no area-wide reports on government communication activities.

One reason no such reports exist is that the government is not now organized so that it can produce them. Until research and planning facilities covering all official communication activities at the local level are strengthened, and until a central review or coordinating body is established in Washington, any picture of U.S. overseas communications is likely to remain segmented along agency lines.[24] This leads to the anomalous situation in which citizens of other countries can obtain a balanced view of U.S. information and cultural programs much more easily than can American citizens.

If reporting on an area as well as an agency basis were introduced, it would be valuable to include sections on the work of private organizations, and on the kinds of private initiative that would be helpful. This would assist nongovernmental organizations in keeping informed about each other's work, and would provide them with a better conception of their own role in the total picture.

In addition to providing brief area summaries of communication activities abroad, official agencies should place more emphasis on furnishing specialized information to individuals and organizations that could use it to good advantage. The role of the government in supplying specialized data to the private sector is well established in such fields as agriculture, commerce, and education. Some beginnings have been made with respect to international communication, as in the case of orientation materials for American tourists going abroad, but there has been little effort made to determine the needs of private organizations and individuals and whether these could be satisfied by materials from official agencies. The government should extend its efforts to provide American publishers, film producers, and radio-TV programmers with relevant information about existing or potential overseas audiences. It could furnish American business, educational, and eleemosynary organizations with data about trends and conditions that are likely to affect their relations with foreign publics, and could indicate areas where existing informational needs could be met by private enterprise. It could also keep private individuals who are in touch with foreign audiences informed about the principal interests of these audiences, about the questions that they usually ask, and about the principal types of information to which they are already exposed.

Expanded government efforts to assist private communication activities can be justified on economic grounds also. Officially operated information services have already helped to create markets that later have been served by private commercial organizations. For instance, U.S.I.A.'s efforts to encourage the distribution of publications abroad have promoted American commercial book exports, and the Information Agency's mobile film units in emerging countries are helping to create habits and tastes that lead to a demand for privately produced films. Educational-exchange activities help to build channels of communication and personal relationships that later may have economic significance. Indeed, it is quite possible that official information and cultural programs have contributed more to the national economy than they have cost the taxpayer. Economic criteria cannot be a controlling consideration, or even a major one, in government communication policies, but neither should they be ignored.

In providing information of use to private individuals and organizations, emphasis should be placed on responding to inquiries rather than on building an extensive series of reports and publications. A central point of contact might be established in the Office of Private Cooperation of the U. S. Information Agency, where interested parties could be informed about available services. Private Americans overseas could, of course, turn directly to Public Affairs officers at U.S. embassies.

The ability of private organizations with overseas programs to cooperate fruitfully with each other could be facilitated through the same mechanism. In some cases, small organizations could be assisted in pooling their resources to accomplish common objectives; in others, organizations with less experience in a given area could be referred to those with more. American groups could also be put in touch with foreign groups that share common interests, as is already being done in the case of American universities and cities that wish to establish relationships with universities or cities abroad.

Another measure that might be taken to promote private-official cooperation would be to appoint to the principal bodies advising government agencies more individuals who are particularly active in international communication in the private sector. This could be done not only in the case of those bodies that are centered in Washington; Americans resident abroad could be utilized more extensively in local advisory groups.

Not all, or even most, of the initiative for private-official cooperation should come from the side of the government. Much more vigorous steps can be taken by private organizations engaged in various aspects of international communication, since governmental influence on the private sector must be exercised circumspectly, while private citizens are free to exert as much pressure on the government, or on each other, as they think proper. Nonofficial groups, especially in education and cultural affairs, already exercise a strong influence on government programs, and more interest in other phases of official communication activities on the part of the private sector is desirable. This has been suggested by Leonard Reinsch, a former Chairman of the U. S. Advisory Commission on Information, who has expressed the hope that private citizens and groups will make their thinking and experience available to official programs, since "no government agency or combination of agencies . . . possesses an exclusive monopoly of ideas and information in the complex ideological field."[25] Creation of a private body that could play a role with respect to information similar to that played by the organization known as Education and World Affairs with respect to education would be desirable.

When it comes to harmonizing the overseas activities of American commercial news and entertainment media with those of other private organizations and the government, the role of official agencies is even more limited. International news activities, insofar as they adhere to the highest professional standards, are among our principal national assets largely because of their completely uncontrolled character, and governmental involvement in them is undesirable. Other communications should be adjusted to them; not they to the others. The same is true of high-quality entertainment and cultural materials. The damaging effects of commercial communications that give a distorted impression of life in the United States, whether these are in the form of news reports, films, television programs, or publications, can never be completely offset, but can be ameliorated. Interpretive comment from both official and private sources will help to put this material in perspective and offset some of its liabilities, and even more can be done by an informed public opinion. If sufficiently conscious of the reactions of foreign audiences, Americans will not just object to exports of this character, but will not want to see them produced for domestic consumption either. Insulting characterizations of foreigners in American popular literature are now rarer than before, and the boisterous and boastful American tourist is less often encountered overseas. Both these developments may be due in part to the pressure of public disapproval. Building a public opinion of sufficient strength to control undesirable exports will be a long and difficult process, and is largely the responsibility of the private sector, but government agencies can on occasion take the lead in pointing out the kinds of effects that private communications are having in other countries.

A somewhat similar prescription is possible in the case of private activities that have the unintended side effect of disseminating political ideas to foreign audiences. These cannot and should not be governed by the plans and regulations of official agencies. Nevertheless, those who are engaged in them should be encouraged to recognize the political implications of what they are doing. If they do not then voluntarily behave in a manner in accord with national interests, they may be prevailed upon to do so by the pressure of an informed public opinion. Such a public opinion is already taking shape within the American business community; it should be encouraged elsewhere.

Strengthening Resources for International Communication

The excellence and effectiveness of American international communications depend heavily on the quality of the resources on which they can draw. These basic resources are provided by the policy branches of government, but even more, in the last analysis, by the private sector: education and research institutions, the press and communication industry—indeed, all organizations that concern themselves in any way with public and international affairs. The extent to which these institutions can help to produce the personnel and ideas that are necessary for effective international communication, and can educate the public to play its part in a fruitful exchange of ideas among nations, largely determines the degree to which the international dialogue will advance or retard the attainment of our national foreign-policy goals. In addition to striving to formulate better policies and to improve the efficiency of their own operations, therefore, government agencies should take a more active part in defining the kinds of personnel that are needed in official communication programs, stimulating private institutions to produce the ideas that are required in these programs, and keeping the necessity for educating the public in the forefront of attention.

The development of ideas that are useful to other peoples is particularly important. The mere existence of extensive channels for international communication is of little significance when compared with the quality and usefulness of the ideas that flow through these channels.

This is recognized by those who emphasize that what the United States does is much more important than what it says, that action and policy are more significant than words. But there is more to it than that. Policies and actions certainly have a greater impact than hortatory phrases, but even more significant are ideas and concepts that help people to deal with the immediate situations that are facing them. Marxism has had a strong influence in emerging countries because intellectuals in these countries often find ideas in the doctrines of Marx that they think will assist them in overcoming poverty and national weakness. In contrast, there is an acute shortage of materials describing other economic and social systems in terms that are meaningful to the leaders of newer nations.[26]

Even scarcer are ideas specifically adapted to the new needs faced in different areas of the world. As African scholars have pointed out, a number of traditional practices in the societies of Africa embody many of the basic concepts of democracy.[27] If scholars can suggest ways that these traditional practices can be adapted to the requirements of the modern era, they will have made a significant contribution to the development of African states. Similarly, little thought has been given to techniques of peaceful revolution. How can an old order that is no longer satisfying the aspirations of a people be overthrown and a new one instituted without conjuring up the specter of instability and war? How does one go about building an interracial society? The only answers that have been made readily available to Africans, Asians, and Latin Americans have been in Communist writings.[28] Scholars in the free world should be able to help develop other formulas for revolution that embody greater respect for civil rights and the dignity of the individual, and do not lead inevitably into a totalitarian straitjacket.

It is often alleged that democratic societies are at a disadvantage when competing with totalitarian states in the realm of ideas, since "official" doctrines regarding history, politics, economics, or social organization cannot be adopted and then propagated through all available means. The opposite is more nearly the case. Since the requirements of different societies are so various, no one doctrine will fit them all, and a choice of solutions to current problems is likely to be far more valuable than a single solution, no matter how vigorously expounded. Even though Communist theorists have shown greater elasticity in recent years, they are still much more rigidly bound than their democratic counterparts. The potentiality for creative thinking about the problems of the new nations is one of the most poorly exploited assets of the free world.

As a veteran Foreign Service officer has observed, the full and stunning concept of the power of ideas has not yet come to government planners.[29] Or as a senior U.S.I.A. official expressed it some years ago: "We have thought too little in terms of creating material that will tell a meaningful story convincingly."[30] Yet, even if they are fully conscious of the importance of the role of ideas in foreign policy, those conducting official communication programs cannot be expected to produce these ideas themselves. They must be painfully thought out and discussed within the institutions that are better adapted to this process: policy-making branches of the government, the universities, the press, business, labor, religious bodies, and many others. Government communication specialists can help mainly by defining the requirements.

Organizations that deal in the production and dissemination of ideas are responsible in the last analysis not only for providing the resources needed by public and private practitioners of international communication, but for making it possible for broad sectors of the public to take part in and support a two-way flow of communications among nations. Educational institutions, the press, and all kinds of organizations concerned with public affairs can help to ensure that all those who are involved in international communication, often without fully realizing it, can contribute constructively to the total process. This is a gargantuan task, and will never be fully achieved. Those who do not want to know will not become informed. Nevertheless, interested segments of the public are large enough to offer a fertile area for cultivation. Even those who are concerned with purely domestic affairs should be assisted in developing an awareness that the eyes of the world may be focused on them. Most people learn to become conscious of the eyes of their neighbors at home; it is to be hoped that more will learn to heed the feelings of their neighbors abroad as well. Henry M. Wriston has noted that "as we gain experience in world affairs, we will learn better how to talk with our own countrymen without needlessly disturbing friendly nations," and the Committee on the College and World Affairs has concluded that "the contemporary world requires of its educated citizens a breadth of outlook and a degree of sensitivity to other cultures unlike any required in the previous history of mankind."[31] Americans traditionally have had a decent respect for the opinions of their neighbors, and will be willing to take these into account if they realize that other peoples are concerned with what they say and do.

At the same time that public awareness of international audiences is encouraged, efforts should be made to improve the ability of interested individuals to take an effective part in intercultural communication. This too is primarily a task for the education system and the press, and a growing body of more specialized literature aimed at Americans who travel abroad or who have contacts with foreigners visiting this country is already available.[32]

More should be done to put research on international communication into a form that will make it accessible to a broader public. Americans need to know more about how to become acquainted with the foreign countries they visit: how to evaluate their observations, and how to learn as much as possible from local media. This is especially important in the case of visitors to totalitarian states. A better flow of information about foreign societies will make it possible to communicate with people from these societies more effectively. Without this, Americans cannot easily obtain a picture of other societies as they are seen by the people who live in them, and they therefore find it difficult to achieve a meaningful exchange of ideas.

Possibly even more important is an understanding on the part of Americans of how our own society works. Robert F. Kennedy has noted that a nice warm feeling in the heart doesn't take the place of adequate knowledge: "Americans who go abroad should do so with a sense of responsibility for providing full and factual answers." [33] Just as foreign students in the United States profit more from their experience if they have an awareness of their own culture, Americans who come in contact with peoples of other countries require an appreciation of their own society.[34]

It would also be valuable if the public could be informed more fully about communications directed to the United States from abroad. Americans are now the target of a constant stream of persuasive ideas from other countries, most of them friendly, but some of them not. Additional knowledge about ways of interpreting these communications would enable Americans to differentiate more clearly among them, to make greater use of some and disregard others. More attention might be paid to the experience of smaller democracies, which have devoted considerable thought to educating their citizens in ways of handling propaganda.[35] The advice of a Belgian authority on ways that the individual citizen can promote international cooperation might be applied equally well to international communication: distrust rumors, never rely on a single source for information, maintain an attitude of critical vigilance, and try to understand the context of international news.[36]

Above all, the individual should have an awareness of the importance of a two-way exchange of ideas. Unless he is willing to listen, he is unlikely to be listened to. As a Michigan State University professor remarked, after conducting a series of seminars for foreign students, the most important tool for explaining the United States to peoples from other countries is "the big ear." A generous measure of humility is useful in maintaining two-way communication. Americans are sometimes annoyed when foreigners come forward with suggestions for improving American society or policy, as for instance when an Indian physician recommended that the United States adopt India's custom of family-arranged marriages at an early age in order to reduce illegitimacy and divorce rates.[37] Suggestions such as these should remind us that many of our own comments about foreign societies sound strange to those on the receiving end.

It is unrealistic to expect that most members of the American public will soon take an interest in the exchange of ideas among nations, or that more than a relatively small minority will be prepared to play an active part in it. Nevertheless, most people are now involved, directly or indirectly, as senders or receivers of messages in international traffic. As more and more recognize this, and act accordingly, the capacity of the United States to make fuller use of the international communication network to help build a peaceful and prosperous world will gradually increase. Specialized governmental agencies and private individuals who have a major stake in foreign affairs will have to take the lead in strengthening American participation in the international dialogue, but in the long run the success of their efforts will depend on the tone of American society as a whole. This is one of the challenges of a shrinking world.

Appendix

Channels for International Communication

The most comprehensive surveys of international communication channels have been made by the United Nations and its affiliated organizations, especially UNESCO. In 1950, 1951, 1956, and 1964, UNESCO issued publications, *World Communications,* summarizing much of the relevant information. Additional data have been compiled in another UNESCO series, *Basic Facts and Figures,* which was discontinued after the 1961 edition. The *U.N. Statistical Yearbook,* in its "Communications" and "Education, Culture" sections, includes information on communication media and channels. Unless otherwise noted, all figures cited below are taken from one of these three sources. Two cautions should be observed in interpreting these figures. First, most of them originate with official agencies of the various nations surveyed, and these agencies use a variety of definitions and qualifications in compiling statistics, so that the data are not always strictly comparable between nations. Also, the sources are sometimes vague as to the exact year to which the figures apply. Some of the statistics in the following pages may therefore be slightly incorrect as to date. Since the purpose in presenting them is to illustrate orders of magnitude, however, relatively minor imperfections in the figures do not affect their utility.

The News Media

As far as transmitting current information from one country to another is concerned, the system made up of reporters, news services (both government and private), and domestic mass media is dominant. People throughout the world receive the bulk of their ideas about events in other nations through the same sources that bring them local news, or from friends or neighbors who pay attention to these sources. The domestic media, in turn, rely mainly on national and international wire agencies.

Five news services are usually classified as "world agencies": Reuters, Agence France-Presse, Tass, the Associated Press, and United Press International. In addition, as of 1962, UNESCO identified some 178 national or specialized news services, most of which also carried some international news. Of these, 23 were organized between 1960 and 1962, with the new states of Africa accounting for a large proportion of them.

The dominance of the large agencies in the international news picture is indicated by the number of local outlets they serve, and by the volume of the news they transmit. Directly or indirectly, they provide most of the foreign information in the press of almost every country. The Associated Press distributes news, features, and photographs to some 7,600 newspapers and radio and television stations in more than 80 countries. By contrast, it served only 38 countries in 1944. United Press International delivers its services to over 6,500 subscribers in 111 countries and territories. Tass dominates the news media of most Communist countries, and also provides material to some media in many others. Reuters has subscribers in 110 nations and territories. Agence France-Presse serves outlets in 104 countries. All the world agencies have agreements with national or specialized news services that give their materials still wider distribution. In 1953, the International Press Institute found that 4 of the world agencies brought some 80,000 words of foreign news to the United States each day—approximately the equivalent of a 200-page book. Western Europe received about 135,000 words a day from global and national agencies combined. Four agencies provided India with approximately 32,000 words of foreign news daily.[1]

The extent to which the files of these international services are used is illustrated by a study of seven leading U.S. dailies, which found that almost 82 per cent of the foreign news in these papers during three months in 1960 came from the two major U.S. agencies. Similarly, seven leading South American papers that were studied for the same period relied almost entirely on the Associated Press, United Press International, and Agence France-Presse.[2] One of the few papers that does not derive most of its international news from the big wire agencies is *The New York Times*. During the same time period, this newspaper received 61 per cent of the foreign news it printed from its own correspondents or from The Times News Service.

The daily press, which is the principal user of news-agency dispatches, is heavily concentrated in North America, Europe, Japan, and Australia. Nevertheless, it has grown appreciably during the past 15 years in the developing countries. In 1949, Indonesia reported 81 papers, with a circulation of about 300,000 per day; by 1962, it had a total of 95, with a circulation of over 1 million. The United Arab Republic reported a sharp decline in the number of dailies between 1950 and 1962, from 55 to 37, although total circulation increased from 350,000 to

500,000. Pakistan, which in 1950 had 34 daily newspapers with a combined run of 120,000, by 1962 had 99 dailies with a circulation of over 600,000. In a few developing countries per capita newspaper circulation declined during this period, mainly because the rate of population growth outstripped newspaper growth.

Fairly stable or gradually declining newspaper circulation figures are characteristic of Western Europe and other industrialized areas. In 1950, the United Kingdom had 135 dailies, with a circulation of 31 million copies; in 1962, there were 112 with a press-run of 26 million. The United States also experienced a slight decline in the number of papers during this period, due chiefly to consolidations; circulation remained slightly below 60 million. An exception is Japan, where the number of dailies increased by 20 per cent and circulation doubled between 1950 and 1962.

Radio and television provide a second major source for information from abroad. In 1962, there were some 12,500 radio transmitters and 400 million receivers throughout the world, of which more than one-third of the transmitters and about half the receivers were concentrated in North America. Nevertheless, the increase in the number of both transmitters and receivers in emerging countries during the past decade has been impressive. Africa, which had fewer than 1 receiver per 100 persons in 1950, now has more than 2.5 per 100 persons. A similar expansion took place in South America, where receivers jumped from 7.5 million in 1954 to some 15.5 million as of 1962. Between 1950 and 1962 the number of sets per 100 people in Asia increased from 1 to 2, while transmitters rose from 444 to 1,220. Much of the increase in receivers is accounted for by battery-powered transistor radios.

Television is spreading at an even more rapid rate, although as a world medium it still cannot rival radio. As of 1950, UNESCO estimated that about 11 million television receivers were in operation. By 1960 the number was 99 million, and by 1962 there were 130 million. Of these receivers, some 60 million were in the United States and 12.5 million in the United Kingdom. By contrast, the UNESCO survey of 1950 had estimated that only half a million receivers existed outside the United States. At that time only France, the Soviet Union, Great Britain, and the United States had organized regular television programs, while 10 years later programming was being done in more than 60 countries. Even in the 5 years between 1954 and 1959 TV receivers in South America multiplied by a factor of 8 to reach 1.6 million, and in Europe they increased fourfold to 20 million. According to U. S. Information Agency surveys, TV receivers in other countries outnumbered those in the United States for the first time in 1961, and by the end of

1963 exceeded 80 million sets, served by over 3,400 transmitters in 83 countries.

Radio broadcasts and telecasts come to the attention of foreign audiences in several ways.[3] Where countries are relatively small, as in Western Europe, it is possible to tune in on long-wave or medium-wave broadcasts, and even television programs, originating in neighboring nations. Indeed, radio stations in several of the smaller states of Europe conduct commercial programs primarily for their larger neighbors. Notable among these are Radio Andorra, Radio Luxembourg, and Radio Monte Carlo. Luxembourg and Monaco also originate commercial television primarily for viewers in near-by countries. Programs that are intended to reach foreign listeners directly, however, are usually broadcast by short-wave radio and are prepared by governmental or quasi-governmental agencies. It is now the rule rather than the exception for even small and less industrialized nations to maintain an international broadcasting service. Lebanon broadcasts to several continents, Thailand has a special program directed to North America, and Iceland's foreign-broadcast service consists of one hour daily and two hours on Sundays. Short-wave broadcasts designed for foreign ears amount to thousands of hours every week, although relatively few listeners have any conception of the number and volume of transmissions available to them.

Since most people cannot receive short wave on their radio sets, or do not regularly monitor the short-wave band even if they can, programs from abroad that are rebroadcast or relayed by domestic stations have many more listeners. The impressive extent of international program exchanges and relays is suggested by the fact that in 1956 the French radio presented its domestic audience with 2,404 hours of programs from other countries, and other nations broadcast 1,890 hours of program material received from France. In December 1955 alone, U.S. radio stations used a total of 4,200 hours of material from the British Broadcasting Corporation, and as of 1963 the BBC was supplying programs to domestic services in 71 countries.[4]

One of the most exciting communication developments in recent times is Eurovision, a creation of the European Broadcasting Union. This organization links the television networks of the non-Communist European nations, as well as those of Israel, Lebanon, Tunisia, and Yugoslavia. International TV programs transmitted through the Eurovision network have been increasing constantly, and by 1963 averaged over twenty per week. There were thirteen Eurovision transmissions from the Vatican on the death of Pope John XXIII and the election of Paul VI; President Kennedy's visit to Europe in 1961 occasioned seventeen. Non-European associate members of the European Broadcasting Union, which take part in some of the international programs it arranges, include the broadcasting organizations of many new African states, most British Commonwealth countries, and Burma, Brazil, and Japan, as well as major U.S. networks.[5]

Radio and TV organizations of the Communist countries, and of a few other nations, are joined in the International Radio and Television Organization (OIRT). Non-Communist members include Finland, which is the only country belonging to both the EBU and OIRT, as well as Iraq, Mali, and Egypt. Interestingly enough, the broadcasting services of some of the individual Soviet republics are listed as members, in addition to the Soviet Union itself. This gives the Soviets a total of seven votes in the governing body of the organization, possibly to help ensure a pro-Soviet majority in the event of differences with such dissidents as Albania and Communist China. In January 1960, the OIRT set up a system for TV program exchanges known as Intervision, which now includes the Soviet Union and six East European countries. Intervision receives some programs from Eurovision, and supplies programs to it.[6] Exchanges are also arranged by such regional organizations as the Asociacion Interamericana de Radiodifusion. The Asian Broadcasting Union and the African Radio Television Union were just getting under way in 1964.

In the United States, the Broadcasting Foundation of America imports radio programs from some 50 countries and offers these to about 330 stations, both commercial and educational. The National Educational Television Center engages in similar operations, and major American networks arrange independently for international programs.

Technological developments, particularly satellite relays, promise an exciting future for international television, and world-wide "live" telecasting will probably become common in this generation.[7] In 1963 and 1964, several experimental international telecasts using the American Telephone and Telegraph Company's Telstar communication satellite were arranged. Soviet TV viewers were able to see some of the events following President Kennedy's assassination direct via Telstar; events from the Olympic Games in Tokyo appeared "live" on American television screens; several televised "Town Meetings of the World" brought together participants in Europe and the United States. By the end of the decade, the communication satellite network may make it possible for a single television program to be seen simultaneously by 1 billion viewers.

Books and Other Publications

Books carry ideas to audiences outside their country of origin either in their original form or in translation. As a rule, those exported in the original language of publication reach a relatively small audience, while those that are translated are read by larger numbers. The spectacular growth of English as an international language, however, and in particular its adoption as a medium of instruction in the schools of many non-English-speaking countries, has made books published in England and the United States a partial exception to this rule. British publishers export over 30 per cent of their entire production. United States commercial book exports in bulk were expected to have a value well over $100 million in 1964—almost a 25 per cent increase over the previous year.[8] Ironically, however, one of the biggest exporters of English-language books is the Soviet Union, which has distributed large quantities of basic Marxist works in English translation throughout Southeast Asia, the Middle East, and Africa.

UNESCO has compiled fairly complete statistics on the number of translations published in recent years. During 1961, for example, it found that nearly 30,000 titles appeared in translation. The Soviet Union reported publishing 4,666 of these, although this figure apparently includes more than 2,000 titles translated from Russian for the benefit of the minority language groups in the Soviet Union. West and East Germany, combined, published 3,304 translations, and other countries publishing more than 1,000 were Czechoslovakia, Belgium, France, the Netherlands, Yugoslavia, Spain, Italy, Sweden, and the United States (which published 1,316). The category "literature" accounted for the largest proportion of translations appearing in most countries, but the Communist bloc states placed much greater emphasis on the sciences than did the democracies. In the Soviet Union, as of 1959, 878 translated titles were devoted to the social sciences, 318 to pure science, and 726 to the applied sciences. For the United States, the corresponding figures were 75, 83, and 67. A similar disparity could be observed between Czechoslovakia and Belgium, and between Rumania and Greece.

English is overwhelmingly the original language of books that are subsequently translated. Of the nearly 30,000 translations appearing in 1961, 11,234 were made from the English. The other major original languages were Russian with 4,930, French with 4,287, and German with 3,096. No other single language provided as many as 1,000 titles, although translations from the three closely related Scandinavian languages exceed this figure.

Magazines, also, have become important carriers of ideas from one country to another. Some export a portion of their regular editions to foreign readers. Approximately 10 per cent of the London *Economist*'s circulation, for instance, is in the United States, and all the major American newsmagazines have an appreciable circulation in Europe.[9] The *National Geographic Magazine,* with over half a million subscribers abroad, probably enjoys the largest foreign circulation of any magazine not directed specifically at an international public, although it is being given stiff competition by *Playboy,* which was selling some 300,000 copies a month in Europe as of the end of 1964.

Other magazines print special editions for readers in other countries. As of 1962, the English-language edition of the French monthly review *Réalités* had a circulation of about 50,000. *The Reader's Digest* publishes 29 international editions with a combined circulation of over 10 million, and the international editions of *Time* and *Life* total approximately 500,000 and 800,000, respectively.

A growing number of magazines are published in one country exclusively for readers in others. The Spanish-language *Visión,* with headquarters in New York, and the Sunday supplement, *Hablemos,* circulate in several Latin American countries, and the weekly *West Africa* is published in London. Most of the periodicals in this group, however, are published by governments as part of foreign information and cultural programs.

Finally, international organizations, both governmental and private, are prolific publishers of magazines for audiences in more than one country. The United Nations and its affiliated organizations issue more than fifty periodicals, many of them in several languages, and numerous associations with members in several countries publish international journals. Scientific and professional organizations are particularly active in this regard.

In addition to periodicals, the international mails are crowded with occasional publications. Some of these advertise goods and promote tourism. Others have a political purpose. Printed matter coming to the United States from all foreign countries totaled more than 500 million items in 1959, and probably has increased appreciably since.[10]

Films, Fairs, and Cultural Events

Films have become an important medium of international communication in part because they are produced mainly in relatively few nations, while projection facilities are widespread. Many countries therefore rely heavily on foreign-produced films.

The world's largest entertainment-film producer by far, in number of titles produced, is Japan, which turned out 652 feature-length films in 1962. Next came India with 319, followed by Hong Kong with 272, and the United States with 254 (in 1961). Other states that produced over 100 films in 1961 or 1962 were Italy, the Soviet Union, France, Great Britain, the Republic of Korea, and the Philippines.

Although there are fewer theaters and mobile projection units in the less developed countries than in heavily industrialized ones (and few indeed in those just starting on the path to nationhood), films are nevertheless the most widely available mass medium, with the possible exception of radio. Furthermore, the developing countries are expanding their screening facilities at a rapid rate. The number of cinemas in Indonesia increased from 260 in 1949 to about 700 by 1960. In Argentina the increase during approximately the same period was from 1,881 to 3,000, while in India theaters and mobile units jumped from 2,060 to 4,300. Part of this increase may be accounted for by better statistics, but even allowing for some inflation in the figures a very rapid rate of expansion is apparent.

The UNESCO survey of communication media in 1951 included information regarding the *sources* of feature films shown in each country. This indicated that while the United States, India, and the Soviet Union drew about 90 per cent of feature films from their own production, the pattern was quite different in most other nations. Great Britain reported that 65 per cent of the films shown there came from the United States, 25 per cent were produced domestically, 4 per cent came from France, 2 per cent from Italy, and the rest from miscellaneous sources. Japan drew half of the feature films shown from its own production, 30 per cent from the United States, 15 per cent from Great Britain and France, and the rest from miscellaneous sources. Argentina obtained half of the feature films shown from the United States, 35 per cent from its own production, 5 per cent from Mexico, and the remainder from minor sources. Since these statistics were compiled, the American film industry's share of the world market has declined from over 70 per cent to about 55 per cent. Nevertheless, it has held its position in Great Britain, and accounts for 55 per cent of screening time in Italy, 29 per cent in West Germany and France, and 21 per cent in Japan.

The number of people who gain some of their ideas about other countries by visiting international exhibitions or watching performing artists or athletes from abroad is not as great as in the case of films, but it is very large. International fairs in countries belonging to the Union des Foires Internationales attract hundreds of thousands of exhibitors and many millions of visitors each year.[11] During 1957, for instance, UFI members sponsored 45 fairs, most of them in Europe, but also in

Algiers, Bogotá, Casablanca, Izmir, Osaka, and Tokyo. The largest one in that year was the Paris International Fair, with 3 million visitors and 2,630 foreign exhibitors. The Brussels Fair the following year included 17,000 exhibits and drew over 40 million visitors. During 1960, members of the UFI sponsored 50 international fairs, the largest being in Milan. In addition, many countries that are not members of the UFI, including the United States, sponsor major fairs and expositions. The New York World's Fair expected to draw some 60 million visitors during 1964-65, about 1.5 million of these from foreign countries.

Cultural events primarily involving foreign artists and art works also attract large audiences. How many people can be reached by even a relatively small exhibit or performance is illustrated by a touring Japanese art display that came to Seattle and several other American cities in 1953. In Seattle alone, it had 73,000 visitors, or one out of every seven adults in the city.[12]

The ideas to which audiences of fairs and cultural events are exposed usually have political implications. Indeed, their very lack of overt political content is one reason they are such an important political instrument. Moscow's use of athletic teams and the Bolshoi Ballet is an outstanding case in point. The psychological impact that a fair can have has been described by a British traveler who visited the Barcelona Exhibition in 1929. He reported that after leaving he searched his mind to discover the principal impression the visit had made on him, and found, somewhat ruefully, that it was that Germany was the industrial leader of Europe, and that anyone who wanted to buy efficient, modern manufacturers should look to German suppliers.[13]

International Travel

During 1963, about 60 million travelers crossed national boundaries, and their numbers are increasing rapidly.[14] The United States, for instance, received about 366,000 foreign visitors in 1950 (not counting the hundreds of thousands coming from Canada and Mexico for brief periods), 500,000 in 1955, and 740,000 in 1963. Some 2 million travelers from abroad now visit the United Kingdom each year. American overseas airlines carried 6.6 million passengers in 1962, as opposed to 2.4 million 10 years earlier.

The significance of travel for international communication may vary widely. A European or Near Easterner visiting relatives in a bordering country is likely to carry with him few ideas that are new to those with whom he has contact, and thousands of American servicemen abroad are fairly well insulated from the societies in which they are stationed. On the other hand, the relatively few citizens who travel from underdeveloped countries to the industrialized nations include a large proportion of present and future leaders, who return with information about a very different world.

As with other forms of international communication, travel leads to further spreading of information through domestic channels. People who have been abroad talk about their experiences, many make formal speeches, and quite a few write articles or books. Indian audiences that have heard about America, and American audiences that have learned about India, through lectures by returned Fulbright grantees have numbered well over 1 million (excluding students in the classroom). When prominent people travel, their experiences are likely to come to the attention of a particularly wide public. After a visit to the United States by the Sardonna of Sokoto, the Premier of the Northern Nigerian region, the story of his trip was published by his Information Ministry and distributed to the schools and tribes of Northern Nigeria.[15]

A major way in which travelers abroad serve as a channel for international communication is by taking part in the educational process in the countries they visit. Americans who have taught at Robert College, the American University of Beirut, and at other American-sponsored schools and colleges throughout the world, have had as students many who later assumed positions of leadership in their own nations. Colleges and universities in most countries are welcoming increasing numbers of visiting professors and speakers from abroad, as well as foreign students. A UNESCO survey found that in 1963 about 130,000 opportunities for international study and travel were offered by 1,686 awarding agencies in 116 states and territories. Of these openings, 36,000 were in the United States. The same survey disclosed that in 1961 about 250,000 students, or approximately 2.3 per cent of all students, were enrolled at institutions of higher education outside their own countries, and an earlier survey suggested that at least as many more were studying abroad without being formally enrolled and counted by the educational institutions concerned.[16] Foreign study by young people from developing countries has increased with particular rapidity. The British Colonial Office has estimated that in the 1920's there were perhaps 30 students from Africa in the United Kingdom; by 1960, there were over 12,000. Three years later, there were reported to be 6,000 Africans studying in Britain, 12,000 in France, 7,000 in West Germany, 4,500 in the United States, and some 3,500 in the Soviet Union.

There is thus a growing group of persons in every country who share with their opposite numbers in other nations the experience of having been exposed to different manners and customs, and of having adjusted with greater or less success to a different way of life. As a result of their foreign experience they are likely to have a continuing receptivity to ideas from or about the part of the world they have visited, and many of them are among the readers of foreign publications and listeners to foreign broadcasts. Some maintain friendships or professional relationships with those they have met abroad, and may keep in touch for many years. Travel helps to create a significant part of the human base for the international communication network.

Organizational Channels

Although public channels, including international travel and the mails, account for the bulk of the ideas that flow from one country to another, they are supplemented by a number of channels that are maintained by organizations. Most international business undertakings, religious groups, and many other associations have developed at least rudimentary facilities for gathering information and transmitting it across national borders.

Of these supplementary channels, by far the most important is made up of government intelligence and diplomatic reporting services. Indeed, the facilities of governments for collecting and transmitting information about other parts of the world are far larger, even though usually slower, than those of the international news services. In every capital there are anywhere from a few dozen to several hundred diplomatic personnel whose duties include gathering material about the host country. Others are engaged in giving out information they receive from their own nation. Most senior diplomats engage in both forms of activity.

The numbers involved in these diplomatic information services are substantial. The Washington *Diplomatic List* for February 1964 lists more than 1,400 persons with diplomatic status in the capital. Of these, nearly 500 are engaged primarily in collecting information—the military attachés, scientific attachés, and so on. Another 100 are more concerned with giving out information—primarily the press attachés, cultural attachés and those concerned with promoting tourism. The remaining 800 cannot be classified on the basis of their diplomatic titles; it is difficult to determine exactly what the duties of a second or a third secretary may involve.* It is probable, however, that a large

* By way of comparison, the Washington *Diplomatic List* for December 1961 showed some 1,200 diplomatic personnel, of whom about 350 were collecting information (according to their titles), and 200 were giving it out. Why the number of diplomats listed as disseminators has declined so sharply while the total

proportion of them are filling speaking engagements in the United States, talking with American newsmen, and writing reports about the United States for transmission back home, as well as doing other things.[17] In addition, we must assume that numerous members of this reporting and intelligence network are not carried on diplomatic lists —either because they lack diplomatic status or because they are operating as undercover agents. As compared with the 2,000 to 3,000 full-time international newsmen, there are probably several times this number of persons primarily involved in the intelligence and diplomatic reporting services of various governments.

Although we do not ordinarily think of the activities of diplomats and intelligence personnel as being in the same category as the operations of international radio and wire services, they nevertheless enter into the public information network at many points. Diplomatic dispatches supplement the information that important officials in every country receive from the mass media. Foreign offices represent a valuable source of news from abroad for the news industry. A domestic dateline on a story dealing with foreign affairs often means that the information in question has made its way through official channels and has been "leaked" to the press, released in an official statement, or secured by an enterprising newsman in an interview. Conversely, information in official dispatches from abroad is often culled from press reports.[18]

In contrast to public communication facilities, which have been the subject of extensive studies, the part played by organizational channels in the exchange of ideas among nations has been given little serious attention. Exploration of their extent and influence should be high on the list of topics deserving further study by those concerned with international communication research.

---

number has risen is not clear. It may be that some countries, in an effort to avoid the appearance of engaging in propaganda, have listed their information and cultural personnel under more neutral titles.

Notes

Chapter 2: The International Network

1. Wilbur Schramm, *Mass Media and National Development* (Stanford, Calif.: Stanford University Press, 1964), pp. 58-63. For an example of the extensive attention given to the United States in Australia and New Zealand, see Richard W. Budd, "U.S. News in the Press Down Under," *Public Opinion Quarterly,* Spring 1964. For an example from Latin America, see James W. Markham, "Foreign News in the United States and South American Press," *Public Opinion Quarterly,* Summer 1961.
2. Alex H. Faulkner, "The United Kingdom in the United States Press," in *As Others See Us* (Zurich: International Press Institute, 1954).
3. Barnard L. Collier, "News and Latin America: A Balance Sheet," *Saturday Review,* October 12, 1963, p. 51.
4. George Seldes, *The Facts Are . . . A Guide to Falsehood and Propaganda in the Press and Radio* (New York: In Fact, Inc., 1942); also Seldes' autobiography, *Tell the Truth and Run* (New York: Greenberg, 1953); Upton Sinclair, *The Brass Check: A Study of American Journalism* (published by the author, Pasadena, Calif., 1919), p. 222; John Lofton, "The Press Manages the News," *The Progressive,* June 1963.
5. "The Press Looks at Itself," *Neue Zürcher Zeitung,* May 27, 1962, Section 4; *Die Feder,* June 1953.
6. John Beaufort, "Image America in the British Press," *IPI Report,* March 1963; Diane Stanley, "The Press in Chile—The Rectification Law," *Nieman Reports,* January 1961.
7. Gladys Engel Lang and Kurt Lang, "The Inferential Structure of Political Communications: A Study in Unwitting Bias," *Public Opinion Quarterly,* Summer 1955.
8. Theodore E. Kruglak, "The Foreign Correspondents," *Nieman Reports,* January 1957, p. 17.
9. Howard L. Lewis, "The Cuban Revolt Story: AP, UPI, and 3 Papers," *Journalism Quarterly,* Autumn 1960.
10. Murray Schumach, "Film to Poke Fun at Both Berlins," *The New York Times,* December 5, 1961.

11. Raymond B. Nixon, "Factors Related to Freedom in National Press Systems," *Journalism Quarterly,* Winter 1960, pp. 18-19.
12. *IPI Report,* February 1961 and December 1962; *The New York Times,* December 31, 1962 (Western ed.), and January 5, 1964.
13. An impressive inventory of regulations governing international communications is given in L. John Martin, *International Propaganda: Its Legal and Diplomatic Control* (Minneapolis, Minn.: University of Minnesota Press, 1958).
14. *Trade Barriers to Knowledge* (rev. ed.; Paris: UNESCO, 1955), Foreword.
15. Akiyoshi Kobayashi, "Kabuki Dancers and Japanese Cowboys," *Overseas,* May 1963, p. 13.
16. *The Problems of Transmitting Press Messages* (Paris: UNESCO, 1956); Llewellyn White and Robert D. Leigh, *Peoples Speaking to Peoples* (Chicago: University of Chicago Press, 1946).
17. Clarence B. Randall, *International Travel* (Washington, D.C.: Executive Office of the President, April 1958), p. 46. This booklet provides a concise summary of the barriers to international travel.
18. Wilbur Schramm, *One Day in the World's Press: Fourteen Great Newspapers on a Day of Crisis* (Stanford, Calif.: Stanford University Press, 1959).
19. Jacques Kayser, *One Week's News: Comparative Study of Seventeen Major Dailies for a Seven-Day Period* (Paris: UNESCO, 1953).
20. *As Others See Us.*
21. Fred Zusy, "Problems of Foreign Correspondents," in David Host (ed.), *The Citizen and the News* (Milwaukee, Wisc.: Marquette University Press, 1962), pp. 166-67; Jacques Champagne, "South Vietnam, Laos, Cambodia," *IPI Report,* November 1963, p. 3.
22. Allen Dulles, "The Craft of Intelligence," *Harper's Magazine,* April 1963, p. 141.
23. United Nations activities with respect to freedom of information up until 1960 are summarized in John B. Whitton and Arthur Larson, *Propaganda* (Dobbs Ferry, N. Y.: Oceana Publications, 1964), pp. 195-209.
24. United Nations Economic and Social Council, *Annual Report on Freedom of Information 1960-61,* by the Secretary-General (New York: United Nations, 1961).
25. The story of the Institute's activities is contained in the monthly *IPI Report,* a series of monographs, and a brief history published in 1962, *IPI—The First Ten Years* (Zurich: International Press Institute, 1962).
26. The IPI has, however, published an excellent survey dealing with countries that do not subscribe to the principle of press freedom: *The Press in Authoritarian Countries* (Zurich: International Press Institute, 1959). A list of the Institute's monographs that had appeared as of 1962 is included in *IPI—The First Ten Years,* pp. 94-95. These have been concerned with the improvement of reporting about specific areas, such as the Soviet Union and Middle East; government pressures on the press; techniques of journalism; the international flow of news; and the requirement for professional secrecy in journalism.
27. Cf. Kent Cooper, *Barriers Down* (New York: Farrar and Rinehart, 1942); Kent Cooper, *The Right to Know: An Exposition of the Evils of News*

Suppression and Propaganda (New York: Farrar, Straus and Cudahy, 1956).

28. *Professional Association in the Mass Media* (Paris: UNESCO, 1959).
29. Armand Gaspard, "Ten Years of the Fight for Freedom," *IPI Report*, July 1962, p. 17.
30. *Directory of Cultural Relations Services* (loose-leaf; Paris: UNESCO, 1959).

Chapter 3: Impact of Communications on the Individual

1. Martin Kriesberg, "Dark Areas of Ignorance," in Lester Markel *et al.*, *Public Opinion and Foreign Policy* (New York: Harper & Bros., 1949), pp. 51-52; Herbert H. Hyman and Paul B. Sheatsley, "Some Reasons Why Information Campaigns Fail," *Public Opinion Quarterly*, Fall 1947.
2. Literature on level of information on foreign affairs in the United States is summarized in Alfred O. Hero, *Americans in World Affairs* (Boston: World Peace Foundation, 1959), pp. 6-14. Public opinion poll results relating to American awareness of world affairs are presented in Hazel Gaudet Erskine, "The Polls: Exposure to International Information," *Public Opinion Quarterly*, Winter 1963.
3. Andrew Berding, *Foreign Affairs and You!* (Garden City, N. Y.: Doubleday & Co., 1962), p. 18; Robert J. Manning, "Journalism and Foreign Affairs," *Department of State Bulletin*, July 30, 1962, p. 190; *Department of State Appropriations Hearings, Fiscal Year 1964*, U. S. House of Representatives (Washington, D. C.: Government Printing Office, 1963), p. 511; Ben H. Bagdikian, "Have U.S. Readers Outdistanced the Editors?," *IPI Report*, June 1964.
4. *The American Public's View of U.S. Policy Toward China* (New York: Council on Foreign Relations, 1964), p. 5.
5. Elisabeth Noelle and Erich Peter Neumann, *Jahrbuch der Oeffentlichen Meinung 1957* (Allensbach, 1957), p. 339.
6. This account is taken from Shirley A. Star and Helen MacGill Hughes, "Report on an Educational Campaign: The Cincinnati Plan for the United Nations," *American Journal of Sociology*, January 1950.
7. Elisabeth Noelle-Neumann, "Mass Communication Media and Public Opinion," *Journalism Quarterly*, Fall 1959, p. 406.
8. *Psychology—Briefer Course* (Torchbook ed.; New York: Harper & Bros., 1961), p. 84.
9. Formulations along these lines have been made by a number of social psychologists. See, for example, Hadley Cantril, *The "Why" of Man's Experience* (New York: Macmillan Co., 1950), especially pp. 66, 103-4; Gardner Murphy and Rensis Likert, *Public Opinion and the Individual* (New York: Harper & Bros., 1938); Franklin Fearing, "Social Impact of the Mass Media of Communication," in Nelson B. Henry (ed.), *53rd Yearbook of the National Society for the Study of Education* (Chicago: University of Chicago Press, 1954), pp. 172-73.
10. George Katona, *The Powerful Consumer* (New York: McGraw-Hill, 1960), p. 9.
11. M. Brewster Smith, "Functional and Descriptive Ananlysis of Public Opinion" (Department of Social Relations, Harvard University, September 1947);

William A. Scott, "Rationality and Non-rationality of International Attitudes," *Journal of Conflict Resolution,* March 1958.

12. David Riesman and Nathan Glazer, "The Meaning of Opinion," *Public Opinion Quarterly,* Winter 1948-49, pp. 645-46.
13. Leon Festinger, *A Theory of Cognitive Dissonance* (Evanston, Ill.: Row, Peterson, 1957). See also Leon Festinger, "The Theory of Cognitive Dissonance," in Wilbur Schramm (ed.), *The Science of Human Communication* (New York: Basic Books, 1963), pp. 18-19.
14. Leon Festinger, Stanley Schachter, and Kurt Back, *Social Pressures in Informal Groups* (New York: Harper & Bros., 1950); M. Brewster Smith, "The Combat Replacement," in Samuel A. Stouffer *et al., The American Soldier: Combat and Its Aftermath* (Princeton, N. J.: Princeton University Press, 1949), Vol. II, pp. 243-72; Theodore M. Newcomb, *Personality and Social Change* (New York: Dryden Press, 1943).
15. See, for example, "The Image of America Abroad" (a symposium under the chairmanship of Leo P. Crespi), *Public Opinion Quarterly,* Fall 1960, pp. 517ff; Ithiel DeSola Pool and Kali Prasad, "Indian Student Images of Foreign Peoples," *Public Opinion Quarterly,* Fall 1958; Lloyd A. Free, *Six Allies and a Neutral* (Glencoe, Ill.: The Free Press, 1959); Franz M. Joseph (ed.), *As Others See Us: The United States Through Foreign Eyes* (Princeton, N. J.: Princeton University Press, 1959); Richard D. Lambert (ed.), "America Through Foreign Eyes," *The Annals,* September 1954; William Buchanan and Hadley Cantril, *How Nations See Each Other* (Urbana, Ill.: University of Illinois Press, 1953). This last survey is of particular interest in that it found that attitudes of one nationality toward another are likely to be the result of the state of relations between the two governments, rather than the cause of them. In other words, people tend to change their attitudes toward other nations when it will help them to adjust to the current facts of political life.
16. Elisabeth Noelle, "Die Wirkung der Massenmedien," *Publizistik* (Bremen), November/December 1960, pp. 536-37.
17. Kenneth P. Adler and Davis Bobrow, "Interest and Influence in Foreign Affairs," *Public Opinion Quarterly,* Spring 1956, p. 94.
18. Elihu Katz and Paul F. Lazarsfeld, *Personal Influence: The Part Played by People in the Flow of Mass Communications* (Glencoe, Ill.: The Free Press, 1955), pp. 234-308; Katona, *The Powerful Consumer,* pp. 147-48.
19. Carl I. Hovland and Walter Weiss, "The Influence of Source Credibility on Communication Effectiveness," *Public Opinion Quarterly,* Winter 1951-52, pp. 635-50; William H. Whyte, Jr., *Is Anybody Listening?* (New York: Simon and Schuster, 1952), p. 22; John Tebbel, "What News Does the Public Believe?," Arville Schaleben, "What Survey Do You Believe?," and Eric Hodgins, "The Believability Survey," *Saturday Review,* March 10, May 12, and June 9, 1962.
20. L. S. Harms, "Listener Judgments of Status Cues in Speech," *Quarterly Journal of Speech,* April 1961.
21. Stein Rokkan and Angus Campbell, "Norway and the United States of America," *International Social Science Journal,* XII, No. 1 (1960), pp. 78-79;

Philip E. Converse and Georges Dupeux, "Politicization of the Electorate in France and the United States," *Public Opinion Quarterly,* Spring 1962, p. 6.

22. Felix M. Keesing and Marie M. Keesing, *Elite Communication in Samoa* (Stanford, Calif.: Stanford University Press, 1956), p. 181.
23. Hadley Cantril, Hazel Gaudet, and Herta Herzog, *The Invasion from Mars* (Princeton, N. J.: Princeton University Press, 1940).
24. Richard Wallen, "Ego-Involvement as a Determinant of Selective Forgetting," *Journal of Abnormal and Social Psychology,* January 1942; John T. Doby, "Some Effects of Bias on Learning," *Journal of Social Psychology,* February 1960.
25. Charles A. McClelland, *College Teaching of International Relations,* A Report to the Carnegie Corporation (San Francisco, June 1961), pp. 269ff; Eunice Cooper and Helen Dinerman, "Analysis of the Film 'Don't be a Sucker': A Study in Communication," *Public Opinion Quarterly,* Summer 1951. See also Jean S. Kerrick and Daniel A. McMillan, III, "The Effects of Instructional Set on the Measurement of Attitude Change Through Communications," *Journal of Abnormal Psychology,* February 1961, pp. 113ff.
26. Arthur R. Cohen, Herbert I. Terry, and Charles B. Jones, "Attitudinal Effects of Choice in Exposure to Counterpropaganda," *Journal of Abnormal and Social Psychology,* May 1959, pp. 388ff.
27. Ralph K. White, "The New Resistance to International Propaganda," *Public Opinion Quarterly,* Winter 1952-53.
28. Gordon W. Allport and Leo J. Postman, "The Basic Psychology of Rumor," in Daniel Katz *et al.* (eds.), *Public Opinion and Propaganda* (New York: Dryden Press, 1954).
29. Eunice Cooper and Marie Jahoda, "The Evasion of Propaganda: How Prejudiced People Respond to Anti-Prejudice Propaganda," *Journal of Psychology,* January 1947.
30. Survey by International Research Associates, Inc. for the U. S. Information Agency. Printed in *Review of United States Information Agency Operations,* Hearings before the Subcommittee on State Department Organization and Foreign Operations of the Committee on Foreign Affairs, U. S. House of Representatives, 85th Cong., 2d sess. (Washington, D. C.: Government Printing Office, 1958), pp. 127ff; Robert T. Holt, *Radio Free Europe* (Minneapolis, Minn.: University of Minnesota Press, 1958), pp. 194ff.
31. Irving L. Janis and Seymour Feshbach, "Effects of Fear-Arousing Communications," *Journal of Abnormal and Social Psychology,* January 1953, pp. 78ff; Joseph C. Ingraham, "Study Finds Horror Films Fail to Reform Hair-Raising Drivers," *The New York Times,* June 24, 1963.
32. Jean Oberlé, *Jean Oberlé vous parle* (Paris: La Jeune Parque, 1945), pp. 122, 213.
33. Bruce M. Russett, "International Communication and Legislative Behavior: The Senate and the House of Commons," *Journal of Conflict Resolution,* December 1962, p. 304.
34. Wilhelm Bauer, *Die Oeffentliche Meinung in der Weltgeschichte* (Potsdam: Akademische Verlagsgesellschaft Athenaion, 1929), p. 176.
35. Robert K. Merton. "Patterns of Influence: A Study of Interpersonal Influence

and of Communications Behavior in a Local Community," in Paul F. Lazarsfeld and Frank N. Stanton (eds.), *Communications Research 1948-49* (New York: Harper & Bros., 1949), pp. 203ff.

36. Jerome M. Levine and Gardner Murphy, "The Learning and Forgetting of Controversial Material," in Theodore M. Newcomb and Eugene L. Hartley (eds.), *Readings in Social Psychology* (New York: Henry Holt, 1947); Paul F. Lazarsfeld, Bernard Berelson, and Hazel Gaudet, *The People's Choice* (New York: Columbia University Press, 1948), esp. pp. 80-84; Angus Campbell, Philip E. Converse, Warren E. Miller, Donald E. Stokes, *The American Voter* (New York: John Wiley, 1960), pp. 171-72; Jörgen Westerståhl, Bo Särlvik, and Esbjörn Janson, "An Experiment with Information Pamphlets on Civil Defense," *Public Opinion Quarterly,* Summer 1961; and Guido H. Stempel, III, "Selectivity in Readership of Political News," *Public Opinion Quarterly,* Fall 1961. This last-named article summarizes research showing that people tend to expose themselves to points of view they expect to agree with; it also reports an experiment in which this generalization was not borne out.
37. Leon Festinger, Henry W. Riecken, and Stanley Schachter, *When Prophesy Fails* (Minneapolis, Minn.: University of Minnesota Press, 1956); May Brodbeck, "The Role of Small Groups in Mediating the Effects of Propaganda," *Journal of Abnormal and Social Psychology,* March 1956, pp. 166ff.
38 Wilbur Schramm, Jack Lyle, and Edwin B. Parker, *Television in the Lives of Our Children* (Stanford, Calif.: Stanford University Press, 1961), pp. 1, 169.
39. Matilda White Riley and John W. Riley, Jr., "A Sociological Approach to Communications Research," *Public Opinion Quarterly,* Fall 1951, p. 456.
40. J. C. Mathur and Paul Neurath, *An Indian Experiment in Farm Radio Forums* (Paris: UNESCO, 1959), pp. 40-41, 93.
41. Donald R. Murphy, "Do Farmers Believe What They Read?," *Journalism Quarterly,* Winter 1960; Elisabeth Noelle-Neumann, "Mass Communication Media and Public Opinion."
42. Albert D. Annis and Norman C. Meier, "The Induction of Opinion through Suggestion by Means of Planted Content," *Journal of Social Psychology,* February 1934.
43. Ithiel DeSola Pool, "Public Opinion and Elections," *NEA Journal,* September 1957.
44. Reo M. Christenson, "The Power of the Press: The Case of 'The Toledo Blade'," *Midwest Journal of Political Science,* August 1959, pp. 227-40.
45. Carl I. Hovland, Arthur A. Lumsdaine, and Fred D. Sheffield, *Experiments on Mass Communication* (Princeton, N. J.: Princeton University Press, 1949), pp. 36, 210; Richard I. Evans *et al.,* "The Effect of Experience in Telecourses on Attitudes Toward Instruction by Television and Impact of a Controversial Television Program," *Journal of Applied Psychology,* February 1961; Mabel N. Reese, "Crusades Are Not Cheaper by the Dozen," *Grassroots Editor,* January 1960.
46. Maurice L. Farber, "Toward a Psychology of Political Behavior," *Public Opinion Quarterly,* Fall 1960, p. 459.

47. James C. Davies, "Some Relations Between Events and Attitudes," *American Political Science Review,* September 1952; Albert H. Cantril, Jr., "The Indian Perception of the Sino-Indian Border Clash," *Public Opinion Quarterly,* Summer 1964, pp. 238ff; Herbert H. Hyman and Paul B. Sheatsley, "Attitudes Toward Desegregation," *Scientific American,* July 1964, p. 20.
48. Gabriel A. Almond, *The Appeals of Communism* (Princeton, N. J.: Princeton University Press, 1954), pp. 240-42, 297ff; R. H. S. Crossman (ed.), *The God That Failed* (New York: Harper & Bros., 1949).
49. Lazarsfeld, Berelson, and Gaudet, *The People's Choice,* p. 102.
50. Joseph T. Klapper, *The Effects of Mass Communication* (Glencoe, Ill.: The Free Press, 1960), p. 62; derived from Bernard Berelson, Paul F. Lazarsfeld, and William N. McPhee, *Voting: A Study of Opinion Formation in a Presidential Campaign* (Chicago: University of Chicago Press, 1954), p. 23, Table 3.
51. Klapper, *The Effects of Mass Communication,* pp. 11-12.
52. Frank Luther Mott, *American Journalism: A History, 1690-1960* (3d. ed.; New York: Macmillan Co., 1962), pp. 719-20; Donald McDonald, *The Press* (interview with Mark Ethridge) (Santa Barbara, Calif.: Center for the Study of Democratic Institutions, 1961). Mott believes that—regardless of editorial position—most papers gave adequate coverage to all major candidates.
53. Oliver Garceau and Corinne Silverman, "A Pressure Group and the Pressured," *American Political Science Review,* September 1954, p. 688; Lester W. Milbrath, *The Washington Lobbyists* (Chicago: Rand McNally, 1963), pp. 340-45.
54. Stanley Kelley, Jr., "Merchandising Doubt," *Professional Public Relations and Political Power* (Baltimore, Md.: Johns Hopkins Press, 1956).
55. Hans Speier and W. Phillips Davison, *West German Leadership and Foreign Policy* (Evanston, Ill.: Row, Peterson, 1957), p. 259.
56. Bernard C. Cohen, "The Present and the Press," *World Politics,* October 1960, p. 165; Bernard C. Cohen, *The Press and Foreign Policy* (Princeton, N. J.: Princeton University Press, 1963), pp. 224-29.
57. Paul F. Lazarsfeld and Robert K. Merton, "Mass Communications, Popular Taste, and Organized Social Action," in Lyman Bryson (ed.), *The Communication of Ideas* (New York: Harper & Bros., 1948), pp. 101-2; Robert K. Merton *et al., Mass Persuasion* (New York: Harper & Bros., 1946), p. 84; Anthony Sampson, "Gossip," *Encounter,* December 1959, p. 15.
58. Paul F. Lazarsfeld, "Mass Culture Today," in Norman Jacobs (ed.), *Culture For the Millions* (Princeton, N. J.: D. Van Nostrand, 1961), p. xiv.
59. Klapper, *The Effects of Mass Communication,* pp. 167-205.
60. Serge Chakotin, *The Rape of the Masses: The Psychology of Totalitarian Political Propaganda,* trans. by E. W. Dickes (New York: Alliance Book Corporation, 1940).
61. Cf. Edwin B. Parker, "Subliminal Stimulation and Voting Behavior," *Journalism Quarterly,* Autumn 1960; Marvin Zuckerman, "The Effects of Subliminal and Supraliminal Suggestion on Verbal Productivity," *Journal of Abnormal Psychology,* May 1959; Institute of Practitioners in Advertising,

"Unterschwellige Kommunikation," *Rundfunk und Fernsehen,* VIII, No. 3/4 (1960). Additional literature on subliminal perception is summarized in Bernard Berelson and Gary A. Steiner, *Human Behavior: An Inventory of Scientific Findings* (New York: Harcourt, Brace & World, 1964), pp. 93-95.

62. Robert J. Lifton, "Psychiatric Methods of Chinese Thought Reform," in *Methods of Forceful Indoctrination: Observations and Interviews* (New York: Group for the Advancement of Psychiatry, 1957), pp. 250-51.

63. H. T. Willetts, "Pavlov or Khrushchev? Soviet Methods in Political Warfare," *The World Today,* October 1960, p. 429.

64. Claire Selltiz, June R. Christ, Joan Havel, and Stuart W. Cook, *Attitudes and Social Relations of Foreign Students in the United States* (Minneapolis, Minn.: University of Minnesota Press, 1963), chaps. vi and ix. This book summarizes some of the research previously reported in other studies sponsored by the Committee on Cross-Cultural Education of the Social Science Research Council, as well as presenting new data. Another valuable summary is contained in Josef A. Mestenhauser (ed.), *Research in Programs for Foreign Students* (New York: National Association of Foreign Student Advisers, 1961). An admirable selective bibliography of research in this area has been compiled by the External Research Staff of the Department of State, "Cross-cultural Education: A Bibliography of Government-sponsored and Private Research on Foreign Students and Trainees in the U.S. and in Other Countries, 1946-1964," March 1965 (mimeographed).

65. U. S. Advisory Commission on International Educational and Cultural Affairs, *A Beacon of Hope* (Washington, D. C.: Government Printing Office, 1963), p. 21.

66. Jeanne Watson and Ronald Lippitt, *Learning Across Cultures* (Ann Arbor, Mich.: Institute for Social Research, University of Michigan, 1955), p. 31.

67. The observations of State Department escort-interpreters have been summarized in Bryant M. Wedge, *Visitors to the United States and How They See Us* (Princeton, N. J.: D. Van Nostrand, 1965).

68. Prodosh Aich, *Farbige unter Weissen* (Cologne: Kieppenheuer und Witsch, 1962), p. 250.

69. Raymond A. Bauer, Ithiel DeSola Pool, and Lewis A. Dexter, *American Business and Public Policy: The Politics of Foreign Trade* (New York: Atherton Press, 1963), p. 170.

70. Hero, *Americans in World Affairs,* pp. 6-14.

71. Samuel A. Stouffer, *Communism, Conformity, and Civil Liberties* (Garden City, N. Y.: Doubleday & Co., 1955), pp. 58-66.

72. Ithiel DeSola Pool, *Communication and Values in Relation to War and Peace* (New York: Institute for International Order, 1961), p. 27. A recent survey of Indian newspaper readers found that 80 per cent were primarily interested in news from India, while only 8 per cent mentioned foreign news. The rest said "both." (A. B. Bose, "The Newspaper Reader in India," *Indian Journal of Social Research,* April 1964, p. 38.)

73. Viggo Graf Blücher, "Die Intensivuntersuchung mit Halbstruktuierten Interviews," *Zeitschrift für Politik,* June 1962, pp. 140-41; DIVO Pressedienst, Release No. 2, June 1962.

74. Robert C. Doty, "Average Parisian Is Calm in Crisis," *The New York Times,* February 7, 1962, p. 3.
75. W. Phillips Davison, *The Berlin Blockade: A Study in Cold War Politics* (Princeton, N. J.: Princeton University Press, 1958), pp. 365-67.
76. *The Economist,* February 17, 1962, p. 627.
77. Don Smith, "Is There a U.S. Audience for International Broadcasts?," *Journalism Quarterly,* Winter 1962.
78. Leo Bogart, "Measuring the Effectiveness of an Overseas Information Campaign: A Case History," *Public Opinion Quarterly,* Winter 1957/58, pp. 493-94.
79. Louis Lochner (ed.), *The Goebbels Diaries* (Garden City, N. Y.: Doubleday & Co., 1948), p. 43.
80. The Psychological Warfare Division, Supreme Headquarters, Allied Expeditionary Force, *An Account of Its Operations in the Western European Campaign 1944-45* (Bad Homburg, Germany: October 1945), p. 53.

Chapter 4: COMMUNICATION AND ORGANIZATION

1. S. N. Eisenstadt, "Communication Systems and Social Structure," *Public Opinion Quarterly,* Summer 1955; Daniel Lerner, "Communication Systems and Social Systems," *Behavioral Science,* October 1957; Wilbur Schramm and Richard F. Carter, "Scales for Describing National Communications Systems" (Stanford University, mimeographed, n.d.).
2. Eugene Walton, *A Magnetic Theory of Organizational Communication* (China Lake, Calif.: U. S. Naval Ordnance Test Station, January 1962).
3. Jiri Kolaja, *A Polish Factory: A Case Study of Workers' Participation in Decision-Making* (Lexington, Ky.: University of Kentucky Press, 1960), p. 136.
4. Norton E. Long, "The Local Community as an Ecology of Games," *American Journal of Sociology,* November 1958, p. 260.
5. George T. Matthews (ed.), *News and Rumor in Renaissance Europe: The Fugger Newsletters* (New York: Capricorn Books, 1959).
6. Wilhelm Bauer, *Die Oeffentliche Meinung in der Weltgeschichte* (Potsdam: Akademische Verlagsgesellschaft Athenaion, 1929), pp. 86, 223-24.
7. Bernard C. Cohen, *The Press and Foreign Policy* (Princeton, N. J.: Princeton University Press, 1963), p. 138.
8. Gerald Freund, *Germany Between Two Worlds* (New York: Harcourt, Brace & World, 1961), p. 199.
9. The classic treatment of government public relations in the United States is James L. McCamy, *Government Publicity* (Chicago: University of Chicago Press, 1939); see also J. A. R. Pimlott, *Public Relations and American Democracy* (Princeton, N. J.: Princeton University Press, 1951).
10. For a concise statement regarding the necessity of government information programs from a British source, see Michael Balfour, *States and Mind* (London: Cresset Press, 1953), pp. 72-90. A sample of Mr. Balfour's prose: "Snobs may dislike having to persuade the people just as they may dislike having to wash the tea-things—but evasion of either task only leads to trouble piling up" (p. 73).

11. H. A. Innis, *Empire and Communications* (Oxford: Clarendon Press, 1950), pp. 11-12; "An Account of the Chinese Progressive Press," *The Democratic Journalist,* August 1957; Fumio Yamamoto, "Reporting in Ancient Japan," *Gazette* (Leiden), II, No. 1 (1956).
12. Robert B. Holtman, *Napoleonic Propaganda* (Baton Rouge, La.: Louisiana State University Press, 1950); Albert Norman, *Our German Policy: Propaganda and Culture* (New York: Vantage Press, 1959), pp. 20-21; see also Hans-Joachim Netzer, "Die Neue Zeitung," *Gazette,* II, No. 1 (1956), pp. 13ff; Nikola Kern, "Jugoslav Press and Publications During the 1941-45 Revolutionary Period," *Training of Journalists,* No. 15 (1963), p. 40.
13. *The New York Times,* November 11, 1962.
14. *12 Decisive Battles of the Mind* (New York: Greystone Press, 1942).
15. Hans Jessen, "Wo Kommt der Aviso her?," *Gazette,* I, No. 3 (1955), p. 182.
16. William S. Ellis, "Nasser's Other Voice," *Harper's Magazine,* June 1961, pp. 54-57; Daniel Lerner, *The Passing of Traditional Society* (Glencoe, Ill.: The Free Press, 1958), p. 255; Sir John Baggott Glubb, *A Soldier With the Arabs* (London: Hodder and Stoughton, 1957), pp. 395ff.
17. *Saturday Review,* December 2 and 23, 1961; March 24 and June 2, 1962.
18. Philip H. Ennis, "The Social Structure of Communication Systems: A Theoretical Proposal," *Studies in Public Communication,* Summer 1961, pp. 130 and 135.
19. Jessen, "Wo Kommt der Aviso her?," p. 185.
20. *Gazette,* I, No. 1 (January 1955), contains several excellent reviews of studies of the Dutch and Danish underground press; T. Bor-Komorowski, *The Secret Army* (New York: Macmillan Co., 1951), pp. 23-24.
21. Rudolf Hoess, *Commandant of Auschwitz* (Cleveland and New York: World Publishing Company, 1959), p. 129.
22. Bor-Komorowski, *The Secret Army,* pp. 50-51.
23. Olav Brunvand, "The Underground Press in Norway," *Gazette,* IX, No. 2 (1963), pp. 131-32.
24. Stanley Kelley, Jr., *Professional Public Relations and Political Power* (Baltimore, Md.: Johns Hopkins Press, 1956), pp. 62-63.
25. Bernard C. Cohen, "The Present and the Press," *World Politics,* October 1960, p. 172.
26. Joseph Kraft, "The Future of The New York Times," *Esquire,* April 1961.
27. Karl W. Deutsch, *Nationalism and Social Communication* (New York: Technology Press and John Wiley, 1953), pp. 43-45; Karl W. Deutsch, "Political Community at the International Level: Problems of Definition and Measurement," Foreign Policy Analysis Project, Princeton University, September 1953 (multilithed). *See also* Morton A. Kaplan, *System and Process in International Politics* (New York: John Wiley, 1957), p. 53.
28. Morroe Berger, *The Arab World Today* (New York: Doubleday & Co., 1962), p. 426.
29. Roderic H. Davison, *Reform in the Ottoman Empire, 1856-1876* (Princeton, N. J.: Princeton University Press, 1963), pp. 175-87; Serif Mardin, "Some Notes on an Early Phase in the Modernization of Communications in Tur-

key," *Comparative Studies in Society and History,* April 1961, pp. 252, 266-67.

30. Kent Cooper, *The Right to Know* (New York: Farrar, Strauss & Cudahy, 1956), pp. xi, 41.
31. It has been suggested that the amazingly rapid economic development in West Germany following World War II was dependent in part on the growth of technical journals to train specialized personnel. (Wilhelm Lorch, "Die Entwicklung der Fachpresse der Bundesrepublik seit 1945," *Gazette,* VI, No. 2 [1960], pp. 119-20.)
32. Bauer, *Die Oeffentliche Meinung in der Weltgeschichte,* chapters i-iv. The murder of Wallenstein during the Thirty Years War was probably the first occasion in modern European history when the impact of a multinational public opinion could be observed. The popular reaction to this event is described in Heinrich Ritter von Srbik, *Wallenstein's Ende* (Vienna: L. W. Seidel & Sohn, 1920), especially pp. 230 and 248. For further descriptions of phenomena involving public opinion in the seventeenth and eighteenth centuries see Charles MacKay, *Extraordinary Popular Delusions and the Madness of Crowds* (Boston: L. C. Page, 1932).
33. Hans Speier, "The Historical Development of Public Opinion," *Social Order and the Risks of War* (New York: George W. Stewart, 1952), pp. 323ff.
34. *Gespräch unter vier Augen,* 1798.
35. A number of ways of looking at public opinion are discussed by V. O. Key, Jr., *Public Opinion and American Democracy* (New York: Alfred A. Knopf, 1961), pp. 7-15. These definitions are all usable, but each refers to a slightly different phenomenon. It is apparent that several expressions are needed to take the place of the single one that is now used to describe different things.
36. Charles H. Cooley, *Social Organization* (Glencoe, Ill.: The Free Press, 1956), p. 121.
37. Ferdinand Tönnies, *Community and Association,* trans. by Charles P. Loomis (London: Routledge and Keegan Paul, 1955), p. 256; Alfred Sauvy, *L'opinion publique* (Paris: Presses Universitaires de France, 1956).
38. A fuller account of this view of the formation of public opinion is given in W. Phillips Davison, "The Public Opinion Process," *Public Opinion Quarterly,* Summer 1958.
39. James Bryce, *The American Commonwealth* (London and New York: Macmillan, 1888), Vol. II, p. 210.
40. J. Paul-Boncour, *Sur les chemins de la défaite* (Paris, 1946), p. 293, quoted by Nathan Leites, *On the Game of Politics in France* (Stanford, Calif.: Stanford University Press, 1959), pp. 32-33.
41. Paul Kecskemeti, *The Unexpected Revolution* (Stanford, Calif.: Stanford University Press, 1962), p. 86.
42. *The New York Times,* July 31, 1960.
43. Friedrich Lenz, *Werden und Wesen der Oeffentlichen Meinung* (Munich: Verlag Pohl, 1956).
44. *The History of the Times, Written at the Office of the Times* (London, 1935), Vol. I, *"The Thunderer" in the Making, 1785-1841,* pp. 35-36.

45. "The Hungarian Listeners to Western Broadcasts—An Audience and Attitude Survey Based on 315 Personal Interviews With Hungarian Refugees," Audience Analysis Section, Radio Free Europe, Munich, October 1957, pp. 76-78 (mimeographed).
46. Bernard C. Cohen, *The Influence of Non-Governmental Groups on Foreign Policy-Making* (Boston: World Peace Foundation, 1959). Although concerned primarily with organized pressure groups, this survey also discusses the relative size of publics interested in various aspects of foreign policy.
47. George Katona, *Psychological Analysis of Economic Behavior* (New York: McGraw-Hill, 1951), p. 79.
48. Marguerite Perrot, *La monnaie et l'opinion publique en France et en Angleterre de 1924 à 1936* (Paris: Librairie Armand Colin, 1955), p. 241.
49. Hans Speier, "German Rearmament and the Old Military Elite," *World Politics,* January 1954, pp. 163-68.
50. Bauer, *Die Oeffentliche Meinung in der Weltgeschichte,* p. 137.
51. Pierre Sardella, *Nouvelles et spéculations à Vènise au début du XVIe siècle* (Paris: Librairie Armand Colin, 1948), pp. 50-53.
52. H. Gabriëls, "House Journals Within the Royal Dutch/Shell Group," *Gazette,* VI, No. 2 (1960).
53. Philip Cortney, "The ICC in War and Peace," *Foreign Service Journal,* July 1958.
54. *Yearbook of International Organizations* (Brussels: Union des Associations Internationales, 1962), pp. 14-15.
55. John B. Whitton and John H. Herz, "Radio in International Politics," in Harwood Childs and J. B. Whitton (eds.), *Propaganda by Short Wave* (Princeton, N. J.: Princeton University Press, 1942), pp. 8-9.
56. O. W. Riegel, "Residual Effects of Exchange of Persons," *Public Opinion Quarterly,* Fall 1953, p. 325. See also U. S. Advisory Commission on International Educational and Cultural Affairs, *A Beacon of Hope* (Washington, D. C.: Government Printing Office, 1963), pp. 3, 27-28.
57. Armand Daussin, "Ein Europaischer Oeffentlicher Dienst," *Europa Archiv,* XV (1960), Folge 21, pp. 655ff. See also "Global Careers: A Program," *Overseas,* January 1962.
58. *Department of State Bulletin,* August 5, 1959, pp. 319-25.
59. Ernst Fraenkel, *Oeffentliche Meinung und Internationale Politik* (Tübingen: Mohr, 1962); Hans J. Morgenthau, "Is World Public Opinion a Myth?," *The New York Times Magazine,* March 25, 1962.
60. Karl W. Deutsch, "Towards Western European Integration: An Interim Assessment," *Journal of International Affairs,* XVI, No. 1 (1962).
61. Deutsch, "Political Community at the International Level: Problems of Definition and Measurement," p. 7.

Chapter 5: The Political Role of Communication in Democracies

1. Cf. Fred S. Siebert, Theodore Peterson, and Wilbur Schramm, *Four Theories of the Press* (Urbana, Ill.: University of Illinois Press, 1956). These authors

distinguish between a "libertarian" and a "social responsibility" theory of the press.

2. Henry M. Wriston, *Diplomacy in a Democracy* (New York: Harper & Bros., 1956), p. 108; John S. Dickey, "The Secretary and the American Public," in Don K. Price (ed.), *The Secretary of State* (Englewood Cliffs, N. J.: Prentice-Hall, 1960), p. 164.
3. Deutsches Institut für Zeitungskunde, *Handbuch der Weltpresse, 1931* (Berlin: Duncker Verlag, 1931), pp. 227-31.
4. *Handbuch der Weltpresse,* II Auflage (Berlin: Duncker Verlag, 1934), pp. 154ff; *Handbuch der Weltpresse,* III Auflage, (Leipzig and Frankfurt a.M.: Armanen Verlag, 1937), p. 153. (It should be noted that the director of the institute that published these volumes was not editor of the two later editions, this function having been taken over by a Nazi Party official.)
5. Frank Luther Mott, *American Journalism: A History, 1690-1960* (3d ed.; New York: Macmillan Co., 1962), p. 818.
6. Raymond B. Nixon and Jean Ward, "Trends in Newspaper Ownership and Inter-media Competition," *Journalism Quarterly,* Winter 1961.
7. Herbert Brucker, *Freedom of Information* (New York: Macmillan Co., 1949), pp. 282-83.
8. Robert D. Leigh, "Problems of Freedom," in Lyman Bryson (ed.), *The Communication of Ideas* (New York: Harper & Bros., 1948), p. 204. Dr. Leigh served as staff director of the Commission. A fuller exposition of its ideas is found in its report, *A Free and Responsible Press* (Chicago: University of Chicago Press, 1947), and in two supplementary volumes by members of the Commission: Zechariah Chafee, Jr., *Government and Mass Communications,* and William Ernest Hocking, *Freedom of the Press: A Framework of Principle,* both published by the University of Chicago Press in 1947.
9. The other side of the coin is that no part of the audience should be excessively annoyed. This accounts for the disappearance of many outspoken columnists and commentators from the press and airwaves. (Karl E. Meyer, "Don't Annoy the Sponsor," *The Progressive,* December 1963.) Nevertheless, some newspapers have opened their advertising columns even to points of view with which they know their readers are in overwhelming disagreement. ("The Birch Advertisement," editorial in *The New York Times,* December 20, 1963.)
10. This was made explicit in a decision of the Federal Communications Commission early in 1964, renewing the licenses of the Pacifica network's three FM stations. (Anthony Lewis, "F.C.C. Sanctions Provocative TV," *The New York Times,* January 23, 1964, pp. 1, 63.)
11. Even repugnant extremists are sometimes given elaborate attention by the news media. Complaining about the front-page treatment accorded American Nazi leader George Lincoln Rockwell by British tabloids, the London *Economist* observed that as a direct result the number of "self-appointed nitwit fuehrers" would go up, and the British and American Nazi leaders would get more bemused recruits. ("Helping Hands," August 11, 1962, p. 514.)
12. Winston L. Brembeck and William S. Howell, *Persuasion: A Means of Social Control* (New York: Prentice-Hall, 1952), p. 9.

13. Leigh, "Problems of Freedom," p. 204; Siebert, Peterson, and Schramm, *Four Theories of the Press,* pp. 87-92.
14. Friedrich Schönemann, *Die Kunst der Massenbeeinflussung in den Vereinigten Staaten von Amerika* (Stuttgart: Deutsche Verlags-Anstalt, 1924). *The Bulletin,* Press and Information Office of the Federal Republic of Germany, Bonn, October 23, 1956.
15. David B. Truman, *The Governmental Process* (New York: Alfred A. Knopf, 1951), pp. 157-67.
16. Selig S. Harrison, *India: The Most Dangerous Decades* (Princeton, N. J.: Princeton University Press, 1960).
17. Bernard C. Cohen, *The Influence of Non-Governmental Groups on Foreign Policy-Making* (Boston: World Peace Foundation, 1959), pp. 2-3.
18. V. O. Key, Jr., *Public Opinion and American Democracy* (New York: Alfred A. Knopf, 1961), pp. 154-68.
19. Gabriel A. Almond, *The American People and Foreign Policy* (New York: Frederick A. Praeger, 1960), pp. 186-87.
20. Bernard C. Cohen, *The Political Process and Foreign Policy: The Making of the Japanese Peace Settlement* (Princeton, N. J.: Princeton University Press, 1957); also, Cohen, *The Influence of Non-Governmental Groups on Foreign Policy-Making,* p. 7.
21. Cohen, *The Influence of Non-Governmental Groups on Foreign Policy-Making,* pp. 11-17.
22. Lloyd A. Free, "France: The Sick Man of Europe" (Washington, D. C., January 1954, mimeographed).
23. Joachim Remak, in a review of Stephen D. Kertesz (ed.), *American Diplomacy in a New Era* (Notre Dame, Ind.: University of Notre Dame Press, 1961), in *Saturday Review,* September 9, 1961, pp. 36-37.
24. Truman, *The Govermental Process,* pp. 448-49, 511-12.
25. Almond, *The American People and Foreign Policy,* p. 138; Lewis A. Dexter, "What Do Congressmen Hear: The Mail," *Public Opinion Quarterly,* Spring 1956, p. 19.
26. Lester Markel, "What We Don't Know *Will* Hurt Us," *The New York Times Magazine,* April 9, 1961.
27. "The Angry Reservists," editorial in *The New York Times,* August 8, 1962.
28. Ithiel DeSola Pool, *Communication and Values in Relation to War and Peace* (New York: Institute for International Order, 1961), p. 34; see also, chapters on "Intensity," "Stability," and "Latency," in Key, Jr., *Public Opinion and American Democracy.*
29. Floyd H. Allport, "The J-Curve Hypothesis of Conforming Behavior," *Journal of Social Psychology,* May 1934, pp. 141-83. This article deals mainly with compliance with traffic regulations. Examples of consensus involving social security, Communists in government, influence of big business, and other matters are given in Key, Jr., *Public Opinion and American Democracy,* pp. 27-53.
30. Michael Balfour, *States and Mind* (London: Cresset Press, 1953), p. 119.
31. Charles A. Siepmann, "American Radio in Wartime," Paul F. Lazarsfeld and

Frank N. Stanton (eds.), *Radio Research, 1942-1943* (New York: Duell, Sloane & Pearce, 1944), pp. 131-33.

32. Alex S. Edelstein, "Propaganda and Economic Policy," *Gazette,* IV, No. 4 (1958), pp. 319ff.
33. Frederick S. Siebert, *Freedom of the Press in England, 1476-1776* (Urbana, Ill.: University of Illinois Press, 1952), p. 4.
34. Kenneth Rose, "The Growth of Freedom in the Reporting of Parliamentary Debates," *Gazette,* II, No. 4 (1957).
35. Samuel L. Becker, "Presidential Power: The Influence of Broadcasting," *Quarterly Journal of Speech,* February 1961.
36. James Reston, "How to Overbalance the Political Scales," *The New York Times,* May 9, 1962, p. 42; Ben H. Bagdikian, "Television—'The President's Medium'?," *Columbia Journalism Review,* Summer 1962.
37. "The Press Looks at Itself," *Neue Zürcher Zeitung,* May 27, 1962, Section 4.
38. Alfred Sauvy, "Opinion and Power," *Diogenes,* Fall 1956, pp. 33-34.
39. Constantine Melnik and Nathan Leites, *The House Without Windows* (Evanston, Ill.: Row, Peterson, 1958), p. 16.
40. Ward S. Just, "The Day the News Managers Quit," *The Reporter,* May 9, 1963. This is a whimsical account. For a more grudging acknowledgment of the value of government handouts, see Arthur Krock, "Press vs. Government—A Warning," *Public Opinion Quarterly,* April 1937, p. 46.
41. Wilhelm Bauer, *Die Oeffentliche Meinung in der Weltgeschichte* (Potsdam: Akademische Verlagsgesellschaft Athenaium, 1929), pp. 175-77; Siebert, *Freedom of the Press in England, 1476-1776,* p. 5.
42. Karl Buchheim, "Preussische Pressepolitik zur Zeit der Olmützer Punktation, 1850-51," *Publizistik,* January-February, 1958.
43. Jean de Soto, "Remarks on Information in a Democratic System," *Training of Journalists,* Autumn 1960, pp. 50-51.
44. Albert G. Pickerell, "Access to News in the United States," *Gazette,* IV, No. 1 (1958), p. 79; see also James Russell Wiggins, *Freedom or Secrecy?* (London and New York: Oxford University Press, 1956).
45. Kurt Baschwitz, "Zeitungswissenschaft für Staatsmänner," *Gazette,* I, No. 1 (January 1955), pp. 18ff.
46. Bruce Lannes Smith, "Democratic Control of Propaganda Through Registration and Disclosure I," *Public Opinion Quarterly,* Spring 1942.
47. *Activities of Nondiplomatic Representatives of Foreign Principals in the United States,* Hearings before the Committee on Foreign Relations, U. S. Senate, 88th Cong., 1st sess., 1963, especially Parts III and VI; James A. Wechsler, "Propaganda in the Press," *The Progressive,* August 1963.
48. *Activities of Nondiplomatic Representatives of Foreign Principals in the United States,* Part I, pp. 11ff.
49. Harwood L. Childs, "America's Short-Wave Audience," in Harwood L. Childs and John B. Whitton (eds.), *Propaganda by Short Wave* (Princeton, N. J.: Princeton University Press, 1942), pp. 313, 323, 341.
50. O. John Rogge, *The Official German Report* (New York: Thomas Yoseloff, 1961), chaps. x and xi.

Chapter 6: Communication in Communist States

1. Frederick C. Barghoorn, *Soviet Foreign Propaganda* (Princeton, N. J.: Princeton University Press, 1964), pp. 32-33.
2. Alex Inkeles, *Public Opinion in Soviet Russia* (Cambridge, Mass.: Harvard University Press, 1950), p. 173; "Castro Sustains Air of Revolution," *The New York Times,* December 20, 1963, p. 12; Lo Lieh, "An Account of the Chinese Progressive Press," *The Democratic Journalist,* August 1957.
3. Summary of Remarks of Edward Crankshaw (of the London *Observer*), in IPI Assembly, *The Professional Panels* (Zurich, 1952), p. 18.
4. Leo Gruliow, "The Soviet Press," *Journal of International Affairs,* X, No. 2 (1956), p. 165.
5. Seweryn Bialer, "Ich Wählte die Wahrheit," *Hinter dem Eisernen Vorhang* (Munich, October 1956), p. 20.
6. Paul Kecskemeti, "Totalitarian Communications as a Means of Control," *Public Opinion Quarterly,* Summer 1950, p. 232; Alex Inkeles and Raymond A. Bauer, *The Soviet Citizen* (Cambridge, Mass.: Harvard University Press, 1959), p. 175.
7. Antony Buzek, *How the Communist Press Works* (New York: Frederick A. Praeger, 1964), p. 51.
8. J. Sylla, "The Periodical Press in the People's Democratic Republics," *Gazette,* VI, No. 2 (1960), pp. 181ff; J. Sylla, "The Bulgarian Press After the Second World War," *Gazette,* IV, No. 4 (1958); A. Kotlyar, "Newspapers in the U.S.S.R.," trans. by Fred Holling (mimeographed publication of Research Program on the U.S.S.R., New York, 1955), p. 46.
9. Donald Dunham, *Kremlin Target: U.S.A.* (New York: Washburn, 1961), p. 246; Theodore E. Kruglak, *The Two Faces of Tass* (Minneapolis, Minn.: University of Minnesota Press, 1962), pp. 44, 93-94; Leo Gruliow, review of *The Two Faces of Tass,* in *IPI Report,* October 1962, p. 9.
10. Gruliow, "The Soviet Press," p. 157; Bruno Kalnins, *Der Sowjetische Propagandastaat* (Stockholm: Tidens Förlag, 1956), p. 169.
11. Margaret Mead, *Soviet Attitudes Toward Authority* (New York: McGraw-Hill, 1951), p. 28; Hadley Cantril, *Soviet Leaders and Mastery Over Man* (New Brunswick, N. J.: Rutgers University Press, 1960), pp. 7-8; Robert Magidoff, *The Kremlin vs. the People* (Garden City, N. Y.: Doubleday & Co., 1953), pp. 223-24.
12. Raymond A. Bauer, *The New Man in Soviet Psychology* (Cambridge, Mass.: Harvard University Press, 1952), pp. 181-82.
13. Helmut Roske, "The Textbook Factory," *The Atlantic,* December 1963, p. 91; Stephen Viederman, "Coexistence English," *Columbia University Forum,* Fall 1960.
14. Matthew P. Gallagher, *The Soviet History of World War II* (New York: Frederick A. Praeger, 1963); "Reds Claim Germany Lost Before D-Day," *Washington Post,* January 22, 1961; Barghoorn, *Soviet Foreign Propaganda,* pp. 75-76.
15. Nicholas DeWitt, "Our Image in the Soviet School Books," *The New York Times Magazine,* March 26, 1961, p. 11.

16. Edwin L. James, "Moscow Gives Lesson in Proper Journalism," *The New York Times,* April 20, 1947.
17. A. K. Uledov, "Public Opinion as the Subject of Social Science Research," *Voprosi Filosofy,* No. 3, 1959. (In *Prod Translations,* February 1960.)
18. Soviet and East German sources are cited in Friedrich Lenz, *Werden und Wesen der Oeffentlichen Meinung* (Munich: Verlag Pohl, 1956), pp. 105-6.
19. Kotlyar, "Newspapers in the U.S.S.R.," pp. 41-46.
20. Magidoff, *The Kremlin vs. the People,* pp. 232-33.
21. Kotlyar, "Newspapers in the U.S.S.R.," pp. 18-19; Inkeles, *Public Opinion in Soviet Russia,* p. 205.
22. Inkeles, *Public Opinion in Soviet Russia,* p. 281; *The Press in Authoritarian Countries* (Zurich: IPI, 1959), p. 27.
23. J. Sylla, "The Periodical Press in the People's Democratic Republics," p. 182; Frederick T. C. Yu, "Communications and Politics in Communist China," in Lucian W. Pye (ed.), *Communications and Political Development* (Princeton, N. J.: Princeton University Press, 1963), p. 276. A fuller account of the Communist Chinese press is found in Frederick T. C. Yu, *Mass Persuasion in Communist China* (New York: Frederick A. Praeger, 1964).
24. Gruliow, "The Soviet Press," p. 159; Kruglak, *The Two Faces of Tass,* pp. 79-80.
25. Leo Gruliow, "What the Soviet Readers *Never Knew,*" *IPI Report,* December 1962; Edward Crankshaw, "Case History of an Unfree Press," *The New York Times Magazine,* December 2, 1962.
26. "U.S. Editors Find Yes is Nyet in Soviet Report on Interview," *The New York Times,* July 17, 1962, p. 3.
27. Seymour Topping, "Moscow Censors Rebuked by Thant," *The New York Times,* September 1, 1962, p. 2. The texts of the U.S. and Soviet notes on Berlin are printed in *The New York Times,* October 14, 1961, p. 2.
28. *World Communications* (Paris: UNESCO, 1964), pp. 364-65.
29. *Basic Facts and Figures* (Paris: UNESCO, 1962), p. 105; "Knigi," *Sovjetskaya Pechat,* November 1959, p. 35 (cited in *Journalism Quarterly,* Summer 1960, p. 470).
30. *World Communications,* p. 364.
31. *Ibid.;* Alex Inkeles, "Recent Developments in Soviet Mass Communications," *Gazette,* IV, No. 4 (1958), pp. 291ff.
32. *World Communications,* p. 369.
33. Inkeles, "Recent Developments in Soviet Mass Communications," pp. 291ff; Yu, "Communications and Politics in Communist China," p. 282.
34. *Die Sowjetzonale Spielfilmproduktion, 1946-1960* (Bonn: Bundesministerium für Gesamtdeutsche Fragen, 1961), pp. 34-36, 45.
35. Inkeles, "Recent Developments in Soviet Mass Communications," pp. 288-90; Kalnins, *Der Sowjetische Propagandastaat,* p. 67.
36. Kalnins, *Der Sowjetische Propagandastaat,* pp. 99-132.
37. Yu, "Communications and Politics in Communist China," pp. 267-68.
38. Kalnins, *Der Sowjetische Propagandastaat,* p. 164; Yu, "Communications and Politics in Communist China," pp. 279-80; Eric Bourne, "Red Loudspeakers Assailed," *Christian Science Monitor,* March 27, 1963.
39. Kalnins, *Der Sowjetische Propagandastaat,* pp. 38-39. See also Inkeles, "The

Administration of Propaganda and Agitation," in *Public Opinion in Soviet Russia,* pp. 26-37.

40. Inkeles, "Recent Developments in Soviet Mass Communications," pp. 285ff.
41. Gruliow, "The Soviet Press," pp. 155-57; Inkeles, *Public Opinion in Soviet Russia,* p. 152; Heinz-Dietrich Fischer, "Funfzig Jahre Prawda," *Publizistik,* March/April, 1962; Philip E. Mosely, "How the Kremlin Keeps Ivan in Line," *The New York Times Magazine,* February 19, 1961, p. 68.
42. *World Communications,* p. 367; Viatcheslav Tchernychev, "The Cultural and Educational Mission of the Soviet Radio," *Cultural Radio Broadcasts—Some Experiences,* Reports and Papers on Mass Communication, No. 23 (Paris: UNESCO, December 1956), p. 28.
43. Richard Tuber, "A Survey of Programming on the Central Studios of Television, Moscow, U.S.S.R.," *Journal of Broadcasting,* Fall 1960.
44. Wilbur Schramm and John W. Riley, Jr., "Communication in the Sovietized State, as Demonstrated in Korea," *American Sociological Review,* December 1951, p. 757.
45. Deming B. Brown, *Soviet Attitudes Toward American Writing* (Princeton, N. J.: Princeton University Press, 1962); Melville Ruggles, "American Books in Soviet Publishing," *Slavic Review,* October 1961, pp. 431-32; Robert Magidoff, "Readers and Writers in Moscow," *The New York Times Book Review,* March 16, 1947.
46. Klaus Mehnert, *Soviet Man and His World* (New York: Frederick A. Praeger, 1962), p. 279.
47. Bernard Lewis, *The Emergence of Modern Turkey* (London and New York: Oxford University Press, 1961), p. 426.
48. Wilson P. Dizard, *The Strategy of Truth* (Washington, D. C.: Public Affairs Press, 1961), pp. 78-81.
49. Frederick C. Barghoorn, *The Soviet Cultural Offensive* (Princeton, N. J.: Princeton University Press, 1960), p. 154.
50. International Commission of Jurists, *The Berlin Wall: A Defiance of Human Rights* (Geneva, 1962), p. 52.
51. Nathan C. Leites, *A Study of Bolshevism* (Glencoe, Ill.: The Free Press, 1953), p. 371; Barghoorn, *Soviet Foreign Propaganda,* pp. 235ff.
52. Survey by International Research Associates, Inc., for the U. S. Information Agency. Printed in *Review of United States Information Agency Operations,* Hearings before the Subcommittee on State Department Organization and Foreign Operations of the Committee on Foreign Affairs, U. S. House of Representatives, 85th Cong., 2d sess. (Washington, D. C.: Government Printing Office, 1958), p. 128; *Der Rundfunk in der Sowjetzone* (Bonn: Bundesministerium für Gesamtdeutsche Fragen [1960?]), p. 12; Dizard, *The Strategy of Truth,* p. 85.
53. Harrison E. Salisbury, " 'Lost Generation' Baffles Soviet," *The New York Times,* February 9, 1962.
54. James H. Billington, " 'They Know So Much, Understand So Little,' " *The New York Times Magazine,* August 13, 1961, p. 7.
55. Mehnert, *Soviet Man and His World,* p. 278; Inkeles, "Recent Developments in Soviet Mass Communications," p. 294.

56. Y. Arbatov, "Imperialist Propaganda of the United States—A Threat to the Peace and Security of Nations," *Kommunist,* No. 7 (May 1955).
57. Karel Vanek, "Abusers of Our Profession," *The Democratic Journalist,* December 1956.
58. F. W. Schlomann, "Der Boese Sender Luxemburg," *SBZ Archiv* (Bonn), 2 Maiheft 1961.
59. *Der Abend* (Berlin), August 16, 1961.
60. Hadley Cantril, *Soviet Leaders and Mastery Over Man* (New Brunswick, N. J.: Rutgers University Press, 1960), pp. 83-84.
61. A number of Communist definitions of political concepts are discussed by Ambassador Thomas C. Mann in "Theories, Dogmas, and Semantics of Communism," *The Department of State Bulletin,* March 26, 1962. See also Cantril, *Soviet Leaders and Mastery Over Man,* p. 27; and Stefan T. Possony, *Wordmanship: Semantics as a Communist Weapon,* A Study Prepared for the Senate Subcommittee to Investigate the Administration of the Internal Security Act (Washington, D. C.: Government Printing Office, 1961).
62. *The Democratic Journalist,* April 1957.
63. Saxton Bradford, "Corporal LeBlond Comes Home," *Foreign Service Journal,* March 1958, p. 21.
64. Ernst G. Riemschneider, "Das Wort als Verständigungsmittel . . . ," *SBZ Archiv,* 1 Oktoberheft, 1961.
65. International Press Institute, *The Press in Authoritarian Countries,* p. 35.
66. Kotlyar, "Newspapers in the U.S.S.R.," p. 33.
67. International Press Institute, *The Press in Authoritarian Countries,* pp. 30-31.
68. Leon Gouré, *The Siege of Leningrad* (Stanford, Calif.: Stanford University Press, 1962), pp. 70-71, 304-5.
69. Alexander Dallin, "Odessa, 1941-44: A Case Study of Soviet Territory Under Foreign Rule," Research Memorandum 1875, The RAND Corporation, Santa Monica, California, February 14, 1957; U. S. Strategic Bombing Survey, Morale Division, *The Effects of Bombing on German Morale* (2 vols.; Washington, D. C.: Government Printing Office, 1946 and 1947).
70. Helmut Roske, "The Textbook Factory," p. 91.
71. Uledov, "Public Opinion as the Subject of Social Science Research."
72. *Sovetskaya Pechat,* October 1960, pp. 27-28 (cited in *Journalism Quarterly,* Winter 1961, p. 122); Alex Inkeles and Raymond A. Bauer, *The Soviet Citizen* (Cambridge, Mass.: Harvard University Press, 1959), p. 161.
73. Kalnins, *Der Sowjetische Propagandastaat,* pp. 70-74; Buzek, *How the Communist Press Works,* p. 27.
74. Paul Kecskemeti, *The Unexpected Revolution* (Stanford, Calif.: Stanford University Press, 1961), p. 118.
75. Inkeles and Bauer, *The Soviet Citizen,* p. 178; *Der Spiegel* (Hamburg), September 26, 1956.
76. Lindley M. Fraser, *Propaganda* (London: Oxford University Press, 1957), pp. 131-32; Mehnert, *Soviet Man and His World,* p. 224.
77. Heinz Kersten, "Der Zonefilm und Sein Publikum," *SBZ Archiv,* 2 Novemberheft, 1962.
78. Elena Calas, "Readers' Interpretation of Newspaper Materials in the Soviet

Union," in Margaret Mead (ed.), "Studies in Soviet Communication" (mimeographed publication of the Center for International Studies, Massachusetts Institute of Technology, 1952), Vol. I, pp. 37ff; Inkeles and Bauer, *The Soviet Citizen,* pp. 162, 181-84.

79. Inkeles and Bauer, *The Soviet Citizen,* p. 163.
80. Margaret Mead, "Oral Communication in the Soviet Union," in "Studies in Soviet Communication," Vol. I, pp. 175ff; Dunham, *Kremlin Target: U.S.A.,* p. 37; Paul Underwood, "Rumors of Soviet Pullout Buoy Hungarian Hopes," *The New York Times,* July 23, 1963, p. 5; "News for Poles Isn't for Regime," *The New York Times,* May 5, 1964, p. 46.
81. Robert R. Brunn, "Conversations in U.S.S.R.," *Christian Science Monitor,* February 4, 1963.
82. Hermann H. Wolff, "West German Television and Television in the Soviet Zone," *Gazette,* II, No. 4 (1957), pp. 235ff.
83. Nicolai Verta, *Literary Gazette,* April 1952, quoted in Magidoff, *The Kremlin vs. the People,* p. 237; Kecskemeti, *The Unexpected Revolution,* pp. 57-63; Daniel Kubat, "Writers in a Totalitarian State: Czechia, 1945-56," *American Journal of Sociology,* January 1962.
84. Carl Hauptmann, "Die Manipulation der Oeffentlichen Meinung im Ostblock," *Publizistik,* July/August 1963. See also, "Youth of Soviet Zone is Holding Out Against Dictatorship," *The Bulletin,* Press and Information Office of the Federal Republic of Germany, July 23, 1963.
85. David Burg, "The Voice of a Dissenter," *Harper's Magazine,* May 1961, p. 131.
86. Alex Inkeles, "Recent Developments in Soviet Mass Communication," pp. 294-95; Barghoorn, *The Soviet Cultural Offensive,* pp. 138-39.
87. Kalnins, *Der Sowjetische Propagandastaat,* p. 233-34.
88. Harrison E. Salisbury, " 'Lost Generation' Baffles Soviet," p. 1; Inkeles and Bauer, *The Soviet Citizen,* p. 169; Peter H. Rossi and Raymond A. Bauer, "Some Patterns of Soviet Communications Behavior," *Public Opinion Quarterly,* Winter 1952-53, pp. 662, 665.
89. Barghoorn, *Soviet Foreign Propaganda,* pp. 72-73; "Pravda Presents New View of U.S.," *The New York Times,* December 26, 1963, p. 3; "Soviet Novelist Warms to U.S.," *Christian Science Monitor,* March 4, 1963.
90. Hauptmann, "Die Manipulation der Oeffentlichen Meinung im Ostblock"; Buzek, *How the Communist Press Works,* pp. 183, 189.
91. "News of the World's Press," *IPI Report,* October 1963, p. 9; "Strengere Kontrolle des Kulturlebens in Polen," *Neue Zürcher Zeitung,* July 9, 1963, Section 2.
92. Burg, "The Voice of a Dissenter," p. 127.
93. R. L. Shayon, "Russian T-V News Updates Itself," *Saturday Review,* June 9, 1962; E. M. Herrmann, "Grundzüge der Marxistisch-Leninistischen Pressetheorie," *Publizistik,* January/February 1961, p. 49.

Chapter 7: Communication in Developing Nations

1. *Mass Media in the Developing Countries* ("Reports and Papers on Mass Communication," No. 33) (Paris: UNESCO, 1961), p. 16.

2. Rohan Rivett, "Quadrupling Circulation in Ten Years," *IPI Report,* March 1963; Armando J. Malay, "Journalism Training Methods in the Philippines," *Training of Journalists,* Winter 1961-62, p. 57; *Developing Information Media in Africa* ("Reports and Papers on Mass Communication," No. 37), (Paris: UNESCO, 1962), p. 11.
3. Helen Kitchen (ed.), *The Press in Africa* (Washington, D. C.: Ruth Sloan Associates, 1956), p. 56; Arno G. Huth, *Communications Media in Tropical Africa,* report prepared for the International Cooperation Administration, Washington, 1961, p. 133.
4. Milton Hollstein, "The Press in Burma: Its Hopes and Problems," *Journalism Quarterly,* Summer 1961, p. 352; *Developing Mass Media in Asia* ("Reports and Papers on Mass Communication," No. 30) (Paris: UNESCO, 1960), p. 61.
5. Marvin Alisky, "Havana Havoc: Too Many Dailies," *Nieman Reports,* April 1956; "How Turkey's Advertising Board Works," *IPI Report,* December 1962.
6. Esuakema Udo Oton, "The Press of Liberia: A Case Study," *Journalism Quarterly,* Spring 1961.
7. Edward Shils, "Political Development in the New States (I)," *Comparative Studies in Society and History,* April 1960, p. 292.
8. Jacques Léauté, "The Development of Mass Communications and Professional Training in Africa," *Training of Journalists,* Autumn 1961, pp. 39-40.
9. James W. Carty, Jr., "The Loma Tribe Is in the Know," *Nieman Reports,* January 1957.
10. "Meeting on Development of News Agencies in Asia and the Far East, Bangkok, December 19-22, 1961," UNESCO/MC/44 (Paris, February 1962), p. 6.
11. Francis Bebey, *La Radiodiffusion en Afrique Noir* (Issy-les-Moulineaux: Editions Saint-Paul, 1963), pp. 4-5.
12. *Developing Information Media in Africa,* p. 25. Even lower cost figures for radio receivers have been mentioned. See, for example, *Hearings before the Subcommittee on International Organizations and Movements,* U. S. Committee on Foreign Affairs, House of Representatives (Washington, D. C.: Government Printing Office, 1963), Part I, p. 30. Subcommittee Chairman Dante B. Fascell suggests that a suitable transistor radio might sell for less than $1.
13. Bebey, *La Radiodiffusion en Afrique Noir,* pp. 57-58.
14. *Telecommunications Journal,* February 1962.
15. Daniel Lerner, *The Passing of Traditional Society* (Glencoe, Ill.: The Free Press, 1958), p. 235; James N. Mosel, "Communications Patterns and Political Socialization in Transitional Thailand," in Lucian W. Pye (ed.), *Communications and Political Development* (Princeton, N. J.: Princeton University Press, 1963), pp. 196-97.
16. *Developing Information Media in Africa,* p. 30; Huth, *Communications Media in Tropical Africa,* p. 51.
17. J. C. Mathur, "Television in India," *Gazette,* VI, No. 2 (1960), pp. 249ff; Bebey, *La Radiodiffusion en Afrique Noir,* pp. 182-84; "Nepal Plans Television Station," *The New York Times,* May 24, 1963; "TV Abroad Shows an Increase," *The New York Times,* May 19, 1964.
18. Herbert Feldman, "The Press in Pakistan," *Gazette,* II, No. 2 (1956), p. 96; Mosel, "Communications Patterns and Political Socialization in Transitional

Thailand," p. 207; Jacques Champagne, "South Vietnam, Laos, Cambodia," *IPI Report,* November 1963.

19. Kenneth E. Olson and Abdul G. Eirabie, "Radio Pakistan: Voice of a New Nation," *Journalism Quarterly,* Winter 1954; Huth, *Communications Media in Tropical Africa,* p. 28; Ibrahim Abu-Lughod, "The Mass Media and Egyptian Village Life," *Social Forces,* October 1963, p. 101.
20. "Training of Journalists in Asia," *Training of Journalists,* Winter 1961-62, p. 8; A. G. P. Vittachi, "The Next Steps in Asia," *IPI Report,* July 1962; Jacques Janvier, "An African Experiment: The Ministry of Information, Press and Broadcasting in the Republic of Senegal," *Training of Journalists,* Autumn 1961, p. 83.
21. Edward Shils, "Demogogues and Cadres in the Political Development of the New States," in Pye (ed.), *Communications and Political Development,* pp. 69-70.
22. Albert G. Pickerell, "The Press of Thailand: Conditions and Trends," *Journalism Quarterly,* Winter 1960, p. 96.
23. Information taken from Janvier, "An African Experiment: The Ministry of Information, Press and Broadcasting in the Republic of Senegal," p. 71.
24. David Halberstam, "Touré's Country—'Africa Incarnate,'" *The New York Times Magazine,* July 8, 1962; Janvier, "An African Experiment: The Ministry of Information, Press and Broadcasting in the Republic of Senegal."
25. *Developing Information Media in Africa,* p. 13.
26. *Mass Media in the Developing Countries,* p. 17.
27. Rohan Rivett, "Quadrupling Circulation in Ten Years," *IPI Report,* March 1963; *The New York Times,* August 20, 1961.
28. J. C. Mathur and Paul Neurath, *An Indian Experiment in Farm Radio Forums* (Paris: UNESCO, 1959), pp. 16-17.
29. Hifzi Topuz, "News Agencies in Africa," *Training of Journalists,* Summer 1961, pp. 54ff; Bebey, *La Radiodiffusion en Afrique Noir,* pp. 180-81.
30. *U.S.I.A. Appropriations Hearings, Fiscal Year 1963,* U. S. House of Representatives (Washington, D. C.: Government Printing Office, 1962), p. 90.
31. *Developing Information Media in Africa,* p. 11.
32. Wilbur Schramm, "Communication Development and the Development Process," in Pye (ed.), *Communications and Political Development,* p. 55.
33. United Nations, Economic and Social Council, Commission on Human Rights, "Seminar on Freedom of Information" (New Delhi, February 20, 1962), pp. 14-15.
34. Charles A. H. Hayes, "Press Report from Kenya," *Nieman Reports,* April 1962; Tom Mboya, "This Is What the Press Must Do," *IPI Report,* June 1962.
35. Morroe Berger, *The Arab World Today* (New York: Doubleday & Co., 1962), p. 452.
36. H. R. Jolliffe, "Developing Journalism in an Emerging Nation—Afghanistan," *Journalism Quarterly,* Summer 1962, pp. 357-58; *IPI Report,* June 1963, p. 18.
37. UNESCO was instrumental in the establishment of these centers and has been a major force in the training of personnel for the information services. A re-

port on the Strasbourg center and an account of UNESCO's work in this field is found in *The Training of Journalists* (Paris: UNESCO, 1958).

38. "Meeting on the Development of News Agencies in Asia and the Far East, Bangkok, December 19-22, 1961," UNESCO/MC/44, p. 9.
39. "Seminar on Freedom of Information," p. 20.
40. Allan R. Holmberg, "Changing Community Attitudes and Values in Peru," in Richard N. Adams *et al., Social Change in Latin America Today* (New York: Harper & Bros., 1960), pp. 104-5; Lucian W. Pye, *Politics, Personality, and Nation Building: Burma's Search for Identity* (New Haven, Conn.: Yale University Press, 1962), pp. 20-21.
41. *Developing Mass Media in Asia,* p. 87.
42. Leonard W. Doob, *Communication in Africa* (New Haven, Conn.: Yale University Press, 1961), p. 78.
43. "Communications Behavior and Political Attitudes in Four Arabic Countries: A Quantitative Comparison" (mimeographed publication of the Bureau of Applied Social Research, Columbia University, 1952), cited in Charles R. Wright, *Mass Communication* (New York: Random House, 1959), pp. 47-48; Abu-Lughod, "The Mass Media and Egyptian Village Life," pp. 100-101.
44. Lerner, *The Passing of Traditional Society,* pp. 151, 190, 319-25.
45. Doob, *Communication in Africa,* p. 289.
46. Herbert Hyman, "Mass Media and Political Socialization," in Pye (ed.), *Communications and Political Development,* pp. 134-36.
47. Doob, *Communication in Africa,* pp. 199-200; S. Biesheuvel, "Methodology in the Study of African Attitudes," *Journal of Social Psychology,* May 1958, p. 176; Holmberg, "Changing Community Attitudes and Values in Peru," p. 105; Robert T. Oliver, *Culture and Communication* (Springfield, Ill.: Charles C. Thomas, 1962).
48. Doob, "An Experimental Approach to the Press in Underdeveloped Areas," *Gazette,* III, No. 1 (1957), p. 25; Lerner, *The Passing of Traditional Society,* p. 252.
49. Nicholas Vakar, *The Taproot of Soviet Society* (New York: Harper & Bros., 1961), p. 17.
50. *Developing Mass Media in Asia,* p. 87.
51. Doob, *Communication in Africa,* pp. 288-89.
52. Berger, *The Arab World Today,* pp. 425-26, 449-50; Lerner, *The Passing of Traditional Society,* pp. 52, 202-3, 326; Daniel Lerner, "Toward a Communication Theory of Modernization," in Lucian W. Pye (ed.), *Communications and Political Development,* p. 332; Louis Wirth, "Research in Racial and Cultural Relations," *Proceedings of the American Philosophical Society,* November 12, 1948, p. 381.
53. *U.S.I.A. Appropriations Hearings, Fiscal Year 1962,* U. S. House of Representatives (Washington, D. C.: Government Printing Office, 1961), p. 121; Peter Hooper, Jr., "Letter From Kampala," *Foreign Service Journal,* December 1959, pp. 47-48; Albert G. Sims, "Africans Beat on Our College Doors," *Harper's Magazine,* April 1961; Lerner, *The Passing of Traditional Society,* pp. 232-33.

54. Frederick W. Frey, "Political Development, Power, and Communications in Turkey," in Pye (ed.), *Communications and Political Development*, pp. 308-12; Mosel, "Communications Patterns and Political Socialization in Transitional Thailand," p. 198; Lerner, *The Passing of Traditional Society*, p. 395; Felix M. Keesing and Marie M. Keesing, *Elite Communication in Samoa* (Stanford, Calif.: Stanford University Press, 1956), pp. 161, 164.
55. Lerner, *The Passing of Traditional Society*, pp. 331-32; Doob, *Communication in Africa*, pp. 110, 320; Ithiel DeSola Pool, *Communication and Values in Relation to War and Peace* (New York: Institute for International Order, [1961]), p. 19; Herbert Passin, "Writer and Journalist in the Transitional Society," in Pye (ed.), *Communications and Political Development*, p. 101.
56. Schramm, "Communication Development and the Development Process," pp. 53-54.
57. Berger, *The Arab World Today*, p. 427; Lerner, *The Passing of Traditional Society*, p. 412; Mosel, "Communication Patterns and Political Socialization in Traditional Thailand," p. 228.
58. Passin, "Writer and Journalist in the Transitional Society," pp. 111-13. Passin notes that similar "Renaissance man" leaders emerged at roughly the same stage in the development of Japan, India, and Spain.
59. Berger, *The Arab World Today*, pp. 427-28.
60. "New Methods and Techniques in Education: Report of a Meeting of Experts," UNESCO Doc. Ed/190 (Paris, 3 April 1962), pp. 7-10; Report by the Director General of UNESCO on a Meeting on Development of Information Media in Latin America, Santiago, February 1-13, 1961, ECOSOC document E/3437, February 16, 1961.
61. Schramm, "Communication Development and the Development Process," pp. 48-49; Bebey, *La Radiodiffusion en Afrique Noir*, p. 177.
62. P. P. Singh, "Mass Communication in India," *Training of Journalists*, Winter 1961-62, p. 83; Mathur and Neurath, *An Indian Experiment in Farm Radio Forums;* Mathur, "Television in India," pp. 249ff; Janvier, "An African Experiment: The Ministry of Information, Press and Broadcasting in the Republic of Senegal," pp. 80-81.
63. Vidya Joshi, "Attitude Towards Reception of Technology," *Journal of Social Psychology*, October 1962; Wilbur Schramm, *Mass Media and National Development: The Role of Information in the Developing Countries* (Stanford, Calif.: Stanford University Press, 1964), pp. 31ff.
64. Léauté, "The Development of Mass Communications and Professional Training in Africa," p. 34. Léauté cites information and recreation as the main functions of the media in older countries, and believes that in addition they should serve education and animation in the new ones.
65. Dagulf D. Müller, "Die Bewusstseinsbildung der Indier durch die Massenmedien," *Publizistik*, January/February 1962, p. 28.
66. Bebey, *La Radiodiffusion en Arique Noir*, pp. 5-6; Justus M. van der Kroef, "The Press in Indonesia: By-product of Nationalism," *Journalism Quarterly*, Summer 1954.
67. Berger, *The Arab World Today*, p. 427; Lerner, *The Passing of Traditional Society*, p. 216.

68. R. B. Ooi, "Professional Training of Journalists in Malaya," *Training of Journalists,* Winter 1961-62, p. 48; Feldman, "The Press in Pakistan," pp. 95-96.
69. Lerner, *The Passing of Traditional Society,* pp. 176-77, 268; Mosel, "Communication Patterns and Political Socialization in Transitional Thailand," pp. 210-13.
70. Bernard L. Collier, "News and Latin America: A Balance Sheet," *Saturday Review,* October 12, 1963; Huth, *Communications Media in Tropical Africa,* p. 40.
71. Mosel, "Communication Patterns and Political Socialization in Transitional Thailand," pp. 213-14.
72. *Basic Facts and Figures 1961* (Paris: UNESCO, 1962), pp. 64-71.
73. Prodosh Aich, *Farbige Unter Weissen* (Cologne: Kieppenheuer und Witsch, 1962), p. 68.

Chapter 8: The Structure of International Communication Programs

1. A number of examples of psychological warfare in ancient times, from both the Mediterranean world and the Far East are given by Paul M. A. Linebarger, *Psychological Warfare* (2d ed.; Washington, D. C.: Combat Forces Press, 1954), pp. 3ff. A brief summary of the history of propaganda activities is found in John B. Whitton and Arthur Larson, *Propaganda* (Dobbs Ferry, N. Y.: Oceana Publications, 1964), pp. 12-52.
2. Lyman H. Butterfield, "Psychological Warfare in 1776: the Jefferson-Franklin Plan to Cause Hessian Desertions," *Proceedings of the American Philosophical Society,* 1950, pp. 233-41, reprinted in William E. Daugherty and Morris Janowitz (eds.), *A Psychological Warfare Casebook* (Baltimore, Md.: Johns Hopkins Press, 1958).
3. Gorham Munson, *Twelve Decisive Battles of the Mind* (New York: Greystone Press, 1942), p. 38; Burton J. Hendrick, *Propaganda of the Confederacy* (New York: Literary Guild, 1939), pp. 389-99, reprinted in abridged form in Daugherty and Janowitz, *A Psychological Warfare Casebook.*
4. James R. Mock and Cedric Larson, *Words That Won the War* (Princeton, N. J.: Princeton University Press, 1939), pp. 235ff; George Creel, *How We Advertised America* (New York: Harper & Bros., 1920); Harold D. Lasswell, *Propaganda Technique in The World War* (New York: Alfred A. Knopf, 1927).
5. Charles A. H. Thomson, *Overseas Information Service of the United States Government* (Washington, D. C.: Brookings Institution, 1948), pp. 40ff; Charles A. Thomson and Walter H. C. Laves, *Cultural Relations and U.S. Foreign Policy* (Bloomington, Ind.: Indiana University Press, 1963), pp. 35ff.
6. Edward W. Barrett, *Truth Is Our Weapon* (New York: Funk & Wagnalls, 1953), pp. 72-100.
7. Report of the Attorney General to the Congress of the United States on the Administration of the Foreign Agents Registration Act of 1938, as amended, for the Calendar Year 1962, Washington, 1963 (mimeographed).
8. John Useem and Ruth Hill Useem, *The Western-Educated Man in India* (New York: Dryden Press, 1955), pp. 83, 192-93.

9. R. H. Bruce Lockhart, *Comes the Reckoning* (London: Putnam, 1947), pp. 168ff.
10. Wallace Carroll, *Persuade or Perish* (New York: Houghton Mifflin, 1948), p. 7.
11. Marjorie Fiske and Leo Lowenthal, "Some Problems in the Administration of International Communications Research," *Public Opinion Quarterly,* Summer 1952, p. 149.
12. A fascinating description of the operation of the Swiss tourist office is given by Eric Mann, *Neue Zürcher Zeitung,* March 24, 1962, Section 20.
13. Hans Speier, "Psychological Warfare Reconsidered," in *Social Order and the Risks of War* (New York: George W. Stewart, 1952), pp. 436-40.
14. *Washington Post,* July 14, 1953.
15. Andrew Berding, *Foreign Affairs and You!* (New York: Doubleday & Co., 1962), p. 180.
16. David B. Truman, *The Governmental Process: Political Interests and Public Opinion* (New York: Alfred A. Knopf, 1951), p. 235; see also "The A & P Campaign," *Propaganda Analysis,* December 1, 1938.
17. The writer is indebted for this example to Mr. Shepard Stone.
18. Berding, *Foreign Affairs and You!,* pp. 65-66.
19. James Reston, "The Number One Voice," in Lester Markel *et al., Public Opinion and Foreign Policy* (New York: Harper & Bros., 1949), p. 74.
20. This point is made in many treatments of public relations. See, for example, Charles H. Prout, "Organization and Function of the Public Relations Department," in Philip Lesly (ed.), *Public Relations Handbook* (2d ed.; Englewood Cliffs, N. J.: Prentice-Hall, 1962), p. 785.
21. Berding, *Foreign Affairs and You!,* p. 180.
22. W. Phillips Davison, "Policy Coordination in OWI," in Daugherty and Janowitz (eds.), *A Psychological Warfare Casebook,* pp. 305-6.
23. Richard H. S. Crossman, "Supplementary Essay," in Daniel Lerner, *Sykewar* (New York: George W. Stewart, 1949), p. 338.
24. William R. Young, "Announcing the Chinese Communist Intervention in Korea," in Daugherty and Janowitz (eds.), *A Psychological Warfare Casebook.*
25. Murray Dyer, *The Weapon on the Wall: Rethinking Psychological Warfare* (Baltimore, Md.: Johns Hopkins Press, 1959), p. 87.
26. Sefton Delmer, *Black Boomerang* (New York: Viking Press, 1962), pp. 69-70, 146-49.
27. Harlan Cleveland, Gerard J. Mangone, and John Clarke Adams, *The Overseas Americans* (New York: McGraw-Hill, 1960), p. 33.
28. Howard Becker, "The Nature and Consequences of Black Propaganda," *American Sociological Review,* April 1949.
29. The names of "Axis Sally" and "Lord Haw-Haw" will be remembered from World War II, as will the efforts of the Communists to use captured Americans as propaganda spokesmen during the Korean War. In both wars, Americans and their allies sought the help of cooperative captured personnel in composing propaganda messages.
30. "The Lazarsfeld-Stanton Program Analyzer," in Paul F. Lazarsfeld and

Frank N. Stanton (eds.), *Radio Research, 1942-1943* (New York: Duell, Sloan & Pearce, 1944).

31. Extensive investigations into the responses of Soviet defectors to various propaganda themes have been conducted by the Inwood Project on Intercultural Communication. See, for example, Ivan D. London and Miriam B. London, "Differential Reactions of Recent and Earlier Defectors to Anti-Soviet Propaganda Themes," *Psychological Reports,* 1956, pp. 285-92; or Ivan D. London and Nikolai P. Poltoratzky, "Contemporary Religious Sentiment in the Soviet Union," *Psychological Reports,* 1957, pp. 113-30.
32. Especially the Human Relations Area Files at Yale and associated universities, and the published extracts from these files prepared by the Washington Office of the Human Relations Area Files.
33. Alain Touraine *et al.,* "Thèmes et Vocabulaire d'une Campaigne Electorale," in Maurice Duverger *et al.* (eds.), *Les Elections du 2 Janvier 1956* (Paris: Librairie Armand Colin, 1957).
34. Katherine Holtzclaw, "More than Translating . . . ," and John W. Heckman, "Information Must Actually Reach People," both in *The Multiplier in International Development* (published by the Agency for International Development), January-May 1962; Peter Bart, "Advertising: Tips on What Foreigners Like," *The New York Times,* January 2, 1964.
35. Herbert I. Abelson, *Persuasion: How Opinions and Attitudes Are Changed* (New York: Springer, 1959).
36. Winston S. Churchill, *Their Finest Hour* (Boston: Houghton Mifflin, 1949), p. 586.
37. *Ibid.,* p. 404.
38. Louis De Jong, *The German Fifth Column in the Second World War* (Chicago: University of Chicago Press, 1956), p. 159; George Seldes, *The Facts Are . . .* (New York: In Fact, 1942), p. 63.
39. "Sport as a Soviet Tool," *Foreign Affairs,* April 1956.
40. Public reactions to Soviet space achievements in several Western European countries are summarized by Gabriel A. Almond, "Public Opinion and the Development of Space Technology: 1957-60," in Joseph M. Goldsen (ed.), *Outer Space in World Politics* (New York: Frederick A. Praeger, 1963). See also Donald N. Michael, "The Beginning of the Space Age and American Public Opinion," *Public Opinion Quarterly,* Winter 1960.
41. Arnold L. Horelick, "The Soviet Union and the Political Uses of Outer Space," in Goldsen, *Outer Space in World Politics.*
42. "How to Detect Propaganda," *Propaganda Analysis,* November 1937. The other three characteristics were the transfer device, the testimonial device, and the card-stacking device.
43. Leonard W. Doob, "Goebbels' Principles of Propaganda," *Public Opinion Quarterly,* Fall 1950.
44. John W. Riley, Jr., and Leonard S. Cottrell, Jr., "Research for Psychological Warfare," *Public Opinion Quarterly,* Spring 1957, pp. 153-55; R. H. S. Crossman, "Supplementary Essay," p. 336; Oren Stephens, *Facts to a Candid World* (Stanford, Calif.: Stanford University Press, 1955), pp. 90-93.
45. Dyer, *The Weapon on the Wall,* pp. 23-28; Lindley Fraser, *Propaganda* (Lon-

don and New York: Oxford University Press, 1957), pp. 208-9; *BBC Handbook* (London: BBC House, 1960), p. 88.

46. Martin F. Herz, "Some Psychological Lessons from Leaflet Propaganda in World War II," *Public Opinion Quarterly,* Fall 1949, pp. 471-72.
47. John S. Dickey, "The Secretary and the American Public," in Don K. Price (ed.), *The Secretary of State* (Englewood Cliffs, N. J.: Prentice-Hall, 1960), p. 164; Michael Balfour, *States and Mind* (London: Cresset Press, 1953), pp. 77-78, 133.
48. Jean Oberlé, *Jean Oberlé vous parle* (Paris: La Jeune Parque, 1945), pp. 161, 218-19.
49. For example, Yole G. Sills, "U.S.A. and U.S.S.R. English Language Publications Distributed in India" (mimeographed publication of the Bureau of Applied Social Research, Columbia University, January 1962).
50. Crossman, "Supplementary Essay," p. 330; Alexander H. Leighton, *Human Relations in a Changing World* (New York: E. P. Dutton, 1949), pp. 55-56, 87-95.
51. An outstanding example is the analysis of group structure and morale in the German Army by Edward A. Shils and Morris Janowitz: "Cohesion and Disintegration in the Wehrmacht," *Public Opinion Quarterly,* Summer 1948.
52. *U.S.I.A. Appropriations Hearings, Fiscal Year 1961,* U. S. House of Representatives (Washington, D. C.: Government Printing Office, 1960), p. 66.
53. "Communicating with the People Behind the Iron Curtain," remarks by Howland H. Sargeant, President of the American Committee for Liberation, The New School, New York, April 4, 1957; *Sparks into the USSR: The Story of Radio Liberation* (New York: American Committee for Liberation, 1957), p. 8.
54. Joseph T. Klapper and Leo Lowenthal, "The Contribution of Opinion Research to the Evaluation of Psychological Warfare," *Public Opinion Quarterly,* Winter 1951-52; Konrad Kellen, remarks in session of the American Association for Public Opinion Research on "Public Opinion Research and the Cold War," *Public Opinion Quarterly,* Winter 1955-56, p. 440.
55. *Sparks into the USSR,* pp. 15-18; also *The Most Important Job in the World* (New York: Radio Liberty, 1962), pp. 11ff.
56. Holmes Alexander, *Boston Herald,* February 6, 1958.
57. For a popular account of the effectiveness of psychological warfare in Korea, see "Psychological Warfare in Korea: An Interim Report," *Public Opinion Quarterly,* Spring 1951.
58. Leo Bogart, "Measuring the Effectiveness of an Overseas Information Campaign," *Public Opinion Quarterly,* Winter 1957-58.
59. Paul W. Massing, "Communist References to the Voice of America," *Public Opinion Quarterly,* Spring 1952; "Reds' Angry Blasts at 'Voice' Delight Washington," *New York World Telegram,* March 19, 1955; *Sparks into the USSR,* p. 12.
60. Michael Padev, *Dimitrov Wastes No Bullets* (London: Eyre and Spottiswoode, 1948), p. 40.
61. Arthur Goodfriend, *The Twisted Image* (New York: St Martin's Press, 1963), p. 141.

Chapter 9: COMMUNIST INTERNATIONAL COMMUNICATIONS

1. John B. Whitton and John H. Herz, "Radio in International Politics," in Harwood L. Childs and John B. Whitton (eds.), *Propaganda by Short Wave* (Princeton, N. J.: Princeton University Press, 1942), pp. 4-5.
2. Quoted by J. L. Reinsch, in *Hearings before the Subcommittee on International Organizations and Movements,* Committee on Foreign Affairs, U. S. House of Representatives (Washington, D. C.: Government Printing Office, 1963), Part I, p. 50.
3. Nathan Leites, *A Study of Bolshevism* (Glencoe, Ill.: The Free Press, 1953), pp. 30-34, 509.
4. Harry Schwartz, "Propaganda in Space," *The New York Times,* August 12, 1962; "Arms and Propaganda," editorial in the *Washington Post,* October 3, 1954.
5. Herbert Passin, *China's Cultural Diplomacy* (New York: Frederick A. Praeger, 1963), p. 3.
6. Seymour Topping, "Soviet Military Priority," *The New York Times,* November 18, 1961.
7. Evron M. Kirkpatrick (ed.), *Year of Crisis: Communist Propaganda Activities in 1956* (New York: Macmillan Co., 1957), pp. 34ff. Although details of Communist propaganda structure have changed since this analysis was published, the basic characteristics have remained the same. See also Frederick C. Barghoorn, *The Soviet Cultural Offensive* (Princeton, N. J.: Princeton University Press, 1960), p. 160; and Frederick C. Barghoorn, *Soviet Foreign Propaganda* (Princeton, N. J.: Princeton University Press, 1964), pp. 244ff.
8. Theodore E. Kruglak, *The Two Faces of Tass* (Minneapolis, Minn.: University of Minnesota Press, 1962), p. 218; *World Communications* (Paris: UNESCO, 1964), p. 366; Antony Buzek, *How the Communist Press Works* (New York: Frederick A. Praeger, 1964), p. 207.
9. Donald Dunham, *Kremlin Target: USA* (New York: Washburn, 1961), p. 247; Kruglak, *The Two Faces of Tass,* pp. 207-8.
10. *Journalism Quarterly,* Spring 1961, p. 259; *World Communications,* p. 367; "Introducing the Novosti Press Agency," *USSR-Soviet Life Today,* June 1964.
11. Kruglak, *The Two Faces of Tass,* pp. 134-35.
12. Max Frankel, "Moscow Accuses American Press," *The New York Times,* October 26, 1957, p. 2.
13. Kruglak, *The Two Faces of Tass,* p. 59; *IPI Report,* February 1961, pp. 5-6; U.S.I.A., *18th Review of Operations,* January 1-June 30, 1962 (Washington, D. C., 1962), p. 36.
14. *The New York Times,* October 19, 1962; *U.S.I.A. Appropriations Hearings, Fiscal Year 1964,* U. S. House of Representatives (Washington, D. C.: Government Printing Office, 1963), pp. 23, 180. The latter source gives total Soviet international broadcasting as 1,205 hours per week, an increase of 13 per cent over 1961. The rapid growth of Communist broadcasting is described in Simon Costikyan, "Twelve Years of Communist Broadcasting: 1948-1959," mimeographed publication of the U. S. Information Agency (n.d.).
15. *U.S.I.A. Appropriations Hearings, Fiscal Year 1964,* pp. 466-67.

16. U.S.I.A., *18th Review of Operations,* p. 34; Barghoorn, *Soviet Foreign Propaganda,* pp. 282-83; *The New York Times,* August 8, 1956.
17. "Ulbrichts 'Zweites Programm'," *Kurier* (Berlin), June 6, 1961.
18. U.S.I.A., *18th Review of Operations,* p. 35; *U.S.I.A. Appropriations Hearings, Fiscal Year 1964,* p. 180; Dorothy Dillon, *International Communism and Latin America* ("Latin American Monographs," No. 19) (School of Inter-American Studies, University of Florida, March 1962), p. 18.
19. "Sino-Soviet Bloc Publishing in Non-Bloc Languages," *Publishers' Weekly,* September 25, 1961; U.S.I.A., *19th Review of Operations,* July 1-December 31, 1962 (Washington, D. C., 1963), p. 33.
20. *Toward a National Effort in International Educational and Cultural Affairs* (Washington, D. C.: Department of State, July 1961), pp. 42-43.
21. "Sino-Soviet Bloc Publishing in Non-Bloc Languages," and U.S.I.A. *18th Review of Operations,* p. 35.
22. *U.S.I.A. Appropriations Hearings, Fiscal Year 1963,* U. S. House of Representatives (Washington, D. C.: Government Printing Office, 1962), p. 28.
23. Murray G. Lawson (ed.), *Communist Propaganda Around the World* (Washington, D. C.: U.S.I.A., 1962), p. 147; U.S.I.A., *18th Review of Operations,* pp. 36-37.
24. Lawson, *Communist Propaganda Around the World,* pp. 85ff.
25. Frederick T. Merrill, "Contacts With the Soviets," *Foreign Service Journal,* March 1959, p. 19; Barghoorn, *The Soviet Cultural Offensive,* p. 96.
26. Barghoorn, *The Soviet Cultural Offensive,* pp. 97, 188.
27. Passin, *China's Cultural Diplomacy,* pp. 1-2.
28. Lawson, *Communist Propaganda Around the World,* p. 113.
29. Passin, *China's Cultural Diplomacy,* p. 118.
30. Barghoorn, *The Soviet Cultural Offensive,* p. 159.
31. *Ibid.,* pp. 160-66; "News and Notes," in *Overseas,* September 1961, pp. 30-31; Barghoorn, *Soviet Foreign Propaganda,* p. 245.
32. *Newsletter,* Experiment in International Living (Putney, Vermont), April 1963.
33. Passin, *China's Cultural Diplomacy,* p. 121.
34. *Ibid.,* pp. 124, 127.
35. Eugene Lyons, *Beware! Tourists Reporting on Russia,* An Analysis of Tourist Testimony on Soviet Russia prepared for the Subcommittee to Investigate the Administration of the Internal Security Act, Committee on the Judiciary, U. S. Senate (Washington, D. C., 1960).
36. Harry Schwartz, "K-Day in the Propaganda War," *The New York Times Magazine,* September 18, 1960, p. 15.
37. Henry M. Halstead, III, "Receiving Soviet Guests" (mimeographed publication, Washington, D. C., 1959), pp. 126ff; Barghoorn, *The Soviet Cultural Offensive,* p. 12.
38. "Greater Freedom Asked for Russians Who Tour Abroad," *The New York Times* (international ed.), January 14, 1963.
39. Emilia Wilder, "America as Seen by Polish Exchange Scholars," *Public Opinion Quarterly,* Summer 1964; Harry Schwartz, "Soviet Scientist Asks More Funds," *The New York Times,* April 29, 1962.

40. *The United States Through the Eyes of Soviet Tourists,* An Analysis of Their Published Reports Prepared by the Staff of the Subcommittee to Investigate the Administration of the Internal Security Act, Committee on the Judiciary, U. S. Senate (Washington, D. C., 1960), p. 26; James A. Fixx, "Books in Communications," *Saturday Review,* February 9, 1963, p. 60.
41. *U.S.I.A. Appropriations Hearings, Fiscal Year 1962,* U. S. House of Representatives (Washington, D. C.: Government Printing Office, 1962), pp. 152, 170; "More Go To Russia to Study," *The New York Times,* September 5, 1963; Passin, *China's Cultural Diplomacy,* pp. 5-6.
42. "Moskaus 'Universität der Völkerfreundschaft'," *Neue Zürcher Zeitung,* November 4, 1961, Section 5; Priscilla Johnson, " 'Friendship U' in Moscow," *Harper's Magazine,* December 1960; Barghoorn, *Soviet Foreign Propaganda,* pp. 150-52.
43. Quoted by the Committee on Educational Interchange Policy, *Educational Exchange in the Economic Development of Nations* (New York, July 1961), p. 11. See also, George Feifer, " 'The Red and the Black:' Racism in Moscow," *The Reporter,* January 2, 1964.
44. *The Bulletin,* Press and Information Office of the Federal Republic of Germany, Bonn, March 12, 1963.
45. Barghoorn, *The Soviet Cultural Offensive,* p. 255.
46. These figures are from *World Strength of the Communist Party Organizations,* Bureau of Intelligence and Research, Department of State (Washington, D. C., January 1964). Most of the figures are estimates, although some represent Communist claims. The report cautions that such statistics are difficult to obtain and are not subject to verification. An estimated total of 6 million Communist Party members in non-bloc states is given by Suzanne Labin, *The Technique of Soviet Propaganda,* a study presented by the Subcommittee to Investigate the Administration of the Internal Security Act, Committee on the Judiciary, U. S. Senate (Washington, D. C., 1960), p. 2.
47. Kirkpatrick, *Year of Crisis,* p. 43.
48. "Troubled International Fronts," *Youth and Freedom,* VI, No. 1-2 (1964).
49. Lawson, *Communist Propagnda Around the World,* pp. 212, 318-20, 369-74, 408; Passin, *China's Cultural Diplomacy,* p. 57.
50. Labin, *The Technique of Soviet Propaganda,* p. 9; Kirkpatrick, *Year of Crisis,* p. 41.
51. These programs are summarized in Lawson, *Communist Propaganda Around the World,* pp. 139-60. See also, *International Trade 1962* (Geneva: GATT, 1963); and *World Economic Survey 1963* (New York: United Nations, 1964), Vol. I, p. 273.
52. Paul Kecskemeti, "The Soviet Approach to International Political Communication," *Public Opinion Quarterly,* Spring 1956, pp. 303-4.
53. Studies of conversions to Communism and Communist voting behavior have found that doctrinal appeals have played a relatively insignificant role. (Gabriel A. Almond, *The Appeals of Communism* [Princeton, N. J.: Princeton University Press, 1954], pp. 99ff.) In Sweden and France surveys of Communist voters indicated that their primary motivation was resentment against the existing order. (Hadley Cantril, *The Politics of Despair* [New York: Basic

Books, 1958]; Sven Rydenfeld, *Kommunismen i Sverige* [Lund: Gleerupska Universitetsbokhandeln, 1954].)

54. Labin, *The Technique of Soviet Propaganda,* p. 18.
55. Ithiel DeSola Pool, "The Mass Media and Politics in the Modernization Process," in Lucien W. Pye (ed.), *Communications and Political Development* (Princeton, N. J.: Princeton University Press, 1963), pp. 239-40.
56. *U.S.I.A. Appropriations Hearings, Fiscal Year 1964,* pp. 185-86.
57. Whitton and Herz, "Radio in International Politics," p. 5; Kirkpatrick, *Year of Crisis,* pp. 111-12.
58. John B. Whitton and Arthur Larson, *Propaganda* (Dobbs Ferry, N. Y.: Oceana Publications, 1964), p. 92; Pieter Lessing, *Africa's Red Harvest* (New York: John Day, 1962), pp. 87, 112, 121-22.
59. Lessing, *Africa's Red Harvest,* pp. 110-12; Edward J. Tyburski, "Few African Students Who Fled Reds Are Found Qualified for U.S. Colleges," *Philadelphia Bulletin,* March 31, 1963.
60. Passin, *China's Cultural Diplomacy,* p. 11.
61. Dunham, *Kremlin Target: USA,* pp. 79-86.
62. Lessing, *Africa's Red Harvest,* p. 124; Dillon, *International Communism and Latin America,* p. 17.
63. Kirkpatrick, *Year of Crisis,* p. 232.
64. Wilbur Schramm, *One Day in the World's Press: Fourteen Great Newspapers on a Day of Crisis* (Stanford, Calif.: Stanford University Press, 1959); Bernard C. Cohen, "The Present and the Press," *World Politics,* October 1960, p. 165.
65. Vladimir Reisky de Dubnic, *Communist Propaganda Methods: A Case Study on Czechoslovakia* (New York: Frederick A. Praeger, 1960), pp. 33ff; Costikyan, "Twelve Years of Communist Broadcasting," p. 9.
66. *The Democratic Journalist,* May 1957; speech of IOJ Vice-President K. M. Rydberg at the Executive Committee Meeting in Peking.
67. Arthur Goodfriend, *The Twisted Image* (New York: St. Martin's Press, 1963), p. 248; Alex Inkeles, "Communist Propaganda and Counter-Propaganda," *Proceedings of the Twenty-eighth Institute of the Norman Wait Harris Memorial Foundation* (Cambridge, Mass., 1952), p. 271.
68. Howland H. Sargeant, "American Information and Cultural Representation Overseas," in Vincent M. Barnett, Jr., *The Representation of the United States Abroad* (rev. ed.; New York: Frederick A. Praeger, 1965), p. 77.
69. "Russians Impale U.S. on Own Barbs," *The New York Times,* December 8, 1957.
70. Kecskemeti, "The Soviet Approach to International Political Communication," p. 305.
71. Arnold L. Horelick, "The Soviet Union and Political Uses of Outer Space," in Joseph M. Goldsen (ed.), *Outer Space and World Politics* (New York: Frederick A. Praeger, 1963); H. T. Willetts, "Pavlov or Khrushchev? Soviet Methods in Political Warfare," *The World Today,* October 1960, pp. 430-31; Reisky de Dubnic, *Communist Propaganda Methods,* p. 123. The author concludes that the concept of "socialist science" is the most preposterous of all the weapons in the Communist propaganda arsenal, yet in the long run is likely to be the most dangerous to the free world.

72. George Liska, "The Politics of Cultural Diplomacy," *World Politics,* April 1962, p. 534; Hans Speier, "Atomic Blackmail," *German Rearmament and Atomic War* (Evanston, Ill.: Row, Peterson, 1957).
73. This summary of the peace campaign follows the more complete treatment given by Marshall D. Shulman in *Stalin's Foreign Policy Reappraised* (Cambridge, Mass.: Harvard University Press, 1963), pp. 80ff. See also Barghoorn, *Soviet Foreign Propaganda,* pp. 117-21. Barghoorn points out that a foundation for the peace campaign had been laid by Lenin and Stalin (pp. 80ff.).
74. This account is based largely on an article by Maarten Schneider, "Bacteria as a Propaganda Weapon," *Gazette,* IV, No. 1 (1958), pp. 47ff. A more complete account of the campaign, including some fascinating examples of propaganda documents, is contained in John C. Clews, *Communist Propaganda Techniques* (New York: Frederick A. Praeger, 1964), pp. 179-268.
75. *Communist Anti-American Riots,* Staff Study of the Subcommittee to Investigate the Administration of the Internal Security Act, Committee on the Judiciary, U. S. Senate (Washington, D. C., August 26, 1960), pp. 4-5, 17-19.
76. Alex Inkeles, "Communist Propaganda and Counter-Propaganda," p. 270.
77. Lawson, *Communist Propaganda Around the World,* pp. 281-82, 425; "Ankara to Counter Red Radio Station," *The New York Times,* April 30, 1961.
78. *Communist Forgeries,* Hearings Before the Subcommittee to Investigate the Administration of the Internal Security Act, Committee on the Judiciary, U. S. Senate (Washington, D. C., June 2, 1961), pp. 6, 8, 14, 22.
79. *Ibid.,* pp. 30-32, 37-40.
80. Elizabeth Wiskemann, "Berlin Between East and West," *World Today,* November 1960, p. 464.
81. "Psychologische Kriegsführung," *SBZ Archiv,* Erste Juniheft, 1960, p. 164.
82. *The Bulletin,* Press and Information Office of the Federal Republic of Germany, January 17, 1961.
83. Henry Cabot Lodge, in the *Foreign Service Journal,* July 1958, p. 35; Barghoorn, *The Soviet Cultural Offensive,* p. 177.
84. Labin, *The Technique of Soviet Propaganda,* p. 16.
85. James Baldwin, "A Negro Assays the Negro Mood," *The New York Times Magazine,* March 12, 1961.
86. "Moskau's Propaganda durch den Rundfunk," *The Bulletin,* Press and Information Office of the Federal Republic of Germany (German ed.), June 12, 1957.
87. *Ibid.,* and Thomas W. Wilson, Jr., "Red Propaganda Can Be Beaten," *The Reporter,* March 31, 1953, p. 15.
88. Leites, *A Study of Bolshevism,* pp. 68-69.

Chapter 10: Foreign Information and Cultural Activities of the United States

1. No inventory or description of the total private American information and cultural program overseas is currently available. As of 1964, however, the Subcommittee on International Organizations and Movements of the Foreign Affairs Committee, U. S. House of Representatives, was reported to be pre-

paring a directory of private American organizations engaging in information activities abroad.

2. *U.S.I.A. Appropriations Hearings, Fiscal Year 1964,* U. S. House of Representatives (Washington, D. C.: Government Printing Office, 1963), p. 565.
3. Statement of James B. Conkling, President, International Educational Broadcasting Corporation, in *Hearings before the Subcommittee on International Organizations and Movements,* Committee on Foreign Affairs, U. S. House of Representatives (Washington, D. C.: Government Printing Office, 1963), Part V, p. 623.
4. Robert W. Sarnoff, *America's Mirror Image,* National Broadcasting Company, June 1962; text of a speech delivered in Philadelphia on June 14, 1962. See also "U.S. Found Gaining Friends Overseas With TV Programs," *The New York Times,* December 30, 1963, pp. 1, 41.
5. Herbert Hyman, "Mass Media and Political Socialization," in Lucian W. Pye (ed.), *Communications and Political Development* (Princeton, N. J.: Princeton University Press, 1963), p. 128.
6. *Hearings before the Subcommittee on International Organizations and Movements* (Washington, D. C.: Government Printing Office, 1964), Part VII, pp. 934ff.
7. Sir Stephen G. Tallents, *The Projection of England* (London: Faber & Faber, 1932), p. 30.
8. *The Democratic Journalist,* I, No. 1 (November 1953), pp. 5-7.
9. C. Edda Martinez and Edward A. Suchman, "Letters from America and the 1948 Elections in Italy," *Public Opinion Quarterly,* Spring 1950.
10. Robert T. Holt, *Radio Free Europe* (Minneapolis, Minn.: University of Minnesota Press, 1958); *1963-A Year of Change* (New York: Free Europe Committee, 1964); testimony of John Richardson, President, National Committee for a Free Europe, *Hearings before the Subcommittee on International Organizations and Movements,* Part V, pp. 603ff; Lewis Galantiere, "The Role of Radio Free Europe," in John B. Whitton (ed.), *Propaganda and the Cold War* (Washington, D. C.: Public Affairs Press, 1963).
11. *The Most Important Job in the World* (New York: Radio Liberty, 1963).
12. *Hearings before the Subcommittee on International Organizations and Movements,* Part V, pp. 570ff.
13. *Newsletter,* Experiment in International Living (Putney, Vermont), October 1961. A popular description of the Experiment's activities is found in William Peters, *Passport to Friendship* (Philadelphia: S. B. Lippincott, 1957).
14. Harold R. Isaacs, *Emergent Americans: A Report on "Crossroads Africa,"* (New York: John Day, 1961); "In View: Stephen Galatti," *Overseas,* November 1963, p. 23.
15. Howland H. Sargeant, "Information and Cultural Representation Overseas," *The Representation of the United States Abroad* (New York: Frederick A. Praeger, 1965), p. 101.
16. "Cultural Exchanges After 25 Years," *Department of State Newsletter,* August 1963, p. 24.
17. Peter S. Jennison, "American Books Abroad," *Bulletin of the Atomic Scientists,* December 1963, p. 33.

18. *Directory of Organizations Giving Services to International Visitors in the Greater Washington Area* (Washington, D. C.: Foreign Student Service Council, 1961); *The New York Times,* February 18, 1962.
19. Lucius D. Battle, "The Importance of the Private Sector in Educational and Cultural Affairs," *Department of State Newsletter,* August 1962, p. 15. See also James M. Davis, "Fifty Thousand Foreign Students to Advise," *Overseas,* September 1961.
20. William Dawson, "Forty Thousand Good-Will Ambassadors," *Overseas,* May 1962.
21. Harrison E. Salisbury, "U.S. Found Ill-Prepared to Serve Foreign Tourists," *The New York Times,* April 24, 1961.
22. U. S. Department of Commerce, *U.S. Business Investment in Foreign Countries* (Washington, D. C.: Government Printing Office, 1960). Most figures in this Commerce Department report are as of 1957. The estimates used here are based on these figures but are updated and include certain additional categories of business.
23. Raymond A. Bauer, Ithiel DeSola Pool, and Lewis Anthony Dexter, *American Business and Public Policy* (New York: Atherton Press, 1963), pp. 164-65.
24. D. H. Radler, "Our National Talent for Offending People," *Harper's Magazine,* August 1961; Thomas Aitken, Jr., *A Foreign Policy for American Business* (New York: Harper & Bros., 1962); Harlan Cleveland, Gerard J. Mangone, and John Clarke Adams, *The Overseas Americans* (New York: McGraw-Hill, 1960), p. 111; Charles E. Allen, *Public Opinion—Achilles Heel of U.S. Business Overseas?,* Training Program for International Business Executives, The American University, Washington, June 1960, p. 4.
25. George Hall, "Dollars and Sense," *Overseas,* May 1962.
26. Theodore Geiger, with the assistance of Liesel Goode, *The General Electric Company in Brazil* (Washington, D. C.: National Planning Association, 1961). (Ninth in a series of case studies by the National Planning Association of the performance of U.S. business abroad. Similar case studies have been conducted in Mexico, Peru, the Philippines, Venezuela, Liberia, Indonesia, Ethiopia, and Central America.) A number of other business activities in international communication are described in the *Hearings before the Subcommittee on International Organizations and Movements,* Part II, pp. 198ff, including those of W. R. Grace & Co., the Gulf Oil Corporation, and the Standard Oil Company of New Jersey.
27. *The New York Times,* June 16, pp. 55, 60, and June 22, 1964, pp. 38-39; Adam Wiener, "Tools for Freedom Aids Schools Abroad," and Ann Morse Walker, "Aid by Mail for Developing Nations," *Overseas,* March 1964.
28. George C. Lodge, *Spearheads of Democracy: Labor in the Developing Countries* (New York: Harper & Row, 1962), pp. 78-87.
29. Tad Szulc, "Role of U.S. Labor Grows in Latin-Aid Program," *The New York Times,* September 17, 1963.
30. *Open Doors 1963* (New York: Institute of International Education, 1963), pp. 2, 4.
31. John L. Thurston, "The Education Explosion: Foreign Student Enrollments in the U.S., *Overseas.* March 1963, p. 2.

32. Edward W. Weidner, *The World Role of Universities* (New York: McGraw-Hill, 1962), pp. 5-6. The author presents an excellent summary of the activities of American universities involving international communication and many fascinating examples of specific programs.
33. Stephen A. Freeman, *Undergraduate Study Abroad* (New York: Institute of International Education, 1964). This report is critical of the failure of some colleges conducting these programs to define their objectives clearly and evaluate their results realistically.
34. J. L. Morrill *et al., The University and World Affairs* (New York: Ford Foundation, 1961), p. 2; Weidner, *The World Role of Universities,* p. 288; H. Field Haviland, "Federal Programs of International Education," in Charles G. Dobbins (ed.), *Higher Education and the Federal Government* (Washington, D. C.: American Council on Education, 1963), p. 79.
35. W. McNeil Lowry and Gertrude S. Hooker, "The Role of the Arts and the Humanities," in Robert Blum (ed.), *Cultural Affairs and Foreign Relations* (Englewood Cliffs, N. J.: Prentice-Hall, 1963), p. 61; Jennison, "American Books Abroad," p. 32; more up-to-date information is provided by the Franklin Book Programs *Newsletter.*
36. Philip M. Glick, *The Administration of Technical Assistance: Growth in the Americas* (Chicago: University of Chicago Press, 1957), p. 4; Kenneth Dole, "News of the Churches," *Washington Post,* July 8, 1961.
37. *North American Protestant Foreign Mission Agencies* (5th ed.; New York: Missionary Research Library, December 1962), pp. 117-19. The introduction to this survey notes that the data in it are not complete, since some bodies did not respond to the questionnaire, and lists the total number of Protestant missionary personnel as exceeding 27,000 (p. iv).
38. *U.S. Catholic Overseas Missionary Personnel* (Washington, D. C.: Mission Secretariat, August 1960). This report points out that although only a small proportion of Catholic missionary personnel come from the United States (about 5 per cent of Catholic missionaries in Africa are Americans), the United States is the major financial supporter of Catholic world missions.
39. Mary Hornaday, "Protestantism Takes to Air," *Christian Science Monitor,* February 5, 1963; John C. Thiessen, *A Survey of World Missions* (rev. ed.; Chicago: Moody Press, 1961), pp. 117, 205.
40. A concise description of the communication activities of major federal agencies, ranging from the U. S. Information Agency to the Social Security Administration has been prepared by Allan S. Nanes of the Library of Congress for the Subcommittee on International Organizations and Movements, Committee on Foreign Affairs, U. S. House of Representatives: *The U.S. Ideological Effort: Government Agencies and Programs* (Washington, D. C., January 3, 1964).
41. Most of the data in this chapter regarding the operations of the U.S.I.A. and the State Department are taken from the House of Representatives or Senate hearings on appropriations. In some cases, U.S.I.A. and State officials have been helpful in providing more up-to-date figures.
42. There is no single source describing AID training programs, although many individual projects have been dealt with in specialized articles and mono-

graphs. Programs relating to communication are described in *The Multiplier in International Development,* a bimonthly publication of the Communications Techniques Branch of the Communications Resources Division of AID.

43. *Overseas Military Information Programs,* Thirteenth Report by the Committee on Government Operations, House Report No. 1549, 87th Cong., 2d Sess. (Washington, D. C.: Government Printing Office, 1962), pp. 20, 42.
44. The Peace Corps is described in more detail in Maurice L. Albertson, *New Frontiers for American Youth* (Washington, D. C.: Public Affairs Press, 1962); and Ray Hoopes, *The Complete Peace Corps Guide* (New York: Dial Press, 1962).
45. Quintus C. Wilson, "What Japan Reads About America," *Nieman Reports,* October 1955.
46. *Ibid.*
47. Wilson P. Dizard, *The Strategy of Truth* (Washington, D. C.: Public Affairs Press, 1962), p. 126.
48. "Foreign Correspondents Center Marks Its Second Year," *Department of State Newsletter,* October 1963; U.S.I.A., *18th Review of Operations,* January 1-June 30, 1962 (Washington, D. C.: Government Printing Office, 1962), pp. 27-28.
49. "If Maine Can Do It, You Can Do It Too," *Saturday Review,* April 14, 1962, p. 55.
50. Dizard, *The Strategy of Truth,* p. 123.
51. *The New York Times,* November 5 and 6, 1961; testimony of Edward R. Murrow, *U.S.I.A. Appropriations Hearings, Fiscal Year 1963,* U. S. House of Representatives (Washington, D. C.: Government Printing Office, 1962), p. 23.
52. "To Millions VOA Means Voice of Integrity," *Department of State Newsletter,* March 1963, pp. 11-12; U.S.I.A., *20th Review of Operations,* January 1-June 30, 1963 (Washington, D. C.: Government Printing Office, 1963), p. 11; *U.S.I.A. Appropriations Hearings, Fiscal Year 1963,* pp. 91, 115.
53. Dizard, *The Strategy of Truth,* p. 114.
54. U.S.I.A., *18th Review of Operations,* p. 19; see also *Presenting America Abroad Through Television* (Washington, D. C.: U.S.I.A., 1960).
55. A U.S.I.A. official has added that there were thirty-three government agencies producing films as of 1963, but that there was little cooperation among them. U.S.I.A. is able to use quite a few films made by other agencies and could use more if closer cooperation during the production process could be assured. Canada has solved a similar problem by setting up a Canadian Film Board, which makes films for all government agencies. This avoids dissipation of skilled personnel and technical facilities among many small production units.
56. Roger W. Tubby, "Industry Communications Programs in Support of U.S. Foreign Policy," *Department of State Bulletin,* February 5, 1962, p. 214.
57. *The Multiplier in International Development,* March-June, 1963.
58. "Books in Latin America" (New York: Franklin Publications, 1962), pp. 63-64 (mimeographed).
59. U.S.I.A., *17th Review of Operations,* July 1-December 31, 1961 (Washing-

ton, D. C.: Government Printing Office, 1962), p. 25; Edward R. Murrow, "To Fill the Reading Gap," *Saturday Review,* April 27, 1963, p. 33.

60. *Overseas,* February 1963, p. 26.
61. *Publisher's Weekly,* November 13, 1961; Peter S. Jennison, "American Books Abroad," *Bulletin of the Atomic Scientists,* December 1963, p. 32.
62. *Department of State Bulletin,* October 29, 1962, p. 666; *Publisher's Weekly,* December 3, 1962, p. 23.
63. *Department of Commerce Appropriations Hearings, Fiscal Year 1963,* U. S. Senate (Washington, D. C.: Government Printing Office, 1962), pp. 538-43.
64. Eugene M. Braderman, "BIC and Commercial Officers Boost Trade as Never Before," *Department of State Newsletter,* January 1964; *Department of Commerce Appropriations Hearings, Fiscal Year 1963,* pp. 491-95.
65. *U.S.I.A. Appropriations Hearings, Fiscal Year 1964,* p. 715.
66. Henry Tanner, "U.S. Graphic Show Closes in Moscow," *The New York Times,* January 16, 1964, p. 22.
67. Ralph K. White, "Soviet Reactions to Our Moscow Exhibit," *Public Opinion Quarterly,* Winter 1959-60; "American Guides in Moscow," *Foreign Service Journal,* October 1959, p. 54; Dizard, *The Strategy of Truth,* pp. 184-85.
68. Catherine D. Norrell, "Roads to International Understanding," *The Department of State Bulletin,* February 11, 1963; *Educational and Cultural Diplomacy—1962,* Department of State Publication 7612, December 1963; Lucius D. Battle, "The Need to Explore Inner Space," *Department of State Bulletin,* July 27, 1964, p. 114.
69. *Experiment in International Understanding,* A Report of the Board of Foreign Scholarships (Washington, D. C., October 1963), p. 72.
70. *Toward a National Effort in International Educational and Cultural Affairs,* Department of State Publication 7238 (Washington, D. C.: Government Printing Office, 1961), p. 46.
71. Lucius D. Battle, "Human Relations and International Relations," *Department of State Bulletin,* September 17, 1962, p. 423.
72. No single publication adequately describing the Military Assistance Training Program is available. Certain aspects of the program are described in Waldemar A. Nielsen, "Huge, Hidden Impact of the Pentagon," *The New York Times Magazine,* June 25, 1961, and Clare H. Timberlake, "Military Schools as Instruments of Societal Change," *Foreign Service Journal,* November 1962; see also Nanes, *The U.S. Ideological Effort: Government Agencies and Programs,* pp. 36ff, and Committee on Educational Interchange Policy, Institute of International Education, "Military Assistance Training Programs of the U. S. Government" (CEIP Statement Na. 18, July 1964).
73. Lucius D. Battle, "The Educational and Cultural Exchange Programs of the United States," *Department of State Bulletin,* July 16, 1962, pp. 111-12.
74. Battle, "The Need to Explore Inner Space," p. 114.
75. *Department of State Appropriations Hearings, Fiscal Year 1964,* U. S. House of Representatives (Washington, D. C.: Government Printing Office, 1963), pp. 1610, 1624-25; *Department of State Bulletin,* October 28, 1963, p. 685; Lawrence Davies, "Hawaii Nurtures U.S.-Asian Amity," *The New York Times,* June 2, 1963.

76. *The Citizen's Role in Cultural Relations,* Department of State Publication 6854 (Washington, D. C.: Government Printing Office, September 1959).
77. Institute of International Education, Annual Report for 1963. In that year, the Institute's income totaled $2,867,643, of which $1,018,118 was received for administering government programs.
78. Cf. Stephen P. Duggan, *A Professor at Large* (New York: Macmillan Co., 1943). This autobiography by the founder of the Institute describes the early years of its growth.
79. Catherine D. Norrell, "Roads to International Understanding," *Department of State Appropriations Hearings, Fiscal Year 1963,* U. S. House of Representatives (Washington, D. C.: Government Printing Office, 1962), pp. 709-10, 744.
80. Lucius D. Battle, "Foreign Students in America: Problems, Progress, and Prospects," *Department of State Bulletin,* May 13, 1963, p. 756.
81. Lowry and Hooker, "The Role of the Arts and the Humanities," pp. 43-45, 70; Dizard, *The Strategy of Truth,* pp. 178-79.
82. Roy E. Larsen and Glenn G. Wolfe, "Report of Survey, Cultural Presentations Program," mimeographed publication of the Department of State, December 1962.
83. *Department of State Bulletin,* June 11, 1962, p. 959.
84. Frederick T. Merrill, "Contacts with the Soviets," *Foreign Service Journal,* March 1959; Lawrence C. Mitchell, "Soviet-American Exchange of Scientists," and Stephen Viederman, "Academic Exchange—A Narrow Bridge," both in *Bulletin of the Atomic Scientists,* February 1962.
85. Edward Weintal, "Analysis of Our Moscow Link," *The New York Times Magazine,* August 6, 1961, pp. 10ff.
86. William Benton, "Should We Continue the Cultural Exchanges with the USSR?," *Saturday Review,* October 27, 1962.
87. *Four International Training Programs in Communication,* School of Education, University of Indiana, 1963 (pamphlet); Robert W. Kitchen, "Training for Communications," *The Multiplier in International Development,* June 1964.
88. *Department of State Bulletin,* June 11, 1962, p. 959; Battle, "The Need to Explore Inner Space," p. 113.
89. *Department of State Bulletin,* September 21, 1959, pp. 422-28.
90. *Sixteenth Report of the United States Advisory Commission on Information* (Washington, D. C.: Government Printing Office, 1961), p. 18; *U.S.I.A. Appropriations Hearings, Fiscal Year 1962,* U. S. House of Representatives (Washington, D. C.: Government Printing Office, 1961), p. 122.
91. *Times Literary Supplement,* London, August 10, 1962. This special issue, entitled "A Language in Common," reviews English creative writing in Commonwealth and other countries where it is not a native language.
92. Walter Johnson, *American Studies Abroad,* U. S. Advisory Commission on International Educational and Cultural Affairs, Washington, July 1963; Sigmund Skard, *American Studies in Europe—Their History and Present Organization* (2 vols.; Philadelphia: University of Pennsylvania Press, 1958).
93. *25th Semiannual Report to Congress, Educational and Cultural Exchange*

Program, January 1-June 30, 1960, Department of State Publication 7191 (Washington, D. C.: Government Printing Office, 1961), p. 61; Edna Duge, "International Alumni Groups," *Overseas,* December 1963, pp. 9-10.

94. Robert M. Cullers, "Return to Japan," *Overseas,* November 1962, p. 22.
95. *Hearings before the Subcommittee on International Organizations and Movements* (Washington, D. C.: Government Printing Office, 1963), Part I, p. 41.
96. Andrew Tully, *CIA—The Inside Story* (New York: William Morrow, 1962); Allen W. Dulles, *The Craft of Intelligence* (New York: Harper & Row, 1963).
97. David Wise and Thomas B. Ross, *The Invisible Government* (New York: Random House, 1964), pp. 313ff; Ben H. Bagdikian, "Unsecretive Report on the C.I.A.," *The New York Times Magazine,* October 27, 1963, p. 108.
98. V. Valentinov, "CIA Intrigues in Latin America," *International Affairs* (Moscow), June 1964.
99. *U.S. Information Service Activities in Africa,* Hearings before the Subcommittee on Africa, Committee on Foreign Affairs, U. S. House of Representatives (Washington, D. C.: Government Printing Office, 1963), p. 13.
100. "Human Skills in the Decade of Development," *Department of State Bulletin,* December 3, 1962.

Chapter 11: Focusing Official American Communication Programs

1. Leo Bogart, "A Study of the Operating Assumptions of the U.S. Information Agency," *Public Opinion Quarterly,* Winter 1955-56, pp. 370-71.
2. *Department of State Appropriations Hearings, Fiscal Year 1947,* U. S. House of Representatives (Washington, D. C.: Government Printing Office, 1946), p. 10.
3. *Ibid.*
4. *Sixteenth Report of the United States Advisory Commission on Information* (Washington, D. C.: Government Printing Office, 1961), p. 3.
5. "USIA Mission Redefined by President Kennedy," *Department of State Newsletter,* October 1963, p. 9; "To Millions VOA Means Voice of Integrity," *Department of State Newsletter,* March 1963, p. 11.
6. Edward L. Bernays, "What Do We Say to the World?," Part I, "Unpopularity is Unnecessary," *Saturday Review,* September 17, 1955, p. 12; *U.S.I.A. Appropriations Hearings, Fiscal Year 1964,* U. S. House of Representatives (Washington, D. C.: Government Printing Office, 1963), p. 179.
7. Edward W. Barrett, *Truth is Our Weapon* (New York: Funk & Wagnalls, 1953), pp. 78-79.
8. *The New York Times,* October 29, 1953; "USIA Mission Redefined by President Kennedy," p. 9.
9. *U.S.I.A. Appropriations Hearings, Fiscal Year 1964,* p. 421. (When told about this exhibit, the Chairman of the appropriations subcommittee remarked: "I thought your business was to describe America to African nations rather than to describe Africa to African nations.")
10. *U.S.I.A. Appropriations Hearings, Fiscal Year 1963,* U. S. House of Repre-

sentatives (Washington, D. C.: Government Printing Office, 1962), p. 22; *U.S.I.A. Appropriations Hearings, Fiscal Year 1964*, p. 6.

11. *Department of State Appropriations Hearings, Fiscal Year 1963*, U. S. House of Representatives (Washington, D. C.: Government Printing Office, 1962), pp. 700, 781.
12. "Survey of United States Information Service Operations—Western Europe," Report to the Senate Appropriations Committee (Washington, D. C.: Government Printing Office, February 1957), p. 16.
13. Arthur Goodfriend, *The Twisted Image* (New York: St Martin's Press, 1963), pp. 145-61.
14. "Secretary Greets Voice of America on 20th Anniversary," *Department of State Bulletin*, March 26, 1962, p. 510; *Department of State Appropriations Hearings, Fiscal Year 1963*, pp. 108, 684; *Department of State Appropriations Hearings, Fiscal Year 1964*, U. S. House of Representatives (Washington, D. C.: Government Printing Office, 1963), p. 189.
15. *Nineteenth Report to Congress* (Washington, January 1964), pp. 6-8.
16. *U.S.I.A. Appropriations Hearings, Fiscal Year 1964*, pp. 538-39; U.S.I.A., *20th Review of Operations*, January 1-June 30, 1963 (Washington, D. C.: Government Printing Office, 1963), pp. 42ff.
17. *Hearings before the Subcommittee on International Organizations and Movements*, Committee on Foreign Affairs, U. S. House of Representatives (Washington, D. C.: Government Printing Office, 1963), Part I, p. 39.
18. Goodfriend, *The Twisted Image*, pp. 194-95; *United States Information Operations in Africa*, Hearings before the Subcommittee on Africa, Committee on Foreign Affairs, U. S. House of Representatives (Washington, D. C.: Government Printing Office, 1962), pp. 9-10; U. S. Advisory Commission on Information, *Nineteenth Report to Congress*, pp. 9-10; U. S. Advisory Commission on Information, *Twentieth Report to Congress* (1965), p. 7.
19. U. S. Advisory Commission on International Educational and Cultural Affairs, *A Beacon of Hope* (Washington, D. C.: Government Printing Office, 1963).
20. Nancy Dammann, "Thai Villagers and Communications," *The Multiplier in International Development*, June 1964.
21. Coordination efforts during and immediately after World War II are described in Charles A. H. Thomson, *Overseas Information Service of the United States Government* (Washington, D. C.: Brookings Institution, 1958). More recent efforts are described in Murray Dyer, *The Weapon on the Wall* (Baltimore, Md.: Johns Hopkins Press, 1959).
22. Roy M. Melbourne, "Coordination for Action," *Foreign Service Journal*, March 1958; Brigadier General Dale O. Smith, "What is OCB?," *Foreign Service Journal*, November 1955; James Reston, "Problem for the U.S.I.A.," *The New York Times*, April 23, 1957, p. 15; "For Coordination of Educational and Cultural Policies," *Department of State Newsletter*, March 1964, p. 38.
23. Walter H. C. Laves, *Toward a National Effort in International Educational and Cultural Affairs*, Department of State Publication 7238 (Washington, D. C.: Government Printing Office, July 1961), pp. 8-9; *The Ambassador and The Problem of Coordination*, Subcommittee on National Security, Committee

on Government Operations, U. S. Senate (Washington, D. C.: Government Printing Office, 1963); John D. Jernegan, "The Ambassador and the Country Team," *Department of State Newsletter,* July 1963; *A Beacon of Hope,* p. 53.

24. Walter Joyce, *The Propaganda Gap* (New York: Harper & Row, 1963), p. 88.
25. Charles A. Thomson and Walter H. C. Laves, *Cultural Relations and U.S. Foreign Policy* (Bloomington, Ind.: Indiana University Press, 1963), pp. 69ff.
26. Howland H. Sargeant, "American Information and Cultural Representation Overseas," in Vincent M. Barnett, Jr., *The Representation of the United States Abroad* (rev. ed.; New York: Frederick A. Praeger, 1965), 1956, p. 96.
27. Robert H. Thayer, "Role of the Humanities in International Relations," *Department of State Bulletin,* October 12, 1959, p. 511; Donald Edgar, "Cultural Exchange and the Foreign Service Officer," *Foreign Service Journal,* June 1959, pp. 38ff; "Fulbright Urges a Larger Program," *The New York Times Magazine,* August 13, 1961, p. 10; *A Beacon of Hope,* pp. 12-14.
28. Thomson and Laves, *Cultural Relations and Foreign Policy,* pp. 109ff.
29. *U.S.I.A. Appropriations Hearings, Fiscal Year 1964,* pp. 565-66.
30. Ted Olson, "USIA's FSCR: A Salute and a Caveat," *Foreign Service Journal,* May 1963, p. 23.
31. Laves, *Toward a National Effort in International Educational and Cultural Affairs,* p. 55.
32. *Department of State Appropriations Hearings, Fiscal Year 1963,* p. 507.
33. *Hearings before the Subcommittee on International Organizations and Movements,* Part I, p. 29.
34. *U.S.I.A. Appropriations Hearings, Fiscal Year 1964,* p. 578.
35. *U.S.I.A. Appropriations Hearings, Fiscal Year 1963,* pp. 193, 223.
36. *U.S.I.A. Appropriations Hearings, Fiscal Year 1964,* p. 502.
37. Lucius D. Battle, "The Importance of the Private Sector in Educational and Cultural Affairs," *Department of State Newsletter,* August 1962, p. 15.
38. Letter from Robert F. Byrnes and Stephen Viederman, *The New York Times Magazine,* August 20, 1961, commenting on "Analysis of Our Moscow Link," by Edward Weintal, in *The New York Times Magazine,* August 6, 1961. A similar letter from William B. Edgerton, Acting Chairman of the Inter-University Committee on Travel Grants, appeared in the *Times* on September 18, 1960. Professor Edgerton deplored the idea that educational values "should be sacrificed for the sake of scoring a few points in the ideological struggle."
39. Alvin Shuster, "Murrow Fails in Effort to Keep Film on Migrants off British TV," *The New York Times,* March 23, 1961. See also Jack Gould's column in the same issue.
40. John S. Dickey, "The Secretary and the American Public," in Don K. Price (ed.), *The Secretary of State* (Englewood Cliffs, N. J.: Prentice-Hall, 1960), p. 156.
41. Reuben S. Nathan, "Westliche Aussenpolitik und Westliche Propaganda," *Aussenpolitik,* August 1962, p. 538.
42. Roy A. Gallant, "More Psycho Than Logical," *Reporter,* March 31, 1953.
43. Robert Blum, "The Flow of People and Ideas," in *Cultural Affairs and For-*

eign Relations (Englewood Cliffs, N. J.: Prentice-Hall, 1963), p. 4. The complex of attitudes toward cultural relations described by Mr. Blum is reflected in the case of information programs by Eugene W. Castle in *Billions, Blunders and Baloney* (New York: Devin-Adair Co., 1955), p. 66. Mr. Castle cites the loss of votes of Italian middle-of-the-road parties in 1953 as a reflection on the efficacy of American propaganda.

44. *Congressional Record,* April 13, 1949, pp. 4536-38.
45. Ralph Block, "Propaganda and the Free Society," *Public Opinion Quarterly,* Winter 1948-49.
46. Monteagle Stearns, "Democratic Diplomacy and the Role of Propaganda," *Foreign Service Journal,* October, 1953; Philip M. Coombs, *The Fourth Dimension of Foreign Policy: Educational and Cultural Affairs* (New York: Harper & Row, 1964), p. 35.
47. Walter Lippmann, "Wanton Carelessness," *Washington Post,* May 7, 1954.
48. The story of what is probably the most chaotic era in the information program's history is told in Martin Merson, *The Private Diary of a Public Servant* (New York: Macmillan Co., 1955). See also Leo Cherne, "What Do We Say to the World: The Loin Cloth or the Rajah," Part 2, *Saturday Review,* September 17, 1955, p. 13.
49. George V. Allen, "What the U.S. Information Program Cannot Do," in John B. Whitton (ed.), *Propaganda and the Cold War* (Washington, D. C.: Public Affairs Press, 1963), p. 61.
50. John F. Melby and Duane Ray Burnor, "Future Leaders of Africa," *Saturday Review,* August 18, 1962, p. 50.
51. James Reston, "How to Make Things Worse Than They Really Are," *The New York Times,* October 27, 1961.

Chapter 12: Roles of the U. S. Government in International Communication

1. Meg Greenfield, "How We Got Protected From Communist Propaganda," *The Reporter,* October 25, 1962.
2. Frank Tannenbaum, "The United States and Latin America," *Political Science Quarterly,* June 1961, pp. 173-76.
3. This case is recapitulated in David Dempsey, "The Case of the Improper Imprint," *Saturday Review,* June 13, 1964; it also received considerable publicity in the daily press.
4. *U.S.I.A. Appropriations Hearings, Fiscal Year 1964,* U. S. House of Representatives (Washington, D. C.: Government Printing Office, 1963), p. 14. U.S.I.A. material is, however, labeled when "local law or custom" requires it.
5. "News-Flow Clause in Treaties Proposed," *Christian Science Monitor,* February 11, 1963. (This suggestion was advanced by Palmer Hoyt, publisher of the Denver *Post.*)
6. Harlan Cleveland, "The Uses of Diversity," *Department of State Bulletin,* September 23, 1963, pp. 461-62.
7. Felix M. Keesing and Marie M. Keesing, *Elite Communication in Samoa* (Stanford, Calif.: Stanford University Press, 1956), pp. 167-68.

8. Homer D. Higbee, *The Status of Foreign Student Advising in United States Universities and Colleges* (East Lansing, Mich.: Michigan State University, 1961), pp. 49-50.
9. Howland H. Sargeant, "American Information and Cultural Representation Overseas," in Vincent M. Barnett, Jr. (ed.), *The Representation of the United States Abroad* (rev. ed.; New York: Frederick A. Praeger, 1965).
10. Pat M. Holt, "Making Democracy Work in Latin America," *Overseas,* January 1964, p. 8.
11. Frederick C. Barghoorn, *Soviet Foreign Propaganda* (Princeton, N. J.: Princeton University Press, 1964), p. 306.
12. Francis E. Dart, "The Rub of Cultures," *Foreign Affairs,* January 1963.
13. Peter S. Jennison, *American Books in the Near East, Central Africa and Asia* (New York: R. R. Bowker Co., 1957), p. 4; *Overseas Information Programs of the United States,* Committee on Foreign Relations, U. S. Senate, Report No. 406 (Washington, D. C.: Government Printing Office, June 1953), p. 175.
14. Benjamin Franklin, "Remarks Concerning the Savages of North America," 1784, reprinted in *Foreign Service Journal,* July 1958, p. 25.
15. U. S. Advisory Commission on International Educational and Cultural Affairs, *A Beacon of Hope* (Washington, D. C.: Government Printing Office, 1963), p. 34.
16. *U.S. Information Service Activities in Africa,* Hearings before the Subcommittee on Africa, Committee on Foreign Affairs, U. S. House of Representatives (Washington, D. C.: Government Printing Office, 1963), p. 19.
17. "For an Audience Abroad," *Saturday Review,* May 25, 1963, p. 26.
18. "The American Image Series": Kenneth S. Lynn (ed.), *The American Society;* Ernest R. May (ed.), *The American Foreign Policy;* Leonard W. Levy and John P. Roche (eds.), *The American Political Process;* and Jesse W. Markham (ed.), *The American Economy* (New York: George Braziller, 1963).
19. Julius Momo Udochi, "The Conflict Involving Communism in Mid-Africa," *Annals of the American Academy of Political and Social Science,* July 1962, pp. 19-20.
20. Welles Hangen, "USIA in the Next Decade," *Foreign Service Journal,* July 1963, pp. 22-23.
21. *Memorandum on the Postwar International Information Program of the United States,* Department of State Publication 2438 (Washington, D. C.: Government Printing Office, 1945). The summary report of the Hickenlooper Committee is entitled *Overseas Information Programs of the United States* (see note 13). The unclassified portion of the Jackson Committee's report was published in *The New York Times,* July 9, 1953. For a portion of the Sprague Committee report, see *Department of State Bulletin,* February 6, 1961. (Reprinted in Urban G. Whitaker, Jr. (ed.), *Propaganda and International Relations* (rev. ed.; San Francisco: Chandler Publishing Co., 1962).
22. *Hearings before the Subcommittee on International Organizations and Movements,* Committee on Foreign Affairs, U. S. House of Representatives (Washington, D. C.: Government Printing Office, 1963), Part V, p. 690.

23. Charles A. Thomson and Walter H. C. Laves, *Cultural Relations and U.S. Foreign Policy* (Bloomington, Ind.: Indiana University Press, 1963).
24. A start in the direction of viewing American overseas activities as a whole has been made by the Policy Planning Council of the Department of State, which prepares unified statements of national policy toward certain critical areas. These papers include attention to "psychological, or ideological factors." They are, of course, for internal government use. (See testimony of W. Averell Harriman and Walt W. Rostow in *Hearings before the Subcommittee on International Organizations and Movements,* Part VI, pp. 715, 736).
25. *Hearings before the Subcommittee on International Organizations and Movements,* Part I, p. 51.
26. Adolf A. Berle, *Latin America: Diplomacy and Reality* (New York: Harper & Row, 1962), pp. 72-73.
27. Julius Momo Udochi, "The Conflict Involving Communism in Mid-Africa," *The Annals of the American Academy of Political and Social Science,* July 1962, p. 16.
28. John M. Cates, Jr., "Democratic Dilemma," *Foreign Service Journal,* November 1963, p. 22.
29. Saxton Bradford, "Ideas: The Ultimate Weapon?," *Foreign Service Journal,* November 1963, p. 25.
30. Oren Stephens, *Facts to a Candid World* (Stanford, Calif.: Stanford University Press, 1955), p. 109.
31. "Voices of America," *Foreign Affairs,* January 1954, p. 189; John W. Nason *et al., The College and World Affairs* (New York: Ford Foundation, 1964), p. 65.
32. See, for example, Louise Winfield, *Living Overseas* (Washington, D. C.: Public Affairs Press, 1962), if only for her general injunction: "Behave like a guest and feel like a student" (p. 163). Even more has been written for the guidance of Americans offering hospitality or assistance to visitors to this country. The American Home Economics Association has published several booklets in a series entitled "Entertaining Foreign Visitors." These include Mollie and Russell Smart, *How to Cherish an Indian Guest,* and Helen S. Mitchell, *When East Meets West* (on welcoming Japanese guests). As of 1964, a State Department booklet on ways that American communities and families can assist foreign students was in preparation. The most comprehensive treatment of psychological problems involved in communicating with foreign visitors is that of Bryant M. Wedge, *Foreign Visitors to the United States and How They See Us* (Princeton, N. J.: D. Van Nostrand, 1965). A more general pamphlet on the role of the individual in international communications, entitled *Challenge to Americans: The Struggle We Face and How to Help Win It,* was issued by the Advertising Council in 1963.
33. Robert F. Kennedy, "A Free Trade in Ideas," *Saturday Review,* February 16, 1963, p. 44.
34. Margaret L. Cormack, "Three Steps to Better Orientation," *Overseas,* September 1963, pp. 11ff.
35. "Spectator," *Svenskarna och Propagandan* (Stockholm: Gebers, 1943); Bjørn

Christiansen, *Krig og Internasjonal Propaganda* (Oslo: Forsvarets Psykologiske Avdeling, 1956), pp. 133-34; Helmut Bohn (ed.), *Siegen Ohne Krieg* (Cologne: Markus Verlag, 1959) contains an essay on defense against propaganda in various Western European countries.

36. Louis Verniers, *International Cooperation and You,* Document No. 12, Union of International Associations (Brussels, 1962), pp. 77-79.
37. "Letters to the Editor," *Saturday Review,* January 19 and February 16, 1963.

Appendix: Channels for International Communication

1. *The Flow of the News* (Zurich: International Press Institute, 1953).
2. James W. Markham, "Foreign News in the United States and South American Press," *Public Opinion Quarterly,* Summer 1961, pp. 257-58.
3. General information on international broadcasting is taken primarily from George A. Codding, Jr., *Broadcasting Without Barriers* (Paris: UNESCO, 1959).
4. Burton Paulu, *British Broadcasting* (Minneapolis, Minn.: University of Minnesota Press, 1956), pp. 406-7; *BBC Handbook, 1964* (London: British Broadcasting Corporation, 1963), pp. 98-100.
5. O. Lund Johansen, *World Radio-TV Handbook* (Copenhagen, 1964), pp. 22-24, 26; Georges Hansen, "Eurovision—Some Technical Aspects," *Gazette,* VII, No. 3/4 (1962).
6. G. Ratkowski, "Television in the Countries Affiliated to the International Broadcasting and Television Organization," *Gazette,* VII, No. 3/4 (1962).
7. *Space Communication and the Mass Media,* Reports and Papers on Mass Communication, No. 41 (Paris: UNESCO, 1963).
8. Peter S. Jennison, "American Books Abroad," *Bulletin of the Atomic Scientists,* December 1963, p. 33; "U. S. Book Exports and Imports, 1962," *Publisher's Weekly,* December 2, 1963, p. 25; U. S. Department of Commerce, *Printing and Publishing* (Washington, D. C., July 1964), p. 13. (Since Commerce Department figures do not include individual export shipments valued under $100, the total value of books exported is far larger than the figures indicate.)
9. L. John Martin, "American Newsmagazines and the European Scene," *Gazette,* VI, No. 2 (1960).
10. Union Postale Universelle, *Statistique Reduite des Services Postaux 1959* (Berne, 1961).
11. Publications of the UFI include *Vade-Mecum,* its annual directory, and the periodical, *Les Foires Internationales,* both published in Paris.
12. Robert T. Bower and Laure M. Sharp, "The Use of Art in International Communication," *Public Opinion Quarterly,* Spring 1956, pp. 221-23.
13. Sir Stephen G. Tallents, *The Projection of England* (London: Faber & Faber, 1932), pp. 36-37.
14. Estimate from *ASTA Travel News,* reported in *The New York Times,* April 6, 1964, p. 60. See also U. S. Department of Commerce, *Survey of International Travel* (Washington, D. C.: Government Printing Office, 1956);

and S. W. Bryant, "What Jet Travel Does to Your Metabolic Clock," *Fortune,* November 1963.

15. Norman Dawes, *A Two-Way Street* (New York: Asia Publishing House, 1962), p. 114; Albert G. Sims, "Wanted: A Certain Quality of Free Enterprise," *Overseas,* September 1961, p. 11.
16. *Study Abroad, 1963* (Paris: UNESCO, 1962), pp. 7, 682; and *Study Abroad, 1961* (Paris: UNESCO, 1960), p. 17.
17. Lord Strang, *The Diplomatic Career* (London: André Deutsch, 1962), pp. 16-17.
18. Thomas A. Donovan, "Political Reporting Trends," *Foreign Service Journal,* November 1963. The writer whimsically suggests that the best way to improve diplomatic reporting would be to improve journalism in foreign countries.

Index

COUNCIL ON FOREIGN RELATIONS

Officers and Directors

PUBLICATIONS

FOREIGN AFFAIRS (quarterly), edited by Hamilton Fish Armstrong.

THE UNITED STATES IN WORLD AFFAIRS (annual). Volumes for 1931, 1932 and 1933, by Walter Lippmann and William O. Scroggs; for 1934-1935, 1936, 1937, 1938, 1939 and 1940, by Whitney H. Shepardson and William O. Scroggs; for 1945-1947, 1947-1948 and 1948-1949, by John C. Campbell; for 1949, 1950, 1951, 1952, 1953 and 1954, by Richard P. Stebbins; for 1955, by Hollis W. Barber; for 1956, 1957, 1958, 1959, 1960, 1961, 1962 and 1963, by Richard P. Stebbins.

Documents on American Foreign Relations (annual). Volume for 1952 edited by Clarence W. Baier and Richard P. Stebbins; for 1953 and 1954, edited by Peter V. Curl; for 1955, 1956, 1957, 1958 and 1959, edited by Paul E. Zinner; for 1960, 1961, 1962 and 1963, edited by Richard P. Stebbins.

Political Handbook and Atlas of the World (annual), edited by Walter H. Mallory.

African Battleline: American Policy Choices in Southern Africa, by Waldemar A. Nielsen (1965).

NATO in Transition: The Future of the Atlantic Alliance, by Timothy W. Stanley (1965).

Alternative to Partition: For a Broader Conception of America's Role in Europe, by Zbigniew Brzezinski (1965).

The Troubled Partnership: A Re-Appraisal of the Atlantic Alliance, by Henry A. Kissinger (1965).

Remnants of Empire: The United Nations and the End of Colonialism, by David W. Wainhouse (1965).

The European Community and American Trade: A Study in Atlantic Economics and Policy, by Randall Hinshaw (1964).

The Fourth Dimension of Foreign Policy: Educational and Cultural Affairs, by Philip H. Coombs (1964).

American Agencies Interested in International Affairs (Fifth Edition), compiled by Donald Wasson (1964).

Japan and the United States in World Trade, by Warren S. Hunsberger (1964).

Foreign Affairs Bibliography, 1952-1962, by Henry L. Roberts (1964).

The Dollar in World Affairs: An Essay in International Financial Policy, by Henry G. Aubrey (1964).

On Dealing with the Communist World, by George F. Kennan (1964).

Foreign Aid and Foreign Policy, by Edward S. Mason (1964).

The Scientific Revolution and World Politics, by Caryl P. Haskins (1964).

Africa: A Foreign Affairs Reader, edited by Philip W. Quigg (1964).

The Philippines and the United States: Problems of Partnership, by George E. Taylor (1964).

Southeast Asia in United States Policy, by Russell H. Fifield (1963).

UNESCO: Assessment and Promise, by George N. Shuster (1963).

The Peaceful Atom in Foreign Policy, by Arnold Kramish (1963).

THE ARABS AND THE WORLD: Nasser's Arab Nationalist Policy, by Charles D. Cremeans (1963).

TOWARD AN ATLANTIC COMMUNITY, by Christian A. Herter (1963).

THE SOVIET UNION, 1922-1962: A Foreign Affairs Reader, edited by Philip E. Mosely (1963).

THE POLITICS OF FOREIGN AID: American Experience in Southeast Asia, by John D. Montgomery (1962).

SPEARHEADS OF DEMOCRACY: Labor in the Developing Countries, by George C. Lodge (1962).

LATIN AMERICA: Diplomacy and Reality, by Adolf A. Berle (1962).

THE ORGANIZATION OF AMERICAN STATES AND THE HEMISPHERE CRISIS, by John C. Dreier (1962).

THE UNITED NATIONS: Structure for Peace, by Ernest A. Gross (1962).

THE LONG POLAR WATCH: Canada and the Defense of North America, by Melvin Conant (1962).

ARMS AND POLITICS IN LATIN AMERICA (Revised Edition), by Edwin Lieuwen (1961).

THE FUTURE OF UNDERDEVELOPED COUNTRIES: Political Implications of Economic Development (Revised Edition), by Eugene Staley (1961).

SPAIN AND DEFENSE OF THE WEST: Ally and Liability, by Arthur P. Whitaker (1961).

SOCIAL CHANGE IN LATIN AMERICA TODAY: Its Implications for United States Policy, by Richard N. Adams, John P. Gillin, Allan R. Holmberg, Oscar Lewis, Richard W. Patch, and Charles W. Wagley (1961).

FOREIGN POLICY: THE NEXT PHASE: The 1960s (Revised Edition), by Thomas K. Finletter (1960).

DEFENSE OF THE MIDDLE EAST: Problems of American Policy (Revised Edition), by John C. Campbell (1960).

COMMUNIST CHINA AND ASIA: Challenge to American Policy, by A. Doak Barnett (1960).

FRANCE, TROUBLED ALLY: De Gaulle's Heritage and Prospects, by Edgar S. Furniss, Jr. (1960).

THE SCHUMAN PLAN: A Study in Economic Cooperation, 1950-1959, by William Diebold, Jr. (1959).

SOVIET ECONOMIC AID: The New Aid and Trade Policy in Underdeveloped Countries, by Joseph S. Berliner (1958).

RAW MATERIALS: A Study of American Policy, by Percy W. Bidwell (1958).

NATO AND THE FUTURE OF EUROPE, by Ben T. Moore (1958).

AFRICAN ECONOMIC DEVELOPMENT, by William Hance (1958).

INDIA AND AMERICA: A Study of Their Relations, by Philips Talbot and S. L. Poplai (1958).

NUCLEAR WEAPONS AND FOREIGN POLICY, by Henry A. Kissinger (1957).

MOSCOW-PEKING AXIS: Strength and Strains, by Howard L. Boorman, Alexander Eckstein, Philip E. Mosely and Benjamin Schwartz (1957).

RUSSIA AND AMERICA: Dangers and Prospects by Henry L. Roberts (1956).